# *American Foundations*

## Politics, Economics, Culture

### SECOND EDITION

## HYRUM LEWIS

Copyright © 2017 Hyrum Lewis

ALL RIGHTS RESERVED.
No part of this work covered by the copyright herein may be reproduced or used in any form or by any means–graphic, electronic, or mechanical, including photocopying, recording, taping, web distribution or information storage and retrieval systems–without the written permission of the publisher.

ISBN: 9781611650303
For more information or permission to use material from this text or product contact:
BYU Academic Publishing
3991 WSC
Provo, UT 84602
Tel (801) 422-6231
Fax (801) 422-0070
academicpublishing@byu.edu

To report ideas or text corrections email us at:
textideas@byu.edu

1st Printing

# CONTENTS

1. Introduction . . . . . . . . . . . . . . . . . . . . . . . . 1

## PART ONE:
## THE POLITICAL FOUNDATIONS OF AMERICA

2. Basic Principles I: Agency & Accountability . . . . . . . 7

3. Basic Principles II: The Rights & Equality of Humans . . . 21

4. Basic Principles III: The Rule of Law . . . . . . . . . . . 35

5. Independence I: Origins of American Self-Government . . 43

6. Independence II: The Creed & The Conflict . . . . . . . 55

7. Constitutionalism I: The Conditions of Freedom . . . . . 79

8. Constitutionalism II: Realism . . . . . . . . . . . . . . . 87

9. U.S. Constitution I: The Convention . . . . . . . . . . . 97

10. U.S. Constitution II: Power in Government . . . . . . . 111

## PART TWO:
## THE ECONOMIC FOUNDATIONS OF AMERICA

11. Market Principles I: The Secret of Wealth . . . . . . . . 125

12. Market Principles II: Market Morality . . . . . . . . . . 143

13. Economic Challenges I: American Economic Development  151

14. Economic Challenges II: Varieties of Political Economy . . 165

15. Depression and Solutions I: Keynesianism . . . . . . . . 179

16. Depression and Solutions II: Monetarism. . . . . . . . . 189

## PART THREE:
## THE CULTURAL FOUNDATIONS OF AMERICA

17. Political Culture I: Religion in America . . . . . . . . . 199

18. Political Culture II: Ideology in America . . . . . . . . . 215

19. Exclusion & Inclusion I: Diversity, Immigration,
    & The Creed . . . . . . . . . . . . . . . . . . . . . . . 229

20. Exclusion & Inclusion II: Fulfilling the Founding . . . . . 237

21. Technology, Socialization, Communication I: Possibilities . 249

22. Technology, Socialization, Communication II: Limits . . . 261

23. America & the World I: History . . . . . . . . . . . . . 275

24. America & the World II: Approaches. . . . . . . . . . . 285

25. Bibliography . . . . . . . . . . . . . . . . . . . . . . . 293

# Chapter 1

# INTRODUCTION

The United States is a fascinating place. It is the most powerful economic and military entity in history, a nation that holds a preeminence in world affairs not seen since Rome. It is a country of remarkable diversity, energy, and opportunity, but most importantly, it stands for extraordinary ideals. Such a unique nation deserves special consideration regardless of one's nationality. While we may quibble over the meaning of "American Exceptionalism," there is no question that America occupies a notable place in world affairs and history.

The study of America[1] is not only fascinating, it is also instructive. We can be inspired by America's core principles and institutions, as well as its heroes—people with names like Lincoln, Washington, King, and Stanton. British Historian Paul Johnson wrote,

> The creation of the United States of America is the greatest of all human adventures. No other national story holds such tremendous lessons, for the American people them-

---

1 This book will use the term "America" as an abbreviation for "The United States of America."

selves and for the rest of mankind . . . if we can learn these lessons and build upon them, the whole of humanity will benefit in the new age that is now opening.[2]

Since the U.S. is likely the most politically successful nation ever—in that it has given more freedom to more people over more time than any other—all of us, Americans or not, have much to learn by studying its past and present.

This study will be more than just an appreciation of American ideals; it will also illuminate universal human problems. Every society must deal with the social pathologies of crime, corruption, abuse of power, poverty, inequality, and ignorance. We can find partial solutions to these problems by studying America's successes and failures, which can inspire and guide, but also warn. Americans, of course, will profit by reading this book, but so will Canadians, Chinese, Rwandans, Spaniards, Chileans, and Australians.

This book will also provide readers of all nationalities with universal intellectual skills and cultural literacy. An educated person is equipped with *mental capital*, a knowledge of terms that allows them to comprehend and converse at a high level.[3] So this book will attempt to expand our intellectual capital by giving us a working definition of terms like "economic stimulus," "First Amendment," "foreign policy realism," and "ethnocentrism," which are often used in the news, journals of opinion, educated conversation, board rooms, and seminar tables. Those equipped with this knowledge can more effectively navigate the complex world of ideas.

The value of this book is more than historical. This is a cross-disciplinary work in which core principles are illustrated *through* history. While history is not the end in itself, it is the proving ground for the ideas under consideration. Not only is the past the laboratory in which we test social theories, but we often learn principles best by embedding them in a story (as the scriptures do with gospel truths).

In summary, the goals of this book are to help us *know*, *do*, and *become*. After reading, we should *know* the basic principles, truths, and history of America. This should allow us to *do* important things like converse knowledgeably and respectfully on public issues, apply social theories to contemporary situations, and appreciate and defend the universal principles of the American Founding. And learning and applying the content of this book should help us *become* more effective disciple-leaders in our communities.

This book looks at America from the viewpoint of the three basic realms of human activity: politics, economics, and culture. Politics is the use of coercive power in society, particularly by those bodies given a monopoly on the use of force: governments. Economics is the study of decisions regarding exchanges and the use of scarce resources. How and why does our free market system work so well, how does it generate so much wealth, and what are some ways we might improve it? Culture is the realm of traditions, beliefs, val-

---

2 Johnson (1999, pg. 3).
3 Hirsch (1987).

ues, perspectives, and religion. It's the "software" of society and may ultimately prove more important than the "hardware" of society—politics and economics—because ideas probably influence people even more than laws, prisons, armies, corporations, or dollars. The old adage "the pen is mightier than the sword" may be correct.

A note on the tone: while I make no apologies for the celebration of American institutions in this book, that doesn't mean it is uncritical. The U.S. needs to both conserve the principles of its founding, but also progress by extending liberty and opportunity to marginalized segments of society. A celebration of America's success entails the progressive obligation to fulfill the Founding through criticism and reform. Novelist John Steinbeck, when asked why he criticized his country in his books, would always reply, "Because I love it. If I did not, I would not bother."[4] My good-faith criticisms of the USA have the same source. The Founders themselves worked towards a "more perfect Union" and we should continue that ongoing project.

My hope is that the extolling of America in this book does not lead to complacency and jingoism, but to gratitude and a consciousness of the need for improvement, in both ourselves and society. In that sense, this book is as much a call to action as it is an appreciation. Only by asking where America falls short can we build upon these successes and extend the promise of American life to all.[5]

Yes, this book aims for objectivity, inasmuch as that means being true to the facts, but I also make no attempt to conceal my personal attachment to my country and its principles. If this appears naïve and patriotic to some readers, I can only say that I don't believe patriotism is outdated or unjustified. Patriotism is a virtue if it means loving that which is lovable, a vice if it means loving that which is simply one's own. I love America inasmuch as it deserves to be loved. To reject patriotism because it is unfashionable among cultural elites would be both snobbish and intellectually dishonest. The patriotism of the American masses, which I share, is well-founded both emotionally and intellectually. If a cynical world scoffs at this patriotism, then so much the worse for that world.[6]

Finally, please note that this book is *a* Latter-day Saint perspective, not *the* Latter-day Saint perspective. All of the content and conclusions are grounded in my own understanding of LDS doctrine, but it is only one person's view of the topic and by no means the

---

4 Benson (1990, pg. 932).

5 I often refer to America as "our" nation. I do this assuming that most of the readers will be American citizens. I hope my international readers will forgive this. Speaking in a personal, affectionate tone about America will be more heartfelt and natural.

6 Too many historians have assumed that you must either be either, 1) informed and cognizant of America's crimes (racism, slavery, unjust wars, Native American genocide, etc.) and therefore fashionably non-patriotic, or 2) ignorant and patriotic. They are wrong. Many of us have weighed the nation's defects against its virtues and have found it still, on balance, worthy of veneration (especially when contrasted with other powerful nations throughout history).

official one. While I had much help in producing this book (especially from Stan Kivett, Grover Quinn, and Professor Quinn's Spring 2017 editing class), all errors are mine alone.

## CHAPTER 1 SOURCES/FURTHER READING

Abcarian, Robin. "American Exceptionalism: We think we're special. Is that so wrong?," *Los Angeles Times*, September 12, 2013. <http://articles.latimes.com/2013/sep/12/local/la-me-ln-american-exceptionalism-20130912>, accessed Feb 2, 2014.

Benson, Jackson J. *John Steinbeck, Writer: A Biography*. New York: Penguin, 1990.

Crunden, Robert. *A Brief History of American Culture*. New York: Paragon House, 1998.

Hirsch, E.D. *Cultural Literacy: What Every American Needs to Know*. Boston: Houghton-Mifflin, 1987.

Johnson, Paul. *A History of the American People*. New York: Harper Perennial, 1999.

Lipset, Seymour Martin. *American Exceptionalism: A Double-Edged Sword*. New York: W.W. Norton, 1997.

Schuck, Peter H. and James Q. Wilson. "Looking Back." In Peter H. Schuck and James Q. Wilson, eds., *Understanding America: The Anatomy of an Exceptional Nation*. New York: Public Affairs, 2008.

Wilson, James Q. "American Exceptionalism," *The American Spectator*, October 2, 2006. <http://spectator.org/articles/46395/american-exceptionalism>, accessed February 2, 2014.

# Part One:
## The Political Foundations of America

# Chapter 2

# BASIC PRINCIPLES I: AGENCY & ACCOUNTABILITY

## ALEXANDER HAMILTON: THE POWER OF CHOICE

*What does it mean to be human?* This is a simple but profound question. So profound, in fact, that all political ideas and systems depend upon the answer one gives. Since the rest of this book will make no sense until we understand what makes humans unique, we must spend a whole chapter learning the inspired, correct answer.

We begin by turning to the life of one of the most important and under-appreciated Founding Fathers: Alexander Hamilton. Unlike most of the Founders, Hamilton did not inherit the privileges of the American elite. In fact, he was not from America at all, but was born on the remote Caribbean island of St. Croix to an impoverished mother and no father. Any social scientific calculation would have predicted a future of poverty, insignificance, and probably even crime for this child.

But Hamilton defied all of the laws of social science and took hold of his destiny at a young age. After his mother's death, he approached a local merchant and asked if he could help out in the man's store for a few pennies. The storeowner agreed and put him to work doing menial tasks (sweeping, cleaning, stocking shelves). Hamilton took this small stewardship seriously. He made sure all of his duties were performed with exactness and went the extra mile to improve the store in other ways. Because of his diligence, the owner gave him responsibilities keeping the books for the firm. At night, when the other kids of St. Croix were home playing or listening to bedtime stories, Hamilton would light a candle and read everything he could about business management. Based on what he learned, he suggested a few ways his employer might improve the store's operations. The ensuing success led to even more responsibilities, this time in management. Eventually, the boy performed so well in his

# Chapter 2

management role that the owner put young Hamilton in charge of the entire business. This orphan with nothing had gone from charity case to business wizard.[1]

Hamilton's employer and other elites of the island decided it would be a shame to let the boy's talents go to waste, so they pooled their resources to provide him with a scholarship to attend King's College in New York City (now Columbia University). In 1772, he set off for his new home in America: Hamilton the waif-islander had become Hamilton the American. The loyalty he felt to his adopted country would make him the leading nationalist of the Founding generation.

In college, Hamilton excelled in his legal studies, but at night, while all the other students frolicked and wasted time, Hamilton would light a candle and study military matters—strategy, organization, and artillery. He saw war brewing and he wanted to be able to defend his adopted country if disputes with the British came to blows. Of course, war did break out and Hamilton immediately enlisted. Although he began in the lowest ranks, his expertise caught the attention of his superior officers and he began to rise, eventually becoming a Colonel and the top aide to General George Washington himself.

That's not the end of Hamilton's remarkable story. He was not only a distinguished soldier and indispensable officer in Washington's Army, Hamilton was also preparing for the next phase of his life. After long days of military drilling, marches, planning, or battle, and while the other officers were carousing in the local tavern, Hamilton would again light his candle and open his books, this time studying international finance. The topic intrigued him and he thought that someday he might put this knowledge to good use.

He was right. After the war ended and the Constitution had created a permanent American government, President Washington chose Hamilton as the first Secretary of the Treasury. So much energy and brilliance did Hamilton bring to the position that he became, without question, the most important Treasury Secretary in U.S. history. Thanks to Hamilton, the new country developed a system of strong credit, sound currency, and efficient taxation, all of which made the new nation financially stable. Most other newly independent countries descend into hyperinflation, anarchy, and eventually military dictatorship because of financial chaos. The U.S., on the other hand, ascended to become the most stable government in the world, largely thanks to Hamilton.

Here was Hamilton at the height of his powers. He had risen from nothing to the highest positions of political and economic influence, yet it all came crashing down. One night, his wife and children were away visiting his in-laws in upstate New York. Hamilton was up with his candle and his books (as usual) when he heard a knock on the door. He answered and there stood a beautiful young woman wearing rags. She poured out a sad tale of poverty and hardship and asked if Hamilton could help.

Hamilton, a compassionate man of means, wanted to assist, but he instead made the

---

1  Brookhiser (1999).

biggest mistake of his life. He thought he could be alone with this young woman without any problem. His intentions were pure, but hers were not. The result was a sex scandal, betrayal, blackmail, and the ruin of the reputation he had worked so hard to establish. Hamilton failed to put barriers around his behavior and, in this moment of foolishness, squandered everything he had achieved.[2]

So what does Hamilton's life story illustrate? *The power and burden of agency.* Early in his life, he had nothing: no favorable environment or illustrious ancestry that would have bespoken success. Yet he triumphed in spite of these obstacles. He could have looked at his bleak prospects and resigned himself to a life of poverty, but instead he put aside all excuses and through sheer willpower rose to become one of the greatest statesmen in U.S. history. Conversely, later in life, he had every reason not to fail and yet he did because of a poor choice. Hamilton's life helps us see how humans are defined by the capacity to choose.

This view contradicts theories put forward by scholars. Biologists might say that humans are defined by certain evolved characteristics, such as brain size or bipedalism. Economists might say that humans are defined by their productive capacity. Technological theorists might say that humans are defined by the ability to use tools. But the great advantage of modern revelation and scripture is that we get to look at what the Lord himself says.

## GOD'S IMAGE

It all begins in the book of Genesis chapter 1. God created the cosmos, the sun, the stars, the earth, the animals, the elements, and the land, and then, in verse 26, created His crowning achievement: "And God said, Let us make man in our image, after our likeness." Humans, unlike everything else in creation, would be *like* God in a fundamental sense. Not only would they look like Him, but they would also share a particularly important attribute with the Creator: "And the Lord God said, Behold, the man is become as one of us, to know good and evil" (Gen 3: 22). We humans are godlike because we are conscious of our actions, can reflect on them as good or evil, and then can decide for ourselves what to do.

There are those who attempt to discredit the Church by calling Latter-day Saints "God-makers." We might not phrase it that way, but if they mean that we believe humans share God's nature and can grow to become more like him, then our response must be "guilty as charged." Latter-day Saints are alone in taking the Bible seriously when it says we are all "children of God." Just as children have the potential to grow up to become like their earthly parents, so we believe that humans, as children of God, can grow, progress, and become more like their spiritual parents.

But the profundity of agency doesn't stop there. The Book of Abraham teaches, "yet these two spirits, notwithstanding one is more intelligent than the other, have no begin-

---

2 Chernow (2004).

ning; they existed before, they shall have no end, they shall exist after, for they are gnolaum, or eternal" (Abr. 3:18, 21-22). Doctrine and Covenants section 93 adds: "Man was also in the beginning with God. Intelligence, or the light of truth, was not created or made, neither indeed can be. All truth is independent in that sphere in which God has placed it, to act for itself, as all intelligence also; otherwise there is no existence. Behold, here is the agency of man, and here is the condemnation of man" (vs. 29-31).

In other words, the essential "you" is not a physical characteristic like height, weight, hair color, eye color, muscle mass, looks, or athleticism. Those attributes will all die with your body. The essence of your being is "intelligence," "agency," "light and truth"—the capability of knowing and acting independently on that knowledge. God didn't only create us to exercise agency; we have always had that agency. This is the "you" independent of the body. You had it forever before this life and will have it forever after.

Many other religions believe that God brought your soul into existence out of nothing at some point in the past, but Latter-day Saints believe that the essence of you—that conscious capacity to know and choose, which we call "intelligence"—has existed for as long as God has—forever. The name of God in the Hebrew Scriptures is "Jehovah," or "YWH," which means, "I Am"—denoting an uncreated self-existence. The great secret is that we are self-existent too—just like the great Jehovah (a point that Christ made many times during his life, but which aroused the violent hatred of the religious authorities and intellectuals of his time just as it continues to arouse pharisaical wrath today). We outdo all other religions in our commitment to the transcendent and sacred nature of agency as the key to eternal progress. It's what allows us to become more like the God in whose image we are made.[3]

In fact, since our agency is the one thing that God didn't give us, He completely respects our use of it. It's not just that He *won't* take it away, *He can't*. Some people ask hard questions like, "Why does God allow wars, torture, genocide, and oppression?" The answer is that He *must*. He has to let all of His children exercise their agency—even villains like Hitler, Stalin, or Mao. Agency, then, gives at least a partial answer to the perennial question of suffering.

The prophet Lehi gave further insight on the meaning of agency in 2 Nephi 2. Here we have one of the great sages of history on his deathbed imparting a lifetime of accumulated wisdom and prophetic insight to his children. Among his final teachings was, "There is a God, and he hath created all things, both the heavens and the earth, and all things that in

---

[3] According to Apostle Neal A. Maxwell, "The submission of one's will is really the only uniquely personal thing we have to place on God's altar. The many other things we 'give' . . . are actually the things He has already given or loaned to us." Maxwell (1995, p. 24). This statement might seem puzzling given that there are scriptures which suggest that God did give us our agency (e.g., Moses 7:32 or 2 Nephi 2:16 given below). How do we reconcile this with other scriptures that say our agency is eternal (such as D&C 93)? According to the former Dean of Religious Education at BYU, Robert Millett, man, as an eternal being, has always had the capacity to think, will, and feel, but his capacity to choose was only made operative in mortality when God gave humans choices. In that sense, God gave man his agency. Millett (2015).

them are, both things to act and things to be acted upon . . . Wherefore, the Lord God gave unto man that he should act for himself" (vs. 14, 16).

For centuries scholars have been trying to classify everything in the universe, but here Lehi gives us the most accurate categorization of all: there are things to act (subjects), and things to be acted upon (objects).[4] Objects, such as rocks, furniture, basketballs, and even planets, are all passive and without will. They have no capacity to act independently. They simply react to the natural forces that control them. Subjects, on the other hand, are choosing, supernatural beings who act independently of external forces. God is an acting being, and so are you.[5]

If you think about it, this is the most liberating idea of all times. It means you can choose not only what you do, but also what you will become. You are in charge of your own destiny. Everything else in this universe lacks that capacity: a rock, amoeba, chimpanzee, or star is stuck with whatever it is programmed to be. What they do and become is completely determined. You, on the other hand, are not just an object subject to the causal forces of physics, but a causal force yourself.

One member of the Church was reading 2 Nephi 2 one day and this idea radically changed his whole outlook on life. The actions of all other creatures, he realized, are determined by stimuli, but in humans there is a gap between stimulus and response in which choice takes place. This makes us *responsible* (response-able) beings. Nothing else in the universe (save God) has that capacity. Humans, this man concluded from 2 Nephi 2, are "proactive" rather than "reactive." He took this insight, wrote a bestselling book, and created a consulting company that taught people to apply this principle to their lives and businesses.[6] In the process, he became a millionaire and one of the most influential management gurus in the world.

## FIRST CAUSE

The act vs. acted upon distinction gives new meaning to the core insights of St. Thomas Aquinas, the greatest philosopher of the Middle Ages. Aquinas wrote a masterwork of many volumes called the *t* in which he put forward a number of arguments for the existence of God. One of these was the "first cause" argument.

To understand the first cause argument, imagine you have a five-year-old niece who one

---

[4] We even find this duality built into our language. In the sentence "John threw the ball," John is the subject who acts, "threw" is the action he performs, and "the ball" is the object acted upon.

[5] Lehi's act/acted upon framework also helps us see one of the many reasons that pornography is so damaging. It turns a child of god (actor) into an *object* of lust to be acted upon. Many other grievous sins do the same. American slavery, for instance, treated human beings like cargo to be piled into a boat, shipped across an ocean, and then unloaded, examined, and lashed like animals—objects to be used and acted upon, rather than free subjects made in the image of God.

[6] Covey (1989).

day asks you, "Why is the weathervane on Grandpa's barn turning"? You answer, "Because the wind is blowing." But she's not going to let you get off that easy: "Why is the wind blowing?" You do a quick Google search and then kindly inform her, "The wind is blowing because of convection currents created by the heating and cooling of the earth's atmosphere." You think you are done but she is not: "Why does the atmosphere heat up?" You don't need to Google this one: "The sun does it." She comes back, "Why is the sun hot?" Back to Google: "The sun is hot because of nuclear fusion that converts hydrogen to helium and releases the excess matter in the form of energy." Still not done: "What causes nuclear fusion?" Your response: "Gravity. The sun is so vast that it pulls the elements together and fuses them by the force of its immense gravitational pull." "Why is there gravity?" OK, now you are really stuck and Google can't help you. At this point you throw up your hands and say, "Gravity just *is*. There is no further explanation. God just wanted it that way. God caused it."

Aquinas's point was that there has to be a God because there has to be a final cause at which all of the "whys" stop. There has to be an uncaused cause that is at the end of the chain of causation: the weathervane is caused by wind, the wind is caused by convection, convection is caused by heat, heat is caused by fusion, fusion is caused by gravity, gravity is caused by God's will, but God's will is the end. It is *uncaused*.

Aquinas was right on that point, but here's what he missed: *you are also a final cause*, just like God. Because you have agency, the buck stops with you. Why are you reading this book? Why did you go to work yesterday? Why did you have a sandwich for lunch? Why did you complete a term paper? You *chose* to. Nothing caused you to do it, it was an expression of your will.

Shakespeare illustrated this in his play *Julius Caesar*. Remember that Caesar refused to go to the Senate House for a meeting and Brutus pressed him as to why. What would Brutus tell the senators when he showed up without Caesar?

### DECIUS BRUTUS
Most mighty Caesar, let me know some cause,
Lest I be laugh'd at when I tell them so.

### CAESAR
The cause is in my *will*: I *will* not come;
That is enough to satisfy the senate.

Shakespeare demonstrates here (perhaps with some irony)[7] that a human's will—Caesar's—is a final cause from which one need not seek a further cause. Thus it is with all of us. We don't invoke further causes for our actions because there is no further cause. The cause

---

[7] Since Caesar ends up fulfilling a pre-determined destiny by attending the senate anyway and being assassinated, it's possible that Shakespeare was actually mocking the idea of free will in this passage.

is our will. God, as Aquinas showed, exists outside of the chain of causality, but so do you. That's why you are a child of God.

## NATURAL MAN

But most of us at some time or another *do* explain our actions as having a prior cause. We blame our actions on circumstances, other people, or limitations. Why do we do this? Why do we sometimes reject this most liberating idea of all times? The answer is that with agency comes responsibility—a heavy burden that accompanies this power.

This tendency to deny responsibility is built right into our human nature. Alongside our godly nature is our animal nature. We are beings to act, but because of the fall we have the temptation to submit to outside forces and allow ourselves to be acted upon. Mosiah 3:19 teaches that "the natural man is an enemy to God, and has been from the fall of Adam, and will be, forever and ever, unless he yields to the enticings of the Holy Spirit, and putteth off the natural man and becometh a saint through the atonement of Christ the Lord." The spiritual, godly man exists side by side with the natural man.

In other words, Darwin was right: you are an animal (a natural being) with all of the base instincts, inbuilt programming, carnality, and limitations that this entails. But he was only half right: you are also a spiritual being with free agency who can defy and overcome all of those limitations.[8]

Animals are among the things to be acted upon. They follow instinct and deserve no praise or blame for doing so since their actions are completely determined. They have no choice. But the human animal is different in that he can "put off" the natural man. This is what self-mastery and self-control are all about: the spirit dominating the body, agency dominating matter, your godly self dominating your animal self.

There is a tug-of-war occurring in your soul every day. Our dual nature means we are caught between animals and gods and must decide which way to go. You become more like God each time you resist carnal inclinations (vengeance, lust, anger, etc.), but become more like an animal/object each time you indulge them. Consider what this means for fasting: your body is telling you to eat, but you are telling your body you won't. Animals can't do that. They automatically consume food according to instinct. But you can decide *not* to eat by an act of will. When you fast, you are practicing godhood—you are exercising your spiritual muscles and putting off that natural/animal man.

On the other hand, when we behave like animals and refuse to take responsibility for

---

[8] As you can see, it's not that Darwinism isn't the truth (it is as true as such scientific theories can be), but that it is not "the whole truth and nothing but the truth." This is where the Neo-Darwinian atheists go wrong. They misuse this scientific theory by turning it into a totalizing explanation that excludes gospel truths. They might speak of humans as "mere machines" programmed to do what they do, but deep down they know that people are responsible for their own actions and that there is much more to being human than "animalness." But since they can't prove this scientifically, they dogmatically deny it.

our actions by saying, "I couldn't help it," we become less like God and more like the chimpanzee, the amoeba, and the dirt. When we reject our agency, we relinquish our status as subjects and put ourselves back in the chain of causation with all other objects. We surrender our godhood.

As you can see, agency is double-edged. The upside is that you are like God himself with the possibility of light, progress, and glory beyond your wildest imaginings. The downside is that you are *accountable* for your actions. It's *hard* to be like God. It means taking responsibility. It means you are to blame for your own mistakes. Objects have it easy. Nothing is ever their fault. If a rock tumbles down a hill, it is neither good nor bad, but just what happened. It's a morally neutral event—objects obeying causation have no responsibility and deserve neither praise nor blame. The reality of human agency is not only the most liberating idea of all times, it is also the most terrifying since we can't claim "I couldn't help it."

Since agency means progress towards godhood, you can understand why Satan worked so hard to destroy it in the pre-existence. He failed there, but he is succeeding remarkably here in the modern world. Every day, more people take the easy way out, deny their agency, behave like mere animals, and then find something to blame (upbringing, parents, poverty, or "the system"). While the Lord asks us to be proactive, put off the "natural" man, and take responsibility for our actions, the world teaches us to just follow our base instincts like any other animal/object. Denial of agency is also a self-fulfilling prophecy (something recent scientific research has confirmed). The more you deny your agency, the less agency you *think* you have; the less agency you think you have, the less ability you *actually* have to exercise it.[9]

In that sense, we are not too much different than the Nephites. When King Mosiah finally abolished the monarchy and set up a free system of judges (Mosiah 29), he was elated. Now that the people were politically free to exercise their own agency, they, not he, would be responsible for their actions and their own sins. And yet in subsequent books, we find periodic movements among the Nephites to bring back kings (such as King-Men or Gadianton robbers). They didn't want the responsibility for their actions that comes with freedom. We 21st century Americans often do the same: we vote against freedom and in favor of greater controls over our lives. Like the Nephites, we don't want the responsibility. We would surrender our godhood to have this burden removed.

## WORLD'S PARADIGM

If we are objects in the world's eyes, what are the forces that control us? The most common answers are: heredity (nature) and environment (nurture). In this view, everything we are, everything we do, and everything that happens to us is pre-determined by the biological genes inherited from our parents and the environment within which these genetic

---
9  Tierney (2011, p. D1).

traits develop. Sociologist Charles Murray says that your destiny is almost 100% a function of your genetically inherited IQ; Neo-Darwinist biologists claim that humans are just machines for the unconscious transmission of DNA; sociobiologist Edmund Wilson says your life is like a recently snapped polaroid—the picture is already set, but just needs to be developed. Pavlov proved that dog behavior is a function of stimulus-response and behaviorists like B.F. Skinner claimed that this was the same for humans—all of our actions are simply reactions to external stimuli. In this view, we are responsible neither for our mistakes nor our successes because both are merely the result of what our environment made us do. To the world the natural man is all there is.

Many religious people enter the debate, begging that we admit a third factor into the nature vs. nurture framework—free will. Of course heredity and environment mostly shape who we are, they say, but doesn't choice give us a little wiggle room within these constraints?

Latter-day Saints not only reject the world's "nature-nurture only" view, but also the standard religious view. Our focus on the centrality of agency means that we don't just see free will as one factor among three; rather, our agency is so powerful that, through Christ, it can actually *overcome, and dominate the other two*. In other words, the godly capacity for choice is so real and decisive that heredity and environment don't only choose you, *you can choose them*.

## CHOOSE ENVIRONMENT

Let's take a closer look at what it means to choose one's environment. In this dispensation, one of the first commandments to Joseph Smith and the early saints was to gather to Zion (initially Ohio and Missouri). Later the Lord told them to gather to Illinois, then Utah, and eventually to the stakes across the world. Gathering to Zion is a major theme throughout the scriptures and what is this gathering if not choosing a gospel environment? The handcart pioneers felt this commandment so deeply that many of them gave their lives in their attempt to come to Zion.

The scriptures command, "Stand ye in holy places" (D&C 45:32, 87:8). You chose your environment when deciding where to go to college or what job to accept. You choose your environment every time you attend church, associate with certain friends, go to a wholesome activity, walk out of an objectionable film, leave a party, close a sketchy internet site, or turn off an offensive TV show. We choose our environment literally hundreds of times a day.

Does a bad environment cause people to do bad things? Of course. There is a reason crime is much higher in inner-city environments, but we can *choose* to escape those bad environments and thereby reverse the chain of causation. As you can see, agency means you can choose your environment instead of letting your environment choose you.

*Chapter 2*

## CHOOSE HEREDITY

While the idea of choosing one's environment might make sense, some have much more difficulty accepting the idea that we can choose our heredity. The genetic traits we were born with are fixed, right? We can't change our biology can we?

Actually, if we are to believe true prophets (rather than the false prophets of the world), *we can*. Read the scriptures again and this time pay special attention to the "House of Israel" theme. What is the House of Israel if not an open genetic line for anyone who wants to join by choosing covenants? All members of the Church are of the Blood of Abraham and it doesn't matter if that is their *actual* lineage or not. It becomes their bloodline by their choices. The House of Israel motif is an ever-present scriptural reminder of how choices override biology.

Dozens of other examples prove this point. The Old Testament tells of a Moabite woman, Ruth, who decided she would join the people of Israel. Their people would be her people and their God would be her god (Ruth 1:16- 17). But she wasn't *really* a member of the House of Israel, right? Actually, the entire line of Israelite Kings was descended from Ruth (David, Solomon, even Christ himself). If she wasn't a "true Israelite" then nobody was. Conversely, the Pharisees bragged about their genealogy that traced back to Abraham, but John the Baptist rebuked them by pointing out that their wicked choices had voided their claims to this chosen ancestry (Matthew 3:9).

We often think of the Book of Mormon as a history of two races—the descendants of Nephi and the descendants of Laman/Lemuel—but in reality, race has very little to do with it. We find many examples of Lamanites converting and *choosing* to live according to the traditions of the Nephites and, indeed, *becoming* Nephites (e.g., 3 Nephi 2:12-16). Likewise, we find Nephites dissenting from their traditions and becoming Lamanites. And lest one think these dissenting Nephites were never "true Lamanites," note that some of them became Kings and rulers over the Lamanites (e.g., Amulon, Amalickiah, Ammoron). They were as Lamanite as Lamanite could be.[10]

We all face the same decision. When we choose baptism we become daughters and sons of Christ. This is what the "re-birth" theme in scriptures is all about—getting a new you, a new lineage through covenants and ordinances that sanctify, elevate, renew, and change our bodies (which carry our genes). In fact, the change that comes with covenants is so profound that we even get a whole new name, symbolizing our new identity (see D&C 130:11). A man named Abram chose to follow the Lord and make covenants and received the new name "Abraham." A man named Simon chose to become a disciple of the Lord and was given the new name "Peter." A man named Saul had a conversion experience on the road to Damascus and was given the new name "Paul." Choice gave them a new identity, a

---

10 Ammoron even wrote an epistle to Moroni in which he declared without equivocation, "I am a Lamanite," even though his ancestors were all Nephites. Choice, not ancestry, was decisive (see Alma 43:4).

new lineage—symbolic of their escape from the constraints of their heredity. Many people convert to the gospel and are disowned by their families. This is tragic, but has profound symbolic import.

But isn't this "rebirth" talk just metaphorical? We don't *really* change our actual biological attributes do we?

Actually we do. Consider this: in the early 20$^{th}$ century scientists wanted a fixed standard of inborn intelligence so they developed the "Intelligence Quotient" (I.Q.)—not a measure of how much knowledge or ability somebody had obtained, but their unchangeable, genetic mental capacity. And yet they gave the tests to thousands of people, followed up decades later with the same people, and found that this "fixed" biological trait had changed for many of them. Some had diligently worked to improve their minds and their IQ's increased, while some had let their minds atrophy and their IQ's dropped. That wasn't supposed to happen. By the reckoning of the time, it was scientifically impossible. That is the power of agency.

Also consider the Latter-day Saints themselves. Many of the first converts were poor, hapless people from the working classes of England. Today, their descendants are Fortune 500 CEO's, Ivy League professors, national politicians, Rhodes Scholars, and millionaires. LDS success rates are disproportionate to their population.[11] That's not supposed to happen. That's the power of agency.

Even scientists are now realizing that will can influence biology. Many of them now understand that our DNA is not so much a program that controls us, but more like a library with many books we can choose to open. Our traits vary depending upon which genes we choose to unlock. Even the most hardened of biological determinists now accept *neuroplasticity*—the view that mental characteristics can be changed, improved, suppressed, or unlocked via an act of will. "Rather than being predestined by DNA and development in the uterus," says Columbia psychologist Walter Mischel, "the architecture of our brains is more malleable than had been imagined, and we can have an active hand in shaping our fates by how we live our lives."[12] Stanford psychologist Carol Dweck notes that by adopting a "growth" mindset, humans can actively change qualities that used to be considered fixed.[13] Even our health, as the placebo effect has long shown, is affected by our will.

Consider finally the example of Heber J. Grant. Like Hamilton, he was an impoverished orphan with no money or gifts. In fact, he had nothing but an unconquerable will and a determination to succeed in life against all odds.

The kids on the playground called him a "sissy" because of the way he threw the ball. He spent months throwing at a target on the side of a barn until his baseball skills were

---

11 See Chua & Rubenfeld (2014).

12 Mischel (2014, p. 273). Also see Chapter 7, "Is It Prewired? The New Genetics."

13 Dweck (2006).

such that he led his team to a territorial championship. He had terrible handwriting and someone said it looked like a chicken with ink-dipped feet had walked across his paper. He took this as a challenge and practiced with a copybook until he had such fine handwriting that people from all over would ask him to pen formal documents. The local university even asked him to teach penmanship courses. Of course, Heber also worked his way up from utter poverty to become one of the wealthiest businessmen in the American West.

Tone-deaf Heber could not hit a note when singing—too bad because surely one's vocal cords are fixed by biology. But Heber belted out hymns at every chance, often driving his traveling companions crazy. Finally, after decades of practice, Heber sang, for the first time in his life, a full song without missing a note. His children were astonished, but since he was late in life, they were also saddened that he had worked so hard to acquire this talent which he would never put to full use. But Heber didn't see it that way—it wasn't so much about the singing itself, but the conquest of his biological limitations. This all wasn't supposed to happen. That is the power of agency.[14]

## CONCLUSION

All of the above shows that agency is the essence of our godly nature and can overcome and conquer biological or environmental limitations. President Benson well understood this and summarized it all in this inspired statement:

> The Lord works from the inside out. The world works from the outside in. The world would take people out of the slums. Christ takes the slums out of people, and then they take themselves out of the slums. The world would mold men by changing their environment. Christ changes men, who then change their environment. The world would shape human behavior, but Christ can change human nature.[15]

Let's circle back and tie all of this in to the topic at hand. What do agency and the meaning of humanity have to do with American Foundations? The answer is: *everything*. God's truths have profound implications for everything we will learn in the rest of this book. A correct understanding of humans as free agents created in the image of God gives us a foundation upon which we can build correct political, economic, and cultural institutions. Mistaken ideas, on the other hand, will take political and economic institutions in the direction of oppression, tyranny, and misery. It is to the political implications of agency that we next turn.

---

14 There is some dispute about how old President Grant was when he finally learned to sing. See Madsen (2004) and Oviatt (1984).
15 Benson (1985).

## CHAPTER 2 SOURCES/FURTHER READING

Benson, Ezra Taft. "Born of God," General Conference of the Church of Jesus Christ of Latter-day Saints, October 1985.

Brookhiser, Richard. *Alexander Hamilton, American*. New York: Free Press, 1999.

Chernow, Ron. *Alexander Hamilton*. New York: Penguin, 2004.

Chua, Amy & Jed Rubenfeld. *The Triple Package: How Three Unlikely Traits Explain the Rise and Fall of Cultural Groups in America*. New York: Penguin, 2014.

Covey, Stephen R. *The Seven Habits of Highly Effective People*. New York: Simon and Schuster, 1989.

Darwin, Charles. *On the Origin of Species* (1859). New York: Signet Classics, 2003.

Dweck, Carol S. *Mindset: The New Psychology of Success*. New York: Random House, 2006.

Givens, Terryl and Fiona. "Man was in the beginning with God," in *The God Who Weeps: How Mormonism Makes Sense of Life* (Salt Lake City: Ensign Peak, 2012), 38-54.

Madsen, Truman G. *Presidents Of The Church: Insights Into Their Lives And Teachings*. Salt Lake City: Deseret Book, 2004.

Maxwell, Neal A. "Swallowed up in the Will of the Father," *Ensign*, Nov. 1995, 22-24.

McCraw, Thomas K. *The Founders and Finance: How Hamilton, Gallatin, and Other Immigrants Forged a New Economy*. Cambridge, MA: Belknap Press, 2012.

Millett, Robert. "Joseph Smith and the Recovery of 'Eternal Man,'" Truman G. Madsen Lecture, Wheatley Institution, Provo, UT, Dec 3, 2015.

Mischel, Walter. *The Marshmallow Test: Mastering Self-Control*. Boston: Little, Brown, and Company, 2014.

Oviatt, Joan. "I Have Learned to Sing": President Heber J. Grant's Struggle to Sing the Hymns of Zion," *Ensign* (September 1984).

Tierney, John. "Do You Have Free Will? Yes, It's the Only Choice," *New York Times*, March 22, 2011, D1.

Walker, Ronald W. *Qualities That Count: Heber J. Grant As Businessman, Missionary, and Apostle*. Provo: BYU Press, 2003.

# Chapter 3

# BASIC PRINCIPLES II: THE RIGHTS & EQUALITY OF HUMANS

## JOHN LOCKE: DISCOVERING LIBERTY

We spent the last chapter learning about agency and how our capacity to freely choose is what makes us humans created in "God's image." Now we turn to the implications this truth has for politics. How does our free will translate into a theory of government and what do we mean when we speak of liberty, rights, and equality?

To understand the origin and meaning of these concepts, we must turn to the philosopher who gave them their first and perhaps greatest expression—John Locke. No thinker has been more foundational to American freedom and the liberal- democratic order that much of the world aspires to in the 21st century. In that sense, he may have been one of the most important people to have ever lived.

Locke was born in 17th century England to a middle-class family. His father, a soldier in the royal military, scraped together enough money to send his precocious son to Oxford University where it was customary to study philosophy and theology in preparation for the ministry. Young John was interested in these subjects, but he didn't like the questions the Oxford theologians were asking nor their methods for receiving answers. Drawing on the medieval scholastics, Oxford scholars would use logic to theorize about lofty, abstract principles that seemed to Locke unimportant and unprovable (e.g., "how many angels can dance on the head of a pin?"). Instead of becoming a clergyman, Locke decided to go into medicine, a field that he felt had more promise for someone of his mindset.

But even as he practiced medicine, Locke was still interested in the philosophical questions that he felt he never received answers to: "How do we know anything? What is human nature? What are governments for?" In pursuing answers to these questions, he founded a school of philosophy called *empiricism,* which says that knowledge comes primarily through the senses—sight, hearing, touch, smell, and taste—not from innate ideas (as philosophers such as Plato had claimed). He presented this philosophy in his book, *An Essay Concerning Human Understanding*, which revolutionized the theory of knowledge.

But Locke also had much to say on theology. He wrote a lesser-known work, *The Reasonableness of Christianity*, in which he gave empirical arguments for religious knowledge. He believed the scholastics had failed to address the great strength of Christian theology—its reasonableness in appealing to the senses. By focusing on the utter mysteriousness of God, the medieval scholars had missed the empirical character of the gospel. We know God is real, he said, not because of complex mental calculation, but because of the testimony of those who have *seen, heard,* and *touched* Him. When Jesus was resurrected from the dead and appeared to the doubting apostles, He didn't say, "Go check out the metaphysical arguments for God's existence," rather, He said, "Handle me and see" to know that I Am (Luke 24:39). The reality of God is found in empirical experience—the testimony of witnesses and the observable effect that God has on our lives. Unfortunately, Locke's religious teachings, unlike the rest of his philosophy, went largely ignored. It took Joseph Smith and the Restoration to find an audience for this "theological empiricism."

For the purposes of this book, Locke's greatest contributions were in the philosophy of politics. Lockean liberalism[1] would inspire the Founding Fathers and become our *American Creed*—the set of common ideals that define our country. Democrats, Republicans, and independents alike pay homage to Locke every time they speak about liberty, rights, or equality—terms that he introduced into common political discourse and established as worthy political goals.

## WHAT IS FREEDOM?

Let's use Locke as our guide to understand the proper meaning and application of these much used (and misunderstood) terms: liberty, rights, and equality.[2] We start with liberty (i.e., freedom). What does it mean to say that someone is free or that America is a free country? Clearly it doesn't mean freedom to do anything, since none of us is free to flap our arms and fly like birds, read minds, or leap buildings in a single bound. So what does freedom mean?

---

1 Liberalism, in this sense, means a political system in which the government exists to protect the rights of individual citizens.

2 The parts of Locke's political philosophy discussed in this chapter are found in his *Second Treatise on Government* (1689).

## STATE OF NATURE

Locke gave us a tool to help us out of this difficulty—a thought experiment with which we can conceptualize freedom and apply it to politics.[3] Imagine, he said, that you live in a "state of nature"—a place like a deserted island where there are no other humans or human creations, only you and nature. You would be alone with the birds, palm trees, sand, clouds, and ocean. There would be no human artifacts such as schools, laws, hospitals, businesses, or buildings.[4]

Locke said that in this state of nature you would be perfectly free. Now, you might think to yourself: "Perfectly free? I've seen *Castaway* and Tom Hanks was not happy on his island. He was lonely, poor, had no healthcare (he had to remove a decayed tooth with an ice skate), had little food, and enjoyed no companionship other than a volleyball. This was not a pleasant situation." But Locke would reply that even though it was not pleasant, it was *free* in the sense that a person alone on a deserted island is free to exercise his agency however he wants *without anyone else there to stop him*. If Tom Hanks wanted to make a fire on the beach, pick up handfuls of sand, hike into the hills, build a raft, or go fishing he was free to do it.

In the state of nature, nobody is there to stop you from exercising your agency and this is what Locke meant by "liberty." To be free doesn't mean having all of your wishes and desires fulfilled, because nature still constrains you. You would not be "free" to fly like a bird or control the weather or even receive quality dental care. We are not talking about freedom *from nature*, we are talking about freedom from *other people*. We are always subject to God and God's laws (we are never free from the law of gravity, for instance), but in the state of nature we are free from the compulsion of others.

This freedom to exercise agency, said Locke, translates into *natural rights*. They are natural because we humans did not invent them (just like a mountain stream is natural—not human-made). Natural rights are God-given and inborn. Our status as beings with agency entitles us to these rights. Since no human gave them to us, no human should take them away.

*Rights* are claims on others that we are justified in using force to secure. When we ask, "What rights do we have?" we are actually asking, "What can we demand from others using

---

3  Some people attack Locke's thought experiment on the grounds that it's only hypothetical, but that's beside the point. Thought experiments help us arrive at truth even if what we are thinking about never actually occurred. For instance, Albert Einstein gave us the theory of general relativity by sitting in his office and thinking about what would happen if he flew into space as fast as a beam of light. That Albert Einstein never flew and caught up to a beam of light is irrelevant. The thought experiment yielded truth even if it only took place in his imagination.

4  This point is somewhat unclear in Locke's *Second Treatise* because he uses the term "State of Nature" in two senses. He starts by describing it as a state of solitary freedom, and then later shifts to speaking of it as a social, pre-government situation.

force?" To Locke, we have three overarching natural rights, each of which encompasses many specific rights.

First, because we are free from anyone else coming to kill us in the state of nature we have a *right to life*. Does this mean that a coconut won't fall on our heads and kill us, a wave won't wash us out to sea, or a lightning bolt won't strike and fry us? No. Nature and nature's God might kill us at any time (and, in fact, will certainly kill us all eventually), but this is not a violation of our right to life because no *other person* is there to kill us. We can never be free from nature, but it *is* possible to be free from other people murdering us.

Second, since there is nobody in the state of nature to imprison us, silence us, beat us, kidnap us, prevent our worship, and so forth, we have a *right to liberty*. By this, Locke meant the right to be free from the arbitrary control and dominance of others.

Third, and most importantly, since there is nobody around to steal from you in the state of nature, you have a *right to property*. If you work to build a hut, then it's your hut and you have a right to it. If you go into the ocean and catch fish, then you have, by your labor, made those fish your own. If you pick coconuts from the jungle and husk them, they are yours. You have taken the natural resources that God put there, mingled your labor with them, improved them, laid claim to them, and made them yours. The fruits of your labor become your property.

So the three over-arching natural rights that encompass all of our sub-rights are *life, liberty, and property*.

## IMPORTANCE OF PROPERTY

Some people are suspicious of natural rights, especially the right to property. They say that property is just filthy money ("the root of all evil," in the Apostle Paul's words; 1 Timothy 6:10), but Locke saw property rights as *foundational* to all other natural rights. That is, if someone does not have property rights, they will sooner or later lose their rights to life and liberty as well. Property is the means by which we pursue our goals and we cannot secure life or liberty without the right to own and control property. Could you really have freedom of expression if you weren't allowed to own and control a printing press? Could you have the freedom to assemble if you had no property on which to meet? Could you have freedom of religion if you were not allowed to own buildings in which to worship? Without property, one cannot protect their other rights. If the government (or anyone else) can take your property, they can effectively take your other rights as well. For this reason, Locke saw property rights, seemingly the most insignificant of the three, as the foundation of all others.[5]

When Locke advanced this idea, he had little historical evidence to back it up, but

---

5 Mandelbaum (2002) summarizes the vast literature on this point, saying, "It was the protection of property that gave birth, historically, to political rights" (pg. 271).

events of the 20th century have proven him remarkably prescient. Every single regime that has taken away property rights has eventually taken away all other rights as well. Think of Pol Pot's Cambodia, Stalin's Russia, or Hitler's Germany—all socialist regimes that controlled property first and then ended up controlling life and liberty as well.

Another illustration of the necessity of property rights for freedom is found in Mao's China. When the Chinese Communist Party came to power, Mao Zedong proclaimed that the government would control and distribute all of the property in the country, but the people would be free to enjoy life and liberty, particularly free speech (letting "100 flowers bloom").

Meanwhile, Mao's nemesis Chiang Kai Shek, after losing the civil war to the Communists, fled the mainland for Taiwan where he set up a dictatorship. There would be no free speech rights, no political dissent, no democracy, and life would be subject to the whims of Chiang and his henchmen. But, unlike on the mainland, Chiang did allow private property rights in Taiwan.

Mao's regime promised *all rights* except for property and Chiang's offered *no rights* except for property. Thirty years later, what had happened? Chiang's regime had become a full-blown liberal democracy with all of the freedom, prosperity, and rights it entails—speech, press, religion, etc.—while the story on the mainland was the opposite. The people under Mao's regime had lost *all* of their rights and some 70 million people had been killed by the government. If anyone spoke out against the government, Mao would withhold their ration of food and starve them and their families. Without property none were at liberty to speak out or challenge those in power and millions were persecuted, beaten, and jailed just for holding certain opinions. Without property the Chinese under Mao had no rights to life or liberty either.

A similar contrast is found in North vs. South Korea. Both began as dictatorships after the Korean War, but South Korea allowed its people to own property while North Korea adopted socialism. Over six decades later, South Korea is one of the wealthiest and freest nations in the world, while North Korea is one of the poorest and most oppressive. Every day people starve to death in the North under the communist tyranny of the Kim family while the average South Korean lives a thriving, abundant life.

We find a similar illustration in the history of the Church. In the 1830s, Missouri mobs sought to silence Mormons by destroying their printing office and press. Thus, the destruction of LDS private property rights was the destruction of freedom of speech. More recently, during the debate over Proposition 8 in California, police officers stood on the perimeter of LDS temple property, protecting the right of saints to go in and out. All that stood between the Latter-day Saints and those who wanted to take away their freedom of worship was property.

## Chapter 3

Locke was right: property is the foundation of freedom. There never has been, nor will there ever be, a free country without private property rights.

### CONSECRATION AND PROPERTY

Before proceeding further, it's important to clear up a misconception that some members of the Church have about property rights and the gospel. Many mistakenly believe that communism (or other forms of socialism) and the law of consecration are "basically the same" since, under both systems, wealth is distributed from rich to poor. They believe that if we were truly righteous, we would all live under a socialistic system and there would be no private property at all.

There are three major problems with this reasoning: first, the law of consecration as given in the scriptures does not take away private property rights, but, in fact, speaks extensively of them as a stewardship from God. Prophets such as Harold B. Lee and Marion G. Romney have been abundantly clear on this point. You cannot consecrate something you don't own; property is the *precondition* of consecration, not its negation.

Second, socialism is administered by the government, while the law of consecration is administered by the Church. How can one say both systems are the same when the Church is an inspired organization led by God's prophets while the government is led by politicians following the philosophies of men?

Third, and most importantly, the law of consecration preserves agency while socialism takes it away. This means that the difference between the two systems is the same as the difference between charity and theft. Let's look at two scenarios to illustrate this.

> Scenario A: John is walking down the street, sees impoverished Mike, feels compassion for him, and hands Mike $100.

> Scenario B: John is walking down the street and Mike grabs John's wallet and runs off with $100.

Is it fair to say that Scenarios A and B are "basically the same" because in both cases $100 has gone from John to Mike? In the first example, John gave his money voluntarily and in the spirit of charity. In the second example Mike took the money by force. The giving in Scenario A is based on compassion and free will—godly principles—while the taking in Scenario B is based on envy and compulsion—satanic principles.

This is exactly the relationship between the law of consecration and communism. In consecration, you freely give; in communism, they take by force. Consecration is based on agency and charity. Communism and other forms of socialism are based on force and control ("institutionalized plunder" in President Benson's words).[6] Communism is taking; consecration is giving. It's that simple. We should live the law of consecration by covenant and agency, but remember that D&C 121:41 says, "No power or influence can or ought to be maintained by virtue of the priesthood, only by persuasion." There is all the difference in the world between theft and charity, and there is all the difference in the world between communism and consecration. Let us not any longer be misled to say that they are "basically the same" when their fundamental principles are so diametrically opposed.

## NATURE OF GOVERNMENT

Although Locke outlined the rights we have in the state of nature, we do not actually live in that state. We all live in societies composed of millions of people. But to Locke this didn't matter. We don't surrender our natural rights in society because we still have the same agency we would have in the state of nature. We retain our natural rights because we retain our agency.

Unfortunately, many people would violate our rights. Unlike on the deserted island, there are people in society who will kill us, silence us, kidnap us, beat us, imprison us, or steal from us. In the state of nature, I can say "Kim Jong-un is a jerk" and thereby exercise part of my natural right to liberty (free speech), but in society, Kim Jong-un might send me to prison for saying this. In the state of nature, I can pick coconuts, husk and eat them and keep them for later—nobody is there to take them from me—but here in society, other people can steal those coconuts. In the state of nature, I can worship the sun, but in society other people can shoot me for worshipping the sun. To Locke, this was fundamentally wrong: no person gave these rights to us (nature and nature's God did), so no person should be able to take them away (except God and nature). Locke concluded that this justified the use of force against others to protect our natural rights.

This is where governments come in. Government is the body to which we delegate the power to exercise force over society. When we ask, "What should the government do?" it is the same as asking, "What should we force people to do?" Locke said we should only use force to protect our natural rights. The government can and should use force to stop people from killing us, imprisoning us, silencing us, preventing our worship, stealing from us, and so on.

## SOCIAL CONTRACT

Unlike natural rights, governments are artificial. We humans create governments and delegate to them the power to protect our natural rights. We do this, says Locke, through

---

6  Benson (1968).

a *social contract*, meaning that we agree to obey the laws and pay taxes to support the government, and the government agrees to defend our natural rights. It's a deal—a mutually beneficial bargain through which we find protection. We relinquish our personal right to enforce our will on others in the hope that the government can more justly and efficiently protect everyone.

## BY THE PEOPLE

Locke's theory was revolutionary in a couple of ways. First, he taught (drawing on Thomas Hobbes) that governments are *created by the people*. Before Locke, people thought that government power and authority could not be challenged because that authority came from sacred tradition or even from God himself (so said the *divine right* principle). If a man was king, the thinking went, then God must have ordained him to that position; how dare anyone try to place limits on the king's God-given authority. A monarch's subjects had to accept that their life, liberty, and property were at the government's disposal.

Locke's theory turned this all on its head. The king did not have power because God gave it to him; the *people* gave him his power through social contract. They delegated authority to the king so that he might protect their rights. The king wasn't master, and the people weren't servants; the people were masters, and the king was a servant. Notice the change in language that reflects this new understanding: citizens of a country used to call themselves "the king's subjects," but today we refer to our elected leaders as "public servants"—a verbal legacy of Locke's theory.

The idea that a just government will be democratic comes from Locke as well. Since governments only govern by social contract, then the government can only act with the consent of the people. Yes, we submit to be governed, but only by laws and rulers that we agree to through elections. The government doesn't just do whatever it wants; it does what the people *authorize* it to do. In that sense, we renew the social contract with every election. It's also no coincidence that the first words of the U.S. Constitution are "We the People." It was a Lockean idea that the people of the U.S. in 1787 used to create a government just as Locke said—by social contract.

## LIMITS TO GOVERNMENT

The second revolutionary idea in Locke's theory is that government power should be *limited*, not absolute. Governments can't just do whatever they want, they can only perform the core functions we delegate to them. Governments must have armies to protect us from external threats to our rights (foreign invaders), and must have police and legal systems to protect us from internal threats to our rights (criminals), but, according to Locke, that's where their authority should end.

Since natural rights are the only things we can claim by force from other people, it follows that natural rights are the only things government can use force to preserve. The government shouldn't use its force to make us righteous, to give us luxuries, to make us join a church, or say something we don't believe. People can only legitimately use force to protect themselves, so the same rule applies to the governments to whom we have delegated a monopoly on force. If government goes beyond protecting our natural rights, then it is, by definition, taking them away.

## RIGHT TO REVOLUTION

Now here's where Locke's philosophy was not just revolutionary in concept, but actually had revolutionary consequences for American history: Locke said that if the government was not performing its single valid function—preserving natural rights—then it had violated the social contract that created it, making that contract null and void. This meant that the people were no longer bound by the contract and could establish a new government altogether. Under the Divine Right idea, if the king violated the people's rights, they simply had to accept it as tough luck. Under John Locke's theory, the people could throw out the old government and create a new one. As the American Revolution proved, this was a revolutionary doctrine in every sense.

## EQUALITY

The final major idea of Locke's philosophy was *equality*. What Locke meant by equality was that even though we are unequal in our attributes, possessions, or characteristics, we are nonetheless equal in the most fundamental sense—our status as humans with agency who are endowed by our creator with natural rights. This *natural equality*, said Locke, entails *political equality*—meaning the government should protect everyone's natural rights equally.

LeBron James is certainly taller, wealthier, and more athletic than the majority of the population, but, according to Locke's theory, he should not have any more rights and political privileges than anyone else. People are naturally equal in their rights to life, liberty, and property so we should have the same rights before government that we have before God. The government preserves LeBron James's rights in the same way and to the same degree that it preserves the rights of the poorest, shortest, and least athletic. That's what Locke meant by equality.[7]

---

[7] Many have used Locke's ideas to advocate economic equality through socialism. Anyone who has read Locke's staunch defense of property rights will recognize such reasoning as a perversion rather than an application of Locke's ideas.

*Chapter 3*

## LOCKE AND THE GOSPEL

Now, if you are a Latter-day Saint, Locke's doctrines should have particular interest for you, because you belong to the only church in the world in which the basics of Locke's political theories are scriptural. It says clearly in D&C 134 that governments exist to "secure to each individual the free exercise of conscience, the right and control of property, and the protection of life" (v. 2). This is a confirmation of Locke's idea that governments should protect life, liberty, and property. D&C 134 further states that governmental powers should be limited to these core functions. They are not "to infringe upon the rights and liberties of others," says verse 4, nor should they "interfere in prescribing rules of worship to bind the consciences of men, nor dictate forms for public or private devotion." The governments should protect our rights by "restraining crime" and "punishing guilt," but should "never control conscience" or "suppress the freedom of the soul." These revealed principles of government perfectly align with Locke's philosophy, as do many statements of latter-day apostles and prophets.

The overlap in principles does not stop there. Like Locke, Latter-day Saints view the possession of agency as a defining human characteristic. Just as the pre-mortal war was justified because "Satan . . . sought to destroy the agency of man" (Moses 4:3), it is appropriate for us to defend our innate freedoms. Satan failed to control us in the pre-existence, so he continues to try to control us through despotic governments here in mortality.

This puts Latter-day Saints at odds with some worldly philosophies. One extreme position says that individuals do not have rights, and the government should control everything in society. All individuals should subordinate their freedom to an all-powerful state (this was the philosophy behind both fascism and communism). The other extreme position says that there should be no government at all; that any use of force is intrinsically evil and we should therefore abolish all governments (the formal instruments of compulsion). Both of these extremes are untenable for Latter-day Saints. We believe, with Locke, in the necessity of governments, but we also believe in governments limited to a core, protective function.

## CAVEATS

Although we now have a proper understanding of the basic principles of government, we must take caution in how we apply these principles. Although it's clear what the government should do in general, it's not always clear how to translate these principles into practice. We can agree on a limited government that protects rights to life, liberty, and property and still disagree on how to achieve those goals. Democrats and Republicans promote different policies and it is possible to have different opinions on how to apply correct political principles. As we seek to do so, we should proceed with care and humility, understanding that both the Republican and Democratic parties are organizations created and run by fallible humans with all of the corruptions and imperfections this entails. Locke's theory provides us a framework for approaching politics, but often will not provide specific policy answers.

We must also remember that no rights are absolute. For instance, nobody has an absolute right to property because we must, at the very least, pay taxes to support the government that protects our natural rights. Nor does anyone have an absolute right to free speech (we have no right to plan a conspiracy to assassinate the President or shout fire in a crowded theater). Yes we enjoy natural rights, but in civil society they all have some boundaries. How high taxes can become before they have violated our property rights, for example, is a matter for debate, not dogmatism. There are many free governments that protect natural rights around the world and they all have different levels and modes of taxation.

## ARTIFICIAL RIGHTS

Before finishing our discussion of liberty, rights, and equality, we must address one last question: what about those rights that are not natural rights? What about the artificial rights that people invent, such as the right to a trial by jury, the right to due process, the right to vote, or the right to a date with Kaylee on Saturday night? Should governments work to secure these man-made, artificial rights for us or should governments only protect the natural rights that we have from God in the state of nature?

To answer this question, we need to understand that there are two types of artificial rights. First, are *civil rights*—human, legal creations that help protect our natural rights. A trial by jury is an example of a civil right. Even though you don't have the right to a jury trial in the state of nature, good governments still afford us this right because a jury trial is a sound way of protecting natural rights. The right to due process of law is another civil right; it helps protect the innocent from having their lives, liberties, and properties infringed upon through a false criminal conviction.

The second category of artificial rights, opposite civil rights, we might call *pseudo-rights*—false rights people invent that take away natural rights. For example, the right to a date with Mary on Saturday night is a pseudo-right because it would mean compelling Mary to go out with you, thus taking away her natural right to liberty.

Pre-Civil War southerners talked about the "right" to own a slave, but this was clearly a pseudo-right because it took away the life, liberty, and property rights of those they held in bondage. Some talk of a right to certain possessions, but since possessions must come from somewhere, securing such pseudo-rights would require stealing from others. If someone claimed that they had a right to a yacht, a million-dollar salary, or another man's wife, we would oppose such claims as pseudo-rights since using force to secure them would infringe upon the natural rights of others.[8]

So when confronted with someone talking about a "right," we need to ask ourselves, "Does this right fall under the category of natural rights, civil rights, or pseudo-rights?" If it is a natural right or a civil right, we should favor government securing it through force. If it is a pseudo-right, on the other hand, we should oppose government using force to secure it, since it will take away natural rights. Determining a pseudo-right is often difficult since many call them natural rights or civil rights hoping to confuse us into accepting them. We must be vigilant: just because something is labeled a civil or natural right doesn't make it so.

## CONCLUSION

As you can see, Locke's ideas are both revolutionary and powerful. If they seem commonplace to you, it is only because his ideas have spread so widely in the modern world. What may have seemed radical and even absurd in the 18$^{th}$ century is now taken for granted. As we shall see in coming chapters, Locke's ideas are particularly revolutionary for this country—they constituted the philosophy of the Founding Fathers expressed in the Declaration of Independence. Just as importantly, Locke's ideas are the American Creed that continues to define and underpin our political institutions.

## CHAPTER 3 SOURCES/FURTHER READING

Benson, Ezra Taft. "The Proper Role of Government," *Conference Report*, October 1968, pp. 17-22.

Berlin, Isaiah. *Two Concepts of Liberty.* New York: Oxford University Press, 1958.

Fried, Charles. *Modern Liberty and the Limits of Government.* New York: W.W. Norton, 2007.

Hayek, Friedrich Von. *The Road to Serfdom.* Chicago: University of Chicago Press, 1944.

_____. *The Constitution of Liberty.* Chicago: University of Chicago Press, 1978.

Huemer, Michael. *The Problem of Political Authority: An Examination of the Right to Coerce and the Duty to Obey.* New York: Palgrave Macmillan, 2013.

Locke, John. *Second Treatise of Government* (1689).

Madsen, Truman G. *Five Classics.* Salt Lake City: Eagle Gate, 2001.

Mandelbaum, Michael. *The Ideas that Conquered the World: Peace, Democracy, and Free Markets in the Twenty-first Century.* New York: Public Affairs, 2002.

Mill, John Stuart. *On Liberty* [1859]. Mineola, New York: Dover, 2002.

Nozick, Robert. *Anarchy, State, and Utopia.* New York: Basic Books, 1974.

---

8 Note that the question of "states' rights" has been hotly debated throughout U.S. history and into the present because some believe that states' rights protect our natural rights from federal government power, while others believe states' rights are a pseudo-right invoked to oppress minorities.

Popper, Karl. *The Open Society and Its Enemies*. Princeton: Princeton University Press, 2013.

Rawls, John. *A Theory of Justice*. Cambridge, MA: Belknap Press, 1999.

Romney, Marion G. "Political Thought and Life of J. Reuben Clark Jr.," BYU Devotional, November 21, 1972. <http://speeches.byu.edu/?act=viewitem&id=371>.

_____. "Socialism and the United Order Compared," *Conference Report*, April 1966, pp. 95-101.

Smith, Joseph. *Lectures on Faith*. Salt Lake City: Deseret Book, 1985.

# Chapter 4

# BASIC PRINCIPLES III: THE RULE OF LAW

### JOHN ADAMS: LAW OVER WILL

John Adams was without question one of our most important Founding Fathers.[1] Adams grew up in Braintree, Massachusetts. His father wanted him to become a minister, so young John dutifully studied and won admission to the top clergy training school in the colony—Harvard College. After graduation, Adams decided the ministry wasn't for him, so he cast about for a different career. He taught school for a while, but when he began reading law in a local attorney's office, he realized he had found his calling. Adams finished his legal studies and moved to Boston where, because of his forceful reasoning and fluid speech, he became one of the most sought-after lawyers in New England. It was in this situation that Adams was thrust onto the public stage in one of the key events in U.S. History.[2]

In 1770, the English government had been taxing the colonists without their consent and sent soldiers to enforce their oppressive measures. These soldiers were, in the minds of the colonists, the very embodiment of English tyranny. So the people of Boston treated these soldiers accordingly—insulting them, spitting on them, and perhaps even throwing rocks from time to time. The soldiers themselves were mostly young, lower-class men simply trying to make a living. They had come to America not out of any animus towards the colonists, but because their military superiors had ordered them.

On March 5, the tension turned into violence. A few angry colonists surrounded some of the soldiers and began hurling insults, then snowballs, and finally rocks, sharp shells, and

---

1 Traditionally, he has also been among the most underappreciated, but this may be changing. We have seen a surge of Adams scholarship over the last two decades, which found its fullest expression in David McCullough's 2001 Pulitzer Prize-winning biography and its adaptation into an HBO miniseries.

2 For the John Adams example and much of the conceptual framework of this chapter I am indebted to Fox and Pope (1990).

## Chapter 4

other hard objects. Soon a crowd formed as dozens more joined in the fun. The soldiers, fearing for their lives, got into formation and ordered the crowd to disperse. Instead, the tragic logic of crowds took over and the mob inflamed further. One of the panicked soldiers accidentally discharged his weapon. This touched off a full volley of fire and, when the smoke cleared, five American colonists lay dead in the snow. A tragedy? Yes. A massacre? No. The killing had been done in self-defense and largely by accident.

Nonetheless, the Bostonians wanted vengeance. This was their chance to indulge their wrath against the king's troops and everything they stood for. The governor of Massachusetts arrested the soldiers and assured the colonists that they would be put on trial for their alleged crimes.

But who would represent them in court? This is where John Adams came in. As much as anyone in the colonies, Adams opposed British tyranny and was considered a radical for freedom. In fact, it would later be said that Jefferson was the pen of Independence while Adams was the voice. If anyone hated the presence of British soldiers and what they symbolized, it was John Adams. But he also understood that an important principle, more fundamental than "no taxation without representation," was at stake. To uphold this principle, he would defend these soldiers in court when nobody else would.

In the minds of many colonists, Adams had now become a traitor to the cause. And where they had previously spit upon, persecuted, and vilified the soldiers, they now did the same to Adams. Former friends refused to speak with him and people turned their backs as he walked down the street. But Adams consoled himself with an ancient passage: "If, by supporting the rights of mankind and of invincible truth, I shall contribute to save from the agonies of death one unfortunate victim of tyranny . . . his blessing and tears of transport will be sufficient consolation to me for the contempt of all mankind."

Then began the first great show trial in US history. In court, Adams affirmed as strongly as he could that it was not so important how the colonists *felt* about these soldiers and British tyranny. All that mattered was what those soldiers had actually *done* and what the law said about those actions. They could not rule based on personal feelings, prejudice, or passions for or against the defendants. Even though everyone may have hated the soldiers and what they stood for, said Adams, this was irrelevant to the situation: the jury must let the *law* rule, not anyone's desires or will. He quoted Algernon Sidney who had said, "The law no passion can disturb. 'Tis void of desire and fear, lust and anger. 'Tis deaf, inexorable, inflexible." Adams then pointed out to the jury the key distinctions the law makes regarding the taking of life. Yes, the soldiers had killed, but this was *homicide excusable* (self defense) not *homicide felonious* (murder). The soldiers had only taken life to defend their own.

Adams's argument was ultimately successful and the jury voted to acquit six of the soldiers and let the other two off with light sentences. Adams understood that convicting the soldiers as murderers could have rallied the colonies further towards his cause—freedom from British oppression—but it also would have betrayed and corrupted the key principle their freedom depended upon.

What principle was that? What crucial ideal was at stake in the trial of the Boston Massacre defendants?

The answer is: *the Rule of Law.*

In the previous two chapters we discussed agency and how it translates into natural rights. In this chapter, we will learn about the Rule of Law as protector of those natural rights in society.

We might best understand the Rule of Law by contrasting it with its opposite—the *Rule of Will.* "Rule" means controlling others by force. By itself, there is nothing inherently wrong with this; we need rule and rulers for protection (the twelfth Article of Faith affirms this). "Will" means individual exercise of agency according to one's desires. As with rule, there is nothing inherently wrong with will—the exercise of agency is how we can progress and become like God.

"Rule" and "Will" alone are harmless, but when joined they form a poisonous combination. The Rule of Will means that the will of one person or group rules over another person or group and thereby takes away their natural rights.

For example, there is nothing wrong with wanting property and using your agency to make choices to acquire property, but there is something wrong with using *rule* (force) over other people to take their property (a natural right) according to your *will*—we call it theft. There is nothing wrong with wanting marriage and using your agency to choose a spouse, but there is something wrong with ruling over someone to compel them to marry you. It is fine to will that your arms swing back and forth, but it is not fine for you to rule over another person by choosing to swing your fist into their nose (taking away their right to liberty or, if you have lifted enough weights, their right to life).

As you can see, the distinction between mere "will" (the exercise of agency) and the "Rule of Will" is crucial and clear. We can and should exercise our will, but not in a compulsory way that rules over others. The Rule of Will—using force to deprive others of their natural rights to life, liberty, or property—is *the* central political problem of all history.

## ANARCHY

The Rule of Will comes in two forms. The first, we call *anarchy*. In anarchy, people take away rights by force because there is no government there to stop them. Anarchy, then, is defined as the Rule of Will in the *absence of government*. With no restraining government power, all become the enemy of all. Avarice and fear drive people to take the lives, liberties, and properties of others. The strong dominate the weak by theft, rape, enslavement, and murder.[3]

Anarchy is the more brutal of the two forms of the Rule of Will and unfortunately, there have been many instances of anarchy throughout history. For instance, we often picture the 19th century American West as a time of honorable cowboys, peaceful sunsets, cattle drives, and heroic conquest of untamed land, but the reality was far crueler. Bandits sacked cabins, roving thugs raided wagon trains, men shot each other in the streets, and because of their remote location out West, little authority was there to stop them.

Anarchy is what finally killed the prophet Joseph Smith. The local authorities arrested and placed him in jail, but then withdrew all government protection and allowed mobs to come and lynch him. It is ironic that mobocracy killed the prophet since he had spent a lifetime combatting this evil. He had seen the saints persecuted by lawlessness in New York, Ohio, and Missouri and he constantly petitioned the government for help. President Van Buren's response "I can do nothing for you," summarized the unwillingness to stop the anarchy that caused such suffering among the Saints. When Senator Calhoun wrote Joseph Smith that he would also do nothing for the LDS if elected president because the Federal Government's powers were "limited and specific," Joseph responded in a lengthy letter of righteous anger. Senator Calhoun, Joseph argued, failed to understand that the most basic function of government is to protect the rights of the people under its jurisdiction. A senator or president who failed to "reinstate expelled citizens to their rights," he said, was a "monstrous hypocrite fed and fostered from the hard earnings of the people."[4]

But isn't anarchy a thing of the past? This kind of mobocracy might have happened in the 19th century, but not the 21st, right? Actually, it does. Numerous third-world countries are run by local warlords and gangs because their governments are too weak to impose order. There are pockets of anarchy in our country government rule is weaker than that of local criminals. Furthermore, anarchy can break out at any moment as exemplified in post-Katrina New Orleans when looters took liberty and property after the government evacuated.

## TYRANNY

Let's now turn to the other, more common, form of the Rule of Will: *tyranny*. While anarchy is the Rule of Will in the absence of government, tyranny is the Rule of Will *through* government. In theory, government is the body that prevents us from violating one another's rights, but in practice government itself often takes our rights away. Once empowered, government rulers use this power to compel others according to their own will. We

---

[3] You can read about the brutality of anarchy in the Book of Mormon (e.g.,, after the Nephite reign of the judges broke down) or in contemporary fiction like Cormac McCarthy's *The Road*.
[4] Bushman (2007, p. 514).

cede power to governments to prevent coercion, but then the government itself becomes an agent of coercion.

We could spend thousands of pages listing the examples of tyranny from history and still not even come close to telling its full story. In fact, most of the history of humankind has been the gruesome story of unrestrained, unjust government oppression.

Nazi Germany is just one famous example. Hitler used the force of government to rule over and control millions of Jews, homosexuals, gypsies, and dissidents. He would seize their homes and wealth (taking their right to property), beat them and send them to prison camps (taking their right to liberty), and ultimately execute them with scientific efficiency in gas chambers (taking their right to life). The Nazi tyranny alone is the source of countless stories of unimaginable horror.

You've also heard of the millions killed by Communist tyrants like Stalin, Mao, and Pol Pot, but perhaps not as much about ancient tyrants like Qin Shi Huang Di, who conscripted thousands of laborers to build him a terracotta army to accompany him to the next life. After its completion, he repaid his laborers by killing them because he feared that, if they lived, they might create a similar monument for a future emperor. Millions died to satisfy the egomania of the first emperor of China who ruled over others to realize the madness of his will.

This only scratches the surface. We could go on recounting the tyrannical atrocities of Japanese militarists, Ottoman imperialists, Spanish inquisitors, and American slaveholders. The story of human tyranny is almost endless.

As you can see, the two forms of the Rule of Will are both tragic and pervasive. Either government rulers impose their will on the people, or non-government actors do when government is powerless to stop them. In both cases, people use force to deprive others of their natural rights.

## RULE OF LAW

In contrast to anarchy and tyranny, the Rule of Law means that stable, impartial laws rule over society rather than anyone's will. Government coercion can only be used to enforce non-arbitrary laws designed to protect the public. Under the Rule of Law, power over others is never exercised according to anyone's individual desires, but only as the law demands.

The Rule of Law places everyone on equal footing and gives no one special advantages over others. It provides fair rules for society just like the rules in a board game. One checkers player may *want* to move pieces backwards to gain an unfair advantage, but the rules prevent it. As in checkers, the Rule of Law means that all must abide by universal rules, regardless of what they may want.

Notice also that since the Rule of Law protects individual rights, it also preserves the principles of agency and accountability. It means *you* are responsible for what happens to you. When the Nephites moved to a Rule of Law system, King Mosiah was giddy with relief. No longer would he be responsible for their actions and sins, the people themselves would. Under the Rule of Law, a person's guilt determines punishment, so the people themselves are responsible for the consequences of their behavior. One's actions, not the caprices of a mob or a tyrant, decide their fate.[5]

The conceptual schema of the Rule of Law also provides us with a useful framework with which to analyze politics (much preferable to the silly and unintelligible "conservative-liberal" spectrum so common in political discourse). At one extreme we have anarchy in which the government does too little and is too weak to protect our rights, while at the other extreme we have tyranny in which the government does too much and takes away our rights. Somewhere between those two extremes we have government exercising just enough power to protect our rights and freedom, but no more. There is sufficient government to impose order—thus avoiding anarchy—but the government's actions are predictable and limited to enforcing laws—thus avoiding tyranny.

As founding father James Wilson said, "Bad governments are of two sorts: first, that which does too little; secondly, that which does too much; that which fails through weakness, and that which destroys through oppression." The Rule of Law is Wilson's healthy middle ground between the extremes of tyranny and anarchy.[6] Modern revelation calls this "constitutional government" and says "whatsoever is more [tyranny] or less than this [anarchy] cometh from evil" (D&C 98:7). Accordingly, we should not evaluate government actions as "right-wing" or "left-wing" (such labels are misleading and irrelevant), but as promoting or reducing the Rule of Law. This is a much better way to conceptualize politics.

## CONDITION

Merely having a government of laws is not enough to ensure the Rule of Law. Those laws must apply to everyone equally. When the government enacts laws, it cannot know beforehand to whom that law will apply. For example, laws in the post-Civil War American South dictated that anyone whose grandfather had voted in the past was exempt from a poll tax. This violated the Rule of Law because ex-slaves' grandfathers had been ineligible

---

5 The great tragedy in Dumas's *The Count of Monte Cristo* was that the French government imprisoned Edmond Dantes, a just (albeit naïve) man who had not done anything wrong. A corrupt magistrate wanted Edmond out of the way and there were no impartial laws to protect him from the will of that official.

6 Disagreements about where that "sweet spot" lies for any given issue is the source of virtually all political debates today. For instance, is government phone wiretapping a necessary power to prevent terrorist anarchy, or is it a tyrannical infringement on personal liberty? Is the government healthcare mandate a tyrannical infringement on personal freedom or a necessary corrective to the anarchy of the healthcare market? Such debates are not easily settled.

to vote. These laws singled out African-Americans. If laws don't apply equally to everyone, then the laws themselves can become tools of tyranny.

You can also see that the Rule of Law is of utmost importance because it protects agency and rights. Agency undergirds our godly nature and allows us to claim the natural rights of life, liberty, and property. These rights are, in turn, protected by the Rule of Law. The Rule of Law is crucial: nothing less than the exercise of agency is at stake.

## BIG QUESTIONS

All of this leads to an important question: "How do we get the Rule of Law?" A short look at history shows that most people who have lived never knew what it was to live in freedom or have their rights protected under the Rule of Law. Most of history has just been a sad fluctuation between tyranny and anarchy. Chinese history, for example, is the story of a series of tyrannical dynasties with periods of anarchy and civil war between each. In the 20th century, the tyranny of the Qing dynasty was followed by the tyranny of the Nationalists followed by the anarchy of civil war followed by the tyranny of the Japanese followed by more anarchy and, finally, the tyranny of the Communist Party. Liberty under the Rule of Law has been the exception rather than the rule throughout history.

But even if a society is fortunate enough to establish the Rule of Law, a second and more difficult question remains: "How do we *keep* the Rule of Law once we have it?" We like to think that societies inevitably progress from anarchy to tyranny and finally to liberty, but the reality is that even if a society achieves the Rule of Law, it is usually only a short moment before it descends once again into the cycle of anarchy and tyranny. Germany, for example, briefly escaped tyranny under the liberal Weimar regime, but that only lasted a decade before Hitler came to power and plunged the nation back into tyranny. Maintaining the Rule of Law can be more daunting than establishing it in the first place.

Keeping the Rule of Law is particularly challenging because of three powerful forces working against it. First, people from outside the country can make an open power grab to conquer and enslave. Genghis Kahn made no pretense about his intentions as he plundered all of Asia and much of Europe. Imperial Japan simply marched into China and Southeast Asia with armies in the 1930s and took lives, liberties, and properties by force. During World War II, the Nazis rolled into free countries, conquered, and set up tyrannical puppet regimes. You can lose the Rule of Law from those who want to take away your freedom from without. The United States is unlikely to lose the Rule of Law due to external forces because of its military might and natural defenses.

Second, the Rule of Law can be threatened by subtle internal forces. National leaders can entice us to yield up the Rule of Law in exchange for security, equality, or prestige. The public sells its freedom for a bowl of pottage. This is what happened in countless fascist and communist nations.

Finally, countries lose their freedom because of well-intentioned, but misguided citizens. There are those who sincerely believe that their view is absolutely correct and will therefore impose their will by force on the honest assumption that it's good for others. The Rule of Will, they say, is better for society so long as it is their own, "correct" will. This has been the attitude of Kings, dictators, and despots from time immemorial, but it's also the attitude of many intellectual elites today. Some feminists openly state that they want to take away a woman's freedom to stay home and raise children because, if women make that choice, they are clearly under patriarchal illusions, so we must "liberate" them from this "false freedom" through the force of government. Richard Dawkins hopes to take away religious freedom because he is certain that religion is a harmful delusion. In all cases, these elites believe that government must impose the will of elites for the good of people who are too benighted to know better.

## CONCLUSION

The crucial question this chapter should leave you with is this: given all of the forces working against it, *how does a society get and keep the Rule of Law?* This is the most important of all political questions. Philosophers, politicians, theorists, and concerned citizens have spent thousands of years trying to come up with solutions.

Fortunately for us, there is an answer. It's simple, elegant, and brilliant. In fact, it is just three words long. If you would like to know what it is, stay tuned. The answer will come in a few chapters. But first we must backtrack to tell the story of how America came to be.

## CHAPTER 4 SOURCES/FURTHER READING

Bushman, Richard L. *Joseph Smith: Rough Stone Rolling*. New York: Random House, 2007.

Diggins, John P. *John Adams*. New York: Henry Holt, 2003.

Fox, Frank and Clayne Pope. *American Heritage: An Interdisciplinary Approach*. 5th edition. Dubuque, IA: Kendall/Hunt, 1990.

_____. *City Upon a Hill*. Provo, UT: BYU Academic Publishing, 2007.

Friedman, Charles. *Law in America: A Short History*. New York: Modern Library, 2002.

McCarthy, Cormac. *The Road*. New York: Vintage, 2007.

McCullough, David. *John Adams*. New York: Simon & Schuster, 2001.

Romney, Marion G. "First Presidency Message: Rule of Law," *Ensign* (February 1973): 2.

Smith, Joseph. Correspondence with John C. Calhoun (1843). *History of the Church* 6:155-60.

# Chapter 5

# INDEPENDENCE I: ORIGINS OF AMERICAN SELF-GOVERNMENT

## THOMAS PAINE: CHALLENGING MONARCHY

In previous chapters we learned about John Locke's philosophy and how our status as humans with agency confers upon us natural rights, liberty, and political equality. In the next few chapters, we'll look at how these ideals played out in the creation of the United States of America—the first society in history founded upon Lockean principles. We will learn how thirteen fledgling English colonies became a single nation that secured (and continues to secure) freedom for its citizens under the Rule of Law.

For America to become a nation, it had to gain independence from England. Thomas Paine, more than anyone else, helped turn the hearts and minds of the American colonists in that direction. Paine is fascinating not only because he was one of the great persuasive writers in history, but also because he was so far along in life when he finally found his calling. Paine had tried school teaching, civil service, and small business, but failed at all of them. Finally, at an age exceeding the life expectancy of his day, he put pen to paper and discovered that he had a gift with words. One of the greatest writers of all time didn't even know he was a writer until late in life.

Paine turned his remarkable skills to a remarkable cause when, in 1776, he wrote his masterwork, *Common Sense*. It immediately sold 500,000 copies, saturated the colonies, and convinced the American people that protesting British tyranny was not enough—they should completely sever their ties with the mother country. It was "common sense," said Paine, that America should reject the king's authority, declare independence from England, and become a great nation of its own. That, of course, was the path the nation took and it was largely due to Paine's writing.

However, Paine, for all of his foresight and patriotism, got something wrong. He sub-

## Chapter 5

scribed to a false paradigm which saw the entire English system as hopelessly tyrannical and the American fight for liberty as a struggle against corrupt English traditions. Unfortunately, this view continues to distort much historical perception of the Founding.

The reality is that the colonists were the freest people in the entire world long *before* independence and the English system was a great source—rather than enemy—of American liberty. The colonists did not fight the War for Independence to achieve something new; rather, it was a war to preserve freedoms that they had long enjoyed as "Englishmen." They inherited a remarkable legacy of liberty from England and then added to it.

## BRITISH LEGACY OF LIBERTY

The first inheritance of freedom from England was the tradition of limited government established in 1215 A.D. by the *Magna Carta*. King John had launched a number of expensive wars to aggrandize his kingdom. To finance them, John decided to raise taxes on the landowners. In most countries, the King had absolute power and the people would simply have to submit to oppressive taxation, but in England (for reasons we will examine in Chapter 7) the nobles had power to rival that of the king. These lords gathered their armies and forced John to sign *Magna Carta,* which declared that no English king could raise taxes without the *consent* of those paying them. In other words, it prohibited "taxation without representation." Many people around the world trace their freedoms back to this seminal document.

The colonists also inherited from England the system of common law, a series of judicial decisions standardized by Henry II and handed down over the centuries. The Common Law granted rights and privileges, such as right of due process and trial by jury, to all English subjects. The American settlers brought this legal tradition with them and the Common Law protected the innocent, punished the guilty, and kept the colonists free.

It was also thanks to the English that the colonists understood the meaning and principles of liberty. We Americans like to flatter ourselves as the originators of freedom and democracy in the world, but the truth is we borrowed these ideas from Englishmen with names like Locke, Hume, Hobbes, Burke, Wilkes, and Sidney. One of the great ironies of history is that the English taught freedom to the Americans who then turned those very ideas against them in 1776.[1]

Finally, the colonists inherited the representative traditions established through England's Glorious Revolution (1688). In the 17th century, monarchs all over continental

---

[1] This also happened in India. Mahatma Gandhi, Jawaharlal Nehru, and the other leaders of the Indian independence movement had studied in England, learned the philosophy of democracy and self-government there, and then took those ideals back to India. Like Americans two centuries before, they used English ideals against English imperialism.

Europe were claiming greater authority based on a philosophy of *absolutism*. Some English kings, chafing at the restrictions on their power, tried to do the same.

James II, for example, attempted to assert greater authority to tax and control, but the English Parliament responded in a decisive and dramatic fashion. They saw that the king's daughter was married to the Dutch prince William of Orange so they invited him over to replace James II as King of England. But there were conditions: William had to agree that the elected Parliament would be superior to the monarch, he would have to tolerate other religions, and he would be limited by a Bill of Rights (this is where the Founders got the idea). William agreed to these terms, sailed over with his armies, and replaced James II on the British throne. The power of the British monarch has ever since been subordinate to the elected Parliament.

A Bill of Rights, limited monarchy, representative government, the Common Law—all of these were the great inheritance that the American colonies received from England.

## DISTANCE FROM GOVERNMENT

But it didn't stop there. The colonists built upon the British legacy of liberty with a legacy of their own. The Americans were even more democratic, free, and equal than the English because of the nature of colonial settlement. The colonists disembarked at Massachusetts Bay and Jamestown calling themselves "subjects of the king" and "Englishmen," but the king's government was on the other side of the ocean so they set up their own little parliaments (legislatures) and chose representatives based on regular elections. These governments were largely independent of England.

## LAND OWNERSHIP

There was also widespread land ownership in America. In the old world, owning land was mostly limited to large, hereditary estates. The land was concentrated in a few hands and if you were lucky enough to own some, you were a lord (the origin of the term "landlord"). Most people owned no land and worked for those who did. In America, by contrast, land was readily available to almost anyone.[2]

As in England, only landowners could vote in the colonies, but land was so widely available that there was far more representation and equality among the populace. This broad land ownership meant that nearly everyone had a similar social status and was a "lord" in his

---

[2] Of course, it often required the removal/killing of the Native Americans, but that was a moral consideration that colonists generally did not consider. Today, we rightly see Indian removal as a moral tragedy and yet another way that American freedom, paradoxically, had some of its roots in depriving others of their liberty. Daron Acemoglu and James Robinson even go so far as to argue that the American colonists' inability to effectively enslave the natives, as in the encomienda system of Latin America, accounts for the more democratic, inclusive nature of American institutions.

own right.[3] Hereditary class distinctions did not exist in America. Even low-status males, such as indentured servants, generally owned land after finishing their obligatory seven-year work contract. The society was far more equal and democratic than anything in Europe.[4]

This land ownership and the wealth that came with it also helped entrench economic freedom in the colonies. Nearly everyone had a vested interest in preserving an inclusive system where taxes and economic controls were limited. Since they were nearly all middle-class, Americans became highly protective of commercial freedom and property rights. The longstanding tradition of economic liberty in the U.S. began long before the Revolution.

## PLURALISM

The colonists also had greater liberty than England because of religious and ethnic pluralism. Once American settlement began, people of many different religious persuasions started showing up (e.g., Quakers, Catholics, Baptists, Anglicans). Normally, a nation would establish its dominant religion as the official state religion and then persecute religious minorities as heretics. This was not the case in America because *everyone belonged to a religious minority*. There was no single predominant religion that could gang up on the dissidents. Each sect just had to learn to get along with the others. They were tolerant by necessity.

## GREAT AWAKENING

Finally, a religious fervor swept through the colonies in the mid 18th century—the Great Awakening—which also contributed to American liberty. Although the movement was religious, it had profound political consequences.

The Great Awakening originated with the American sense of religious decline. The Puritan fathers came to North America hoping to establish a "city on a hill"—an example of godliness to the whole world—but a century later, people were focused on commerce and accumulating wealth. Many asked, "What happened to our godly society?" They felt that their community had strayed from its original errand and they needed to repent and halt the slide into worldliness.

Some important religious figures came forward to call Americans to repentance. First, there was the man considered the brains of the Great Awakening: Jonathan Edwards. Edwards entered Yale at age 12, graduated as valedictorian at age 16, and shortly thereafter became a professor of theology, a pastor of a local congregation, and one of the greatest phi-

---

3  This did not include women and racial minorities. They received full rights much later as we shall see in chapter 20.
4  This point was made early on by authors such as De Tocqueville (1830) and Charles and Mary Beard (1921).

losophers in American history. Edwards attempted to reconcile the Calvinist emphasis on predestination with the Enlightenment emphasis on free will. Edwards said that the grace of God was dependent upon a free will acceptance of salvation—your church could not save you, your parents could not save you, the king could not save you, *only Christ* could save you through your choice to accept Him. This religious point led Americans to cherish choice in political matters as an extension of their theological beliefs.

Edwards also initiated the Great Awakening with his preaching. In 1741 he delivered the most famous sermon in American history, "Sinners in the Hands of an Angry God," a fire-and-brimstone homily in which he pounded the pulpit and used terrifying language and imagery. By trying to frighten the American colonists into repentance, Edwards had lit the first sparks of a national religious revival.

These sparks would grow into a raging spiritual fire when the greatest preacher in American History, George Whitefield, showed up. Whitefield came over from England, unknown, and began preaching in the American South. At first people paid him little heed—it was routine for itinerant preachers to show up and give sermons—but soon Whitefield became a blockbuster. His manner of speaking was captivating and entertaining: he elevated his voice, gesticulated, flailed, and pieced together words and pauses for perfect dramatic effect. As members of the audience listened, their ears perked up, their eyes widened, their mouths dropped, and they were finally enraptured by this captivating speaker. They would then encourage everyone they knew to go hear him and change their lives as well. Whitefield's sermons became legendary and soon he was preaching to congregations in excess of twenty thousand—this at a time when there was no voice amplification and the American population was only about a million. Even the skeptical Benjamin Franklin recalled emptying his pockets onto Whitefield's collection plate.

The Great Awakening turned the hearts and minds of the American people towards an even greater sense of liberty, equality, and democracy. Whitefield would preach about sin and eternal damnation for everyone. He didn't except dukes, lords, earls, or even kings. Everyone was a sinner so everyone was equal in the eyes of God and in equal need of salvation. American egalitarianism had strong religious roots.

The Great Awakening also caused the colonists to distrust human authority. Whitefield and Edwards preached the importance of a personal commitment to God. Conversion was the key to salvation, not any particular denomination, institution, or clergyman. This subordinated human authority to divine authority and made earthly rule conditional rather than absolute (you can see how this would go well with what Paine said in *Common Sense*).[5]

It also heightened the American sense of individualism. The emphasis of the Great Awakening preachers on individual salvation created fertile ground on which Locke's philosophy could take root.

---

5 Adams (1818).

Chapter 5

The Great Awakening also made the colonists more comfortable with the religious pluralism that already existed. Whitefield would say that all had to come to Christ for salvation, but didn't mandate that they join a particular church. The specifics of theology were unimportant next to rebirth through Christ making it acceptable for neighbors to have differing religions.[6]

## SUMMARY OF 1760 COLONIES

In summary, because of the Great Awakening, the nature of colonial settlement, and the English legacy, American colonists in 1760 (and this date is very important as we shall see) were already free, equal, independent, and democratic. They enjoyed far more liberty than their European counterparts. Nearly every family was represented in government and all had a sense of status equality. They lived in politically autonomous colonies that made their own laws, levied their own taxes, and governed their own affairs. If a man lived in Virginia, his government was the Virginia House of Burgesses, not the English Parliament. Although the colonists called themselves "Englishmen," their tie with England was mostly nominal. The English government was doing little to them or for them.

## CHANGING RELATIONSHIP

If the colonies were already free, democratic, and independent, why did they have to fight a war for independence? The answer is simple: after 1760 the *relationship with the mother country changed*. The independence, freedom, and democracy they enjoyed were increasingly threatened by an English government that began to crack down on their liberty.

It all began with the French and Indian War. In the 1750s, the American colonies were filling up with people. Immigration and a high birth rate meant that new settlers were flowing west of the Appalachians, taming the frontier, staking out land, cutting down forests, farming, and establishing new agricultural towns. Since land ownership was so central to the American experience, colonists were continually being tugged westward.

At the same time, French trappers were moving south from their base in Canada seeking new waters for trapping. As the English moved west and the French moved south, their paths began to converge and they clashed over who had rights to this land in the North American interior. The first skirmish happened at the confluence of two rivers where the French had established Ft. Duquesne (we call it Pittsburgh today). A young colonel in the Virginia militia went to Ft. Duquesne and ordered the French to leave. When they refused, the Virginians exchanged shots with the French and started the war. One of history's great

---

6  Gaustad (1990); Marty (1984); Butler (1990); and Butler (2000).

ironies is that Virginia Colonel fighting for the British forces was none other than George Washington.

After extensive fighting all over the world (there were even prominent battles on the Indian subcontinent) the English triumphed and replaced France as the dominant power in Europe and North America, meaning that English language and institutions would prevail as the colonies expanded westward.

The French and Indian War left the English two big problems that led directly to the War for Independence. First, the British crown, tired of fighting on the frontier, issued The Proclamation of 1763, which forbade the colonists from moving west of the Appalachian Mountains. To the Americans, this Proclamation would put an end to their liberty and democracy—after all, the availability of free land in the West was the only hope for the growing number of Americans to be full citizens with voting rights and equality.

The second and bigger problem was the cost of the war. The English government had borrowed heavily to defeat the French and needed repay those debts. To raise the revenue, they decided to start taxing the American colonists.

Why would the colonists have had a problem with this? We all understand that we must pay taxes as the price for government services, including military protection. Why was it different with the American colonies?

The answer is extremely important because it gets to the crux of the cause of the Revolutionary War: the colonists did not accept these taxes because they did not accept that the English Parliament could govern them. Each colony had its own representative government to whom they paid taxes. Their local governments could tax them because they were represented in those governments, but they were not represented in the English Parliament. They didn't vote for any of the politicians in London, so who was Parliament to take their money?

Imagine that tomorrow morning an official from the Canadian government knocks on your door and says "Hi, I'm here to collect taxes from you." Naturally, you would refuse and laugh them away. But what if they persisted and brought an army to take the taxes by force? Then you would become angry and protest. That is how the colonists felt.

## BRITISH TAXATION

The first attempts at taxation were small. The British began to enforce revenue-generating Navigation Acts that controlled trade and prohibited the colonists from trading with whoever they wanted. Then they passed a tax on molasses (the "Sugar Tax"), which angered merchants like John Hancock, but didn't generate a widespread outcry.

Then in 1765, the Parliament passed a huge, burdensome tax that fell heavily on colonists of nearly all regions, professions, and classes—the hated Stamp Tax. To the Americans, this abominable tax reached in and stole money right out of their pockets by requiring that all official documents be printed on expensive, government-stamped paper.

The backlash to the Stamp Tax was widespread and dramatic. Up to this point in their history, the colonists had been free, independent, and democratic, but this tax took away their property rights and ability to legislate for themselves. The cry of "no taxation without representation" went up in all the colonies. Politicians like Patrick Henry gained prominence speaking out against it. Underground organizations, such as the Sons of Liberty, arose to protest the tax and terrorize tax collectors.

The Stamp Tax also represents the beginning of American unity. Before 1765, there were thirteen independent colonies, as different from one another as Australia is from New Zealand today, and yet this grievance gave them common cause. In order to fight the Stamp Tax, the colonies created a congress to unify, coordinate, and strengthen their protest. For the first time in U.S. history, all of the colonies were working together. This congress, in a modified and reconstituted form, is still with us in Washington D.C. and the states still send representatives to congress as they began doing in 1765.

Parliament realized that their plan had backfired. The colonists opposed this tax with so much energy and violence that it cost the government more to enforce it than they collected in revenues. It only made British finances worse.

When their plan failed, the British tried to save face. Parliament repealed the Stamp Tax in 1767, but simultaneously passed The Declaratory Act which asserted their right to control the colonies "in all cases whatsoever." The British wanted to make clear to the colonists that, even though they were not taxing them anymore, they *could* do so anytime they wanted.

To prove it, they tried again later that year by passing the Townshend duties. These were sales taxes on goods like paint, glass, lead, and tea that they hoped would succeed where the Stamp Tax had failed.

The British judged wrong. The colonists protested the Townshend Acts just as vociferously as they had the Stamp Tax. The Sons of Liberty revived their underground protest and began to terrorize tax collectors and enforce boycotts. Things became so chaotic that the British had to send soldiers to enforce their decrees. This further enflamed the colonies and led to the Boston Massacre.

At this point, the British politicians realized that it was no longer about raising revenue, but showing the colonists who was in charge. To prove their point, they repealed all of the taxes except one: the tax on tea. The British knew it would only raise a token amount of money, but it would at least uphold the principle of Parliament's right of taxation and prove to the colonists that they *would* be obedient to English authority.

The colonists saw the Tea Tax for what it was and fought against it accordingly. They were fighting for the principle of "no taxation without representation" regardless of whether the tax was of one penny or one million pounds. To show their unwillingness to submit, Sons of Liberty boarded the East India Company ships in 1773 and threw the taxed tea into Boston Harbor. We call this the Boston Tea Party.

This destruction of royal property enraged King George III. In his view, the colonists were behaving like spoiled children defying a parent and had to be taught a lesson. He and the Parliament would punish them.

They did so through the Coercive Acts (the "Intolerable Acts" to the colonists), a series of laws passed to bring the Boston tea partiers to justice and force them to pay for the tea they destroyed. There were four major parts of the Coercive Acts: First, they closed the port of Boston. This was a major blow to the New England Economy. Merchants would go broke, ship crews and stevedores would lose their jobs, and even those in unrelated professions (like silversmith Paul Revere) would lose business from the depressed economy. The English hoped to squeeze the colonists into submission.

Second, the Acts required colonists to house British soldiers on their private property. In other words, they were forced to accommodate their enemies and had their natural right to property violated.

Third, the Acts said that any person accused of a crime would be tried in England, not by a sympathetic jury in the colonies that would probably acquit them. This violated the fundamental Common Law right to a trial by a jury of *one's own peers*.

To cap it all off, the Acts disbanded the Massachusetts legislature, taking away their democracy and representative government. Their right to self-government had become subject to his majesty's whims. Not only would Parliament tax without representation, but the colonists could also lose their representative assemblies.

As you can see, a major shift had occurred between 1763 and 1774. The British government had stripped the colonists of key elements of their freedom, independence, and democracy. The English government had turned away from its very own legacy of liberty.

## ROAD TO WAR

The colonial actions against the Coercive Acts were bold and decisive. First, they called a "Continental Congress"—a united body consisting of representatives from all the colonies—to protest British actions and serve as an independent government. Even though the Coercive Acts were directed primarily at Massachusetts, the colonies now had a sense of solidarity. An attack on one was an attack on all. If Parliament could do this to Massachusetts, the other colonies could be next. The Congress then called for a boycott of British goods and for a day of fasting and prayer (Washington himself spent the entire day at his local church in Virginia). Most telling of all, the Congress called for the colonists to begin forming militia, stockpiling weapons, and preparing for war.

The British ministers saw what was going on and sent General Thomas Gage to stop this incipient rebellion by seizing the colonists' weapons at Concord and arresting the "radical" leaders (Sam Adams and John Hancock). Gage decided to avoid conflict with the colonists by carrying out these orders at night and heading for Concord covertly.

This is where Paul Revere comes into the picture. The Sons of Liberty had developed an elaborate system of signals to communicate British actions. Apprised of "Redcoat" movements, Revere set off in the middle of the night to warn the militia of each town that was on the road to Concord.

Early on the morning of April 18, 1775, the British regulars drew up to the Lexington Green. The ever-ready Minutemen of the local militia were there to meet them. The British ordered them to disband without success. After a few moments, a shot came from an unknown source and war was on. The British mowed over their untrained American adversaries and this scuffle at Lexington is considered the first battle in the War for American Independence.

But then the American advantage kicked in. As the British soldiers continued their march to Concord, the Americans began to use the tricks that had been used against them in the French and Indian War. Instead of lining up and fighting the British European style, they hid behind walls, trees, and houses and took potshots at the soldiers marching down the road. These guerilla tactics were so effective that the British never made their objective and had to beat a hasty retreat back to the safety of Boston.

## CONCLUSION

The Americans had scored an important victory, but the die was cast. The British, now fully aroused to anger, threw the weight of the mightiest economic and military power on the planet towards subduing their unruly colonies. Reconciliation between the two sides became less tenable and the momentum for independence began to rise.

## CHAPTER 5 SOURCES/FURTHER READING

Adams, John to H. Niles, February 13, 1818. <http://www.constitution.org/primarysources/adams-niles.html>.

Beard, Charles and Mary. *History of the United States*. New York: Macmillan, 1921.

Boorstin, Daniel. *The Americans: The Colonial Experience*. New York: Vintage, 1964.

\_\_\_\_\_. *The Americans: The Democratic Experience*. New York: Random House, 1973.

Butler, Jon. *Becoming America: The Revolution before 1776*. Cambridge, MA: Harvard University Press, 2000.

Catton, Bruce and William B. Catton. *The Bold and Magnificent Dream: America's Founding Years, 1492-1815*. Garden City, NY: Doubleday, 1978.

# Independence I: Origins of American Self-Government

Churchill, Winston. *History of the English Speaking Peoples*. Edited by Henry Steel Commager. New York: Barnes & Noble, 1994.

De Tocqueville, Alexis. *Democracy in America* (1830). New York: Penguin, 2003.

Franklin, Benjamin. Examination Before The House of Commons (1766).

Hannan, Daniel. *Inventing Freedom: How the English-Speaking Peoples Made the World Modern*. New York: HarperCollins, 2013.

Hitchens, Christopher. *Thomas Paine's Rights of Man*. New York: Atlantic Monthly Press, 2006.

Johnson, Paul. *The Offshore Islanders: A History of the English People*. London: Orion, 1972.

Marsden, George. *Jonathan Edwards: A Life*. New Haven: Yale University Press, 2003.

McDonald, Forrest. *We The People: The Economic Origins of the Constitution*. Chicago: University of Chicago Press, 1958.

Mead, Walter Russell. *God and Gold: Britain, America, and the Making of the Modern World*. New York: Knopf, 2007.

Paine, Thomas. *Common Sense* (1776).

Potter, David. *People of Plenty: Economic Abundance and the American Character*. Chicago: University of Chicago Press, 1958.

Taylor, Alan. *American Colonies*. New York: Viking, 2001.

# Chapter 6

# INDEPENDENCE II: THE CREED & THE CONFLICT

## THOMAS JEFFERSON: AUTHOR OF INDEPENDENCE

It is almost impossible to think of the Declaration of Independence without also thinking of its author, Thomas Jefferson. For his contribution to this founding document alone, Jefferson deserves a place in the pantheon of American heroes.

Unlike Abraham Lincoln, Joseph Smith, Thomas Edison, and other great Americans, Jefferson was born into wealth. His father belonged to the privileged Virginia gentry class and passed on to Jefferson an abundance of land, slaves, and property. Although many in such circumstances would become spoiled and squander their opportunities, Jefferson didn't. As a young man, he went to William & Mary College and studied under professor George Wythe who taught young Thomas to ask questions and diligently seek answers.

This insatiable thirst for knowledge became a guiding principle in Jefferson's life. He wanted to know everything and pretty well succeeded. As an attorney, Jefferson knew the law, but he also mastered science, philosophy, invention, music, poetry, literature, classics, languages, mathematics, and even architecture (his home Monticello remains one of the great examples Greek Revival architecture in America). In fact, when President John F. Kennedy welcomed forty-nine Nobel Prize winners to the White House in 1962 he said, "I think this is the most extraordinary collection of talent and of human knowledge that has ever been gathered together at the White House—with the possible exception of when Thomas Jefferson dined alone."[1]

---

[1] John F. Kennedy, "Remarks at a Dinner Honoring Nobel Prize Winners of the Western Hemisphere," April

*Chapter 6*

Jefferson remains widely revered by Americans of all political persuasions, but he also had glaring weaknesses. He can't escape charges of hypocrisy: the man who enshrined for all the world the proposition, "all men are created equal," also owned many slaves; the man who condemned excess lived in luxury; the man who encouraged fiscal prudence died heavily in debt.

We often excuse 18th century slaveholders on the grounds that "they didn't know any better," but Jefferson did. He knew that the Lockean principles of equality went against slavery (Lincoln would eventually invoke Jefferson's words to abolish slavery), and yet he nonetheless continued to hold human beings in bondage and live off of their labor in order to enjoy upper-class comforts. There is also evidence that he may have fathered children by one of his slaves, Sally Hemmings.[2] There is no question that Jefferson was a great man, but he was also a man of controversy and contradictions.

## JEFFERSON'S RELIGION

Jefferson's religion was as controversial as any aspect of his life. Unfortunately, the debate has come to be dominated by the same binary thinking that has infected much of our political discourse. Many on the religious "right" argue that Jefferson and the other Founding Fathers were evangelical Christians, while many on the secular "left" contend that Jefferson was too smart to believe in God and was an atheist.

The evidence disappoints both sides. Jefferson's religious views were far more interesting and nuanced than can be captured in a simplistic binary. Remember, Latter-day Saints believe that when Christ established the gospel during his mortal ministry it was full of plain and precious truths, but then, through apostasy, these truths were corrupted and lost, particularly as early Christian theologians mingled Christianity with Plato's philosophy and taught that the material world was evil and that God was not a physical being. This way of thinking culminated in the Nicene Creed which established the doctrine of the Trinity—God was immaterial, both one being and three beings at the same time. Humanity eventually pulled out of this apostasy when the plain and precious truths of Christ were restored in their purity through the prophet Joseph Smith.

Jefferson held similar religious beliefs. Once, responding to the accusation that he was not a Christian, he wrote the following to his friend Benjamin Rush:

> My views of [the Christian religion] are the result of a life of inquiry and reflection, and very different from that anti-Christian system imputed to me by those who know

---

29, 1962. Available at Gerhard Peters and John T. Woolley, eds., *The American Presidency Project*. <http://www.presidency.ucsb.edu/ws/?pid=8623>.

2 The DNA evidence is persuasive, but not conclusive. It shows with 95% certainty that *a* Jefferson was the father of the children of Sally Hemmings, but not necessarily *Thomas* Jefferson.

nothing of my opinions. To the corruptions of Christianity I am, indeed, opposed; but not to the genuine precepts of Jesus himself.[3]

But what did it mean to be a true Christian? He answered that question in a letter to Charles Thomson:

> I am a *real Christian*, that is to say, a disciple of the doctrines of Jesus—very different from the Platonists, who call *me* infidel and *themselves* Christians and preachers of the gospel, while they draw all their characteristic dogmas from what its Author never said nor saw.[4]

A true Christian, in other words, was someone who believed in original Christianity, not the corrupt version. Jefferson wrote to John Adams that the teachings of Jesus were, "within the comprehension of a child; but thousands of volumes have not yet explained the Platonisms engrafted on them."[5] The pure doctrines of Christ, in other words, had been corrupted by Plato's anti-material philosophy. People often claim that "Mormons are not Christians" because we don't accept the Platonic (rather than Biblical) elements of the Nicene Creed. Jefferson often faced the same charge for the same reasons.

Jefferson, however, was hopeful for the future of Christianity:

> When we shall have done away the incomprehensible jargon of the Trinitarian arithmetic, that three are one and one is three; when we shall have knocked down the artificial scaffolding reared to mask from view the simple structure of Jesus; when, in short, we shall have unlearned everything which has been taught since His day, and got back to the pure and simple doctrines He inculcated, we shall then be truly and worthily His disciples.[6]

Jefferson's solution to the corruption of Christianity was a return to the pure, original doctrines that Christ himself had taught.

Finally, near the end of his life, Jefferson wrote to his friend Jared Sparks:

> I hold the precepts of Jesus, as delivered by Himself, to be the most pure, benevolent, and sublime which have ever been preached to man. I adhere to the principles of the first age, and consider all subsequent innovations as corruptions of His religion, having no foundation in what came from Him . . . If the freedom of religion guaranteed to us . . . can ever rise . . . truth will prevail over fanaticism, and the genuine doctrines of Jesus, so long perverted by His pseudo-priests, will again be restored to their origi-

---

3  Thomas Jefferson to Benjamin Rush (1803), in Bergh 10:379.
4  Thomas Jefferson to Charles Thomson (1816), in Bergh 14:385.
5  Thomas Jefferson to John Adams (1814), in Bergh 14:149.
6  Thomas Jefferson to Timothy Pickering (1821), in Bergh 15:323.

nal purity. This reformation will advance with the other improvements of the human mind, but too late for me to witness it.[7]

Jefferson died in 1826; Joseph Smith went to the Hill Cumorah in 1827. The truth was indeed restored after his death, just as he predicted. So much for Jefferson the atheist or Jefferson the fundamentalist. The restorationist elements of his religious beliefs disappoint tribalists on both sides of the political spectrum, but sit quite well with Latter-day Saints.

The story doesn't end with Jefferson's death. In 1877, Wilford Woodruff was serving as president of the newly dedicated St. George Temple when a group of men appeared to him in vision, asking that their temple work be done. "These were the signers of the Declaration of Independence," said President Woodruff, "and they waited on me for two days and two nights." In fact, he said, "they argued with me"—they berated President Woodruff for being lax in bringing gospel ordinances to them. "We laid the foundation of the government you now enjoy," they said, "and we never apostatized from it; but we remained true to it and were faithful to God."[8]

We presume Jefferson was speaking here, but "apostasy" is an LDS word. One could be skeptical and say that either Woodruff made this up or used his own language to express their general point. A close look at the writings of Thomas Jefferson shows that he used the term "apostate" often—it was among his favorite ways to describe those who he believed departed from free principles.[9] President Woodruff's testimony is perfectly in line with Jeffersonian language.

## THE DECLARATION'S HISTORY

Now that we've covered Jefferson's religion, let's talk about the masterpiece he and Congress produced in the summer of 1776. At that point, the war was already in full swing and Congress was acting as an independent government, but they had to issue a statement to formalize and explain their break from England.

Sensing the historical significance of their actions, the writers of the Declaration of Independence wanted to produce a worthy document. They carefully selected a drafting committee which included three key, inspired choices.

First, Benjamin Franklin had more prestige than any other American. Congress wanted the colonists, Great Britain, and the whole world to take notice of this Declaration, and Franklin's participation in producing and signing it would have that effect. Franklin was not only the scientist who discovered the workings of electricity, but also a publishing tycoon,

---

7  Thomas Jefferson to Jared Sparks (1820), in Bergh 15:288.
8  Fawcett (2004, p. 103).
9  Jefferson (1859, p. 91). Later, to Lafayette he wrote that his opponents were "strengthened by unsuspecting or apostate recruits from our ranks." Thomas Jefferson to the Marquis De Lafayette, October 28, 1822.

a self-made millionaire, a philosopher, and an inventor. Today we cannot fully comprehend Franklin's fame and cultural power because there is nobody like him. You would have to combine Bill Gates, Ted Turner, Stephen Hawking, Warren Buffet, and Colin Powell all into one person. Because of his prestige, Franklin was an obvious choice to help write the Declaration.

Second, Congress chose John Adams for the committee because he had been the foremost advocate for independence in their debates. Adams was not a great writer; he was a great speaker who could move and persuade through oral communication. It is often said that Adams was the voice of independence, and Jefferson its pen. The problem is that speech vanishes into the air while written words remain indefinitely. That is why we most closely associate Thomas Jefferson with independence rather than John Adams. Jefferson's words are still with us in the National Archives and in millions of reproductions.

Adams also had an eye for talent. It was Adams who had the foresight to nominate George Washington as Commander-in-Chief of the Continental Army, and after Congress had voted for independence, Adams selected Jefferson to write the first draft of the Declaration.

Jefferson was an inspired choice because of his ability to write with the precision and cadence that we all know. It's not just *what* the Declaration says, but *how* it is said. The

# Chapter 6

words themselves, as well as the principles, have stood the test of time. We have Jefferson to thank for that.

## FOUNDING BROTHERS

The relationship between Adams and Jefferson is worth examining for a moment because it is one of tragedy and redemption. In 1776 they were friends, Founding Brothers, fighting for a common cause of freedom. They spent hundreds of hours together working, traveling, and conversing both as colleagues and friends.

But in the early days of the republic the curse of partisanship arose. Jefferson led the Republican Party and Adams drifted towards the Federalists. The Republicans would make terrible accusations against Adams, and the Federalists would make terrible accusations against Jefferson. This wedge drove them apart until they would not even speak to one another. The friends had become *de facto* enemies.

Fortunately, another signer of the Declaration came forward to mend this schism. Seeing the animosity that had developed between these founding giants, Benjamin Rush pondered and prayed over a solution. One night in October 1809, with this problem weighing heavily on his mind, he had a dream that he considered prophetic. He awoke and wrote down what he had seen:

> "What book is that in your hands?" said I to my son Richard a few nights ago in a dream. "It is the history of the United States," said he. "Shall I read a page of it to you?" [so he read] 'Among the most extraordinary events of this year was the renewal of the friendship and intercourse between Mr. John Adams and Mr. Jefferson, the two ex-Presidents of the United States. They met for the first time in the Congress of 1775. Their principles of liberty, their ardent attachment to their country . . . being exactly the same, they were strongly attracted to each other and became personal as well as political friends . . . A difference of opinion upon the objects and issue of the French Revolution separated them during the years in which that great event interested and divided the American people . . . In the month of November 1809, Mr. Adams addressed a short letter to his friend Mr. Jefferson in which he congratulated him upon his escape to the shades of retirement and domestic happiness, and concluded it with assurances of his regard and good wishes for his welfare. This letter did great honor to Mr. Adams. It discovered a magnanimity known only to great minds. Mr. Jefferson replied to this letter and reciprocated expressions of regard and esteem. These letters were followed by a correspondence of several years in which they mutually reviewed the scenes of business in which they had been engaged, and candidly acknowledged to each other all the errors of opinion and conduct into which they had fallen during the time they filled the same station in the service of their country. Many precious

aphorisms, the result of observation, experience, and profound reflection, it is said, are contained in these letters. It is to be hoped the world will be favored with a sight of them ... These gentlemen sunk into the grave nearly at the same time, full of years and rich in the gratitude and praises of their country."[10]

Benjamin Rush sent this account to Adams. Touched by the letter, Adams in turn wrote to Jefferson who then reciprocated. Everything in Rush's dream came true. Adams and Jefferson renewed their friendship with a correspondence that remains a valuable historical window into the minds of the Founders. Most remarkably of all, these men did, indeed, "sink into the grave at nearly the same time." On July 4$^{th}$ 1826, Adams lay dying in his Braintree, Massachusetts home. Before breathing his last, he said, "Jefferson yet lives." He was wrong. Jefferson had died just a few hours before—50 years to the day of the adoption of the Declaration of Independence. President John Quincy Adams saw this not as coincidence, but as "visible and palpable marks of divine favor for which I would humble myself before the ruler of the universe."[11]

Historians have sometimes scoffed at these late-life letters, saying that Jefferson and Adams were merely putting on a show for posterity.[12] But that's exactly the point. They were thinking of future generations as much as they were each other. The hearts of the Founding Fathers were turned to their American "children."

## IMPORTANCE OF THE DECLARATION

The Declaration marked the birth of the United States, but its importance goes beyond that. The Declaration also contains the most concise and understandable statement of true political principles ever written. Others, like Locke, have expressed these same truths of free government, but it took hundreds of pages of dense, philosophical writing. Jefferson did it in just a few short sentences. Jefferson treasured the idea of plain and precious truths in politics as much as in religion. Those who teach obscurity are usually trying to hide something. The Book of Mormon makes clear, "the Lord worketh not in darkness"; the adversary does (2 Nephi 26). Jefferson understood this intuitively and made the Declaration as plain in meaning as possible.

The principles of the Declaration have inspired many throughout the world and continue to do so. Since 1776, peoples worldwide have claimed the right of self-government, consent of the governed, and the rights to life, liberty, and the pursuit of happiness. The spark of the Declaration set the world ablaze with freedom—that fire continues to spread as

---

10 Benjamin Rush to John Adams, October 17, 1809, in Butterfield (1951, pp. 1021-1022).
11 Brookhiser (2002, p. 219).
12 See, for example, Ellis (2002, pgs. 220-45).

## Chapter 6

liberal democracy is increasingly the default form of government worldwide. The principles of the Declaration have become near-universal aspirations.

The Declaration not only created America, but also defines it. America is not an ethnicity, race, geography, or language (as has been historically the case for, say, China, Japan, or Germany)—it is a creed—the set of ideals laid forth by Jefferson in the Declaration. We often hear people accusing others of not being "good Americans" but everyone is a good American who believes in and adheres to the principles found in the Declaration. America was made in 1776 not just because the Declaration formally separated the colonies from Great Britain, but also because it set down the principles that define this creedal nation.

Because of the Declaration's status as a nation-defining document, you can understand why we treat it like sacred scripture. If you walk down Constitution Avenue in Washington D.C. you will find the hustle and bustle of any large city—traffic, honking, vendors shouting, people walking and conversing—and yet if you enter the National Archives you will find complete silence. The crowds are hushed before a 250 year-old parchment; a sacred document that created, defines, and in many ways preserves American liberty.

## CONTENT

Now that we've covered the importance of the Declaration of Independence, let's turn to its contents. The Declaration has four sections. The first is an introduction or statement of purpose. All great writers know that giving a thesis statement up front tells the reader why they are writing. Jefferson understood this too, declaring his intentions in the first paragraph:

> *When in the Course of human events, it becomes necessary for one people to dissolve the political bands which have connected them with another, and to assume among the powers of the earth, the separate and equal station to which the Laws of Nature and of Nature's God entitle them, a decent respect to the opinions of mankind requires that they should declare the causes which impel them to the separation.*

After setting the stage with this statement of intentions, Jefferson then digresses briefly to give us a summary of John Locke's philosophy. Now a reader might wonder why he takes this detour into political philosophy, but, as we shall see, these basic philosophical principles were crucial to the Declaration's purposes. He begins,

> *We hold these truths to be self-evident*

Notice that Jefferson does not say, "We hold these perspectives" or "opinions" to be self-evident, but *truths*. There are relative truths, but there are also eternal truths, and these Lockean principles are among them. They are final, absolute, and independent of time or space. Just like the axioms of math, these political principles were true ten thousand years ago, are true now, and will be true ten thousand years in the future. They are true regardless of your skin color, nationality, or even the planet you live on.[13]

These truths are also *self-evident*, meaning they appeal so directly and forcibly to the common moral sense of mankind that we know them even prior to reflection. We "can't not know" these truths, they are available to all, not just educated elites.[14] Pre-Civil War southerners said that slavery may have been considered morally wrong in the North, but it wasn't immoral in the South. The Southerners were mistaken: slavery is wrong in all places and all times (whether or not people accepted or faced up to it) and always will be. Slaveholders knew deep down—and Jefferson himself was a prime example—that holding fellow humans in bondage and depriving them of rights to liberty and property was wrong. It was self-evident, even to the most hardened slave master.

Then Jefferson lists the relevant self-evident truths of politics. They are,

> *That all men are created equal, that they are endowed by their Creator with certain unalienable Rights, that among these are Life, Liberty and the pursuit of Happiness.*

By "equal," Jefferson didn't mean all were equal in their talents, resources, or the way they looked, but in their intrinsic worth, agency, and natural rights. Regardless of who we are, we possess rights to Locke's trinity of life, liberty, and property. Jefferson even went beyond property to the more expansive, "pursuit of happiness"—not only do we have the right to control property, but also to use that property to pursue happiness as we see fit.

Then Jefferson moves from Locke's view on rights to his social contract theory:

> *That to secure these rights, Governments are instituted among Men, deriving their just powers from the consent of the governed.*

Government exists not by divine right or arbitrary control, but by agreement with the people it is under contract to protect. The power of government is only legitimate if it is fulfilling its end of the bargain—protecting rights. The government doesn't give you rights—they are yours *naturally*—but it is under contractual obligation to protect them. For thousands of years, monarchs, oligarchs, and tyrants had told people that they owed their lives, liberties, and properties to the government. Jefferson turned that on its head. Public servants protect rights only because the people delegate that power to them. (We will later spend a whole chapter on the principle, "consent of the governed.")

---

13 The world is trying hard to convince us otherwise. Moral relativism is a popular doctrine that says humans just invent codes of good and evil. This "postmodern" doctrine is neither post nor modern—it has been around since at least the ancient Greeks. Many who teach this doctrine have ulterior motives. They know in their hearts that what they are teaching is false, but teach it anyway because they want to get away with something that defies traditional morals. Moral relativism is "pleasing to the carnal mind" (Alma 30). In the end, even the most convinced moral relativists know that racism, rape, slavery, murder, and so forth, are wrong for all times and all places.

14 Budziszewski (2003).

# Chapter 6

After taking us through this detour into Lockean Philosophy, Jefferson shows in the next sentence why it matters for the subject at hand:

> *That whenever any Form of Government becomes destructive of these ends, it is the Right of the People to alter or to abolish it, and to institute new Government*

A contract can be created, but contracts can also be violated and thereby rendered null and void. The same is true of the social contract that creates governments. When a government violates its promise to protect our natural rights, then the contract is no longer in force. This justifies rebellion against an unjust government.

But Jefferson needed to add a caution making sure people didn't rebel against their government on a whim:

> *Prudence, indeed, will dictate that Governments long established should not be changed for light and transient causes*

Jefferson wanted to make clear that we cannot just overthrow the government every time we disagree with something it does, such as raise tax rates (as the malcontents in the Shays and Whiskey Rebellions learned a few years later). There must be a "long train of abuses" that reveals a tyrannical design. It's also important to remember that those of us who live in a democratic society can seek redress for government misbehavior at the polls—the founders had no such option. After all their primary bone of contention with Britain was "taxation without *representation*." Without democratic recourse, our founders had no choice but to revolt.[15]

Since the whole principle of independence hinged on whether or not the British government had violated the social contract, Jefferson spent most of the Declaration proving that the British had, indeed, taken away American rights to life, liberty, and property. In this third and most lengthy section, he listed in great detail that "long train of abuses" that brought the colonies to this point.

Then, in a climactic final paragraph—the fourth section—Jefferson takes us to the actual declaration itself. Everything preceding was merely preparation for this grand crescendo:

> *We, therefore, the Representatives of the united States of America, in General Congress, Assembled, appealing to the Supreme Judge of the world for the rectitude of our intentions, do, in the Name, and by the Authority of the good People of these Colonies, solemnly publish and declare, That these United Colonies are, and of Right ought to be Free and Independent States; that they are Absolved from all Allegiance to the British Crown, and that all political connection between them and the State of Great Britain, is and ought to*

---

15 Latter-day Saints should give extra heed to this sentence. The twelfth Article of Faith declares, "We believe in being subject to kings, presidents, rulers, and magistrates, in obeying, honoring, and sustaining the law."

*be totally dissolved; and that as Free and Independent States, they have full Power to levy War, conclude Peace, contract Alliances, establish Commerce, and to do all other Acts and Things which Independent States may of right do. And for the support of this Declaration, with a firm reliance on the protection of divine Providence, we mutually pledge to each other our Lives, our Fortunes and our sacred Honor.*

## THE SIGNERS

We must focus closely on that final line because it alone puts to rest a commonly held view that first gained currency a century ago. In 1913, a book came out called *An Economic Interpretation of the Constitution* that accused the Founders of doing what they did because it was in their narrow economic interest.[16] This book's thesis has since been soundly refuted, but it kicked off a whole industry of Founding Father criticism that continues into the present. Numerous books have been written claiming that the Founders were greedy, exploitative men whose ultimate motivations were money, domination, and power.

While some of this critical tradition has served the useful purpose of helping us to see the Founders' imperfections, much of it makes quite ridiculous claims. We could go one by one through these arguments and refute them with historical evidence, but we don't need to. All we have to do is look at the last four lines in the Declaration of Independence. Who, in pursuit of private wealth and gain, would sign their own potential death sentence and pledge away all of their earthly possessions? Each of the signers would have been executed had the revolution failed. After everyone had signed the Declaration John Hancock said, "Gentlemen we must now hang together," and Franklin, chimed in, "Yes or we most assuredly will hang separately."

Some may say this pledge was just an empty promise, but, actually, over a dozen of the signers did lose everything. Many had their homes ransacked, plundered, and/or destroyed by the British. Some of them were captured or exiled and suffered extreme hardships that led to premature deaths; some had family members taken, others fought as soldiers in the war—physically putting their lives on the line. They did, in fact, give their fortunes and lives to their "support of the Declaration." Had they been seeking power and fortune, they would have recanted at the first sign of sacrifice. None of them did. The truth is the exact opposite of the misguided views of some historians and we need look no further than the last line of the Declaration for proof.

---

16 Beard (1913). In many ways, it's unfortunate that Beard's thesis initiated the anti-Founder tradition because Beard himself was a great historian who had high regard for the American Founding Fathers. His works of history are models of quality historical scholarship and I recommend them to anyone. He put forward a provocative thesis in this book, but didn't mean for it to discredit the Founding or the Constitution. Many who followed him, however, were not nearly as fair-minded or kind. For a sound refutation, see McDonald (1958).

*Chapter 6*

# FREEDOM & VIRTUE

Before leaving our discussion of the Declaration, we must address another question that has long troubled historians. Seeing all of this talk about liberty, freedom, and rights, some historians have asked, "Where in all this talk of liberty is there any concern for virtue?" Didn't the Founders care about morality? Revisionist historians have then countered that the primary concern of the Founders was, in fact, virtue and that liberty was secondary. Which was it, liberty or virtue? Which did the Founders really want?

The answer is that these historians are asking the wrong question. They see liberty and virtue engaged in a tug of war with each gaining ground at the expense of the other, but fail to realize that freedom and virtue are not opposed, but complementary. The fallacy of the libertine is that we need to give up on virtue and focus on freedom; the fallacy of the theocrat is that we need to give up on freedom and focus on virtue. They are both wrong: freedom cannot exist without virtue and vice versa.

This mutually reinforcing relationship between freedom and virtue is illustrated in the scriptures:

> I, the Lord God, make you free, therefore ye are free indeed; and the law also maketh you free. Nevertheless, when the wicked rule the people mourn. Wherefore, honest men and wise men should be sought for diligently, and good men and wise men ye should observe to uphold; otherwise whatsoever is less than these cometh of evil. And I give unto you a commandment, that ye shall forsake all evil and cleave unto all good (D&C 98:8-11).

Similarly, note that Satan's unvirtuous rebellion corresponded with his effort to negate freedom:

> Wherefore, because that Satan rebelled against me, and sought to destroy the agency of man, which I the Lord God, had given him . . . I caused that he should be cast down (Moses 4:3).

No action is truly virtuous unless it is freely chosen. If we are forced at gunpoint to give to the poor, have we really been "charitable"? The scriptures are clear that giving grudgingly is not accounted unto us as righteousness (Moroni 7:8). There is no virtue without freedom because freedom is the *pre-condition* of virtue. Satan understood this and proposed a plan in the pre-existence that would have forced us to be righteous. He knew that force would have destroyed the righteousness itself and thus stopped our eternal progression.

Just as there is no virtue without freedom, there is no freedom without virtue. The Founders understood that humans require control; either they will control themselves internally, by their own virtue ("primary control" in Madison's language), or must be controlled externally by governments. The less virtue we have, the less freedom we will have as

# Independence II: The Creed & The Conflict

well. Freedom and virtue are self-reinforcing—the more virtuous the people are in a society, the more freedom that society will enjoy.[17]

Elder Christofferson made this point in the October 2009 Conference saying,

> The societies in which many of us live have for more than a generation failed to foster moral discipline . . . As a consequence, self-discipline has eroded and societies are left to try to maintain order and civility by compulsion. The lack of internal control by individuals breeds external control by governments.[18]

By all objective measures, freedom in the U.S. has declined since 2000. The Republicans want to blame Obama and the Democrats want to blame Bush, but the blame lies with "we the people." It is our own lack of virtue that is responsible for the decline in our liberty. Our politicians simply reflect the popular will. The bottom line is this: If we fail to internally govern ourselves, we will require a more oppressive external government.

## OPPONENTS OF INDEPENDENCE

The Founders didn't have a debate about freedom *or* virtue, but they *did* have the debate over whether or not to declare independence at all. In retrospect, we assume that anybody who would have opposed the Declaration of Independence must have been a villain, but that's not true. John Dickinson was a patriot, a staunch opponent of British oppression, a faithful public servant, and would later participate in the Constitutional Convention itself. But when it came time to declare independence he broke ranks with his friends Adams, Jefferson, and Franklin. He was not motivated by cowardice or greed (or else he wouldn't have later worked so tirelessly in the War for Independence), so what did motivate him?

First, Dickinson appreciated more than many of the Founders (and certainly more than Thomas Paine) how much America owed its liberty to England. He recognized that American traditions of freedom grew out of the British heritage of representation, limited government, Common Law, and Bill of Rights. If we cut ourselves off from England, said Dickinson, then we cut ourselves off from the source of our liberties.

Second, he did a simple cost-benefit analysis: in Dickinson's estimation, the colonies had more to lose than to gain by declaring independence. Yes things might turn out well, but there was the likelihood that an independent America would be worse than what it replaced. To illustrate, he used a metaphor: imagine that in the middle of winter your

---

17 The sticky problem of governing people without virtue is illustrated in the Book of Mormon. During a period of growing wickedness, Mormon lamented, "For as their laws and their governments were established by the voice of the people, and they who chose evil were more numerous than they who chose good, therefore they were ripening for destruction, for the laws had become corrupted. Yea, and this was not all; they were a stiffnecked people insomuch that they could not be governed by the law nor justice, save it were to their destruction" (Helaman 5:2-3).

18 Christofferson (2009).

## Chapter 6

house develops some serious imperfections—leaks in the roof, chinks in the wall, draftiness. We could understand wanting to patch up the house to make it better, but it would be extremely foolish to burn the house to the ground. Declaring independence, Dickinson said, is like burning down the political house—we should instead correct the imperfections from within. As we shall see, if it were it not for James Madison and the "new house" created by the Constitution, Dickinson would have been right.

Finally, and most prophetically, Dickinson said that if they declared independence from England, it would set a dangerous precedent—what would stop future dissidents from declaring independence from any new government they set up? If anyone can declare independence when they don't like the government's actions, then we stand in jeopardy of civil war and anarchy. As we all know, he was partially right about this. One hundred years later, America fought the bloodiest war in its history for exactly this reason.

### THE WAR FOR INDEPENDENCE

Notwithstanding Dickinson's view, the Congress made independence official by adopting the Declaration on July 4, 1776. Their work, though, had just begun. Now came the near-impossible task of making their independence real by defeating Great Britain on the battlefield.

On paper the Americans didn't have a chance. The British had four major advantages that should have guaranteed their victory. First, they simply had a larger military. Having more troops in the field meant the British would outnumber their colonial counterparts in almost any given engagement. A football metaphor can help here. If the Pittsburgh Steelers put 11 players on the field against only 8 for the Green Bay Packers, oddsmakers would pick the Steelers to win every time.

Second, it wasn't merely that the British had more troops, they also had better troops—*quality* as well as quantity. Their soldiers had been rigorously educated in the military arts. They knew how to march efficiently, maneuver into orderly formations, fire coordinated, accurate volleys, and conduct unified bayonet charges. It's as if the British troops were first-round draft picks while their American counterparts (mostly untrained farmers) were mere benchwarmers.

Third, the British had the greatest navy in the world. This was the same navy that would shortly defeat the mighty Napoleon and then establish the most extensive sea-based empire in history. Their navy gave the British unchallenged supremacy of the seas and an ability to quickly transport men and goods. All of the major colonial population centers (Boston, New York, Philadelphia, and Charleston) were coastal and vulnerable to naval attack.

Finally, the British had a decisive economic advantage. Not only was England a bigger country with more people to tax, but was also the most advanced industrial, capitalist nation on earth. Supplies were always scarce on the American side, but not on the British—

their factories could quickly and efficiently pump out blankets, clothes, supplies, firearms, cannons, and other military products they needed. Given all of the above British advantages, few would have anticipated an American victory.

But the Americans still had a few small advantages of their own that gave them a fighting chance. First, they had deeper reserves. The British had more players on the field, but the Americans always had reserves of militia on the sidelines ready to enter when the starters went down.

Second, they had home field advantage. The colonists knew the forests, hills, rivers, streams, lakes, and mountains that were, quite literally, in their backyard, whereas the British would get bogged down in the dense American frontier. As the home team, they not only knew the field, but also had the "crowd" cheering them on. Civilians would aid the American soldiers, but harass the British at every opportunity.

Third, the Americans were fighting for a cause they believed in, while the British soldiers were simply following orders. The average British soldier really didn't care much (beyond their own survival) about the outcome of the war, but the Americans were fighting for freedom. With their highest ideals on the line, American soldiers would sacrifice and persist far more than their opponents. Call this the "Rocky" factor.[19]

Fourth, the colonists had George Washington. How can one measure the contribution of the greatest man of the 18$^{th}$ century? The British may have had superior strategists with more experience and extensive training in the field, but Washington had courage, wisdom, judgment, integrity, motivational skills, and determination that exceeded that of his British counterparts. By sheer force of character, Washington kept his army together when it should have collapsed. Most importantly, Washington had an ability to lose battles—since losses would be inevitable—without ever allowing the British to land a decisive blow. These attributes are precisely what the colonies needed and nobody else had them as Washington did.

Finally, the Americans benefited from British blundering. The British commanders repeatedly made foolish decisions in key moments that prevented their winning. One of their biggest blunders was to underestimate popular sentiment in the colonies. The British thought that a few hothead ringleaders like Sam Adams, John Hancock, and Patrick Henry were making a fuss, but that most Americans were content with British rule. They didn't understand that these ringleaders *did* in fact represent the common sentiments of the people, or else they never would have been elected as leaders. Ultimately, the British didn't understand American democracy.

Based on this false assumption, the British began the war in the North trying to pacify

---

19 This may partially explain the popularity of American films like *Rocky* and *Star Wars*, which portray the triumph of a scrappy, rebellious underdog against a stronger, better-trained opponent. Notice also that in the original *Star Wars* films, the imperialist villains all spoke with English accents.

# Chapter 6

what they saw as the cauldron of rebellion—Boston. Once that didn't work, they moved to the middle colonies, hoping to control the Hudson River and thereby cut off New England from the other, presumably loyal, colonies. When that didn't pan out, they went down to solidify control over South. Consequently, the war went through three phases: North, Middle, and South.

## WAR IN THE NORTH

After the battles of Lexington and Concord, the British rushed back to Boston, licking their wounds and trying to regroup. The Americans, meanwhile, had moved to occupy the high ground above the city on Breed's (Bunker) Hill. The British, fearing the Americans could use their elevated location to bombard the city, sent three attack waves up to dislodge them. They eventually succeeded in taking the hill, but lost almost 1,000 soldiers in the process while the Americans only lost about 300. The victory was so costly, that the British sacked General Gage as commander and replaced him with General Howe.

After Bunker Hill, Washington arrived on the scene, incorporated the soldiers into a "Continental Army," and came up with a new plan to drive the British out. The colonists could occupy Dorchester Heights and bombard the city from the south, but they needed cannons.

Fortuitously, right about the same time, Ethan Allan and Benedict Arnold captured 60 tons of cannon at Fort Ticonderoga in upstate New York. But lakes, rivers, mountains, and hills stood between the Fort and Boston where the cannons were needed. At this point, Washington turned to one of his officers, Henry Knox, and charged him with crossing the Appalachians, retrieving the artillery, and bringing it back to Dorchester Heights.

Knox was, like most of Washington's officers, an unlikely soldier. Overweight and unsophisticated, Knox's only military "experience" came from what he read in his Boston bookshop. But he had a heart to match his girth and that proved more valuable than the military know-how of British officers. He was exemplary of the American cause not only in his lack of experience, but also in his determination.

In a heroic journey, Knox took his men to Fort Ticonderoga, loaded the cannon onto sleds, and then dragged them in the middle of winter all the way back to Dorchester Heights where they could be used to besiege Boston. The Redcoats, realizing they had been checkmated, had no choice but to evacuate the city. Round one went to the Americans. The first British strategy—controlling Boston and subduing the head of the rebellion—had been thwarted.

# INDEPENDENCE II: THE CREED & THE CONFLICT

## WAR IN THE MIDDLE

The British were not done. After regrouping in Canada, they turned to their second strategy—cutting off New England by capturing the Hudson River. Washington correctly surmised that the mouth of the Hudson—New York City—would be their target so he moved his army down for defense even though chances of success were slim.

Things turned out according to his worst fears. American troops were decimated at Long Island, Kips Bay, Harlem Heights, White Plains, and Fort Washington. After this string of defeats, the war seemed all but lost. Washington loaded what was left of his battered army onto boats and crossed the Hudson and Delaware Rivers, temporarily placing his men outside the grasp of General Howe.

Had he so desired, Howe could have pursued Washington and crushed the Continental Army in one easy, decisive blow, but he decided not to, thinking (for good reason) that Washington's army was so weakened and threadbare that it would just dissipate over the winter. The British could then declare victory in the spring without having to fight any further battles.

Howe was right about the condition of Washington's army. Not only had the Continentals run out of supplies—forcing them to walk hungry, barefoot, and cold in the harsh winter of 1776—but their enlistments were expiring at year's end. The soldiers had no legal obligation to stay on and fight for the cause—a cause that now looked hopeless. The number of loyalists grew daily as patriot enthusiasm flagged.

This was the darkest hour of the war, but also when its greatest heroes were made. That's true of all of us—we are tested to the greatest extent in times of greatest adversity, and that's when our eternal growth is most pronounced. Times of trial, not times of ease, are the crucible of greatness, where our character is formed and where the legend of our life is made.

Few historians will allow Providence as an explanation for American victory in the War for Independence, but when it comes to Trenton, there seems to be no other. Washington realized he needed to act immediately or all would be lost. He only had about 2,400 men left, but in this moment of desperation, Washington risked everything in one of the boldest gambles in military history: he decided to re-cross the Delaware River on Christmas Day and launch a surprise attack on the British forces (German "Hessian" mercenaries) at Trenton, New Jersey. He was outmatched in every way—numbers, skills, morale, and supplies—but he was determined (perhaps under inspiration) that it would work. It had to, or the war would be over. A surprise attack, if successful, would prevent the British from reinforcing the Hessians. If it failed, they would all be massacred. When his officers informed him that the gunpowder was wet and might not fire, Washington simply said with determination, "use bayonets." They were going to fight regardless.

On paper this was a suicide march. The Hessians were some of the most feared soldiers in the world—well trained and ruthless. By almost any rational calculation, the attack

## Chapter 6

would fail. Washington had to somehow convince his men to march into near-certain death without any recompense or financial incentive. How could he do it?

First, he had with him one of the most skilled persuasive writers in the world—Thomas Paine, the author of *Common Sense*. Paine had convinced the colonies to declare independence, now perhaps he could convince the Continental Army to go along with Washington's plan. To that end, he penned the American classic, "The Crisis," a stirring, emotional appeal to the soldiers (and, indirectly, to the American people) asking them to continue on in a cause that seemed hopeless. "These are the times that try men's souls," it began. Anyone, Paine pointed out, could be a "sunshine patriot." It takes no special courage to fight when things are going well, but the heroes are separated from the ordinary in moments of extreme difficulty. Moments like December 1776. Their participation in the attack on Trenton would, like all trials, be an opportunity for the forging of character and legend.

Paine also appealed to something that Washington often referenced—the "millions yet unborn." That is, it wasn't enough to fight for American freedom in the present. One's own freedom may not have been worth the price. But considering those millions who would come later and live under liberty if they held strong in this moment—that was worth fighting for. In the Church we often talk about Malachi 4:5 and the "hearts of the children turning to the fathers" in genealogical work, but we sometimes forget the other half of verse: that the hearts of the *fathers* would turn to the children. Could it be that Malachi's prophecy was fulfilled in this moment when the hearts of these Founding Fathers were turning to their posterity?

The second reason that the soldiers willingly attacked Trenton was Washington himself. Physically, he was a giant—a man of towering height and strength for his time.[20] He dominated every room by his size and regal demeanor. Those who knew him said he was the most dignified and imposing person they had ever encountered.

Not only was he a physical giant, he was a moral giant as well. We talk about the honesty of Abraham Lincoln, the empathy of FDR, or the sense of justice of a Martin Luther King, Jr., but Washington possessed all of these virtues in the highest degree. Parson Weems's story of boy Washington and the Cherry Tree may not be factually true, but it is certainly true in spirit. Many in our modern age wax self-righteous and condemn the Founders, including Washington, for owning slaves, but we forget that owning slaves was not remarkable among 18th century Virginia planters. What *was* remarkable was having the moral insight and self-sacrifice to free one's slaves. Almost alone among men of his time and position, Washington freed and provided pensions for his slaves. He stands supreme not only in his battlefield courage, but in his lack of hypocrisy. We find that young Washington

---

20 There has been some debate about exactly how tall he was. Traditional views and first-hand accounts put him at 6'4, but one of Washington's letters to a tailor puts him at 6'1 (perhaps he know the tailor's reputation for making clothes too large?). Either way, he was well above the average male height of the time.

had many flaws, but with each passing year, he steadily overcame them. He was a model of self-improvement. Over the years, the physically imposing Washington quietly became a moral giant unique in the annals of American history. Napoleon reportedly said on his deathbed, "they wanted me to be another Washington," but there was no other Washington.

He also possessed an almost supernatural aura of immortality. It often seemed that Washington couldn't be killed. It began when, as a young explorer, a treacherous guide fired a rifle point blank at his chest and then ran off into the woods. Washington looked down expecting to see his lifeblood running out, but was unharmed. Had the bullet magically bounced off? He later fell into a raging, icy river in mid-winter which, his companions thought, meant certain death, and yet he found his way to shore and continued as if nothing had happened. At Braddock's defeat in the French and Indian War, nearly all of the British officers on the march were killed. But not Washington, and he later wondered why, noting that four bullets had passed through his coat, hats were shot off his head, and two horses were shot out from under him. Yet Washington was unscathed, as if enemy fire was deflected by an invisible shield.[21] This larger-than-life hero seemed to have had the direct guidance and protection of Heaven.

Following their leader's courageous example and trusting in the Providence that seemed to accompany him, the American soldiers went ahead with the attack on Trenton. They crossed the Delaware (a scene immortalized in Emanuel Gottlieb Leutze's painting) then marched all night in the bitter cold to reach Trenton by dawn. Two freezing young soldiers sat down to rest and never got up again.

Those two young men were the only American casualties of the battle. Washington's gamble paid off spectacularly. The Americans caught the Hessians unaware in their beds, killed 100, captured 900 more and gained a victory that, although not of great strategic significance, kept the tiny flame of revolutionary hope alive. Buoyed up by the victory, colonial soldiers re-enlisted and new recruits trickled in. Howe was wrong: the Americans were not finished yet. Washington would keep fighting and so would his men.

Most importantly, Trenton kept the cause alive long enough for the colonists to win a major battle that was the turning point of the war: Saratoga. General Howe, to achieve their second objective of controlling the Hudson, ordered General Burgoyne to descend from Canada, meet Howe near Albany, and thereby cut New England off from the other colonies.

It did not go as planned. Burgoyne was constantly harassed in the dense American wil-

---

21 There is an apocryphal sequel in which, years later, an aged Indian chief remembered giving his men orders to kill all of the British officers, but eventually saw that they were wasting their bullets on Washington because "The Great Spirit protects that man" See Custis (1860, p. 304). Washington, it seems, later began to take advantage of his invincibility—riding out in front of his line of troops to encourage them. One of his soldiers reported pulling his hat down over his eyes because he couldn't bear to watch the General shredded by the bullets of his own men. And yet when the smoke cleared, there was Washington leading the charge unharmed.

# Chapter 6

derness by American militia who cut his supply lines, threw up barriers, destroyed bridges, and barricaded roads. By the time he neared Albany, Burgoyne was desperate for Howe's help.

But Howe never came. For some reason he went to Philadelphia instead. The American forces led by Benedict Arnold and Daniel Morgan seized the opportunity of Burgoyne's vulnerability, attacked, surrounded him, and forced a surrender on October 17, 1777. General Horatio Gates, although only nominally involved in the battle, received credit for the victory (this misattribution of credit would lead to both the American loss at Camden and Benedict Arnold's defection).

The triumph at Saratoga was a turning point for a number of reasons. Most obviously, it thwarted the second British strategy and prevented their control of the Hudson. But the Americans also captured Burgoyne's entire army along with its weapons and supplies. Most importantly of all, the victory at Saratoga brought France into the war on the side of the Americans. Benjamin Franklin, Congress's ambassador to France, had been trying to enlist French aid for months, but they had hesitated, thinking the war unwinnable. Saratoga convinced them otherwise. The colonies signed a formal alliance and suddenly French ships, men, and money were at work in the American cause. There never would have been American independence without France's help.

England, seeing what was happening, now agreed to all of America's prewar demands—repeal of the Declaratory Act, restoration of self-government, no taxation without representation—but it was too late. The American course was set: independence or nothing.

While Gates was triumphing at Saratoga, Washington was working to defend Philadelphia. He performed admirably, but was outmaneuvered and lost at Brandywine and Germantown. The American capitol fell and some blamed Washington. Conspiracies, such as the Conway Cabal, even threatened to remove him as commander-in-chief. Thankfully for America, the plots came to nothing.

The the threat of sedition was compounded by the harsh winter at Valley Forge where Washington tried, once again, to keep his army together in spite of intense cold, hunger, and deprivation. But there was a bright spot at Valley Forge: Colonel Friedrich Von Steuben. An officer in the Prussian Army who had volunteered in the American cause, Von Steuben was a master of military training who drilled and disciplined Washington's band of threadbare farmers until they became formidable soldiers who could meet the British on their own terms. Once spring came, they proved their new skills at the Battle of Monmouth Courthouse, an American victory that was no fluke. Howe ceded Philadelphia at this point and retreated to New York. Washington had fought the British to a stalemate in the middle colonies. This forced the British to turn to their third and final strategy—control of the South.

# INDEPENDENCE II: THE CREED & THE CONFLICT

## WAR IN THE SOUTH

Initially, the British were successful in the South. General Clinton (who had replaced Howe by this point) seized Charleston, South Carolina, the most important southern city, and then smashed Horatio Gates at the Battle of Camden. Their southern strategy seemed to be working.

But then another American legend was born. Among Washington's many gifts was an eye for talent, and he saw military genius in Nathaniel Greene. Congress had initially passed over Greene in favor of Gates for command in the South, but after Gates's cowardice and failure at Camden, they heeded Washington's advice and sent Greene down to stop Cornwallis. It was the right choice.

Greene, a cripple from a pacifist Quaker family, was an unlikely soldier, but he had tenacity and an uncanny intuition on the battlefield. He was perhaps the greatest tactician on the American side. Unlike Gates, who marched out into the open battlefield to take on Cornwallis European style, Greene knew how to leverage American advantages. He drew Cornwallis into the American backwoods where the British, not the Americans, would be out of their element. He then divided his forces, forcing Cornwallis to do the same, and this allowed Daniel Morgan to win a decisive victory over Colonel Tarleton at Cowpens. Cornwallis finally engaged Greene at Guilford Courthouse, but suffered major losses. Like Burgoyne at Saratoga, Cornwallis was beaten, weakened, and stranded. He stopped chasing Greene, headed for the coast, and hunkered down for relief at Yorktown, Virginia.

Washington knew that this was his chance to end the war and moved immediately. To prevent Clinton from going to the aid of Cornwallis, he spread rumors of an imminent attack on New York and left behind enough men in camp to act as a screen. The ruse worked. Clinton so feared Washington's attack that he didn't go down to rescue Cornwallis until it was too late.

A French fleet under Admiral DeGrasse blocked British reinforcements at the mouth of the Chesapeake while Washington, with the help of French soldiers under Rochambeau, laid siege to Yorktown. After steadily squeezing in on the British position, Washington finally forced Cornwallis to surrender on October 19, 1781.

That was the final blow. Yorktown marked the end of the War for Independence, formalized and made official by the Treaty of Paris two years later.

## THE MEANING OF INDEPENDENCE

This short summary of the American War for Independence has left out what Washington thought was the most important part of all—the hand of Providence. Washington firmly believed that he had only been an instrument in the hands of the Almighty. In fact, said Washington, the hand of Providence was so conspicuous that anyone who doubted it

## Chapter 6

was "worse than an infidel that lacks faith," and "more than wicked" for not acknowledging that obligation to the Creator.

What specifics did he have in mind? We mentioned how Washington's men placed cannons on Dorchester Heights, but this was only possible because a providential fog concealed their activities from the British and gave them just enough cover to finish their fortifications. Once they were done, the fog promptly lifted.

Then, in round two, when the Americans were surrounded on Long Island, the divine hand of Providence intervened again. We justly give credit to Washington for executing a masterful retreat, but it would have been impossible had not another fog appeared that limited British visibility and allowed Washington's army to escape undetected. When the British then tried to move upriver to block the American retreat to Manhattan, a fortuitous downwind prevented it. The survival of Washington's army depended upon miracle after miracle.

Just as bad weather enabled American retreats, it also prevented British ones. At Yorktown, Cornwallis saw the rising besiegement and loaded his men into boats for evacuation. But just as they were about to push off, a severe storm came in and forced them to call off the retreat until it was too late. Were each of these coincidences? Washington didn't think so.

For Washington, the greatest miracle of all was the fortitude of his own men in the face of adversity. These farm boys with little military experience fought with bravery, stamina, and skill far beyond their natural capacities. Against all selfish interest, these men stayed in the cause and fought even when things looked hopeless. They acted as if sustained by Divine Power. In fact, Washington thought that future generations wouldn't even believe the miraculous tale of the Revolution. **"It is more than probable,"** he said,

> That Posterity will bestow on their labors the epithet and marks of fiction; for it will not be believed, that such a force as England has [been] employed for eight years in [our] Country, [but] could be baffled in their plan of subjugating it by numbers infinitely less, composed of men oftentimes half-starved; always in rags, without pay, and experiencing, at times every species of distress which human nature is capable of undergoing.[22]

The hearts of these young soldiers were indeed turned to the children, the millions yet unborn—you and I—and in such a noble cause, the Lord upheld them. All of us can learn from this example: we will, like the Continental soldiers, find ourselves faced with tasks beyond our natural capacities, but with faith, prayer, and effort on our part will find ourselves accomplishing the impossible—just like these young, destitute farmers who defeated the mightiest military force in the world.

---

[22] Ellis (2007, p. 58).

## INDEPENDENCE II: THE CREED & THE CONFLICT

## CONCLUSION

Although this concludes our discussion of independence, it is far from the conclusion of our discussion of the Founding. We have yet to reach a happy ending. America had thrown off the yoke of tyranny, but who was to say that anarchy or another tyranny wouldn't replace it? Who was to say that the American Revolution wasn't just one more phase in that terrible human cycle of suffering under the Rule of Will? Dozens of other ex-colonies have been freed from imperial control only to find themselves ruled by domestic despots. Would America be different? The Founders ensured it would be through their discovery and implementation of the secret to freedom. That is the subject of the next four chapters.

## CHAPTER 6 SOURCES/FURTHER READING

Adams, John. *The Portable John Adams*. Edited by John Patrick Diggins. New York: Penguin, 2004.

Bailyn, Bernard. *The Ideological Origins of the American Revolution*. Cambridge, MA: Harvard University Press, 1967.

\_\_\_\_\_. *The Peopling of British North America: An Introduction*. New York: Vintage, 1986.

Beard, Charles. *An Economic Interpretation of the Constitution of the United States* [1913]. Mineola, NY: Dover, 2004.

Beeman, Richard. *Our Lives, Our Fortunes and Our Sacred Honor: The Forging of American Independence, 1774-1776*. New York: Basic Books, 2013.

Benson, Ezra Taft. *This Nation Shall Endure*. Salt Lake City: Deseret Book, 1977.

Bergh, Albert Ellery, ed. *The Writings of Thomas Jefferson*. 19 Volumes. Washington, D.C.: Thomas Jefferson Memorial Foundation, 1904.

Bobrick, Benson. *Angel in the Whirlwind: The Triumph of the American Revolution*. New York: Penguin, 1997.

Boorstin, Daniel. *The Lost World of Thomas Jefferson*. Chicago: University of Chicago Press, 1993. Covers Jefferson's intellectual outlook.

Brookhiser, Richard. *Founding Father: Rediscovering George Washington*. New York: Free Press, 1996.

\_\_\_\_\_. *The Adamses: America's First Dynasty*. New York: Free Press, 2002.

Budziszewski, J. *What We Can't Not Know: A Guide*. Dallas: Spence Publishing, 2003.

Butterfield, L. H. ed. *Letters of Benjamin Rush* Vol. II. Princeton: The American Philosophical Society, 1951.

Chernow, Ron. *Washington: A Life*. New York: Penguin, 2010.

Christofferson, D. Todd. "Moral Discipline," General Conference, October 2009.

Countryman, Edward. *The American Revolution*. New York: Hill & Wang, 2000.

Custis, George Washington Parke. *Recollections and Private Memoirs of Washington*, edited by Benson J. Lossing. New York: Derby & Jackson, 1860.

# Chapter 6

Declaration of Independence (1776).

Ellis, Joseph J. *Founding Brothers: The Revolutionary Generation*. New York: Vintage, 2002

———. *His Excellency: George Washington*. New York: Knopf, 2004.

Fawcett, Stanley E., ed. *God's Prophets Speak*. Springville, UT: Horizon, 2004.

Ferling, John. *Almost A Miracle: The American Victory in the War of Independence*. New York: Oxford University Press, 2009.

———. *Setting the World Ablaze: Washington, Adams, Jefferson, & The American Revolution*. New York: Oxford University Press, 2000.

Flexner, James T. *George Washington: The Indispensable Man*. Boston: Little, Brown, 1974.

Higginbotham, Donald. *The War of American Independence*. Boston: Northeastern University Press, 1983.

Hitchens, Christopher. *Thomas Jefferson: Author of America*. New York: HarperCollins, 2005.

Isaacson, Walter. *Benjamin Franklin*. New York: Simon & Schuster, 2003.

Jefferson, Thomas. *The Writings of Thomas Jefferson*. New York: Derby & Jackson, 1859.

Johnson, Paul. *George Washington: The Founding Father*. New York: HarperCollins, 2005.

Malone, Dumas. *Jefferson the Virginian*. Boston: Little, Brown & Co., 1948.

McCullough, David. *1776*. New York: Simon and Schuster, 2005.

Middlekauff, Robert. *The Glorious Cause: The American Revolution, 1763-1789*. New York: Oxford University Press, 1982.

Padover, Saul. *Jefferson: A Great American's Life and Ideas*. New York: Penguin, 1952.

Paine, Thomas. *The American Crisis* (1776).

Randall, Willard Sterne. *George Washington: A Life*. New York: Henry Holt & Co., 1998.

———. *Thomas Jefferson: A Life*. New York: Henry Holt & Co., 1993.

Wood, Gordon. *The American Revolution: A History*. New York: Random House, 2002.

———. *The Radicalism of the American Revolution*. New York: Random House, 1993.

# Chapter 7

# CONSTITUTIONALISM I: THE CONDITIONS OF FREEDOM

## BARON DE MONTESQUIEU: DIVIDING POWER

A few chapters ago we encountered this difficult question: "how does a society get and keep the Rule of Law?" It's time for an answer and the man who rediscovered it for modern times can help: Charles-Louis de Secondat, baron de la Brède et de Montesquieu. As you can probably guess from his name, Montesquieu was born into a noble French family with inherited estates and titles. After studying law, he worked as an officer in the French penal system. His job sparked an interest in government so he traveled widely in Europe seeking greater understanding of political systems. During his trip to England he realized that the English were freer and had more rights than people elsewhere. As he studied English government and read about ancient republics, he came to understand the secret to freedom and wrote up his findings in his masterwork, *The Spirit of the Laws* (1748).

While Montesquieu spent hundreds of pages elaborating on the conditions of liberty, we can summarize his findings in just four words. The secret to freedom is:

*The Division of Power*

Sear it into your brain, for this simple, but powerful phrase is responsible for freedom in America and everywhere else it has existed in the world. Inasmuch as political freedom is among the highest earthly goods, Montesquieu's discovery may be one of the most important insights in all of history and among the most important principles you will learn in life. Failure to understand and implement the division of power explains why most of history has been a cycle of tyranny and anarchy rather than liberty under the Rule of Law.

*Chapter 7*

Now, naturally, we can't just leave it at that. We need to further unpack the meaning of the secret to freedom. We must learn how it works, why it works, and how the Founding Fathers institutionalized and formalized divisions of power in the U.S. Constitution.

As we have already seen, freedom existed in Europe, particularly England, prior to the Founding of America. It is important to realize that this happened by chance or, as Latter-day Saints believe, Divine Providence. The secret to freedom was at work before 1776, but nobody planned it that way. Political institutions just evolved naturally in that direction through four major divisions of power in European history.[1]

## DIVISION I: CHURCH AND STATE

First, was the division between church and state. It is hard for us in 21$^{st}$ century America to understand how tightly church and state have been interwoven in almost every society throughout history. Until fairly recently, most people believed that political power should work hand in hand with religious authority. This had always created oppression as governments coerced people into believing and worshipping in a certain way. The government could enforce church dogmas and religious beliefs became political ends. Sometimes, the king was also a religious figurehead or even considered deity. For instance, the King or Queen of England is also head of the Church of England; Egyptian Pharaohs were considered divine (this explains their elaborate entombment); and the Japanese emperor, the head of their government, was also considered a god—a descendent of the Shinto sun goddess.

This began to change in 324 A.D. with Constantine the Great, Emperor of Rome. Constantine had no intention of separating church and state, but he wanted to move his capitol to a more favorable location. The eastern frontier of the empire was more suitable for trade and conquest so he took his advisors and civil servants with him from Rome to a new capitol city—Constantinople.

But here's the key: the leaders of the Church did not go with him. The Pope's authority came from his status as Bishop of Rome so he couldn't leave with the emperor. When Constantine left Rome, the Pope and the Church stayed behind.

With the Pope in Rome, the Church became institutionally and geographically split from the state. The political power of the empire no longer worked hand in hand with the Church and eventually they would even develop an adversarial relationship. The ambition of the state checked the ambition of the Church and vice versa. Kings and Popes engaged in a protracted tug-of-war for power in Europe, which prevented overreaching by either side. The Church limited the power of governments, and governments limited the power of the Church. In that struggle for power a space for freedom started to grow.

---

[1] For the historical framework and much of the information in this chapter I am particularly indebted to Zakaria (2003), Gress (1998), North (2005), and Roberts (1997). The opening line of Gress's work, "liberty grew because it served the interests of power," well summarizes the core principle behind this entire chapter.

## DIVISION II: STATE AND STATE

The second division of power was that between state and state. This came about because of European geography. A look at the map of Europe reveals a continent of remarkable geographic diversity—wide rivers (such as the Rheine, Seine, and Danube), towering mountain ranges (the Alps, the Pyrenees), countless valleys, bays, and peninsulas all chop up Europe into little pieces.[2]

This geographic fragmentation meant that Europe was nearly impossible to conquer and unite into a single political unit (just ask Napoleon, Charlemagne, or Hitler). Powerful military leaders could conquer India, Russia, or China with their flat plains and cohesive, uniform geography, but not Europe.

With so many disparate political units in Europe, none of them could get too strong and conquer all the others. By competing for power, the European kingdoms checked each other and prevented the emergence of a single hegemonic (dominant) state.

When Europe finally did coalesce into nation states, as in England, the local political leaders retained much of their authority. The local leaders only accepted admission into the new order under the condition that they be allowed to keep much of their power. So even the Kings in many parts of Europe were checked by the lords beneath them. This was on display most notably when the English lords forced King John I to sign the *Magna Carta* in 1215 A.D. In Europe, as nowhere else in the world, geography had created both external and internal checks on over-ambitious government power. Part of the importance of this political fragmentation was the diversity and competition which ensued. The need to keep up with neighboring states led to a loosening of stifling practices that might have been imposed without competition.

## DIVISION III: CHURCH VS. CHURCH

The third division of power that created freedom in the West was church vs. church. This division had its background in the *Renaissance*—a French term that means "re-birth." The Europeans weren't proposing ideas that were totally new, but recovering those that had been lost. The 14th century poet Petrarch most forcefully explicated this point of view, saying that Europe had long been stuck in medieval squalor with backwardness in technology and culture and yet things had not always been this way. The classical Greeks and Romans had marvelous wealth, beautiful art, remarkable poetry, and advanced technologies. So Petrarch worked his whole life convincing Europe to restore this classical splendor and wrote his own poetry using classical forms.

Filippo Brunelleschi was another restorer of lost truth. The Florentines wanted to build

---

2 It appears that the first to suggest a relationship between geography and free institutions may have been Montesquieu himself. See *The Spirit of the Laws* book XVII.

# Chapter 7

the largest freestanding dome in the world on a cathedral worthy of God's glory. Brunelleschi offered a plan for such a dome, but nobody on earth knew how to build such a thing. There was, however, a way to find out: Brunelleschi went to Rome and dug in the rubble of ancient buildings to find methods for building freestanding domes. The ascending-chain imbrication technology that he recovered from antiquity allowed him to erect an enormous dome that still dominates the Florentine skyline today.

Renaissance thinkers also restored religious truths. Michelangelo, for instance, subtly communicated the nature of God in his painting of the Sistine Chapel ceiling. He depicted God riding his chariot and extending his finger to Adam to transmit something to him. His chariot, which represents his glory and power, is shaped like a human brain. Michelangelo understood that the Glory of God is intelligence and that God shared this nature with man. We talk about the restoration beginning with Joseph Smith, but he was only the capstone of a restoration that had been going on for hundreds of years. It was the restoration of all things as the Lord poured out his spirit upon all flesh (Joel 2:28 and Joseph Smith History 1:41).

Such truths as revealed in Michelangelo's painting should help us transcend one of the highly contentious but fruitless debates that has raged for generations. One side says that the Renaissance was a terrible moment in world history because Western man stopped glorifying God and started glorifying human accomplishment. The other side says the Renaissance was a great moment in world history because man stopped being captivated by the God delusion and was then liberated to glorify the accomplishments of man. One side says we should downplay human achievement and the other says we should downplay God's achievements.

Both sides are wrong. One of the great truths of the restoration is that man and God are glorified *together*. Human achievements do not diminish those of God, they augment them. That is the whole plan of salvation and the meaning of exaltation. Much of Christ's ministry was dedicated to proving that by doing good works He was glorifying His Father, Himself, and the humans he served. Disciple-leaders will glorify God by discovering new scientific truths in the laboratory, designing new software, practicing the healing arts in medicine, defending the Rule of Law in court, or teaching truths in a classroom. You glorify God with your work if you excel in your professions with an eye single to His glory.

Among the main achievements of the Renaissance were technological advances that created an information revolution, most notably Johannes Gutenberg's invention of the printing press in the 15th century. Previous to Gutenberg, books were incredibly expensive. Each one had to be written out by hand and represented hundreds of hours of tedious work by a scribe. Books and literacy were mostly available only to the clergy. This gave the Church an unchecked monopoly on cultural power. There was little competition of ideas and little room for people to challenge accepted religious practices.

The printing press broke that monopoly. With widespread literacy, common people could learn and think for themselves. Thanks to heroic Bible translators, such as William Tyndale, they could also read the scriptures and learn religious truths unmediated by the Catholic hierarchy.

Martin Luther was one of these people that had access to the Bible and saw that much of what the Church did was inconsistent with its teachings. The practice of indulgences pushed him over the edge and out of the Church altogether. In 1517 Luther wrote up 95 charges against the Catholic Church and nailed them to the door of the Church at Wittenberg. Had he done this 100 years earlier he would have been summarily executed as a heretic, but not now. The printing press meant that others had read the Bible, had read of Luther's protest, and agreed with him (including powerful German princes who gave him protection). Luther gained a following that he could never have had in a pre-printing press world.

Once Luther broke away from Catholicism, others followed suit. John Calvin preached new doctrines and started an autonomous religious community in Geneva while Huguenots rejected Catholicism in France. Henry VIII of England didn't like what the Pope had to say about his marital situation, so he started his own church with himself at the head—the Church of England. Thanks to Luther's precedent, new churches popped up all over the continent.

This movement, which fragmented and weakened the power of the Catholic Church, we call the Reformation. It allowed for greater freedom of thought and action in religious matters. The Church was no longer a monolith with uncontested religious power.

Freedom of religion expanded under this process. All throughout history the attitude had been: "Our country accepts a particular religion so we are going to force your country into accepting our religion too." In the early 17$^{th}$ century there were large pockets of Protestantism in Northern Europe and the Catholic Hapsburgs brought armies to make them renounce their Protestant ways (this was the Thirty Years War). In 1648 they finally gave up fighting each other over religion and, at the Peace of Westphalia, accepted the "crazy" idea of letting each nation decide for itself which faith tradition it would pursue within its own boundaries. This was not yet religious freedom as we know it today, but it was a step in that direction.

## DIVISION IV: ECONOMY VS. STATE

The fourth and perhaps most important division of power was that between the *economy* and the state. Throughout history, those who controlled political power also controlled the economic power. Kings either owned most of the country's resources outright or could seize them at their whim. There were no private property rights or independent pools of wealth to challenge political authority.

# Chapter 7

Then in the 14th century, Europe saw the first stirrings of capitalism—an economic system in which wealth is primarily in private hands. It all started with the Black Death. This was a terrible plague that killed over ¼ of the people in Europe, but when it was all over, there was the same amount of wealth in fewer hands, meaning that wealth per capita had increased. Many who had previously struggled just to survive now had a surplus of money.

Jews, who weren't under the Catholic Church's prohibition of usury (charging interest), could receive these surplus funds as deposits and lend that money out. They would set up shop on park benches in Venice ("bancos" in Italian) and receive deposits, make loans, and pay interest. That was the birth of banking.

This banking system meant two things: 1) the people who deposited their money with these bankers saw their money grow as they received interest, and 2) those who borrowed the money started businesses, which also increased wealth. These banks created a way to pool money—capital—to finance moneymaking ventures (money used for production rather than consumption). The difference between consumer goods and capital goods is the difference between a fish and a fishing boat. The fish is cheap, but the boat is expensive so it requires many people to pool money to build it. Ultimately the fishing boat means far more fish (wealth) and more productivity in catching them. Banking financed capital investment and capital investment meant large amounts of economic power in private hands. This was the beginning of modern capitalism.

The rise of capitalism made an enormous contribution to liberty. The King didn't control the wealth, the emperor didn't control the wealth, the lords didn't control the wealth—private citizens did. Common people without titles or privileged connections to the state now had access to mobility and power that had always been denied them. Part of the magic of capitalism is the power of incentives that are brought to bear when individuals own the fruits of their labor. Barons and Kings were forced to decide between having low producing peasants or highly productive merchants. In the end, they gave up some control in the hope of more profit.

As this capitalist system spread to northern Europe, it married finance to industrial production. Factories and textile mills sprung up and began churning out resources in an abundance never seen before. This created a new, powerful class that was independent of the government—the *bourgeoisie*. Capitalism was non-discriminatory. It did not care if you were aristocratic, Jewish, Christian, immigrant, blond, darker-skinned or whatever—it only cared about efficiency. Capitalism served as a sledgehammer to smash away old forms of arbitrary, hereditary privilege.

Before the rise of capitalism, anytime someone wanted to engage in a large financial project, the government always had to fund it (think Columbus's voyages, the Great Wall of China, or the Taj Mahal). But now private wealth was so vast that it exceeded the fortunes of the richest kings. In fact, kings would often come begging these private citizens for loans and money. It was an unprecedented constraint on their power. The king could no longer seize money at his whim—the bourgeoisie class was too big, powerful, and entrenched.

In order to protect their new status and property, the bourgeoisie demanded political representation. Thus was born the House of Commons in England. Common people (non-nobles) now had rights and a voice in government. Capitalism helped gave birth to incipient democracy and political equality.

## CONCLUSION

This chapter has made clear that these four divisions of power were beneficial, but also accidental (or, if you will, providential). Nobody planned them; they simply emerged by the grace of God. Later we will see that, although it worked for Europe, we don't have to sit back and wait for freedom to emerge through chance divisions of power. Wise statesmen can harness their destiny by consciously designing governments in which power is systematically checked and balanced.

In the next chapter, we turn to the question of why this all works. The secret to freedom is the division of power, but why should dividing power create freedom under the Rule of Law? This is a puzzle that we will solve by looking at human nature, scriptural truths, and the nature of power itself.

## CHAPTER 7 SOURCES/FURTHER READING

Appleby, Joyce. *The Relentless Revolution: A History of Capitalism*. New York: W.W. Norton, 2010.
Burnham, James. *The Machiavellians*. New York: John Day, 1943.
Collinson, Patrick. *The Reformation: A History*. New York: Modern Library, 2004.
Cook, Quentin L. "Restoring Morality and Religious Freedom," *Ensign*, September 2012.
Ferguson, Niall. *Civilization: The West and the Rest*. New York: Penguin, 2011.
\_\_\_\_\_. *The Ascent of Money: A Financial History of the World*. New York: Penguin, 2008.
Fukuyama, Francis. *The Origins of Political Order: From Prehuman Times to the French Revolution*. New York: Farrar, Straus, and Giroux, 2011.
Gleeson-White, Jane. *Double Entry: How the Merchants of Venice Created Modern Finance*. New York: W.W. Norton & Co., 2012.
Gress, David *From Plato to NATO: The Idea of the West and its Opponents*. New York: Free Press, 1998.
Johnson, Paul. *The Renaissance: A Short History*. New York: Modern Library, 2000.
King, Ross. *Brunelleschi's Dome: How a Renaissance Genius Reinvented Architecture*. New York: Penguin, 2000.
Landes, David . *The Wealth and Poverty of Nations*. New York: Norton, 1999.

## Chapter 7

Magnusson, Sally. *The Flying Scotsman: A Biography of Eric Liddell*. NY: Quartet, 1981.

Marty, Martin. *Luther*. New York: Penguin, 2004.

Micklethwait, John and Adrian Wooldridge. *The Company: A Short History of a Revolutionary Idea*. New York: Modern Library, 2003.

Morris, Ian. *Why the West Rules (for now)*. New York: Farrar, Straus, and Giroux, 2010.

North, Douglass C. *Understanding the Process of Economic Change*. Princeton: Princeton University Press, 2005.

Porter, Bruce D. *War and the Rise of the State: The Military Foundations of Modern Politics*. New York: Free Press, 1994.

Roberts, J.M. *A History of Europe*. New York: Penguin, 1997.

Ruggiero, Guido De. *The History of European Liberalism*. Boston: Beacon, 1927.

Zakaria, Fareed. *The Future of Freedom: Illiberal Democracy at Home and Abroad*. New York: W.W. Norton, 2003.

# Chapter 8

# CONSTITUTIONALISM II: REALISM

## REINHOLD NIEBUHR: SIN AND SOCIETY

Now that we've seen how divisions of power created freedom in the West, we turn to the natural follow-up question: why does it work? Why, of all things, does dividing up political power lead to the Rule of Law and how can we best institute divisions to protect our freedom? To help us answer this question, we turn to the life and thought of Reinhold Niebuhr, the great 20th century Protestant theologian.

Niebuhr was born in 1892 to German immigrant parents. His father was a Protestant minister so Reinhold went to Yale Divinity School, hoping to follow in his father's footsteps. After finishing his studies, he took a position as the pastor of a small congregation in Detroit. Through ministering to the working class, Niebuhr was mobilized into social action. He wanted to know how the truths of Christianity could come to bear on the grave problems facing the world. The answers he came up with were so influential that he eventually became a bestselling author, an advisor to Presidents, a sought-after lecturer, and one of the most important intellectuals in the world. He appeared many times on national TV and on the cover of *Time Magazine*.[1]

Niebuhr achieved such eminence because his ideas spoke to the anxieties of America in the mid 20th century. The country had just gone through the worst war in the history of the world, the worst ever economic downturn, and then another world war even more terrible than the first. Once that war had ended, a powerful Soviet Russia emerged, which was every bit as tyrannical and genocidal as Nazi Germany, but also armed with nuclear bombs.

Particularly interesting to Niebuhr was how these developments contradicted expectations of Americans just a few decades earlier. The first years of the 20th century were among

---

1 He also penned the Alcoholics Anonymous Serenity Prayer, which begins, "God grant me the serenity to accept the things I cannot change; courage to change the things I can; and wisdom to know the difference."

# Chapter 8

the most optimistic in U.S. history. Americans of that generation had seen science deliver unprecedented control over the natural world—e.g., automobiles, skyscrapers, new medicines to prolong life, and even machines that allowed humans to fly. There was nothing, it seemed, humans could not accomplish through expert, scientific control. And if scientific control could yield such marvelous results in the natural world, why not apply it in the social world to end injustice, poverty, inequality, and war? Many in the "Progressive Era" believed that, through scientific reform, the world could shortly reach Utopia.[2]

And yet this progressive dream turned into a nightmare—far from delivering utopia, the next decades were the most violent in history, with some of the worst instances of tyranny and anarchy imaginable. The century that had begun with such promise turned into the bloodiest of all time. What had gone wrong?

Niebuhr believed that Christianity held the answer. The world had suffered so terribly, he said, because humans had forgotten the first and most basic of all Christian teachings—*the reality of sin*. The doctrine of original sin appears right at the beginning of the Bible, said Niebuhr, because it holds such profound insight into human behavior.

Now we must be clear that by "original sin" Niebuhr did not mean that all humans mystically inherit Adam's wickedness, rather, he meant that all humans, like Adam, have *free* agency and being truly free, they will often use that freedom to do *wrong*. Therefore, sin is inevitable. Humans, as beings to act rather than to be acted upon, are different than all else in creation and uniquely given to sinfulness. As long as there are humans, there will be sin.

Niebuhr had to remind America that people are not objects for scientific control (like cement, steel, germs, or bricks), but subjects who make choices.[3] Folly and evil are with us and always will be, said Niebuhr; it is as certain and immutable as the law of gravity. We cannot change the fact of original sin, we can only deny it at our own peril.

In his emphasis on the imperfection of humans, Niebuhr was one of the greatest *realists* of the 20th century. Political realism simply means that, when structuring governments, we take people as they are, with all of their flaws, and not as we wish them to be. While Karl Marx and other utopians have assumed that we could perfect people through political control (which, of course, never happens and only leads to mass death and suffering), Niebuhr understood that people have sinfulness hard-wired into them, regardless of circumstances.[4] Efforts at widespread social control backfire because of this basic fact of human nature.

In this chapter, we are going to see how Niebuhr's realist insights can help us understand why tyranny is so pervasive and how we can structure governments to prevent it.

---

2 Perhaps the most naïve was journalist Lincoln Steffens who admired the Communist Revolution in Russia and returned to America declaring, "I have seen the future and it works."
3 Perfection, remember, can only come through Christ, not through the human efforts of scientists and politicians.
4 His realism is also found in the Serenity Prayer, which admonishes us to "Take, as Jesus did, This sinful world as it is, Not as I would have it."

## WHY TYRANNY?

Earlier in the book, we learned that the Rule of Law is rare in human history. There have almost always been governments, but they have usually worked to destroy rather than protect freedom. We can understand why once we examine a couple of political axioms:

*Axiom 1. People must govern*

*Axiom 2: Governments will be as bad as the people who run them*

In other words, since governments are always run by people, governments will inevitably be as imperfect and corrupt as those people. This means tyranny.

Of course, political philosophers have not been ignorant of this fact, but most of them have believed that the solution was simply to find the "good guys" to rule. If the problem of tyranny comes because bad people are governing, then just switch that around and put the good people in charge.

Different peoples throughout history have had different opinions about who those "good guys" were. Medieval theologians thought that the "good guys" were monarchs who governed by divine right. Plato believed that the "good guys" were philosophers who were fit to rule by virtue of their superior understanding of ideal truths. Economist Thorstein Veblen believed that the "good guys" were intellectuals ("social engineers") trained in the scientific method. Karl Marx believed the "good guys" were members of the working class. Today's liberals believe the "good guys" are Democrats while conservatives think that the "good guys" are Republicans.[5] Our political problems will be solved, they all say, if we just give power to the right people.

Niebuhr understood that this "solution" was no solution at all. First of all, everyone, regardless of their ability, party, status, or training is still a human with agency and therefore still given to sinfulness. Belonging to any of the above "chosen" groups does not give one a free pass out of the human condition and the imperfection that comes with it.

Second, and even more tragically, even if you were fortunate enough to find "good people" to rule, the *very act of ruling itself would turn those good people bad*. Power corrupts. It is an unavoidable fact of human nature. Wielding political power turns even the best people into monsters.[6] As you can see, the "good guys" solution doesn't work. We are, seemingly, stuck with tyranny no matter how hard we try to find good rulers.

---

[5] Isn't it highly convenient that those who suggest the group that should rule always just happen to belong to that particular group?

[6] The *Lord of the Rings* trilogy is an extended metaphor on the corrupting influence of power.

*Chapter 8*

## Evidence

To know that the above is correct, we don't have to take Niebuhr's word for it; we have history, science, and even scriptural passages as proof. Attempted political utopias have always failed and power has corrupted even the noblest leaders.[7] The 20th century alone saw over one hundred million people sacrificed to the quest for utopia by corrupt leaders in fascist or communist systems.

The Bible tells of how the Israelites, wanting to be like other nations, rejected the system of judges and demanded that the prophet Samuel choose a king instead. Samuel warned against it, but they said it would be fine as long as Samuel chose the right guy. So Samuel went and found the humblest man in the whole kingdom—Saul, "a choice young man, and a goodly: and there was not among the children of Israel a goodlier person than he" (1 Samuel 9:2). Saul was everything Israel could have wanted in a king. Surely, if ever there was a "good guy" fit to rule righteously, it was Saul. But as soon as Saul took the crown, the power began to work on him. He began launching unjust wars of conquest, attempting to murder rivals, and plundering the kingdom he was chosen to serve. It all ended tragically for Saul and Israel.

Instead of learning their lesson that kings don't work, the Israelites assumed that Samuel had just chosen the wrong person. They asked him to try again. This time Samuel chose a heroic, righteous young man named David who was as near perfection as a person can be. This was the same David who slew Goliath and would write the Psalms. But as soon as David took the crown the power began to work on him as well. Before long he had become so corrupt that he committed the two most serious earthly sins. Clearly the problem was not the men Samuel had chosen, but the corruption that came with the absolute power of kings.

It wasn't just a problem for ancient Israel, it remains a problem today. Every election, new candidates promise to go to Washington and root out the corruption—end pork barrel waste, stop special interest lobbies, pay down the debt, and bring "change" to the country—and yet with each successive election pork barrel spending, waste, lobbying, and debt set new records. We send "good people" to Washington to *clean up* the problem, and yet as soon as they take power they become *part of* the problem. It's not that our politicians are bad people, it's just that they are humans and subject, like all of us, to the corrupting effects of power.[8]

Science has also demonstrated the tendency for power to corrupt. Laboratory experiments have shown that those placed in positions of authority usually turn almost imme-

---

7  There are a handful of exceptions that prove the rule, e.g., George Washington, Mosiah, King Benjamin, Cincinnatus, but this still leaves the problem of corrupt monarchical successors. See Mosiah 29:13.

8  The futility of establishing utopia freed from human sinfulness is also well illustrated in *The Village*, an underrated film by M. Night Shyamalan.

diately into controlling autocrats. The most notable example was the Stanford Prison Experiment carried out by Phillip Zimbardo. Michael Huemer provided a nice summary of the implications of the experiment:

> Power corrupts . . . this has long been apparent from history; now we have experimental evidence as well. When some human beings are given great power over the lives of others, they often discover that the sense of power is intoxicating. They want to exercise their power more frequently and more fully, and they don't want to give it up."[9]

The scriptures also bear out Niebuhr's insights. D&C 121:39 says, "We have learned by sad experience that it is the nature and disposition of almost all men, as soon as they get a little authority, as they suppose, they will immediately begin to exercise unrighteous dominion."

By now it should be clear why there is almost an iron law of tyranny in history: either bad people rule and take away rights, or good people rule, are corrupted by the power, and then take away rights. The people might rise up and overthrow a tyrant, but whomever they choose as their new ruler will almost certainly become as corrupt and oppressive as the man he replaced. This is a huge dilemma and has plagued societies from the beginning.

## Solution

This is all very gloomy, but it helps us understand how the secret to freedom provides a way out of this dilemma. Since those who have unlimited power will almost certainly abuse that power and take away our natural rights, the only way to preserve freedom is to *limit power*, and the only way to limit power is by *dividing it*. In other words, dividing power limits power, and limiting power prevents corruption and abuse. Ergo, *the secret to freedom is the division of power.*

If division of power is the only way out of the above dilemma, how do we actually put divisions of power in place? We saw previously that Europe became partially free by chance as power naturally divided between state, church, and economic actors, but must we just sit back and wait for freedom to happen, or can we seize hold of our destiny and structure governments with divisions of power built in?

To answer this question we turn to Thomas Hobbes, the great 17th century English philosopher and precursor to John Locke. Hobbes lived during the anarchy of the English Revolution and had a low opinion of human nature because he had seen so much interpersonal brutality first hand. Life for humans left to their own devices, he famously said, is "solitary, poor, nasty, brutish, and short."

Because of the inherent tendency of humans to kill, brutalize, rape, enslave, and steal from one another, Hobbes proposed that societies empower an absolute sovereign to stop

---

9  Huemer (2013, p.133).

the predations of one person over another. Holding a monopoly on power, this sovereign (the government) would solve the problem of anarchy by stopping humans from taking away one another's rights. When we move to hurt each other, the sovereign steps in to stop it and reassures us, "don't worry I've got you."

But as you can see, Hobbes's "solution" only introduces a new problem: once we give all power to the sovereign to stop us from preying on one another, *what is to stop the sovereign himself from preying on us?* The sovereign, by being empowered to protect natural rights, is also thereby empowered to take them away. Given the reality of human nature, he will almost certainly do so if given the chance. Hobbes solved the problem of anarchy, but left us with the problem of tyranny. "You've got us," we might say to the government, "but who's got you?"

The solution to the above Hobbesian dilemma is simple: *a constitution.* By constitution we mean a formal mechanism that explicitly divides and limits the government's power. John C. Calhoun, the 19th century U.S. Senator and political theorist, taught that a constitution restrains the government in the same way that the government restrains the people. It divides political power such that each part checks and places limits on the others.

The idea of a constitution means that we don't have to just sit back and hope that chance divisions of power emerge through good fortune, we can design political institutions with inbuilt divisions of power that will check and balance the government to prevent it from going beyond its necessary functions. Such a government restrained and limited by a constitution is called a "constitutional government." Every free country in the world is free only because of constitutional limits placed on those in power.

A constitution, then, is the means by which we achieve the Rule of Law—the sweet-spot middle ground between anarchy (too little government) and tyranny (too much government). We empower a government to protect us, thereby preventing anarchy, but then put constitutional restraints on that government, thereby stopping tyranny.

Great thinkers throughout history have agreed with the need for a constitution. Montesquieu said, "The only safeguard against power is rival power." According to Lord Acton, "Liberty depends upon the division of power." The great sociologist Robert Nisbet said, "In the division of authority and multiplication of its sources lie the most enduring conditions of freedom."

As you can see, the stakes of constitutional government couldn't be higher. A constitution limits government power through divisions, which in turn preserves the Rule of Law, which means that our natural rights are protected, which means that we can exercise our agency. Clearly, achieving and preserving constitutional government is of the utmost importance since it protects that capacity for free choice that allows our eternal progress.

## CONSTITUTION EXAMPLES

Every country needs a constitutional government to be free, but effective constitutions come in many forms. There are a variety of ways to divide and check power so let's look at some examples of effective constitutions both ancient and modern.

One of the first constitutions in history was put in place by Mosiah, the last Nephite King. Mosiah lived at a moment when the Nephite nation had vastly expanded in size by incorporating both the People of Zarahemla ("Mulekites") and the People of Limhi. Not only did the Nephites need a government more adequate to their expanded population, but Mosiah also had the historical records from the Limhites and Jaredites that showed how much damage wicked Kings could do. He had a new awareness of the need for an alternative to the absolute power of a monarch.

As with all those who have ever designed free government institutions, Mosiah began with that important Niebuhrian insight about the sinful tendencies of humans. The judgments of God, he said, are perfectly just, but the "judgments of man are not always just"; therefore, a king is likely to abuse any power entrusted to him. "For how much iniquity doth one wicked king cause to be committed and what great destruction!" It was the fault of King Noah that his people were put into bondage, and his abuses of power deprived the people of their rights through theft, wars, and murder (Mosiah 29:12, 16-20, 36).

Mosiah also had no illusions about simply finding a "good man" to be their king. He understood that the temptations of power would corrupt even the most righteous among them. Some proposed that his oldest son, Aaron, succeed him as king, but Mosiah refused. Was it because Aaron was so bad? No, precisely the opposite: it was because Aaron was so *good*. Mosiah didn't want his son to have to face the temptations of power that could corrupt him. "We have no right to destroy my son [nor] another appointed in his stead," he said. Mosiah understood that the problem of tyranny would not be solved by just finding a "good guy" to rule, it could only be solved through replacing monarchy with a constitution.

So Mosiah proposed a system of judges with a number of ingenious checks and balances that would limit government authority. First, power would be divided between multiple judges rather than concentrated in the hands of a single person. The competition for power among these judges would prevent any one of them from exercising tyrannical authority. Second, there would be a division between *levels* of judges—higher and lower—each checking the other. If a lower judge acted unjustly, a higher judge could reverse that ruling. If a higher judge acted unjustly, then a group of lower judges could check the power of the higher judge. Third, and perhaps most important of all, these judges would not inherit their position but would be elected "by the voice of the people." Democracy itself would check the power of the judges. The Nephite rulers would be restrained knowing that maintaining their power depended upon doing what was in the public interest. This, in essence, divided power among all Nephite citizens (Mosiah 29:8, 29:26-28).

## Chapter 8

Mosiah didn't, however, have any illusions about democracy. Some of us today see democracy as a panacea for all ills or synonymous with the Rule of Law. It is not. The people are often wrong. Alma even taught that if they could always count on having just men as kings (such as Benjamin and Mosiah), then monarchy would be preferable to democracy (Mosiah 23:7-8). But democracy was a necessary check on the tendency of rulers to abuse power (Mosiah 29:13). Mosiah's views align with those of Winston Churchill who said, "democracy is the worst form of government except for all of the others," or with Niebuhr who reminded us that, "Man's capacity for justice makes democracy possible; but man's inclination to injustice makes democracy necessary."[10]

Mosiah's new constitutional government proved remarkably successful (at least in the short term) in establishing the Rule of Law among the Nephites. They had always had just laws, but often those laws were not executed with justice.[11] Now they were, and an equality of rights and liberty was maintained among the Nephites. Most important of all, the new "reign of the judges" preserved the agency and accountability of each person. By limiting the government, this constitution allowed the people to answer for their own sins (Mosiah 29:25, 31-34, 38). Such was one of the great constitutional achievements of the ancient world.

In modern times, the best proposal for a structure of government came from Montesquieu. In his masterwork, *The Spirit of the Laws* (1748), Montesquieu began, like Mosiah, with the crucial realist insight about human fallibility. Humans, he said, are tragically caught between animal and godly status. Humans, unlike animals, have free will, but, unlike God, are imperfect. This means that humans are in the unique position of committing sin—something animals can't do and God won't do. Every free political system, Montesquieu understood, must begin with this proper, realist understanding of human nature.

Of course Montesquieu knew that we should divide power, but his greatest contribution to political theory was to propose dividing government power according to *function*. The tasks of governments, said Montesquieu, are threefold: they make laws, enforce laws, and apply laws. So the best constitutions will divide the government according to these functions. This means three *branches*—a legislative branch, an executive branch, and a judicial branch. The abuses of power that constitutions are designed to prevent are most likely to happen when these functions are combined. By dividing executive, legislative, and judicial functions, said Montesquieu, you get the most effective divisions of power and therefore the most liberty. This is why the English had enjoyed more freedom over the course of their history than had the French. Their constitution evolved naturally to embody these functional divisions.

---

10 Niebuhr (1944, p. xxxii).

11 The laws were probably handed down on the Brass Plates, which gives insight into why it was so crucial for Nephi to secure them from Laban in the first place.

## CONCLUSION

As you've probably guessed by now, Montesquieu became *the* primary inspiration for the U.S. Constitution. At the Constitutional Convention, the Founding Fathers quoted *The Spirit of the Laws* more than any other book except the Bible. In that sense, Montesquieu is to the Constitution what Locke is to the Declaration of Independence. Locke gave us the ideals that government should strive for—preservation of natural rights; Montesquieu provided the mechanism—division of power by function—that would accomplish that goal.

Now that we understand what constitutions are, why they are necessary, and how they work, we will turn in the next chapter to the most successful constitution in human history.

## CHAPTER 8 SOURCES/FURTHER READING

Ariely, Dan. *Predictably Irrational: The Hidden Forces That Shape Our Decisions*. New York: HarperCollins, 2008.

Burnham, James. *The Managerial Revolution: What is Happening in the World*. New York: John Day Company, Inc., 1941.

Calhoun, John C. *A Disquisition on Government* (1848). New York: Peter Smith, 1943.

Diggins, John P. *Why Niebuhr Now?* Chicago: University of Chicago Press, 2011.

Fox, Richard. *Reinhold Niebuhr: A Biography*. New York: Pantheon, 1985.

Hobbes, Thomas. *Leviathan* (1651). New York: Penguin, 1982.

Kahneman, Daniel. *Thinking Fast and Slow*. New York: Farrar, Straus and Giroux, 2013.

King, Ross. *Machiavelli: Philosopher of Power*. New York: HarperCollins, 2007.

Machiavelli, Niccolò. *Discourses on Livy* (1531). Translated by Harvey C. Mansfield and Nathan Tarcov. Chicago: University of Chicago Press, 1998.

_____. *The Prince* (1532). New York: Penguin, 2003.

Montesquieu, Charles de. *The Spirit of the Laws* (1748). Edited by Anne M. Cohler, Basia Carolyn Miller, and Harold Samuel Stone. New York: Cambridge University Press, 1989.

Neuhaus, Richard, ed. *Reinhold Niebuhr Today*. Grand Rapids, MI: William B. Eerdman's, 1989.

Niebuhr, Reinhold. *The Children of Light and the Children of Darkness: A Vindication of Democracy and a Critique of Its Traditional Defense*. Chicago: University of Chicago Press, 1944.

_____. "Why the Christian Church is Not Pacifist," in *The Essential Niebuhr*, edited by Robert McAfee Brown. New Haven: Yale University Press, 1987, pp. 102-119.

_____. *Moral Man & Immoral Society: A Study in Ethics*. New York: Charles Scribner's Sons, 1932.

_____. *The Irony of American History*. New York: Charles Scribner's Sons, 1952.

_____. *The Nature and Destiny of Man*. New York: Charles Scribner's Sons, 1953.

Tetlock, Philip. *Expert Political Judgment: How Good Is It? How Can We Know?* Princeton: Princeton University Press, 2006.

## Chapter 8

Zimbardo, Philip. *The Lucifer Effect: Understanding How Good People Turn Evil*. New York: Random House, 2007.

# Chapter 9

# U.S. CONSTITUTION I: THE CONVENTION

### JAMES MADISON: FATHER OF THE CONSTITUTION

James Madison is considered "the Father of the Constitution" for good reason. He, more than any other Founder, was responsible for designing the Constitution and bringing delegates to the Constitutional Convention. If there were no James Madison, there may have been no Constitution and no United States of America as we know it.

Like many of the other Founders, Madison was a Virginian, but unlike Washington and Jefferson who were tall, athletic, and robust, Madison was small and frail: five feet four inches tall and shy of 100 pounds. But he more than compensated with a capacious, brilliant mind that continues to amaze us over two centuries later.

Madison came into his own as an intellect at Princeton University. He had a great mentor named John Witherspoon—a Scotsman and a signer of the Declaration of Independence—who taught Madison how to think deeply on fundamental issues of government, philosophy, and religion. After completing his education (including time as a graduate student in Hebrew), Madison decided to pursue a career in law. Witherspoon wrote his young protégé a letter of recommendation, which said, "I have never known this young man to do or say an improper thing." Madison had character to match his intelligence.

After Princeton, Madison returned to Virginia where he was elected to the House of Burgesses and soon realized that he faced a different problem than that of the older generation of Founders. Their problem had been that of tyranny—the oppression of King George and the British government—but Madison saw that after the fight for independence came the problem of anarchy. The older generation had thrown off an oppressive British government that infringed upon their natural rights, but had yet to replace it with a government sufficiently strong to protect those rights. Madison realized that they would need a powerful, yet limited government to secure the ideals of the Declaration of Independence. The country no longer needed freedom *from* bad government, but freedom *through* good government.

## ARTICLES AND ANARCHY

The post-independence government that Madison worked to replace was created by The Articles of Confederation. Its problems were legion. First, The Articles of Confederation had just one branch of government—a legislature to make laws, but no executive or judiciary to carry out or apply them. Furthermore, the legislature poorly represented the people—there were thirteen states and each of them had one vote in Congress meaning that, regardless of population, every state had equal power and influence.

Second, under the Articles of Confederation, the government had no way to raise money. Governments obtain funds in three ways: taxing, borrowing, or printing. The Articles of Confederation empowered the government to do none of these. Only the states could tax (since Americans at the time were extremely fearful of taxation, especially from a distant government), the government had no credit (who would lend them money when they had no way to pay the debts back?), and there was no valid national currency. If Congress wanted money they had to beg it from the states and the states rarely obliged. Since all government action requires money, the Congress was powerless to act in any meaningful way.

Third, the country didn't have a foreign policy. Each state had its own foreign relations and trade agreements, but there was no united foreign policy of all the states. There was no military—they had cobbled one together during the Revolution, but that had now dissolved (again, the Founding generation was scared of a standing army—remember the Boston Massacre?); their treaties were toothless since there was no united voice or force to back up those treaties; and the states were engaging in trade wars with each other—slapping tariffs and trade restrictions on the other states and squabbling over navigation rights. Such restrictions prevented Americans from reaping the gains from commerce that a national market would have created. Instead of turning a strong, united national policy to the world, the states fought with one another.

Clearly, the Articles were terribly inadequate for freedom and prosperity. The U.S. government after 1776 was insufficiently strong to protect rights through the Rule of Law. In fact, the weakness of the Articles of Confederation led to two close calls with the Rule of Will.

First, the country had a brush with tyranny that historians call the Newburgh Conspiracy. During the war, Congress had bestowed upon George Washington quasi-dictatorial powers. Washington used this power judiciously and wisely during the war to carry the cause to victory, but after the war was over, would Washington keep this power and set himself up as a King (many thought he would and many thought he should) or would he return power to the civilian authority in Congress?

He was one of the most famous men alive with an army behind him that had just defeated the greatest military force in the world. There was nothing to stop him from becoming another king. However, Washington realized that retaining power would have compromised the principles upon which the Revolution was based. As a result, unlike other military victors throughout history, he decided to voluntarily relinquish his position and hand power back to the civilians represented in Congress. When George III heard of Washington's plan he said, "if he does this, he will be the greatest man in the world." He was right. In a dramatic moment Washington appeared before the Congress in Annapolis, laid down his sword, and resigned his commission.

But not all of Washington's officers had his long-sighted view. Most of them were angry with the Congress. Who could blame them? The weakness of the Articles meant that Congress had no power to raise money to pay the officers their back salaries. These soldiers had given their blood, sweat, and tears to the cause of freedom while their farms and businesses failed and yet they still received almost no compensation. A government that can't pay its military is susceptible to a military coup and the installation of dictatorship. That is what has happened in countless other ex-colonies after independence, and that's what almost happened in the United States.

Congress tried to pacify the military by saying, "Just be patient while we work with the states to get your money." But the officers had already been patient for seven years and had been through enough. They gathered in Newburgh, New York to plan a march on Congress in which they would seize the government and take their money by force. At this heated moment, Washington showed up and begged them not to go through with their plan. If they did, he said, they would squander the principles of self-government for which they had fought and suffered.

But the officers were too angry to heed him, and their determination only escalated until Washington performed an act of symbolic brilliance that saved the country. He asked the officers to remain quiet long enough to hear him read a letter from Congress. He took out the letter, unfolded it, strained at the words, and then drew a pair of spectacles from his pocket, saying, "Gentlemen, you will excuse me. I've grown old and gray in your service and now find myself going blind." This gesture so moved the angry mob of officers that they decided to scotch their plan. If it weren't for Washington (yet again), the United States would have ended in tyranny. The country was dangerously close to becoming yet another failed post-colonial state, throwing out one tyranny to replace it with another.

The second brush with the Rule of Will was also sparked by military veterans from the Revolutionary War. Like the officers at Newburgh, a captain named Daniel Shays had sacrificed greatly for the cause of independence. He was a patriot who understood the injustice

*Chapter 9*

of excessive taxation, but his service in the Revolutionary War left him and other western Massachusetts farmers heavily in debt.

In this difficult situation, Massachusetts tax collectors showed up and demanded payment. Shays was irate. To him, this was completely backward: he shouldn't be *giving* money to the government, he should be *getting* money from the government. They should be paying him for his service and sacrifices during the war, not taking money from him when he could least afford it *because* of that service.

Shays had just finished fighting one war against unjust taxation and he had no problem fighting another one. He organized his neighbors into an armed mob and they ran the tax collectors off, marched on the courts that had ordered these collections, and overthrew the local government. They were heading to seize an arsenal to do the same at the state level when the Massachusetts militia showed up and put down the uprising before it gained unstoppable momentum. In this event—Shays' Rebellion—people lost their lives, liberties, and properties because the government was too powerless to protect them (or collect taxes to pay veterans). It was anarchy.

These close calls made thoughtful Americans nervous. Madison in particular realized that the government under the Articles of Confederation was insufficiently strong to secure liberty. Americans had so despised the tyranny of king George that they had swung too far towards the other extreme of anarchy.

## CALLING THE CONVENTION

Madison's goal was to get the country to come together and form a "more perfect union"—one stronger than that under the Articles, but limited from becoming tyrannical. Only thus, said Madison, could America break the looming cycle of vacillation between anarchy and tyranny.

How could Madison persuade the country to strengthen the national government when they were so afraid of centralized government power? He realized that he couldn't call outright for a new, stronger national government; that smacked of the English oppression they had just fought to get away from. He had to be subtle and move the country towards a constitutional convention in steps.

First, he went to Washington, the most respected man in the country, and asked if he would lend his house for a meeting between states. Washington agreed, so Madison invited delegates from Maryland and Virginia to Mt. Vernon where they could resolve their trade disputes. He was wise to pick Mt. Vernon because the delegates would come knowing that Washington would be in the corner presiding over the meeting and giving legitimacy to its proceedings. At this *Mt. Vernon Conference* (1785), the delegates worked out a united solution to their trade disagreements, proving that states could cooperate to solve their problems with stronger governance. It was a start.

# U.S. Constitution I: The Convention

Madison built on this momentum the next year with the *Annapolis Convention* (1786). He invited delegates from all the states to come to Annapolis, Maryland where they could discuss revising the Articles of Confederation. Delegates from five states showed up (an improvement on the two at the Mt. Vernon Conference) and resolved to assemble in Philadelphia the following summer to revise the Articles of Confederation. They had a year to persuade the other states to join them.

A few things happened after the Annapolis Convention that helped their cause. First, Madison himself was persistent and persuasive. To avoid spooking the delegates, he continued to insist that they would only be "revising" the Articles.

Second, he prevailed upon Washington, "the indispensable man," to come to the Convention. Washington had gracefully retired from public life after the Revolution and was reluctant to return. But Madison explained the stakes to him: if he didn't attend, neither would many undecided delegates and their project of creating a free nation would fail. So Washington changed his mind and agreed to come. Once the delegates from the other colonies heard that Washington would attend the convention they were willing to gamble on the proceedings.

Third, Shays' Rebellion in late 1786 convinced many of the wisdom of Madison's point: they needed a stronger government lest their society degenerate into anarchy. Thanks to each of the above, the states decided to participate in the 1787 Convention at Philadelphia that we now call the Constitutional Convention.

Now that the Convention was set, Madison had to be ready. He knew they would be creating, from scratch, a great republic of freedom to last for the ages. If they got it right, they could create the most effective government in history. If they got it wrong, it would not only destroy freedom in America, but also communicate to humankind that democracy can't work. He asked Jefferson, then living in Paris, to send him books on political theory, philosophy, and history to help him prepare. He read up on Montesquieu, Locke, Gibbon, Hume, and the classics. He knew that there had been free republics in previous epochs, and hoped that the United States could restore that lost freedom.

His study paid off. By the time of the convention, Madison had developed a plan for a stronger, more effective national government to replace the Articles of Confederation. This "Virginia Plan" would become essentially the first draft of the U.S. Constitution.

## GREAT DEBATES

In May of 1787, representatives from the other colonies began arriving in Philadelphia to join him. Some of them you have heard of—George Washington, Benjamin Franklin, and Alexander Hamilton—others you probably have not heard of—Edmund Randolph, the young Virginia governor; Robert Morris, the financial wizard who kept the nation afloat with funds during the Revolution; Gouverneur Morris, the "rake who wrote the Constitution" in its final draft form; and James Wilson, a brilliant Philadelphia attorney who we will talk more about later—but almost all of them were remarkable, wise men who made important contributions to the final version of the Constitution. Their average age was 42. Most had graduated from college and belonged to the elite professions in America (lawyers, planters, and businessmen). Eight had signed the Declaration of Independence and all had extensive political experience in their state governments and/or the Congress. In short, they were well equipped for the task at hand.

After arriving, the delegates immediately got down to business. First, they elected Washington as the President of the convention—this was a foregone conclusion and they would keep him in mind as they designed the office of President of the United States. Washington would say little during the Convention, but he gave a crucial calming, unifying presence to the proceedings.

Next, Madison headed to the front of the hall to take notes. He knew future generations would be interested in the "intentions of the Founders" and only a meticulous record could provide that.

Then Governor Randolph introduced the first motion: to scrap the Articles of Confederation and replace them with Madison's plan for a new government. This was extremely controversial. Many protested that their states had given them instructions not to abolish the Articles and threatened to leave (and many would make good on that threat). But, to their credit, most of the delegates remained to at least see what Randolph had in mind. Randolph's proposal kicked off the first of three major debates that defined the proceedings of the convention for the rest of the summer.

## Debate #1: Large v. Small States

The first debate was between the large states and the small states. This was the most protracted and contentious of all issues and took the majority of the summer to resolve. Remember that since 1776 each of these states was like an independent country and intensely jealous of their autonomy. In 1786, you weren't an American, but a Virginian, New Yorker, Georgian, etc. The Articles of Confederation loosely bound the states, but didn't make these thirteen little nations into one big nation. Congress had been a distant body that didn't do much, which was a good thing in the minds of most because they had fought the Revolution precisely to break free of a distant, central government.

The small state/large state debate hinged on two opposing ideas. The small states feared that their independence would be swallowed up by the large states, while the large states felt that the one-vote-per-state system established in the Articles of Confederation gave disproportionate power to the small states. All of the delegates agreed that a stronger central government was needed, but the real issue was how to determine representation in that new government.

Madison's Virginia Plan proposed a strong national government with three branches and a bicameral legislature, but also proposed that representation be based on population. This was anathema to the smaller states. Under the Articles, each state received one vote—no matter how large or small—and that's the way the small states liked it. This arrangement gave them comparatively more power: a small state would have $1/13^{th}$ of the power even if they only had $1/100^{th}$ of the population. To the large states, on the other hand, Madison's proposal was better and more democratic. Why should a state with far fewer people have the same say in the national government as one with far more people?

Although the delegates would eventually accept the basic structure of Madison's plan, many couldn't accept the idea of a government in which representation was purely popular. Those from smaller states like New Jersey and Delaware knew that representation based on population alone would overwhelm and dilute their say in government, so William Paterson of New Jersey made a counter-proposal which we today call the New Jersey Plan. Paterson's plan would strengthen the national government by giving it more power to tax and act, but would keep the one branch, one-state-one-vote system that had been in place under the Articles of Confederation.

This heated debate—representation by state or population—lasted all summer and almost killed the Convention. It was finally resolved with what we call "The Great Compromise"—aptly named because without the compromise there would have been no United States Constitution. The Great Compromise answered the question of "representation by state or population?" with "both." Since Madison had proposed a "bicameral legislature"—two houses of congress—why not have one of the houses represent according to population and the other represent each state equally? States would send representatives to the House of Representatives based on their population, but would each send the same number of representatives to the Senate (two) regardless of population. This proposal eventually satisfied the delegates from both the large and small states.

The Great Compromise also applies to the selection of the President. We sometimes say that we vote for President, but in reality we vote as a state for electors who in turn vote for the President. How many electors each state receives is determined through a combination of state and popular representation. A state has electoral votes equal to the number of its Senators (state) and Representatives in the House (popular). So if a state's population entitled them to three seats in the House of Representatives, then that state would have five electoral votes for president (3 Representatives + 2 Senators). Thus we see the Great Compromise at work in the selection of all three branches of government (albeit indirectly in the case of the judiciary). With this compromise, the Convention had overcome its greatest hurdle.

## Chapter 9

**Debate #2: North v. South**

The second major debate at the Constitutional Convention was between the northern and southern states. The North-South split was easily the most important division in the history of our country and eventually led to civil war. Although this schism centered on slavery it went beyond into larger cultural and economic questions. The North was commercial and industrial while the South was agricultural and plantation-based. The South had (and still has to a degree) a more communal social system based on kinship ties and honor, while the North had an individualistic culture based on contract.

Delegates from the South understood that they could increase their power at the expense of the North by including slaves in the population count. Remember, a state's say in the new government would be partly determined by the number of its people, so the South wanted to inflate its population numbers by including the slaves in the census. The Northerners responded that Southerners couldn't have it both ways: either the slaves were people entitled to rights and representation (in which case they shouldn't be slaves at all), or they shouldn't be counted in the population at all. Those from the South would not budge on the issue and this put the Convention at another impasse.

Most of the Founding Fathers were against slavery (even though many of them held slaves) and wanted to see it abolished. In fact, George Mason wouldn't even sign the Constitution because it allowed the abominable institution to continue. But most of them were willing to concede on slavery to create a union that they hoped would be capable of abolishing slavery in future generations. That is exactly what happened and we must give credit to the Founders for their foresight on this, even if we also condemn many of them as hypocritical slaveholders.

The agreement they finally came to is called *The Three-Fifths Compromise*. Would the new government count the slaves or not? Sort of. It would count slaves as 3/5 of a person. So if a state had a population of 50,000 free and 50,000 enslaved persons, and if there was one representative in the House per 30,000 persons, then the math works like this: the free are counted as 50,000 people, the slaves are counted as 30,000 people (3/5) so the state's population would ultimately be counted as 80,000 for purposes of representation. This would give them two representatives (and two more electoral votes), instead of the four they would get counting the slaves as a whole person or the one they would get not counting the slaves at all.

Some people in the modern day wax self-righteous and denounce the Constitution and the Founders as racist for considering African-Americans as "less than a full person," but such critics fail to understand that this compromise is precisely what allowed for the eventual abolition of slavery. Counting slaves as a full person would have given more political power to Southern slaveholders and thereby prevented the emancipation that later occurred. Lincoln, the Great Emancipator, would never have been elected if slaves had been

# U.S. Constitution I: The Convention

counted as a full person. In that sense, slavery owes its abolition to the Three-Fifths Compromise.

## Debate #3: Federal v. States

The third and final major debate at the Convention was over the relationship between the states and the new Federal Government. Formal compromises resolved the first two debates, but this one was much trickier since it involved the question of "sovereignty." We don't use the word "sovereignty" much anymore, but it essentially answers the question, "where does the buck stop?" When push comes to shove in government, who has the final say? Prior to 1787 the state governments had clearly been sovereign and acted as their own

little countries. Would they now surrender this sovereignty to the Federal Government under the new Constitution?

Madison and others tried to placate the states by saying that *both* national *and* state governments would be sovereign under the new Constitution. But how could this be when sovereignty, by definition, is indivisible? The whole point of sovereignty is to locate the one final authority in government matters.

They eventually found their way out of this dilemma with words rather than substance. They said that, unlike in a monarchy where the King sat atop the pyramid of authority, America would be a republic with the *people* on top. Ergo, the *people would be sovereign*. So,

Chapter 9

no, we wouldn't and couldn't divide the sovereignty of the people—it was indivisible—but you could divide the *representation* of the sovereign people. States and Federal government could co-exist as two separate expressions of the sovereignty of the American people themselves.

This was not a satisfactory answer. The Founders came up with the slogan *e pluribus unum* to describe the new nation—"out of many, one"—but this debate is still with us. The Federal Government has steadily accrued more power since the Founding, but states still claim prerogatives and the debate over what belongs in the state or federal sphere continues to this day.

## THE MIRACLE AT PHILADELPHIA

After overcoming these three enormous hurdles, the Founders finally declared themselves satisfied with their handiwork and on September 17, 1787, came forward one by one to sign the Constitution. It had taken all summer, but they all realized they had accomplished something remarkable, even supernatural. Many of them referred to the Constitution as a "miracle." Washington, for example, maintained for the rest of his life that God had been with them in the Convention as much as he had been with them on the battlefield. Why would he say that and why do we still speak of a "divinely inspired Constitution" today?

First, the *content* of the Constitution was miraculous. It established a remarkable system of government (not "perfect," but "more perfect" in the Founders' words). This inspired document contains the most effective and appropriate means for dividing power that humans have ever devised. The secret to freedom is the division of power, and our Constitution masterfully sets up a structure of balanced power that created and continues to preserve liberty. It has weathered many storms and prevented the abuses of power that come when power remains unchecked.

Second, the Constitution did nothing less than create the first and most enduring liberal democracy in history.[1] America is not the only free country in the world today, but it has been the freest country over the course of the last three centuries. No other nation comes close to offering so much freedom to so many people for so long. France, Japan, and Germany, for example, are all exemplary free countries today, but were tyrannies as recently as 1945 or even 1989. The Latin-American states never united as did the North American states and the differences are stark: the cycle of tyranny and anarchy is still plaguing many

---

1 Two qualifications: the Constitution was not fully democratic at first (women and minorities were excluded), but did set up a government by the people with broad representation of all strata of society. It was democratic in that sense. Also, there had been popular governments before, but always on a limited scale (tribe or city) and never on a national scale—in that sense the U.S. was the first democratic nation. The continuing quest to fulfill the promise of the Founding by extending democracy and rights to all Americans will be the subject of chapter 19.

states in South and Central America. Divided Europe, while currently stable and free, has been plagued by recurrent civil wars (such as the Napoleonic Wars, Crimean War, Franco-Prussian War, World Wars I and II) that make our Civil War look tame by comparison. Who is to say this would not also have been the fate of America had not the Constitution bound the independent states together? Perhaps only divine inspiration can fully explain this success.[2]

Note also the elegance of the U.S. Constitution. It is as thin as a pamphlet and an educated person can read it thoroughly in less than an hour. Simplicity, clarity, and precision are political virtues and the Constitution has them. Contrast it with the European Union Constitution, which is thousands of pages long and requires weeks of labor and a team of lawyers just to decipher. The U.S. Constitution is like an elegant scientific theory or mathematical equation: Occam's Razor testifies to the truth of its principles. It is direct enough to give us guidance, but open enough for flexibility in application.

Third, the participants themselves were miraculous. Thomas Jefferson once dubbed the Convention an "assembly of demi-gods"—the most gifted assemblage of political minds in history. Almost any one of the delegates would have been the greatest statesman of their time had they lived in any other age, and yet in Philadelphia in 1787, (with a much smaller population to draw from than today) there were 55. The likelihood of this much talent being in one place at one time in such a small country defies the laws of probability. Even secular historians are stumped by this "fantastic coincidence." Once again, providential intervention may be the only adequate explanation.

Fourth and finally, there were miracles in the *compromises* the delegates agreed to. The Spirit of the Lord is the spirit of goodwill, humility, and being willing to listen and understand other viewpoints. Only such a spirit can account for the degree to which the delegates put aside narrow interests and prejudices to create the American nation. In fact, there was one moment in the convention when the fighting was particularly heated and Benjamin Franklin, who had been sitting quietly in the back, finally spoke up. Everyone calmed down, hushed, and listened as the sage of Philadelphia—the great Franklin—said, "the longer I live, the more convincing proofs I see of this truth—that God Governs in the affairs of men. And if a sparrow cannot fall to the ground without his notice, is it probable that an empire can rise without his aid?" This was especially remarkable coming from Franklin who had for much of his life been a Deist—one who believes that God does *not* intervene in the affairs of men but rather wound up the universe like a clock to run on its own. Even though they didn't hire a chaplain to offer formal prayers in the Convention (they lacked funds to pay one) the advice was sound and heeded individually. Compromise only came after Franklin's wise admonition.

---

2  Because of the success of the U.S. Constitution, nations all over the world since 1787 have copied it as a model for their own governments.

## PROPHETIC STATEMENTS

Each of the accomplishments listed above testifies to the miraculous nature of the Constitution, but we also have the words of modern prophets as a witness. Presidents of the Church in this dispensation, from Joseph Smith onward, have stated in no uncertain terms that the U.S. Constitution was inspired and at nearly every General Conference at least one of the speakers reiterates this truth.

But just because the Constitution is "inspired" doesn't mean that it is without flaws, only that its general principles are of Divine origin. Elder Dallin H. Oaks said we see this inspiration in the document's "Great Fundamentals."[3] He identified five of them: 1) The Separation of Powers into Branches, 2) The Bill of Rights, 3) Federalism, 4) Popular Sovereignty, and 5) The Rule of Law. These are the inspired fundamentals that we should seek to protect, preserve, and defend against those who might want to diminish them for political gain or misguided zeal.

The scriptures also tell us that the Constitution was divinely inspired. D&C 101 is the most explicit. At the time of this revelation, mobs were depriving the Latter-day Saints in Missouri of their rights to life, liberty, and property. The Saints wanted to know what the Lord would have them do. The answer that came in verses 76-80 well summarizes everything we have covered so far.

Verse 77 tells the Saints to appeal to the government "According to the laws and constitution of the people, which I have suffered to be established, and should be maintained for the rights and protection of all flesh, according to just and holy principles." Constitutions, in other words, protect our rights. Verse 78 continues, "That every man act in doctrine and principle pertaining to futurity, according to the moral agency which I have given unto him, that every man may be accountable for his own sins in the day of judgment." This means that rights and political liberty are an outgrowth of our agency that God has placed us on this earth to exercise. Then verse 80 says, "And for this purpose have I established the Constitution of this land, by the hands of wise men whom I have raised up unto this very purpose." How do we achieve the rights and liberties that are a function of our agency? Through constitutions that check and balance power, particularly the inspired U.S. Constitution—a miracle that God worked through agents on earth.

## CONCLUSION

As you can see, Americans are the inheritors of a remarkable and miraculous political legacy. Since members of the Church have a unique knowledge of this truth, they also have a unique responsibility to preserve this legacy as the U.S. Constitution will certainly come under increasing attack in the years ahead.

---

3 Oaks (1992).

# CHAPTER 9 SOURCES/FURTHER READING

Articles of Confederation and perpetual Union between the states of New Hampshire, Massachusetts-bay Rhode Island and Providence Plantations, Connecticut, New York, New Jersey, Pennsylvania, Delaware, Maryland, Virginia, North Carolina, South Carolina and Georgia (1781).

Beeman, Richard. *Plain, Honest Men: The Making of the American Constitution*. New York: Random House, 2009.

Benson, Ezra Taft. "Our Divine Constitution," *Ensign*, November 1987.

\_\_\_\_\_. "The Constitution—A Glorious Standard," *Ensign*, May 1976.

Bowen, Catherine Drinker. *Miracle at Philadelphia: The Story of the Constitutional Convention, May to September 1787*. Boston: Little, Brown, & Co., 1966.

Brookhiser, Richard. *Gentleman Revolutionary: Gouverneur Morris: The Rake who Wrote the Constitution*. New York: Free Press, 2003.

\_\_\_\_\_. *James Madison*. New York: Basic Books, 2011.

Derthick, Martha. "Federalism." In Peter H. Schuck and James Q. Wilson, eds., *Understanding America: The Anatomy of an Exceptional Nation*. New York: Public Affairs, 2008.

Ellis, Joseph J. *American Creation: Triumphs and Tragedies at the Founding of the Republic*. New York: Knopf, 2007.

Hamilton, Alexander. "The Continentalist, no. 1," July 12, 1781, in Joanne B. Freeman, ed. *Alexander Hamilton: Writings*. New York: Library of America, 2001. Pgs. 98-101.

Madison, James. *Notes of Debates: In The Federal Convention of 1787*. Oxford, OH: Ohio University Press, 1985.

Oaks, Dallin H. "The Divinely Inspired Constitution," *Ensign*, February 1992.

Stewart, David O. *The Summer of 1787: The Men who Invented the Constitution*. New York: Simon & Schuster, 2007.

Wills, Garry. *James Madison*. New York: Henry Holt, 2002.

Wood, Gordon. *The Creation of the American Republic*. New York: Norton, 1969.

# *Chapter 10*

# U.S. CONSTITUTION II: POWER IN GOVERNMENT

### ALEXIS DE TOCQUEVILLE: DEMOCRACY IN AMERICA

Now that we understand how the U.S. Constitution came to be, let's turn to how it works and why it has been so successful. We'll use as a guide one of the greatest foreign observers of American life—Alexis de Tocqueville.

Tocqueville lived in the early 19$^{th}$ century and came from a French aristocratic family who had been royal advisors at Versailles. Early on, he pursued a legal career, but was also interested in knowing how political systems worked, especially democracy. He wanted to understand why the democratic experiment had failed in France—turning into anarchy, terror, Napoleonic imperialism, and finally the restoration of the monarchy—but had succeeded in the United States.

In order to find out, he came to the U.S. in the early 1830s, traveled around the country, observed American life from the grassroots level, spoke with common Americans on farms, riverboats, shops, and factories, and then returned to France to write up his observations. The result was his masterwork, *Democracy in America* (1835), perhaps the greatest book ever written on either democracy or America.

Tocqueville ultimately concluded that although democracy was a desirable form of government, it was not perfect. He was impressed with what he had seen in America and predicted that democratic government would spread throughout the world, but he also understood that popular rule had some serious drawbacks. In particular, Tocqueville noted the possibility of what he called "*the tyranny of the majority.*"

We often make the mistake of thinking that tyranny and democracy are opposites and tyranny only results when one person or a few people hold all of the power. But actually

# Chapter 10

tyranny is *any* time a government uses its power to take away natural rights—whether it's a government of one person or one million people. Since democracy simply means rule by a majority of the people, it is possible for a majority to vote to tyrannize a minority (e.g., blondes and brunettes could democratically vote to enslave those with red hair). We often naively think that the "will of the people" is an unmitigated good, but Tocqueville saw that this is not so. Many years before Tocqueville's warnings about the possible excesses of democracy, King Mosiah also noted that there are occasions when the majority chooses evil and puts society at risk (Mosiah 29:26-27).

History has proven Tocqueville correct. We have seen tyranny of the majority many times. Hitler was elected Chancellor of Germany through democratic processes, but that doesn't make him any less of a tyrant. During the French Revolution, a democratically elected assembly would vote on a resolution and then guillotine the losers. It was "democratic" in that the majority ruled, and yet members of the minority lost all of their natural rights. Tocqueville saw that Americans are particularly prone to the error of thinking that majority opinion can't be wrong. It often is. The voice of the people is not the voice of God. Majorities can take away rights to life, liberty, and property *through* government just like any other tyrant.

Thankfully, the Founding Fathers foresaw the problem of democratic tyranny and, in the Constitution, established restraints against this and many other tyrannical dangers. Madison often spoke of the virtue of the people as a "primary control" to restrain government power through elections, but he also pointed out that we needed "auxiliary precautions" ("checks and balances" as we sometimes call them), for those times when the virtue of the people fails. Since human beings, especially those in power, are given to corruption, we need a backup plan—something more than just a hope for virtue among the populace. Madison understood we needed checks and balances in the Constitution to restrain all abuses of power, even those of the people themselves.

## DEBATE ON RATIFICATION

To understand these mechanisms at work in the Constitution, it is helpful to look at the debate over ratification. After the signing of the Constitution in Philadelphia, each state held a special "ratifying convention." The Constitution would only become the law of the land if the conventions of at least nine states approved. Many in the states, treasuring their autonomy, resisted ratification. Americans had just fought a war against a centralized government and were fearful of instituting another one. Furthermore, since the Constitution transferred power from the states to the national government, local politicians would have their own power weakened. Their self-interest militated against ratification.

Two political parties arose as a result of the ratification debate. Those who favored ratification of the Constitution were called "Federalists" and those who opposed ratification were called "Anti-Federalists." To convince the American people to ratify the Constitution (especially those in swing states like New York), three gifted Federalist authors, Alexander Hamilton, James Madison, and John Jay, took up their pens and wrote a series of editorials promoting and defending the Constitution. Hamilton later collected and published these editorials as *The Federalist Papers.* Although their purpose was a rhetorical one, an unintended consequence of the *Federalist Papers* the Federalist Papers was to give the world one of the greatest ever works of political philosophy and the best first-hand explanation of the workings and design of the U.S. Constitution.

Like Niebuhr, Montesquieu, and Mosiah, the *Federalist* authors began with an assumption of realism. They understood that we can't wish away or abolish human "ambition" (the tendency to seek power, wealth, and fame) since it is hardwired into human nature. But we can *use* ambition to achieve a positive outcome by structuring government appropriately.

We can understand what they meant by using a parenting example. Imagine that two children—Johnnie and Janey—are fighting over a piece of cake. Now, a parent might *hope* that her children would just be kind and share equally (virtue), but would also accept the fact that this is probably not going to happen. Children are naturally "ambitious" for sugar and will be selfish in trying to get as much cake as they can. So instead of telling the kids to "just share," mom has Johnnie *cut the cake* into two pieces, but then lets Janey *choose* which of the two pieces she wants. This wise parent made it in Johnnie's *interest* to cut the cake as evenly as he can. The parent hasn't abolished Johnnie's selfishness, but has used it to create justice—an auxiliary precaution when virtue fails.

Like the mom with the cake, the Constitution accepts humans as they are with all of their frailties, but contains mechanisms to use that ambition to achieve justice. By setting power against itself, we get liberty. As James Madison said in Federalist #51, "ambition must be made to counteract ambition . . . [thus] supplying, by opposite and rival interests, the defect of better motives."

## HORIZONTAL CHECKS

The Constitution's first and most well-known mechanism for dividing power is the creation of competing *branches* of government—legislative, executive, and judicial. When government power is divided *within* a level of government in this way, political scientists call it a "horizontal" check on power. Madison had read deeply in the works of Montesquieu and understood the importance of dividing government power by function. "The accumulation of all powers, legislative, executive, and judiciary, in the same hands," he said, "whether of one, a few, or many, and whether hereditary, self-appointed, or elective, may justly be pronounced the very definition of tyranny." Notice, he saw that even "elective" (democratic) government had the capacity for tyranny if left unchecked.

But the Founders went even further than Montesquieu in structuring their horizontal checks and balances. Since they believed that legislative power was the most threatening—one cannot execute or apply laws that haven't been legislated—they further checked its power by splitting it into an upper house (the Senate) and a lower house (The House of Representatives). With this "bicameral legislature" each house could check the excesses of the other.

To further contain the legislative branch, the Founders gave the executive a "veto" power over legislation. The President could negate any bill he deemed unjust and dangerous. But the Founders also gave the legislature power to "override" a veto and pass the law over the head of the executive if they had enough votes. The Founders, in their wisdom, placed layers of checks upon checks in the Constitution.

They also added to Montesquieu's basic framework by assigning specific duties to each branch. Yes, the executive would act as commander-in-chief of the military with the power to carry out wars, but this power would be limited by the legislative branch which would retain the power to *declare* war. The executive would make treaties, but that power would be checked by the legislature's right to ratify them. While the executive would have the considerable power of carrying out laws, the legislative branch would have power of the purse, thereby making the executive reliant on the legislature for the financing necessary to put laws into play. The President would appoint federal judges and other officials, but the legislative branch would confirm or reject those appointments. Additionally, the judges would have life terms, thus insulating them from executive pressures and the whims of public opinion. Finally, the legislative branch would hold impeachment power over the other two branches and could try and remove a President or Supreme Court Justice from office. These are only the most salient of the many mechanisms for controlling power contained in the U.S. Constitution.

The effect of all of these checks and balances is to drastically limit the action of the Federal Government. It cannot just "decree" actions quickly and intemperately. There must be long, careful deliberation, compromise, and consensus before action.

In the present day, we often hear the complaint that "our government doesn't get things done" and that it is "paralyzed" by inaction, while certain other nations (like China) act with enviable speed and decisiveness. When you hear this complaint, you should gratefully smile because this is exactly what the Founders intended. Swift, efficient government is the kind most likely to become tyrannical. The governments in Hitler's Germany, Mussolini's Italy, and Stalin's Russia all "got things done" with remarkable speed and efficiency. And yet what they were getting done, in the absence of the limits that checks and balances create, was tyrannical oppression of their people. The Founders understood that "efficiency in government" is generally a vice rather than a virtue. Slow, cautious deliberation and consensus is far preferable. It's too bad that so many of us today have forgotten this crucial principle.[1]

---

[1] It is also factually untrue that our government doesn't get things done. It is often said that we have record gov-

Those determined to live under an "efficient" government that "gets things done" might consider moving to North Korea.

## VERTICAL CHECKS

Beyond the three horizontal divisions of power, the Founders also implemented a number of "vertical" checks, which divide power from *outside* the national government. Most notably, they established a federal system, which separated power between national and state governments. The Constitution increased national government power, but the states retained all powers not explicitly given to the national government. Today police, schools, courts, emergency response, etc., are all under local government jurisdiction. Each level of government has distinct powers and serves as a check on the others.

Vertical checks are also established in the Bill of Rights.[2] The Fifth Amendment, for instance, ensures that economic power remains independent of political power. No person, it says, shall be deprived of "property, without due process of law; nor shall private property be taken for public use, without just compensation." Every time political and economic power have been conjoined, tyranny has ensued. The Founding Fathers foresaw this problem and hedged against it in the Bill of Rights. By specifically enumerating private property in the Constitution, they ensured that the economic sphere would remain largely separate from political control.

The Bill of Rights also guarantees freedom of speech, religion, and the press. This meant that not only economic power, but also *cultural* power would remain independent of the Federal Government. Cultural institutions, such as newspapers, television stations, websites, magazines, and even churches, allow the independent circulation of ideas and can serve a "watchdog" function to expose corruption and wrongdoing among public officials. The Founders understood that free speech is more than just part of the natural right to liberty; it is an important check to keep government power limited and accountable. What kind of democracy would we have if the government controlled the news and told us what to think, who to vote for, and only gave us their side of the story? The power to *criticize* government is a key to preventing tyranny and the First Amendment ensures that citizens retain this right.

---

ernment debt because of federal government inaction and "gridlock" (Fukuyama, 2014). The opposite is the case. Since the turn of the century, our government has passed record amounts of legislation—launching two wars, bailing out banks, creating massive new entitlement programs, paying billions in corporate subsidies, doubling education funding, repeatedly cutting taxes, and spending billions on "stimulus," all of which have increased the national debt. Our government financial problems are not the result of government *inaction*, but of government *hyper-action*. Our debt hasn't come *because* of checks and balances, but *in spite* of them.

2 Madison was initially opposed to a Bill of Rights, thinking that by delineating a few rights, the people would think those were the only rights they had. Do we really need to let people know they have a right to blink or breathe or eat dinner? But in order to placate the anti-Federalists, Madison promised a Bill of Rights, which he eventually guided through the legislature as the first ten amendments to the Constitution.

# Chapter 10

The importance of freedom of the press to check government power was well on display during the Watergate Scandal of the 1970s. Neither the legislative nor the judicial branch exposed this corruption in the Nixon Administration, but two young reporters at the *Washington Post* did. They were outside the government altogether. Thus, a non-government institution served as a "vertical" check on abuse of power by the executive branch.

Of course, the whole idea of "consent of the governed" is itself the most important check of all. In a democracy, the people themselves check government power through periodic elections. Nothing better keeps politicians accountable than knowing they can lose that power by abusing it. In a democracy, the politicians' own lust for power (staying in office) keeps them in line. You can't do away with a politician's ambition, but you can *use* that ambition to create virtuous action—they have an incentive to work for the public good when re-election is on the line.

## CHECKS ON DEMOCRACY

And yet this democratic check on power takes us back to where we started: to Tocqueville's problem of the tyranny of the majority. Yes, we need government by the people, but what is to stop the people themselves from being tyrannical?

The Founders grappled with this dilemma. To them, democracy was a necessary evil: necessary because "government by the consent of the governed" was a cornerstone principle of the Founding, but evil because democracy can turn into "mob rule." *Demos*—the Greek term from which we get democracy—denotes an easily manipulated and impassioned mass of people. Recent psychological studies have confirmed the reality of "groupthink." In large groups, individuals are often stirred up into an emotional frenzy, pressured into unwise action, and feel a lack of responsibility for their behavior (if one person tramples another to death, it is clearly murder; when a mob of 1,000 people tramples a person to death, the responsibility is diffused among the crowd).

For these reasons, the Founders distrusted democracy. They even preferred the term "republic" to "democracy" because of the negative connotations that "demos" carried. This fear led them to build checks on democratic tyranny into the Constitution itself.

The first check on democracy was representation. "The consent of the governed," although necessary, would always be filtered through the process of electing representatives. That is, the people would never rule directly, but would instead select the most virtuous to govern *for* them as representatives (presidents, congresspersons, senators, etc.). Those elected officials, distanced from the whims and passions of the people, would make more stable, wise, and informed decisions than the people themselves. Thus, filtering consent preserves "government by the people," while mitigating the tendency to the rash, mob-like action that the Founders feared.

For some offices, the Founders believed that multiple layers of filtering were necessary.

For instance, U.S. senators would be chosen by state legislatures, who would in turn be chosen by the people.[3] Senators would thereby be distanced from the people by two levels of representation. The Electoral College would elect the U.S. President and those electors would, in turn, be chosen by the people of each state. Most filtered of all are the Supreme Court justices—chosen by the President, who is in turn chosen by the electors, who are chosen by the people. The American people are, indeed, "represented" by the Senate, the Presidency, and the Supreme Court, but only indirectly through multiple levels of filtering. Having these layers of consent, the Founders hoped, would sift out the people's tendency to tyranny, leaving a more virtuous, wise elite at the top insulated from the whims of public opinion.

Second, the Founders hoped to reduce democratic excess by *dispersing* representation in many different bodies. The American people are represented by three branches of government, both houses of the legislature, a state governor, a state house, a state senate, a local town council, a county commission, and more. By being represented in so many different bodies, the American people have no single locus of consent that could carry out the tyranny of the majority. One of the reasons the French Revolutionary government became tyrannical was that the people were represented in one, single assembly without any checks and balances, filters, or dispersion. The decisions of this assembly quickly became tyrannical and thousands of innocents were executed under the terror of the guillotine. Although it is not popular to admit today, indirect representation has virtues over pure, direct democracy. The Founders understood this.

Finally, and perhaps most powerfully, Madison saw that the Constitution would reduce the tyranny of the majority by *diluting factional power*. By "faction," Madison simply meant what we today would call a "special interest group"—a group dedicated to securing its own interest at the expense of the public as a whole. While factions are usually bad, Madison understood that, given human nature, there is no way to get around them in a democracy. Collections of people (potato farmers, investment bankers, clothing retailers, teachers, construction workers, car manufacturers, artists, trial lawyers, etc.) would naturally band together to seek special benefits from the government, even though that would mean taking rights from others. Madison realized that when such a faction controls the government, tyranny of the majority ensues.

Thankfully, he had a solution to this problem. He understood that although we can't do away with factions, we can minimize their tyrannical effects by *multiplying the number of factions through a large republic*. In a small republic, one faction could easily become a majority, get control over the government, and exercise tyrannical controls over others, but in a large republic, the many factions would neutralize one another. The larger the republic,

---

3 This was altered with the 17th Amendment which allowed for the direct election of Senators.

## Chapter 10

the harder it would be for one special interest group to gain majority power since each faction would be but one faction among many.

Montesquieu had argued, and Americans had long assumed, that a republic needed to be small, such that the representatives were local, known, visible, and more directly accountable. But Madison challenged the great Montesquieu on this point, showing that while a small republic had the advantage of keeping power closer to the people, it had the more significant disadvantage of making it possible for a single faction to dominate the government. If eastern Idaho were its own country, for instance, the potato farming faction might be large enough to capture the government, but in the United States of America as a whole, the potato farmers are just one of many thousands of special interest groups all vying for government favor. The factions compete and cancel each other out. In that sense, factions can check and balance each other just like the competing branches of government do. This was among Madison's strongest arguments for uniting the states (small republics) into a federal union under the Constitution (large republic). According to Madison, a large republic would be more stable and less susceptible to both tyranny and anarchy.

To prove that Madison was correct on this point, we need look no farther than our own U.S. history. In the 19th century American South, white Americans—the majority—voted to oppress black Americans through Jim Crow Laws. This discrimination, legally upheld and enforced by the government, came about through majority rule. In the "small republic" southern states, the white-supremacist faction outnumbered the African-Americans and could thereby democratically tyrannize them. But in the large republic of the United States, the white-supremacist faction was diluted and outnumbered by those who wanted more racial equality. This, of course, is what led to the Civil Rights bills. If there had been no union of small republics into a large republic through the Constitution, Civil Rights for blacks would have remained limited.

We also see Madison's wisdom on display in LDS history. When the Latter-day Saints settled in Missouri, an anti-Mormon faction took control of the state government and elected Lilburn Boggs as governor. Boggs then proceeded to issue an extermination order against the Saints. This was a classic example of democratic tyranny. The anti-Mormon faction in Missouri was large and powerful enough to dominate politics. It was just such a "tyranny of the majority" that the Constitution was designed to correct. This is why the Lord admonished the saints to seek redress form the national government since, on the larger scale, anti-Mormons made up a small group without the power to tyrannize. Had there been a U.S. President with the courage to "preserve, protect and defend the Constitution of the United States" as he had sworn to do, the saints would have had their rights restored. Unfortunately, the Saints were left at the mercy of the Missouri militia which tyrannically deprived them of their rights to life (e.g., The Haun's Mill Massacre), liberty (e.g., beatings, rape, imprisonment), and property (confiscation and destruction of homes and possessions).

Finally, we can see Madison's wisdom by comparing the United States of North America to the divided states of South America. After their revolutions against Spanish rule, Latin America remained fragmented into many small nations—such as Ecuador, Bolivia, Nicaragua, El Salvador, Columbia, Chile, and Paraguay. As Madison's theory predicted, these small republics have been riven by instability, military coup, corruption, and hyperinflation because their small size has made them susceptible to factional control.

In this sense, Madison's whole point in Federalist 10 was to show that democracy can act as a check upon itself, and the larger the democracy, the better those checks will function. Skeptics of democracy point out that ill-informed knaves have just as much vote as the wisest, most virtuous citizen. But for the Founders, that was beside the point. Democracy can work even when people seek their narrow interest through factions since this tendency will check that same inclination in other groups. If the primary control of virtue fails, then auxiliary precautions kick in such that even self-interest voting can be channeled to the greater good. It is better that 300 million people make mistakes than a few elites, because the 300 million can balance each other out. Does democracy work because people are wise and good? We would hope so (that's the primary control on government), but the checks and balances, including checks on factional power, can serve as auxiliary precautions even if public virtue fails.

## RATIFICATION

Thanks to the *Federalist* authors, the Constitution was ratified by the necessary number of states in 1788.[4] But the logic of ratification remains a mystery to historians. Why did some people favor the Constitution and others oppose it? Historians have hypothesized geography, national origin, class, and urban vs. rural, and yet none of these explanations seems to hold. The more one studies the ratification of the Constitution, the more mysterious and miraculous it seems.

It is also important to understand how the Constitution relates to the Declaration of Independence. Some misguided scholars have seen the two documents as contradictory and have felt impelled to align themselves with one or the other.[5] The reality is that the documents are not antithetical, but complementary. The Declaration of Independence gives us our goals as a nation—the high principles of liberty, equality, and natural rights—while the Constitution gives us the mechanism of government with which to *secure those goals*. The

---

4 Rhode Island and North Carolina ratified the Constitution after Washington's inauguration.
5 Examples include political philosophers John C. Calhoun and Willmoore Kendall, both of who rejected the Declaration of Independence and its talk of "natural rights," but celebrated the checks and balances of the Constitution.

Declaration contains the *ends* of government, the Constitution provides the *means*. The two primary documents of the Founding harmonize perfectly.

## CONCLUSION

Now that we've completed Part I of this book, let's summarize and tie together what we've learned. We first learned that agency is the essence of what it means to be human and that our ability to exercise agency must be preserved if we are to progress. Next we learned that government under the Rule of Law preserves and protects the exercise of agency (i.e., natural rights). We then learned that, because of human fallibility and tendencies to evil, the Rule of Law is only secure when political power is divided, usually through a written constitution. Finally, we learned how the Founders of our country understood all of the above and actualized these principles in the United States Constitution—the source of the Rule of Law in America. The Constitution, by providing the U.S. with over two centuries of liberty, has made America the most successful country in history—the nation that has provided more freedom to more people than any other. In that sense, the Constitution did better than Madison ever could have hoped. After more than two centuries, it continues to preserve the Rule of Law, secure natural rights ("the blessings of liberty"), and protect the exercise of agency. This is what makes the Constitution the greatest political miracle of all times and places it at the center of the Political Foundations of America.

## CHAPTER 10 SOURCES/FURTHER READING

Bernstein, Carl, and Bob Woodward. *All the President's Men*. New York: Simon & Schuster, 1974.

Constitution of the United States of America (1787).

Fernandez-Armesto, Felipe. *The Americas: A Hemispheric History*. New York: Modern Library, 2003.

Fukuyama, Francis. *Political Order and Political Decay: From the Industrial Revolution to the Globalization of Democracy*. New York: Farrar, Straus and Giroux, 2014.

Hamilton, Alexander, James Madison, and John Jay. *The Federalist Papers*. Edited by Clinton Rossiter. New York: Penguin, 1961.

Hume, David. *Political Essays*. Edited by Charles William Hendel. New York: Liberal Arts Press, 1953. (1741, 1752).

Lichter, S. Robert. "The Media." In Peter H. Schuck and James Q. Wilson, eds., *Understanding America: The Anatomy of an Exceptional Nation*. New York: Public Affairs, 2008.

Morone, James A. and Rogan Kersh. *By the People: Debating American Government*. New York: Oxford University Press, 2013.

Polsby, Nelson W. "The Political System." In Peter H. Schuck and James Q. Wilson, eds., *Understanding America: The Anatomy of an Exceptional Nation*. New York: Public Affairs, 2008.

Surowiecki, James. *The Wisdom of Crowds*. New York: Doubleday, 2004.

Wilson, James Q. and John J. DiIulio, Jr. *American Government*. 8th edition. Boston: Houghton Mifflin Company, 2001.

# Part Two:
## The Economic Foundations of America

# Chapter 11

# MARKET PRINCIPLES I: THE SECRET OF WEALTH

### ADAM SMITH: THE WEALTH OF NATIONS

Now that we've moved on to Part Two of this book—the Economic Foundations of America—you might ask, "what does economics have to do with American Foundations?" The answer is: *everything*.[1] Our nation, more than any other in history, has exemplified the principles of market capitalism. When people think of a capitalist country, their minds immediately turn to the United States. The bottom line is this: you cannot understand America if you don't understand the free-market economy.[2]

To introduce the workings of the market, we'll look at the life and thought of Adam Smith—the man most responsible for discovering basic economic principles. Smith is unquestionably one of the most important thinkers of the past few centuries. His ideas have changed the world incalculably, especially during the last generation as countries around the globe have embraced Adam Smith's theories and have found themselves wealthier, healthier, and better off as a result.

Adam Smith lived in Scotland around the time of the American Founders—in fact, his classic work was published in 1776. Unlike Washington who fought heroic battles or Locke who advised Kings and nobles, Smith lived a simple, undistinguished life. But, like the Founders, he was a child of the Enlightenment. Thinkers of the Enlightenment conceived of the universe as a machine with regular clock-like workings that humans could investigate and understand. Just as one can open a clock to uncover ("dis-cover") the workings of its

---

1 Although we now leave our discussion of the Founding, the principles of agency, rights, and Rule of Law will carry through the next two parts of the book.
2 It is also no coincidence that the most free market nation in history is also the wealthiest. Markets and wealth go hand in hand.

gears, wheels, and hands, so one can use reason to discover the regular, precise workings of the universe.

The greatest Enlightenment thinker was Sir Isaac Newton. It was Newton who did more to push back the frontiers of knowledge than just about anyone else by discovering the physical operations of the universe. When Newton died, the king of France asked his advisor, "do you think there will ever be another Newton?" His advisor thought a moment and responded, "Not until there is another universe to discover." That's how important Newton was to science: he revealed the fundamental operations of the main components of the cosmos (such as gravity, light, and bodies in motion). Newton uncovered the workings of this machine we call the universe.

We have all heard the story of Newton sitting under a tree and being hit by a falling apple, but what made this experience unique was Newton's response. He looked up and said, "Do you see what just happened? The apple used to be up there and now it's down here." Others couldn't understand the profundity of this childlike observation; a falling apple was hardly remarkable. But Newton saw wonder in the event: some mysterious force grabbed the apple and pulled it to the ground as if by magic. This invisible hand is constantly pulling things towards the earth, the earth is constantly pulling the moon, and the sun is pulling the planets in orbit. Newton called this remarkable force "gravity" and developed mathematical models that allow us to explain and predict its workings.

Adam Smith took this Enlightenment-Newtonian paradigm and applied it to the economic realm. There are laws and invisible forces, he said, that govern the production of wealth and these laws work analogous to Newton's laws of the universe. To better understand them, Smith traveled around Europe and upon his return wrote the masterpiece of economics: *An Inquiry into the Wealth of Nations* (1776).

There were two great principles that Smith discovered and outlined in his book. First, Smith discovered the secret to wealth, which explains why some nations are rich while others are poor. Second, Smith discovered the laws that guide the efficient allocation of wealth.

## WHAT IS ECONOMICS?

Before we tackle these principles, we must define and understand the field of economics and the concepts of decision making that it is based upon. When we think of "economics," our minds immediately turn to the realm of money, but that is only one aspect of economics. Economics is a complete science of decision making regarding scarce resources (those that have limited availability); we only think of money because our most quantifiable decisions are made in monetary terms. Money, of course, is finite and therefore scarce, but so are time, energy, and even marital commitment (we only marry one person) so studying our decisions of time, energy, and marriage fall under the domain of economics. Gary Becker won a Nobel Prize for studying the economics of criminal behavior, racial discrimination,

# Market Principles I: The Secret of Wealth

drug use, and families. Steven Levitt wrote a bestselling book, *Freakonomics,* that applied economic analysis to cheating, the naming of children, and even drunk driving. As you can see, economics is an all-pervasive science whose extremely useful tools can be applied to the whole range of decisions we make.

So when we make economic decisions, what guides us? The answer is simply *cost* in the economic sense; that is, *opportunity cost*. We talk about the cost of a box of cereal or pair of shoes, but opportunity cost goes beyond price tags to include whatever we *give up* in making a decision—the next best option. There is, for example, a cost to reading this chapter. What are you giving up? Perhaps you are giving up an hour of sleep, an hour of playing video games, or an hour chatting with someone on the phone. Whatever you are giving up—the next best option—is the opportunity cost of reading this book. Using your time to read is an economic decision. Since the learning gained through reading is probably more valuable than the pleasure of playing a video game, you give up *less* by reading and it is the correct decision from an economic standpoint.

Whether we know it or not, we make decisions this way all day every day. The more consciously and rigorously we make those decisions, the better our lives will be. Often in the gospel we think of choosing right vs. wrong, but in economics it's more like what Elder Oaks outlined in his talk, "Good, Better, Best." It's not that there's a simple good and bad with every decision—both sleeping and going to class are good—it's choosing the best option among those available. The question is not which decision is bad and which is good, but which has the *lowest opportunity cost*. Where do you give up the least? That's economic analysis in a nutshell.

Let's understand the concept of opportunity cost a little better by looking at a major life decision—attending college. When someone asks you what college costs, you probably quote the tuition figure, but that's just the beginning. You give up much more than the few thousand dollars that goes to the university; you also give up rent money, the comforts of home, the money you could have earned working a full-time job, the foregone recreational opportunities, and more. If we calculated the decision to attend college in pure monetary terms, the cost (the money we gave up) would come out to perhaps hundreds of thousands of dollars.

And yet the cost of *not* going to college is much higher. The earning power of a college graduate over the course of a lifetime, in pure monetary terms, is millions of dollars—a much larger amount than the hundreds of thousands you give up to go to college. The cost of college is high, but the cost of foregoing college is much higher still (and that doesn't even include the priceless non-monetary benefits—knowledge, skills, social relationships, experiences, and wisdom). This explains why more young people than ever before are making the rational, economic decision to pursue a higher education.

*Chapter 11*

# THE SECRET TO WEALTH

Now that we understand what economics is and how it works, let's do a quick exercise to flesh things out a little bit further and understand Adam Smith's first insight. Think of an old fashioned yellow, number-two pencil. If you tried to make this pencil by yourself, how long would it take? A pencil is a simple commodity, but its production is enormously complex. Think about its constituent parts: perhaps the wood comes from Lebanon, the graphite from Chile, the yellow paint from a refining plant in Mexico, the rubber from Malaysia, and the steel from a foundry in China. Were you to attempt to make this pencil yourself, you would have to travel to all of these places, extract the resources, process the chemicals, create the production machinery, etc. etc. It would take millions of hours of your time.[3] Assuming that your time is worth, say, ten dollars an hour, you would have to give up millions and millions of dollars just to make one silly little pencil. And yet you can buy this pencil for just a dime at the bookstore!

Why do you save millions of dollars buying this pencil instead of making it yourself? The answer lies in Adam Smith's first great discovery, the secret to wealth. Just like the secret to freedom, it is concise, simple, and elegant, but also incredibly powerful. The secret to wealth is:

*Free Exchange*

These two magic words are the foundation of economic success around the world. They explain why people in some countries are rich while people in other countries are poor.

Let's unpack why free exchange creates wealth. First of all, free exchange presupposes property rights. When you are free to earn and keep property, you have incentives to do economically efficient things like work hard, start businesses, develop new products, make technological improvements, and invest capital. All of these foster economic growth. In a regime without property rights—if the government is too weak to protect the fruits of your labor or the government itself confiscates it—then you will have no reason to engage in growth-producing activities. Humans won't work hard to make money if thieves or tyrants will just take it away. Lack of property rights explains why we see so little growth in tyrannical places like North Korea or anarchic places like Somalia.

Once property rights have been secured, humans next need the freedom to engage in trade with each other. This process of exchange further explains wealth. To see how, think of the last time you ate fast food. Maybe you bought a Seven-Layer Burrito at Taco Bell. You freely gave Taco Bell two bucks and they freely gave you the burrito. You enjoyed the burrito more than the two dollars you gave up. So clearly, since the burrito is better than the two bucks, you ripped off Taco Bell, right?

Of course, you know that Taco Bell didn't feel ripped off. Just as you valued the burrito

---

3  Reed (1958).

more than the two dollars, they valued the two dollars more than the burrito. That's the miracle of exchange at work. By making a trade, both you *and* Taco Bell were better off—each having more of the resources you prefer than you did before. In that tiny transaction, the American economy grew just a little bit.

We engage in exchanges hundreds of times a day and don't think twice about it, just as people of Newton's time saw things fall hundreds of times a day and didn't think twice about it. It took the genius of Newton to describe what was going on when apples fell and it took the genius of Smith to figure out what was going on when people buy and sell.

How is it that both sides can be better off and that an economy grows nearly every time someone buys or sells? The answer is: *specialization and trade.* When someone specializes in producing something (such as pencils or burritos), they *lower the marginal opportunity cost of producing it*—this is just a fancy way of saying that the more we make of something, the less it costs us to make it. When we produce more, we produce cheaper.

Specialization reduces costs because of 1) skill improvement and 2) capital investment. To illustrate, let's assume that there is a set of twins who are equal in natural skill, but one twin spends all week doing dozens of different activities, while the other twin spends all week only shooting free throws. Naturally, the latter twin will shoot a higher free-throw percentage once the week is over. We get better at what we specialize in. The economic benefits of skill improvement are summed up in Emerson's maxim: "That which we persist in doing becomes easier, not because the nature of the thing has changed, but because our ability to do it has increased." The more free throws we shoot, the higher percentage of shots we sink. The more pencils we make, the less time and energy it takes to produce an additional one. The more burritos we cook, the less it costs to make the next burrito. Costs go down as we produce more of something because we get better at it.

But the principle of specialization also works because of capital investment. I have a building contractor friend who is a "jack of all trades"; he frames, roofs, drywalls, plumbs, and wires electrical circuitry. One day when he was stuccoing the exterior of a house one trowel at a time, I asked him if there wasn't a faster, cheaper way to do it. He answered that there was a machine that would stucco the whole house in less than an hour, but it cost hundreds of thousands of dollars. It was not worth it for him to buy that machine since he only stuccoes once in a while.

But what if he worked in stucco all day every day? What if he *specialized*? He could have paid for the machine after completing just a few jobs. So it's not just that we get better at things when we specialize, but we also make capital investments that bring the costs down. We invent or buy tools that make the job easier. This is a major driver of technological advance. Specialization means an increase in both human and physical capital.

In summary, specialization works because our costs generally come down (and efficiency goes up) as we produce more of something. From this insight was born Smith's famous concept of the *division of labor*. In general, the more labor is divided, the more specialization occurs, and the more productivity increases. When people chop up work into ever-narrower jobs, they incur ever-lower costs.

But specialization is not the end of the story. If someone specialized in producing only shirts, they would have plenty of shirts to wear, but no shoes, pants, socks, or hats. So as you can see, specialization alone is not enough to create wealth, it requires *trade* as well.

Each person produces what they are best at producing (in economist jargon: where they have a *comparative advantage*) and then trade those goods or services with another so that both parties are better off. Producing where we have a comparative advantage and then exchanging with others makes us wealthy.

## SPECIALIZATION AND TRADE EXAMPLES

Let's illustrate the miracle of exchange with some examples. Imagine that Crusoe and Friday live on a deserted island and every morning they head their separate ways into the jungle to find food to sustain them that day. There are two ways to get food on their island: 1) picking coconuts, or 2) hunting wild boars. Now, working all day, Friday and Crusoe can each produce, on average, three coconuts and three boar steaks.

One day, Friday pitches an idea to Crusoe: why don't you spend all of your time hunting the boars, and I'll spend all of my time picking and husking coconuts? So they each specialize with predictable results: Crusoe gets better and better at hunting boars, not just because he's getting more expert at where to look and how to track, but also because he fashions a hunting spear (a capital investment). His strength and accuracy throwing the spear improve and soon he is able to kill far more boars than ever before. His efficiency in producing boar steaks goes up.

Meanwhile, Friday is able to produce more and more coconuts. Not only is he getting better at finding, picking, and husking them, but, since he's spending all of his time on coconuts, it is worth his while to fashion a reaping tool that will reach into the tree and cut the coconuts down without him having to climb (yet another capital investment). So now Friday, with his new expertise, can produce 8 coconuts per day while Crusoe, with his new expertise, can produce 8 boar steaks per day.

But then they are confronted with the dilemma: Crusoe says, "Friday, I'm getting a little sick of eating boar steaks all the time," and Friday says, "yeah, and I could do with mixing up my coconut diet and getting a little protein." So they trade: four boar steaks for four coconuts. *Voilà*: both have become one coconut and one boar steak richer than when they started. They have spent the same amount of time and effort in production, but through the magic of free exchange, they both got richer. That's the brilliant truth that Adam Smith discovered: free exchange allows for a division of labor that improves efficiency and creates wealth.

Here's another example to illustrate the magic of free exchange: imagine that there is a man out on the American frontier in the 19th century who grows his own food, builds his own furniture, dips his own candles, tans his own leather, sews his own clothes, and coopers his own barrels. He's a jack-of-all-trades and master of none. One day he decides that he's tired of not being really good at anything so he focuses on just tailoring clothes. The first shirt he makes takes him all day. He is clumsy with the scissors and needle, he doesn't know how to cut the fabric according to a proper pattern, and has to keep correcting mistakes. But by the second day he's getting a little better at it. He's more agile with the needle and knows how to best connect the different pieces of cloth. As his skills in tailoring grow, he gets to the point where he can make three shirts in a day. Then he decides that if he's going to spend all day every day making shirts, he could be more efficient if he had a sewing machine (a capital investment). With the help of the sewing machine, he can now make ten shirts in a day. By specializing, his costs came way down and his productivity went way up.

Of course, now the country tailor has a cabin full of shirts, but he only uses a few of them so he comes up with an idea. He decides to trade shirts to his carpenter friend for a chair, to a candle maker friend for a box of candles, to a farmer friend for a bushel of grain, and to a cooper friend for a barrel. As he starts trading with his neighbors, everyone gets richer: he's good at making shirts, but he also gets all of the other goods he needs. He is now far wealthier than if he had just continued to dabble in every type of work.

For another example, imagine a CPA named Steve is doing taxes one evening and gets a hankering for some pizza. Now, Steve is a good tax accountant and can charge $50 an hour for his services. Steve knows that the parlor next door to his office makes a great pizza for $15 and he's tempted to go over and order one, but he's an accountant and starts doing the math. He realizes that the cost of the ingredients—the flour, cheese, oil, sauce, flour, and pepperoni—is only $10. So he can save $5 by skipping out on an hour of work and going home and making the pizza himself, right?

Wrong. He needs to think like an economist and factor in the principle of opportunity cost. If Steve made this pizza himself he would have to give up that $10 for the ingredients, but *also the hour of his time,* which is worth $50. So he's giving up $60 total. Assuming that Steve equally enjoys making pizza and doing taxes, he's better off by $45 if he goes next door and buys the pizza for $15. Strangely, that pizza parlor, by selling Steve that pizza and sparing him having to make it himself, grew the economy by $45. The pizza parlor specialized in making pizza, Steve specialized in preparing tax returns, and then, through exchange, everyone became better off.

## WHAT IS THE EVIDENCE?

Perhaps you are thinking to yourself, "this is a fine academic theory, but does it actually work in practice?" Absolutely. It's been proven time and time again. The wealthiest nations in the world today are those that engage in the most free exchange—just as Adam Smith predicted—while those with the least free exchange, by contrast, are the poorest. Nations like North Korea, Burma, and India (before 1991) where their governments have prevented free exchange and shut themselves off from world trade, have the poorest people.

To understand why you are one of the richest people who ever lived, look no further than your wardrobe. Go to your closet sometime and look at the tags that tell you where your clothes were produced. You do business with people from China, Honduras, Malaysia, Vietnam, Taiwan, and Turkey every day when you get dressed and you didn't even know it. Every day you make free exchanges with people all over the world and that is why you have more goods at your disposal than almost anyone ever before.

This principle has always been at work. Just as gravity had operated long before Newton discovered it, so the magic of free exchange was in force long before Adam Smith discovered it. Helaman 6:8-9 in the Book of Mormon says, "and thus they did have free intercourse one with another, to buy and to sell, and to get gain, according to their desire. And it came to pass that they became exceedingly rich, both the Lamanites and the Nephites." Ether 10:22 says, "And they were exceedingly industrious, and they did buy and sell and traffic one with another, that they might get gain." Many other scriptures make the same point: wealth correlates with exchange.

## THE INVISIBLE HAND

Now that we know how wealth is produced through free exchange, let's turn to Adam Smith's second insight: the magic of wealth allocation. Who tells everyone what to produce, consume, buy, and sell? Who makes sure that there is enough milk on the shelves, cars on the lots, and gasoline at the pumps? Why is there just about enough housing in a given place to fit all of the people—no more, no less? Adam Smith asked the question about his dinner: why did the butcher always have his favorite cut of meat there for him on his way home to make the evening meal?

To answer, Smith invoked what he called *"the invisible hand."* To understand what Adam Smith meant by the invisible hand, we must first understand the most important economic tool of all—a graph so essential to economic analysis that it's almost sacred. It is the *Graph of Supply and Demand*.

This graph is not just important for economists; it is important for everyone—it is a general intellectual instrument that has application in almost infinite situations. You can use the graph to understand what is happening when you are watching the news, filling up your car with gas, paying your electric bill, or receiving a paycheck.

To understand the graph, we must understand its two curves. Imagine that outside your door there is a little stand that sells delicious, warm chocolate chip cookies. How much would you pay for one? Would you buy one for $1? What about fifty cents? Ten cents?

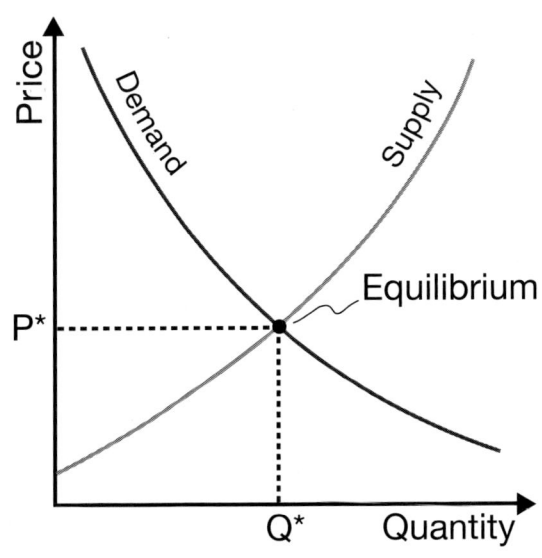

One penny? How many would you buy at each price? In essence, if the cookies only cost a penny, you and everyone else would buy quite a few of them. If they cost a dime, you would buy a few less. At fifty cents, you would buy even less and if they cost ten dollars you would hardly buy any at all. So, the simple insight the thought experiment reveals is this: *the more something costs, the less we want to buy of it; while the less it costs, the more we want to buy of it.* In other words, the lower the price, the higher the quantity demanded. We call this the *Law of Demand*. If we plot this relationship on a graph (with price on the y axis and quantity on the x axis), this curve—the *demand curve*—will slope down to the right.

Now, imagine you are *making and selling* those cookies instead of buying them. How many would you take the trouble to bake and sell if you could get ten dollars for each? Probably quite a few? How about at ten cents? Probably much less and you would probably not make any if you could only sell them for a penny. You would want to sell more at a higher price and sell fewer at a lower price. We call this the *Law of Supply*. If we plotted this relationship on the same graph it would slope upward to the right. This is the *supply curve*.

So people want to buy low and sell high. It's that simple. And that explains why the supply curve slopes up to the right (higher price, higher quantity) and why the demand curve slopes down to the right (lower price, higher quantity).

But how do we resolve this conflict between the buyer, who wants a low price, and the seller, who wants a high price? Does the cookie vendor twist the arm of the buyer and say, "give me a dollar for a cookie or else"? Does the person buying the cookie twist the arm of the seller and say, "give me a cookie for a penny or else"? No, of course not. That's why we call it a *"free exchange"*—there is no compulsion. The buyer and seller agree on a price. And what is that price? It is the point at which the supply and demand curves cross—we call this the *"equilibrium price."* That's how the price of any good in a competitive market is determined: by the intersection of the demand and supply curves that represent the collective

# Chapter 11

agreement of millions and millions of buyers and sellers. The price of a house, an orange, a cell phone, a bag of wheat, or your salary is determined in this way.

So the next time you look at an item for sale and ask, "who decided that price?" the answer is "*you* did." We all did. All buyers and sellers help determine those prices. We signal to a firm our view of acceptable prices every time we pay our bills, buy an item at the store, pump the car full of gas, or clock in at work. Every time we buy or sell something we are "voting" for a price. When we go to the checkout line with a can of chicken noodle soup for fifty cents, we cast a "yes" vote for that price. If that same can costs a dollar and we didn't buy it, we cast a "no" vote. Millions of such votes are the "haggling" that yields the equilibrium prices that we see on all goods and services in our economy.

Now, here's where things get fun: these curves don't sit still. They can move around because the supply and demand relationship moves around. Imagine that tomorrow scientists discovered that eating chocolate chip cookies reduced the risk of cancer by 90%. Given such new information, people would naturally want to buy more cookies (a higher quantity). This means that the entire demand curve would move up (to the right). If the demand curve went to the right, what would happen to the equilibrium price? It would go up too since it would intersect with the supply curve at a higher point.

Conversely, let's say we are talking about supply. What would happen if the amount of chocolate chip cookies suddenly increased (with, say, new efficiencies that allowed us to produce cocoa, sugar, eggs, and flour in greater supply)? Then the price of cookies would go down. As the supply and demand curves move, the price moves with them and to understand how, you only need employ the supply and demand graph.

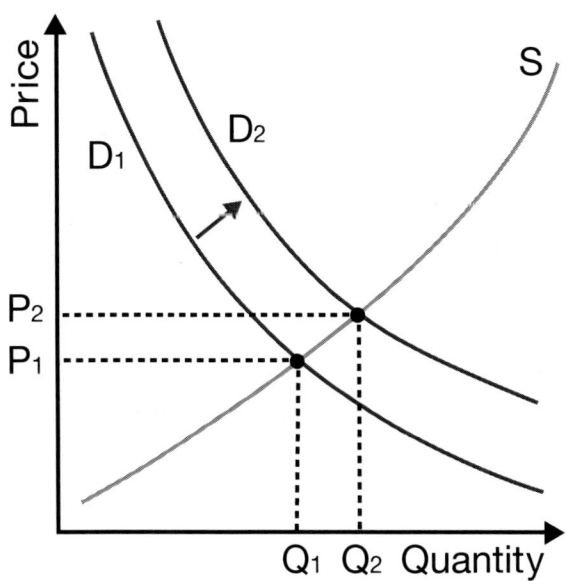

Now, let's see what this has to do with coordinating the production and consumption of goods in the economy by going back to the pencil example: it's not just strange that the pencil gets produced at such a low cost, the bigger miracle is that the pencil gets produced *at all*. Why? Because there is not a single person on the planet who knows how to produce the pencil. It requires the cooperation of thousands of people all over the world just to make this simplest of economic goods.

# Market Principles I: The Secret of Wealth

Who coordinates economic activity between the graphite miner in Chile, the lumberjack in Oregon, the chemist in Japan, the steel manufacturer in China, the rubber farmer in Malaysia, the refiner in Pittsburgh, the engineer in California, and the product designer in England? The answer is *prices*. Prices tell economic actors what it is in their self-interest to do. Who told you to buy the burrito that cost two dollars? The price did. The prices created by supply and demand send signals to economic actors telling them what to do and this coordinates economic activity.

Why does the grocery store always have milk on the shelf for you? Do they send spies to your house to see when your fridge is empty and then stock accordingly? Did your mom call and say, "please be kind and stock milk for my child"? No, nobody had to send out spies and no mothers had to make phone calls. The grocery store stocked the amount of milk they did because the prices told them to.

So prices are like little messengers buzzing around in the market economy persuading people to alter their behavior. People produce and consume not because someone is making them, but because it's in their self-interest. If we demand something, like milk, then that pushes prices up and gives an incentive for farmers to produce milk and stores to stock more of it. If we demand less of something, like pickled pigs' feet, then that pushes prices down and tells stores to stock less of it.

Here's how economist Greg Mankiw put it:

> Prices are the mechanism for rationing scarce resources. Similarly, prices determine who produces each good and how much is produced... Economies are large groups of people engaged in many interdependent activities. What prevents decentralized decision making from degenerating into chaos? What coordinates the actions of the millions of people with their varying abilities and desires? What ensures that what needs to get done does in fact get done? The answer, in a word, is *prices*. If market economies are guided by an invisible hand, as Adam Smith famously suggested, then the price system is the baton that the invisible hand uses to conduct the economic orchestra.[4]

Clearly, the invisible hand described by Smith is a truly incredible force. It brings pencils into existence, stocks milk on shelves, has landlords open up apartments for tenants to live in, and so on.

## THE HAND IN ACTION

Now let's look at some examples of the invisible hand in practice. Imagine that a sudden insect mutation creates a leather-eating bug that consumes most of the shoes on the planet and then dies. This has obviously caused the supply of shoes to go way down, but that low

---

[4] Mankiw (2008, p. 83).

supply will, in turn, cause the price to increase. While we may complain about this higher price, it sends a message to shoe manufacturers to make more shoes; it gives them an incentive to increase production. They solve the problem of low shoe supply just by listening to the price.

Another example: imagine that there is a severe drought. If the supply of water goes down, the curve moves to the left and the price of water goes up. Now, humans can't really produce more water and change the supply curve, but we can modify our behavior and consume differently. At this higher price, it would be in our own interest to take shorter showers, turn off the sink while we scrubbed dishes, and water our lawns less. Cries from environmental groups, decrees from governments, and even a guilty conscience would do far less to conserve water than the messages sent by the price system: expensive water would incentivize us to use less.

Think about energy. Why are companies developing new fossil-fuel extraction methods (such as fracking)? High energy prices gave energy companies an incentive to develop these new technologies. What about the demand side of energy? When gas prices go up, we listen to this "messenger" and adjust our behavior accordingly by driving less. We walk more, bike more, and use public transportation more frequently. This means that high gas prices lead to lower pollution, reduced freeway congestion, decreased traffic fatalities, and even lower obesity rates. This is why one group of economists (called the Pigou Club) advocates higher taxes on gasoline to create incentives for people to drive less, since driving has so many negative side effects. Economists know that since people respond to price incentives, we should increase taxes on what we want less of (e.g., gas usage, smoking, alcohol consumption) and reduce taxes on what we want more of (e.g., efficiency, work, savings, and investment).

But notice how a failure to understand prices has created widespread confusion. Because of economic illiteracy, the media, politicians, and the public blame rises in gas prices on the "greed" of the oil companies. This is silly. If gas companies can just arbitrarily raise prices any time they are feeling a bit greedy, then why aren't they charging $10 a gallon? $20? $100? And if greed causes high prices, then why do gas prices often come down? We don't hear anyone in the media reporting "the charity of oil executives" when gas prices decline.

## SHORTAGE AND SURPLUS

As you can see, price messengers tell us how to change our behavior in producing and consuming gas such that we won't have shortages. And yet many Americans remember a severe gasoline shortage in the early 1970s in which people waited in lines for hours to get a little fuel in their cars. That's not supposed to happen according to Adam Smith's theory, so why did it?

The answer is that the U.S. government didn't let Adam Smith's invisible hand work.

## Market Principles I: The Secret of Wealth

The market didn't create that shortage, government intervention did. It so happened that President Richard Nixon knew that high gas prices were unpopular and he thought he could boost his approval numbers by issuing an executive order forbidding gasoline suppliers from charging more than a fixed amount.

This sounded good, but it was a disaster. The supply and demand graph shows why. Draw a supply and demand curve for gasoline and draw a horizontal dotted line below the equilibrium price. This represents the *"price ceiling"* that the government imposed. Look at what it did: it put supply and demand out of whack. Producers of gasoline could not get a high enough price to make it worth their effort, so they decided to produce less. Consumers on the other hand had an incentive to buy far more gasoline at this lower price. The gas quickly ran out. This gap between the quantity the people wanted to buy, and the quantity the producers wanted to sell is called a *shortage*. That's what government-imposed price ceilings create.[5]

Now, if price ceilings create shortages, price floors create *surpluses*—a situation where the quantity demanded is less than the quantity supplied. While a price ceiling represents the maximum the government will allow you to charge, the price floor represents the minimum. You may be thinking that if a shortage of a something is bad, then a surplus is good, but that's incorrect. A surplus is inefficient and represents wasted resources.

For instance, one popular price floor is the minimum wage: people want to employ and work for the equilibrium wage, but the government won't let them. So if the price floor for labor (the minimum wage) is higher than the equilibrium price, it will create a surplus of labor—we call this "unemployment" (inefficient, idle labor and hardship for those who can't find work). Policies such as a minimum wage sound nice, but they can often hurt the very people they are intended to help.

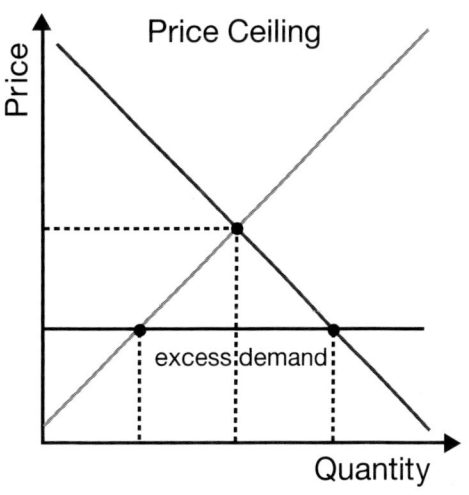

The lesson is that we cannot really "control" prices because the laws of supply and demand are as real as the law of gravity. Adam Smith was merely describing a natural process just as Newton was. Governments can't suspend the laws of supply and demand any more than they can sus-

---

5  It's important to note that, as we shall see in an upcoming lesson, not all government interventions in the economy are bad. In fact, most economists believe that extensive government action is needed to correct market weaknesses. So economists don't oppose government intervention *per se*, but only misguided intervention—like price controls.

pend the law of gravity. They can only ignore the laws of supply and demand (or gravity) at their own peril. If you jump off of a 100-story building you will splatter on the ground even if the government has passed a law "forbidding" gravity from working. It's the same in economics: we can't change prices by government fiat; we can only forbid people from buying and selling at those prices and by so doing create economic chaos. Prices are just messengers and killing the messenger of bad news doesn't do any good (any more than kicking in your TV for telling you bad news will change what happened). Just as we study physics to understand gravity and better work within its constraints, so we should study economics to understand the price system and better work within *its* constraints.

Many people today are questioning the viability of capitalism without realizing that many of the problems they worry about are actually the effects of governments violating the principles of free enterprise. The invisible hand has not failed, it has merely been put in handcuffs.

Thankfully, the USA has been a predominantly free market country since its inception so our few experiments in price controls have been limited in their effects. However, in other countries, where free-market institutions are not as robust, interventions have created disaster.

## MAO'S CALAMITY

For example, in 1949 there was a revolution in China that brought the Communists under Mao Zedong to power. Many Chinese were elated because the Communists promised a society in which the government would make sure that everyone had prosperity, abundance, and equality. This sounded nice (as most anti- market initiatives do), but it was based on economic ignorance and led to one of the worst disasters in world history.

To bring about his communist "utopia," Mao implemented a system in which the government, not prices, would determine who would produce what. Instead of letting people freely exchange and follow price incentives, the government coerced them into economic activity at the point of a gun. Since the price system is characteristic of "evil, exploitive capitalist societies," said Mao, China would live by the "higher" and "more virtuous" principles of Marxist communism.

Mao began by forcing peasants to leave their farms to produce steel so that China could catch up with England and the U.S. in industrial power. A few people protested that peasants didn't know how to produce steel and it was an inefficient use of resources. Mao branded these dissidents, "selfish, greedy, capitalist roaders" and then killed a few of them as an example. The Chinese people quickly learned their lesson and from then on obeyed Mao's decrees, no matter how silly.

To meet their government mandated steel-production quotas, the peasants went into their backyards, set up primitive furnaces, and started melting down anything of value that

# Market Principles I: The Secret of Wealth

contained steel (e.g., bicycles, plows, kitchen utensils). The price system would never have given them an incentive to engage in such economic lunacy, but government coercion did.

So if the peasants were "producing" steel, who was going to produce the food? Again, the government, not prices, would take care of that. Mao appointed a commissar of food and told him to make sure China had enough to feed the population of China. The big problem here was human nature. Remember, people are foolish and evil, including (and perhaps especially) government officials who are susceptible to the corruptions of power. Since the commissar was foolish, he couldn't possibly know how much food was needed to feed the whole population of China and, since he was evil, he would be willing to lie in order to curry favor with Mao.

Predictably, with no price incentives in place, the harvest was far lower than the commissar's target. Instead of telling the truth about the poor food production (which would have gotten him shot), the Commissar told Mao what he wanted to hear: they had produced many times the target amount. He even fabricated propaganda pictures showing children walking atop unimaginably dense fields of grain. The price system would never have rewarded such lies, but corrupt governments do.

But it got worse. Mao reasoned that if they had produced far more food than planned, why not send more farmers to make steel? At the very moment when they needed to make *more* food (when the price system would have been screaming its message to increase food production), Mao was telling them to make less. They couldn't listen to the market, they had to listen to the government.

The results were incomprehensibly tragic. Mao's "Great Leap Forward" created the worst famine in the history of the world. It was completely caused by government control over the economy. Recent estimates put the death toll at 45 to 50 million people. This makes even Hitler's Holocaust look tame by comparison.

Tens of millions perished because Mao didn't understand the basic economic principles outlined in this chapter. Perhaps speaking of millions dying in China is too abstract. Were this famine to have happened in America it would have meant the death of every person in Idaho, Utah, Nevada, Montana, Oregon, Louisiana, Oklahoma, Connecticut, Iowa, Arkansas, Kansas, West Virginia, New Mexico, Nebraska, Maine, New Hampshire, Hawaii, Rhode Island, Delaware, South Dakota, Alaska, North Dakota, Vermont, and Wyoming. Every person in every one of these states would have starved. That's the result of Mao's forbidding free exchange.

Almost every communist revolution in history has been followed by a famine while, as far as we can tell, there has never been a famine in a modern, free-market economy because the prices will reallocate food resources to where they are most needed (signaled by the higher prices). All of this should make clear why studying economics is not just nice, but essential. It can, literally, be a matter of life and death.

*Chapter 11*

## CONCLUSION

In this chapter we've seen that, without question, free markets are efficient, wealth-generating, and even lifesaving. This leaves us with a puzzling question: why are markets controversial? Why do people throughout the world, including many in our own country, oppose the free-market capitalist system? We will turn to this important question in the next chapter and see if this market skepticism is justified.

## CHAPTER 11 SOURCES/FURTHER READING

Bastiat, Frédéric. *The Law*. Irvington-on-Hudson, New York: Foundation for Economic Education, 1998.

Becker, Gary. *The Economics of Life: From Baseball to Affirmative Action to Immigration, How Real-World Issues Affect Our Everyday Life*. New York: McGraw-Hill, 1997.

Becker, Jasper. *Hungry Ghosts: Mao's Secret Famine*. New York: Henry Holt, 1996.

Behravesh, Nariman. *Spin-Free Economics: A No-Nonsense, Nonpartisan Guide to Today's Global Economic Debates*. New York: McGraw-Hill, 2009.

Buchholz, Todd G. *From Here to Economy: A Shortcut to Economic Literacy*. New York: Dutton, 1995.

Chang, Jung. *Mao: The Unknown Story*. New York: Knopf, 2005.

_____. *Wild Swans*. New York: Doubleday, 1991.

Dubner, Steven J. and Stephen Leavitt. *Freakonomics: A Rogue Economist Explores the Hidden Side of Everything*. New York: William Morrow, 2005.

_____. *Superfreakonomics*. New York: William Morrow, 2009.

Friedman, Milton. *Capitalism and Freedom*. Chicago: University of Chicago Press, 1962.

Friedman, Thomas L. *The World is Flat: A Brief History of the Twenty-First Century*. New York: Farrar, Straus, and Giroux, 2005.

Hazlitt, Henry. *Economics in One Lesson*. New Rochelle, NY: Arlington House, 1979.

Heilbroner, Robert L. *The Worldly Philosophers: The Lives, Times, and Ideas of the Great Economic Thinkers*. New York: Simon & Schuster, 1980.

Heilbroner, Robert L. and Lester Thurow. *Economics Explained: Everything You Need to Know About How the Economy Works and Where It's Going*. New York: Simon & Schuster, 1998.

Ip, Greg. *The Little Book of Economics*. Hoboken, NJ: Wiley, 2010.

Kotkin, Joel. *The City: A Global History*. New York: Modern Library, 2005

Krugman, Paul. *Pop Internationalism*. Cambridge, MA: M.I.T Press, 1996.

Lee, Susan. *Susan Lee's ABZs of Economics: Basics to Buzzwords--Everything you Need to Know in Plain English*. New York: Simon and Schuster, 1987.

Mankiw, Greg. *Principles of Economics*. Fifth Edition. Mason, OH: Cengage Learning, 2008.

McCarty, Marilu Hurt. *The Nobel Laureates: How the World's Greatest Economic Minds Shaped Modern Thought*. New York: McGraw-Hill, 2001.

Nasar, Sylvia. *Grand Pursuit: The Story of Economic Genius*. New York: Simon & Schuster, 2011.

Oaks, Dallin H. "Good, Better, Best," LDS General Conference, October 2007. <https://www.lds.org/general-conference/2007/10/good-better-best?lang=eng>

Reed, Leonard. *I, Pencil: My Family Tree as told to Leonard E. Read*. Irvington-on-Hudson, NY: The Foundation for Economic Education, Inc., 1958.

Smith, Adam. *The Wealth of Nations* (1776). New York: Modern Library, 1994.

Sowell, Thomas. *Basic Economics: A Common Sense Guide to the Economy*. 4th Edition. New York: Basic Books, 2011.

Wolf, Martin. *Why Globalization Works*. New Haven: Yale University Press, 2004.

# Chapter 12

# MARKET PRINCIPLES II: MARKET MORALITY

## ANDREW CARNEGIE: THE GOSPEL OF WEALTH

Nothing in Andrew Carnegie's background would have suggested that he would one day become a wealthy business tycoon. He was a Scottish immigrant who came penniless to the United States and then worked as a bobbin boy in a Pittsburgh factory. At that point, he was no different than millions of other impoverished industrial workers in the U.S. simply trying to get by.

But unlike so many others in his situation, Carnegie was determined to succeed in life. He learned and worked diligently and eventually caught the eye of a railroad manager who made Carnegie his assistant. Soon, Carnegie himself was promoted to a managerial position and was earning a stable, middle-class salary.

Even though Carnegie was making more money, he was still spending the same as he had as a factory worker. He carefully invested his surplus income in railroad stock. As his investments increased in value and paid handsome dividends, he still didn't spend lavishly, but reinvested those profits. Eventually, Carnegie had accumulated enough capital to buy a railroad of his own.

As a railroad owner, Carnegie saw that he could increase his profit margins if he didn't have to pay retail price for the steel needed for track and cars, so he expanded into steel production. Carnegie created new smelting processes that made his steel the sturdiest and most flexible in the world. Soon, millions were buying Carnegie steel and his operation was bringing in wealth beyond anyone's wildest dreams. When he finally sold off his businesses in 1900, he was the richest man who had ever lived.

Carnegie decided he wanted to die as poor as he was born. He had spent much of the first half of his life making his millions and would spend most of the second half giving it all away. The world's wealthiest man became the world's greatest philanthropist: he built institutions to promote literacy, music, education, the arts, and peace. He believed in the old adage, "give a man a fish, feed him for a day; teach a man to fish, feed him for a lifetime," so he targeted his philanthropic efforts towards helping others rise as he had (especially by building libraries). Countless people had their lives bettered through Carnegie's generosity.

During his lifetime, Carnegie had provided great quality steel at low prices for his customers, created thousands of jobs for American workers, and gave more money away than any single person in history. And yet, despite all of these good works, Carnegie has come down in the history books as an exploitative "robber baron." Carnegie was evil, many claim, because he pursued his wealth in a ruthless capitalist system based upon self-interest, competition, and profits.

In the following pages, we will see that the unfair assumptions people make about Carnegie stem from the unfair assumptions people make about capitalism itself. In the last chapter we learned about the workings of the market economy, but in this chapter we will learn about the *morality* of the market economy. Most people concede that the free market is efficient, but many still claim that it is nonetheless a wicked system because it operates on the immoral-sounding principles of 1) self-interest, 2) profit-seeking, and 3) competition. Is capitalism as bad as it sounds, or has it been judged too harshly?

## SELF-INTEREST

Let's begin with that much-abused term, *self-interest*. The idea that the free-market system works on the principle of self-interest goes all the way back to Adam Smith. In the *Wealth of Nations*, Smith explained that individual pursuit of self-interest led to coordination of economic activity and collective well-being. Since that time, critics have charged that Smith's economic theory gives license to selfishness.

When we look closely, we see that these charges are mostly unfounded. They come from a misunderstanding of self-interest and the unfortunate coincidence that both "self-interest" and "selfishness" share the common root word, "self." Selfishness, as we all know, means helping oneself at the expense of others. One person gains by hurting someone else—a win-lose scenario. The gospel makes clear that selfishness is always wrong.

Self-Interest, on the other hand, is more complex than selfishness. It simply means pursuing one's own interests and these interests can be either bad or good (and may not even be monetary). For instance, some believe that it is in their self-interest to accumulate a fortune, buy expensive toys, flaunt costly apparel, indulge their base appetites, and join exclusive clubs in an effort to feel superior. On the other hand, it is certainly in your own interest to get an education (a prophet has commanded it), marry someone you love, and, above all, seek eternal salvation. Since God has commanded each of these, but would never command us to do something selfish, it's clear that self-interest and selfishness are different.

# Market Principles II: Market Morality

So how do we distinguish between the two? When is our self-interest bad ("selfishness") and when is it good (*"enlightened self interest"*)? Self-interest becomes enlightened under two conditions: 1) Just Pursuit and 2) Just Intent. In other words, self-interest is justified when pursued in the *right way* and for the *right reasons.*

Just pursuit is concerned with *how* you pursue your self-interest. Do you seek personal gain in a way that is honest, follows the laws, and does not hurt others?[1] In pursuing a higher education, for example, do you cheat in your courses or work honestly for your grades?

Just intent is concerned with *why* you pursue your self-interest. Do you have the intent to do good with the blessings you acquire? Do you have righteous goals? Will you use your college degree to help others and make the world a better place, or arrogantly set yourself up as superior?

If you pursue your interest in the right way and for the right reasons, then that self-interest is enlightened and acceptable. Unfortunately, the world fails to see this. Those without the light of the gospel have developed false paradigms and see benefit in "zero-sum" terms in which there is a fixed pie and more for one person means less for others. Any time you seek your self-interest you *must* be hurting someone else, they say, and therefore you are necessarily "selfish."[2]

Economic science teaches that this is just wrong. The rule in free-market transactions (although there are exceptions which we shall discuss later) is win-win. Both parties mutually consent and mutually benefit. The market isn't characterized by fighting over a bigger slice of the economic pie, but by expanding the *size* of the pie so everyone gets more. Of course there are examples of people acting selfishly within capitalism, but there are also myriad examples of people acting for the good of themselves *and* others—enlightened self-interest.[3]

Even the Prophet Joseph Smith taught the principle of enlightened self-interest. In 1843, he answered the question of whether it was OK to seek one's own self-interest ("self-aggrandizement") and said,

> Some people entirely denounce the principle of self-aggrandizement as wrong, [but] it is a correct principle and may be indulged upon only one rule or plan—and that is to elevate, benefit and bless others first. If you will elevate others, the very work itself will exalt you. Upon no other plan can a man justly and permanently aggrandize himself.[4]

---

1 We should treat others, as philosopher Immanuel Kant admonished, as ends themselves and never as means.
2 The zero-sum fallacy explains, for example, why businessmen are almost invariably portrayed as villains in Hollywood movies or history textbooks.
3 As we shall see, capitalism actually turns selfishness into enlightened self-interest by requiring both parties to enter into transactions freely. In free exchanges, you cannot benefit yourself without offering benefits to others or else they wouldn't do business with you.
4 Andrus (1974, p. 61).

# Chapter 12

In other words, there is no selfless action that does not work for our interest as well in the long term.

Satan wants us to think in terms of win-lose (selfishness), but the Lord works upon the principle of win-win (enlightened self-interest) in which everyone benefits. God's existence is spent bringing to pass "the immortality and eternal life of man," but this work also brings glory to Him (Moses 1:39). Sometimes the Lord will ask us to do something that may seem lose-win, like giving of our time and resources to someone else, but, as Joseph Smith pointed out, by elevating others we cannot help but benefit from these acts of service. The growth, joy, and blessings that come from serving others turn these seemingly lose-win situations into win-win. Recent social scientific evidence has confirmed this, showing that those who give service are happier than those who do not. This is what Jesus meant when He taught that he who loses his life shall find it. His parable of the talents further indicates that the Lord wants us to multiply the resources he has given.

We can find plenty of examples of enlightened self-interest in U.S. history. Some have charged George Washington with being no different than dictators because, like them, he sought power and fame. But such glib accusations fail to acknowledge that Washington's *means* and *ends* were completely different than those of dictators. The *way* he sought power and the *reasons* he sought power make a world of difference. Washington surrendered all political authority and thereby gained the power of example and the esteem of others. He did this to establish freedom in his country, not achieve unrighteous dominion. To say that he and Hitler "both sought their own self-interest and therefore are not really much different" is absurd. Washington pursued his interest according to both Just Pursuit and Just Intent.

Notice that many of the prophets and apostles (starting as early as the patriarch Abraham) have been men of great wealth. Brigham Young was a shrewd businessman who became rich. So was Heber J. Grant. Today among the General Authorities we find many wealthy doctors, lawyers, and businessmen, but we would be wrong to call them "selfish"— they sought their wealth and position in the right way and did so for the right reasons: to bless others and serve the Lord. Their self-interest is enlightened and justified.

Jacob taught enlightened self-interest when he declared, "But before you seek for riches, seek ye for the kingdom of God. And after ye have obtained a hope in Christ ye shall obtain riches, if ye seek them; and ye will seek them for the intent to do good—to clothe the naked, and to feed the hungry, and to liberate the captive, and administer relief to the sick and the afflicted" (Jacob 2:18-19). Consider how much more good you will be able to do in life (missions you can serve, poor you can help, good causes you can fund) if you gain wealth through enlightened self-interest.

The point of all of this is that capitalism is a system of self-interest, but not necessarily of selfishness. If people will seek enlightened self-interest, doing good for others even as they elevate themselves, then the system transcends selfishness. Extractive economic systems, such as feudalism, autocracy, or socialism, are based on the principle of win-lose: one person taking by force from another. Capitalism, on the other hand, can be a system of win-win if the Rule of Law is in place and the people act virtuously.

## COMPETITION

Let's turn next to *competition* in a market economy. Many people recoil at the word "competition" in economics because it sounds so Darwinian—as if competition meant that economic losers are "weeded out" and die in a struggle for survival. They then conclude that competitive capitalism is a ruthless system which should be replaced by one in which firms *cooperate* instead of compete.

Those who say this need to look a little deeper and realize that businesses often *do* cooperate with each—it's called *monopoly*. Without competitors, monopolistic businesses can charge inflated prices, offer poor service and products, and the little guy (the consumer) is at their mercy. Without competition, businesses have no incentive to improve.

Looking at economics rationally, rather than emotionally, we see that competition is an essential part of a market economy because it serves the same function as it does in politics: checking power. Just as we would not want tyrannical groups to cooperate in government and take away liberty, so we don't want economic groups cooperating and forming monopolies.

To realize the value of economic competition, just think about your last trip to the Department of Motor Vehicles (DMV). At the DMV, we often wait in line for hours, the place is drab, the employees are grumpy, and it is an altogether unpleasant place. Why? Because the DMV is a government-run monopoly and *has no competitors* and can't go out of business. If you get poor service or food at a restaurant, you can take your business and go elsewhere. You have no such options with the DMV.

Whereas monopoly means that the producer rules, competition among businesses means that the *consumer* rules. The business owner ultimately has to please the customer or go under. They cannot force us to buy their products, they have to *persuade* us to do so. This means businesses must give the highest quality and lowest prices possible to keep their customers happy. This is the discipline of the market. Business cooperation, although it sounds nice, would hurt consumers.

But does that mean that there is no cooperation in a market economy? Hardly, but that cooperation remains where it should: between the buyer and seller. You cooperate with the supermarket every time you buy groceries. You cooperate with the gas station every time you fill up your car. You cooperate with the bank every time you pay your mortgage. You cooperate with the TV station every time you watch a show. You cooperate with the cinema every time you go to a movie. You cooperate with your employer every time you clock in.

You cooperate with the restaurant every time you eat out. The market economy is full of cooperation, but it is the right kind of cooperation in which both parties win. As you can see, the characterization of capitalism as a system of "nasty competition and no cooperation" is simply not accurate.

It is also important to remember that economic competition does not "weed out" people, only institutions and inefficiencies. Some have lamented the "social Darwinism" of capitalism, assuming it means the poor (the "unfit") are left to starve and die. This is nonsense and, as we shall see in the next chapter, the poor live far better under capitalism than under any alternative system. The reality is that the "social Darwinism" of the marketplace only means that businesses must adapt to remain competitive. This is what drives innovation and wealth creation. The same "social Darwinism" is at work in democracy, where candidates must adapt to the wants of the electorate or be removed from office—they don't die, they are simply replaced. To oppose this kind of "social Darwinism" would be to oppose democracy as well as capitalism.

## PROFITS

Third, and finally, we turn to that nastiest-sounding term of them all: profits. Many believe that those who seek profits in a market economy are simply greedy people concerned only with a fatter pocketbook and a bigger bank account.

This prejudice against profits is more Hollywood than reality. The dictionary defines "greed" as an unhealthy and excessive lust after money—this, of course, is immoral. But profits are not as horrid as they may appear for two reasons. First, profits serve as both a signal and incentive to produce goods and services we need. When the supply of a good is low and demand is high, prices rise, and this promise of higher profits tells producers to make more of that good. The profits reward them for giving us what we want. Without the profit incentives and signals, farmers, contractors, and hospitals would not provide the food, housing, and healthcare we need.

Second, profits are *value neutral*—their morality depends upon what we do with them. Sure, we could greedily hoard profits in a bank account, live lavishly, and indulge vices, but we can also use profits to aid the poor, support education, give to political causes, or advance technology through research and development (computers, light-bulbs, life-saving medicines, automobiles, and more all came about because of companies seeking profits). None of us would say that people earning wages are greedy, and yet the morality of profits, just like wages, depends upon the uses we put them to. We can't see into the hearts of others, so instead of accusing business men and women of being "greedy" for wanting to earn profits, we should probably do as the scriptures say and withhold judgment.

# MARKET PRINCIPLES II: MARKET MORALITY

## CONCLUSION

Maybe you are still uncomfortable with the moral basis of capitalism and just feel in your gut that self-interest, competition, and profit-seeking are wrong. The final point in this chapter is that even if you still feel that way, it simply doesn't matter because of what we know about human nature.

Consider the following illustration. If you go to Albertsons grocery store, you will see shopping carts strewn all over the parking lot. They are often rusty, broken, and neglected. Albertsons has to spend a small fortune hiring a team of employees to constantly find and retrieve the carts.

And yet if you go to Aldi's grocery store, the shopping carts are almost always in mint condition and stacked neatly right next to the entrance. If someone leaves their cart in the parking lot, the next customer will happily return it to the front for them. What has happened? Do good people shop at Aldi's while bad people shop at Albertson's? Does Aldi's use some kind of hypnosis or brainwashing on their customers?

No, it's much simpler than that: unlike Albertson's, Aldi's requires a deposit of one quarter ($.25) for use of their carts. When you return the cart, you receive your twenty-five cents back. One silly little quarter is all the incentive that shoppers need to return their cart promptly to the front.

The point is that even if people are seeking self-interest, profit, and competition for greedy purposes, it's still the case that humans respond to incentives and make the market system work. The free market can turn even selfish motivations to the constructive ends of productivity and growth.

The evidence for this simple truth is overwhelming. Notice that nearly everyone washes their own car, but nobody washes a rental car. Owner-occupied homes are almost always better cared for than rental properties. Private restrooms are better maintained than public restrooms. Books from the public library are more abused than those from a personal collection. This is because of human nature. It is just a fact that we love our own families more than we love the families of others; we love our own children more than we love the children of others; and we love our own possessions more than we love the possessions of others. Right or wrong, this tendency to love our own is an inevitable part of human nature.

As the Aldi's example shows, we even love our quarter more than we love the store's carts. The desire to "do the right thing" is often not sufficient motivation to get people to return them to the front, but the quarter is. If this is "selfishness," then Aldi's (like the capitalist system) has figured out how to use that selfishness to incentivize us to do something constructive.

So the final fallacy about the market economy is that the market *produces* selfishness and greed. That's just not true. The ability to choose evil is at the core of human nature, so greed and selfishness are found in *every* economic system. The only question is whether that

# Chapter 12

selfishness and greed will lead to win-win outcomes. Human nature responds to incentives even if those incentives are less than noble. We cannot eliminate this fact, but, through capitalism, we can channel it to constructive ends. We might say that people *shouldn't* be motivated by self-interest, but we *can't* say that they aren't. Capitalism, like constitutional government, accepts people as they are and proceeds accordingly. It forces greedy people to help others (produce beneficial goods and services) to satisfy their greed. A realistic understanding of human nature explains not only why divisions of power produce freedom, but also why free exchange under capitalism succeeds so spectacularly in producing wealth.

## CHAPTER 12 SOURCES/FURTHER READING

Andrus, Hyrum L. and Helen Mae Andrus, eds. *They Knew the Prophet*. Salt Lake City: Bookcraft, 1974.

Christensen, Joe J. "Greed, Selfishness, and Overindulgence," *Ensign*, May, 1999.

_____. "Reflections on a Consecrated Life." *Ensign* (Nov. 2010).

Livesay, Harold C. *Andrew Carnegie and the Rise of Big Business*, 2d ed. NY: Longman, 2000.

Smith, Adam. *The Theory of Moral Sentiments* (1759). New York: Penguin, 2009.

Sowell, Thomas. *Economic Facts and Fallacies*. Second Edition. New York: Basic Books, 2011.

Tice, Richard. "Greed: When Enough Is Not Enough," *Ensign*, June, 1989.

Tomasi, John. *Free Market Fairness*. Princeton: Princeton University Press, 2012.

# Chapter 13

# ECONOMIC CHALLENGES I: AMERICAN ECONOMIC DEVELOPMENT

## MAX WEBER: CAPITALIST CONDITIONS

In this chapter we turn to the nature and causes of American economic power. Max Weber, the great German sociologist of the early 20th century, will be our guide. Weber was born in Prussia to a wealthy family of industrialists and politicians. After graduating from college, Weber went into law by default rather than conviction—a mistake many graduates make when they are unsure of what to do. He soon found himself bored so he left his job and began a new career in social studies. His passion for the field led him to make some of the most profound and consequential discoveries of the 20th century.

One of the questions he asked, as have many social scientists before and since, was, "Why are some nations richer than others?" Adam Smith answered this question by pointing out that nations prosper when they allow free exchange. Weber didn't disagree, but he also noted that free markets failed to take hold in certain places and that some nations had greater success under capitalism. To explain why, he turned Karl Marx on his head. Marx had argued that economics was so fundamental that it determined everything else in society, including values, beliefs, and religion.

Weber said that Marx had it backwards: it's not economics that determines beliefs, but *beliefs that determine economics.* He noted that Northern Europe had the countries with the most advanced capitalist economies in the world (e.g., Germany, England, Holland), and concluded that this was because of their Protestant religion. Southern European nations, by contrast, largely remained Catholic and less prosperous. Protestants, said Weber in his landmark book, *The Protestant Ethic and the Spirit of Capitalism,* uniquely cultivated the virtues of thrift, hard work, and deferred gratification as a way to signal status as God's elect. To Weber, this "Protestant ethic" helped explain the economic success of nations.

## THE CAPITALIST ETHIC

The Protestant part of Weber's argument has not stood the test of time. Some of the most successful capitalist countries in the world today are not Protestant, but Catholic, Buddhist, Hindu, and even Confucian. However, what he said about deferred gratification leading to capitalist success remains valid.

For example, a person could spend all of their income on consumption goods (vacations, cars, electronics, expensive clothes, etc.), or they could defer the pleasure of consuming immediately and instead *invest* a portion of their money in expectation of a greater future return. This is what the famous "marshmallow experiment" illustrates. Kids willing to put off eating a marshmallow for a few minutes (deferred gratification) receive a second marshmallow as a reward. This experiment has proven to be remarkably predictive of a child's future economic success. Those kids who demonstrated the capacity for deferred gratification have ended up with higher educational levels, higher salaries, and greater levels of life satisfaction.

On a macro level, deferring gratification leads to economic growth because it allows capital accumulation. When people save and invest instead of consuming, they create the pool of capital that entrepreneurs and businesses use to start or expand productive enterprises. Capitalism rests on capital, and we get capital by investing rather than consuming resources. If people don't exercise self-control and spend all of their money on consumption, then capitalism can't work. Worse yet, if people in a society consistently borrow rather than save, the result is economic stagnation. In other words, Weber may have been wrong about capitalist values being tied to Protestantism, but he was right about the values themselves. There are, in fact, moral requisites for capitalism.

Is it any wonder, then, that America hit a financial crisis in 2008 and continues to languish economically? During the 2000s, Gordon B. Hinckley seemed to be the only man in America telling us to get out of debt while everyone from the U.S. President to the local real estate agent assured us that more public and private borrowing would only result in higher incomes, raised standards of living, and never-ending economic growth. We listened to the false prophets of the world instead of the true Prophet of God because buying big homes and maxing out our credit cards sounded more fun than living within our means. Predictably enough, the economy crashed and has so far struggled to recover.

The point is that, contrary to partisan myths, it's not Obama's fault or Bush's fault that our economy tanked. It's *our* fault. We the people shifted from being savers to borrowers and our politicians only bent to our democratic wishes. As citizens, we lost the moral foundation that capitalism needs to work and, collectively, became like the kids who couldn't wait for a second marshmallow. Our success as a nation largely depends upon reversing the decay of deferred gratification and recovering the ethic upon which economic growth rests.

## AMERICA'S WEALTH

Weber's insight not only explains America's economic problems today, but much of our economic success in the past. For Weber, America was the most powerful economic nation simply because America was the most Protestant nation. The early settlers were zealous Puritans (too radical even for Protestant England) who came to this land to establish a "city on a hill."

But that is only part of the story. To fully understand the nature, extent, and causes of American economic power, we must look at a fuller range of explanations. As we examine American economic success, the point is not to congratulate ourselves on our "success," but to induce a sense of humility in all of us. Where much is given much is required, and as we shall see below (in pre-2008 numbers) Americans have been given much indeed.

The statistics on American wealth are staggering. Economists have developed a way to measure national economic well-being called *Gross Domestic Product* (GDP) which essentially tells us the value of all the stuff—cars, pairs of shoes, laptops, washed windows, watermelons, etc.—a nation produces in one year. It's like a huge basket containing all of an economy's goods and services. American GDP in 2007 was around 14 Trillion dollars. We can't comprehend a number that big, so let's put it into other terms: if we had divided it up between every man, woman, and child in this country, it would come out to about $46,000 per person. If you realize that millions of people in the world subsist on less than a few hundred dollars a year, this number is truly astounding. The amount of wealth Americans command is unprecedented.

Think of it this way: most people throughout history have spent almost all of their money and resources just trying to get enough food to survive, yet Americans (even the poorest ones) spend less than a tenth of their money on food and still eat very well. In that sense, most of our income goes to luxuries that have little or nothing to do with survival.

Note also that the U.S. economy at its peak was about as big as the next four largest economies combined. In the "contest" to be the richest nation in the world, there really was no contest. All of the closest competitors—China, Japan, Germany, and England—were miles behind.

America has also been economically blessed with a low *unemployment rate* (a measure of what percentage of the workforce can't find jobs). Historically, we've had an unemployment rate around 5% while poor countries of the world suffer with unemployment rates of 25% or higher. Even when our economy is in recession, the unemployment rate almost never reaches 10% and yet France, a wealthy country, has an unemployment rate that is

# Chapter 13

*almost always* above 10%. Even in bad economic times, we have it much better than most of the world.

In proportional terms, the USA had about 6% of the world's population in 2007 and yet controlled about 30% of the world's resources. In 2007, Asia contained almost 50% of the world's population, but had an economy the same size as America's. That's not just unfair, it's disturbing. The next time you think to yourself, "life isn't fair," your next thought should be one of gratitude; if life were fair, you would be far, far poorer. Most of the world ekes out an existence that makes poverty in America look lavish by comparison. Immigrants come by the millions to be poor in America because it is far preferable to the situation they came from in Cuba, Nigeria, Mexico, India, and other countries.

The American economy is not only the largest "economic pie" in history, but that pie has consistently grown by about 3-4% a year. Little economies can grow very quickly, but big economies are supposed to be lumbering, slow, and stagnant. And yet, the American economy—the largest of them all—has historically plowed forward with surprisingly high rates of growth.

## WHAT IT MEANS

This all means that common Americans are among the wealthiest people ever to have lived. You may not think of yourself as rich, but you are extremely wealthy by historical standards. The grandest kings of medieval times would have changed places with you in a heartbeat. The richest man in the world just one century ago would have gladly given it all up to live as an average American today in order to have the commonplace advantages of modern medicine, television, computers, internet, varied diet, and more. All of the money in the world 100 years ago couldn't have bought cancer radiation treatment, a polio vaccination, or a smartphone—but most Americans have access to these things today. We sometimes say, "It would be nice to win the lottery," but the truth is that you *already have won the lottery*. When you were born to live in America, you won the sweepstakes of life. The chances that you would live in America in the 21$^{st}$ century were one in a million, but that good fortune landed on you.

What does this mean in even more tangible terms when we start talking actual assets? It means the average American home is about 2,500 square feet which surprisingly does not impress us much, but that is the point—you are accustomed to extremely large homes. If you took this average American home and dropped it down in most places in the world, the locals would ask, "Whose castle is that?" Our average houses, which extend to the horizon in thousands of subdivisions across the country, would count as mansions in most places in the world.

The average American household owns two to three cars. In most nations you have to be quite rich to own *just one* car. In much of Asia, Latin America, and Africa the town bigwig drives a beat up old piece of junk, but he is considered rich and powerful because he owns *a* car. Here in the U.S., the average family owns not just one car, but three. We often speak of "starving college students," and yet one of the biggest problems on campuses around the country is parking. The "starving students" in America have so many cars that we can't find places to put them all.

It's not just our cars and homes, it is also what we put into them: appliances, fridges, big screen TV's, video-gaming systems, exercise equipment, couches, and more. Collectively, Americans simply have more stuff than anybody else in the history of the world.

As one of the richest people who has ever lived, you have an obligation to be a wise steward with this blessing. Where much is given, much is required. You will be accountable for your use of every dollar. When the Lord asks you what you did with your wealth, do you really want to report that you "took it easy" and "bought a lot of toys"?

## POVERTY

Does all of this talk of American wealth mean that there were no economic problems in America before 2008? No, there always have been problems, including poverty. Largely because of the breakdown of the family, economic exploitation, the legacy of slavery and racism, and low-skilled immigration, the poverty rate—the percentage of Americans defined as very poor—fluctuates between 10-15%. That is, indeed, a serious problem. In spite of all of our efforts to reduce it through initiatives, private charities, public programs, and even a government "war on poverty," the poverty rate has not come down since the mid 1960s.

Having said that, we do need to keep a little perspective. In other places in the world, living in poverty means being malnourished, ill-clothed, and threatened with starvation. The poor in America, on the other hand, have too much food rather than too little.[1] If you go to a government welfare office—where the poorest of the poor congregate to receive public assistance—you find that they wear adequate, comfortable clothing and are generally overweight. The poor in America have access to clean water, have opportunities for social mobility (most of them will move out of poverty), and own air-conditioners, televisions, microwave ovens, cars, and other resources that would be considered luxuries elsewhere in the world. An Indian wrote a friend in America saying he wanted to immigrate to the United States because he "wanted to live in a country where the poor people are fat." In India the poor are, by definition, skinny and malnourished.

The point is that there is a difference between absolute poverty and relative poverty. In most countries, our poverty line of $18,000 income per year would be considerable wealth.

---

1 Although affording food and healthy food are two different matters.

## Chapter 13

This doesn't absolve us of the moral obligation to do something about poverty in the United States, but it does help put it in perspective.

## HISTORY OF ECONOMIC POWER

We can better understand the sources of American economic power by looking at its history, beginning with the colonial era. The first settlements in this country were established by companies—The Massachusetts Bay Company and the Virginia Company—who created an entrepreneurial energy from the get-go.

Of course, these companies didn't start out making much money. In the case of Massachusetts Bay, becoming rich wasn't even in the plans. They were Puritans who wanted to create a godly example for the world. But this vision didn't last very long. After the first generation, the children of these Puritans cared less about godliness and more about exploiting the vast economic opportunities the colonies had to offer. There were fish to catch, forests to harvest as lumber, ships to build, and mercantile houses to run. There was good money to be made and the Puritans lapsed from their original goal and became materialistic. The Puritan backlash against this commercialism took ugly forms like the Salem witch trials, and some would say it continues in the anti-business prejudices we see in America today.

After the end of the colonial era, the moneymaking continued. The unification of the nation in 1787 created a vast free-trade network that let Adam Smith's magic run wild and made America rich. During the Washington Administration, Treasury Secretary Hamilton established the national bank, the beginnings of a securities exchange, and a business-friendly political environment.

In the early 19th century, the building of roads, canals, and railroads linked the country together and further expanded its trade networks. The Erie Canal is just the most notable example of the infrastructure projects that extended the size of the market for Americans. Millions of immigrants also poured in, bringing all of their gumption and entrepreneurial energy to further fuel economic growth.

Although America fought a costly Civil War from 1861 to 1865, after its conclusion the economy picked up right where it had left off. This time Americans were not just producing crafts and agricultural commodities, but industrial goods for a worldwide market. Steel, textiles, and other products were cranked out of American factories and sent all over the world. America, by the year 1900, had become the greatest economic power in history.

The growth continued in the 20th century and, for the first time, we had hard numerical data to prove the extent of that growth. *Per capita GDP*—the best measure of material well-being (annual wealth per person)—rocketed upward. At the beginning of the century, the average American had to subsist on less than $2,000 a year, but by the year 2000 that had grown to about $40,000. Our wealth per person had multiplied 16 times in real terms (adjusted for inflation) in just a few generations. Although there were economic hiccups in the 1930s and 1970s (we'll discuss those downturns in later chapters), for the most part the United States saw uninterrupted growth in the 20th century.[2]

## OBJECTIONS

Some people grumble about American economic success by claiming that it "only benefits the rich." This is a prevalent myth that we can dispel with the facts. The official statistics from the Congressional Budget Office (CBO)[3] tell us that, throughout U.S. history, the people from every income group (rich, middle class, or poor) have been better off than their parents in material terms. You can pick any generation and see that, rich to poor, it has been better off at the end than at the beginning. It's simply inaccurate to say, as so many glibly do, that in America, "The rich have gotten richer and the poor have gotten poorer." The reality is that America has made the rich *and* poor richer together. This falsifies the predictions of Marxist ideologues.

But things have been even better than these numbers suggest. First of all, the CBO statistics only count income, and not consumption, a much better measure of well-being. Nor do they take into account non-salary compensations, such as employer-provided healthcare, stock options, or retirement plans. Someone could be living in a mansion, eating at the finest restaurants, wearing luxury clothing, and driving fancy cars, and yet still be considered "poor" according to these statistics. (This is the case with many seniors in our country who have high wealth, but low income.) These CBO numbers don't do full justice to the standard of living Americans enjoy.

They also don't account for the higher quality of goods available today that were not available in the past. For example, even most "poor college students" today carry devices in their pockets that act as movie players, cameras, film studios, music players, planners, telephones, video gaming systems, e-book readers, and more. When their parents were in college, all the money in the world could not have purchased such a device. Thirty years ago, nobody had internet access—an invaluable resource—but today, every person in America has it (at the very least through a local public library). There are life-extending medical services that weren't even available to the wealthiest people in the world in previous genera-

---

2 The American stock market is a nice measure of this growth. Anyone who has held diversified stocks for at least a couple of decades has found themselves much wealthier for having done so. Up until now, you haven't had to be lucky in the stock market to make money. Even if you would have invested all of your money on the eve of the Great Crash of 1929, you still would have come out on top just by holding on to your stocks into the 1940s. So the American economy has in the past been a steady, trustworthy economic investment that has provided incredible riches for its participants.

3 See http://www.cbo.gov/publication/43524. This is the official government data, un-interpreted or altered by those of the political left or right who try to make the economy look bad or good depending on whether or not "their side" is in office. Also see: http://www.cbo.gov/publication/42729.

tions, and the benefits of these qualitative improvements have redounded most to the poor.[4] That's why the richest people in the world from a century ago would have gladly changed places with many poor Americans today.

These statistics also do not account for *economic mobility*. That is, we talk about these groupings of people—poor, middle class, rich—as static entities when, in reality, their composition is constantly shifting. Most people move from one group to another during their lifetimes. Very few people who were poor in 1980 remained poor thirty years later because they had moved up into the middle and high income groups, while many of the richest had moved down (think of all of the millionaires who lost their shirts in the crash of 2008). So even if someone was *stuck* in the poor quintile, they were still better off a generation later, but chances are they *weren't* stuck there and moved into a higher bracket (perhaps even the highest). When we talk about "the poor" in 1980 and "the poor" in 2010, we are talking about almost completely different people. The government would classify college students as "poor" today, but most will be considered "middle class" or "rich" thirty years from now. Of those who were in the lowest income bracket in 1975, only 5% remained there 16 years later. Most of them had moved into the two highest income brackets.

In fact, because of immigration, many of today's poor did not even show up on the statistics of the previous generation at all. Most immigrants are impoverished and looking for economic opportunity in America so their presence inflates the numbers of the poorest class and drags down the income statistics. Now, these immigrants are economically much better off than they were before they came here, but the statistics don't indicate that and make it appear that "the poor" are doing only slightly better when, in fact, they are doing considerably better.

Speaking of immigration, nothing better falsifies the claim of America being bad for the poor than immigration itself. Millions of people have risked their lives crossing rivers, deserts, and oceans to *be poor in America*. If this country were so bad for the poor, then the indigent would be fleeing in droves. Instead, they are (often literally) dying to get in. Capitalist countries build walls to keep poor people out, while socialist countries build walls to keep them in.

As you can see, "the poor getting poorer" is not the real problem in America; the real problem is *growing inequality*. Yes, as the above shows, the poor have gotten consistently richer over the course of American history, but the rich have gotten rich *much faster*. This has created an enormous power imbalance that could threaten our democracy and freedom. Remember, the Book of Mormon and modern prophets have warned against stark class divisions and those have been growing since the early 1970s. Politicians will promise easy answers to this problem, but it is caused by numerous technological, political, moral, and

---

[4] The life expectancy of the poorest class, for instance, increased the most dramatically of any income group during the 20th century.

social ills that can't simply be solved by legislative fiat. This is yet another task that disciple-leaders of the future must confront.

## SOURCES OF AMERICAN WEALTH

Having examined America's economic power, we now return to the question we began with: What has made this nation so rich and driven its spectacular economic growth? There are three primary reasons, two of which are essential, one of which is supplemental.

The first essential is the free market. Nations that have free economies do well because they allow the free exchange that Adam Smith identified as the secret to wealth. The most important step a nation can take to improve the material well-being of its people is to liberalize the economy.

While most countries in the world have only moved towards a free market during the last few decades, the United States has been capitalistic almost from the beginning. Ironically, those who first settled this country—the Pilgrims and those at Jamestown—actually tried socialism at first. You've all heard that half the Pilgrims starved during the first winter, but this, according to their governor William Bradford, was due to their experiment in communal economics. Bradford noted that, with no incentives in place, few people worked and that led to food shortages and starvation.[5] Communist experiments cause famines, and this was also the case in our early colonial experience. Thanksgiving should be a day of thanks for the free market system that the Pilgrims finally implemented.

Starvation also befell the Jamestown colony for the same reason. They tried socialism in their first years and most of them perished. Fortunately, the U.S. learned its lesson about the folly of socialism early on, quickly switched to a market system, and never looked back.

While the early colonial settlers established economic freedom, the Founding Fathers led an effort to preserve it. Remember, the Founders' revolt against Great Britain was primarily to stop British infringements on their freedom of trade and property rights. No wonder that U.S. citizens have historically treasured these freedoms so highly. Free markets, with the strong private property rights and the incentives to produce and exchange that they entail, explain America's wealth more than anything else.

The second essential to economic growth is a favorable culture—those values, habits, and virtues that Weber identified. This includes the commercial traditions that the first wave of American settlers brought with them from England. The English were an entrepre-

---

5 Some, like Kate Zernike of the *New York Times*, have disputed the characterization of these colonies as "socialist" on the grounds that they were run by private corporations and were therefore examples of "free enterprise" rather than "socialism." See Zernike (2010, p. WK1). What Zernike fails to understand is that corporations can act as a government if they exercise coercive power. After all, nobody disputes that India was politically oppressed in the 19$^{th}$ century, despite being run by a "company" (East India Company) in the same sense that Plymouth or Virginia were. Companies could and did implement socialism so yes, Ms. Zernike, the Pilgrims were socialists.

neurial people, a "nation of shopkeepers," who believed in starting businesses and making money. Americans inherited this British legacy of commerce, just as they inherited the British legacy of freedom.

The "immigrant" ethic is also a part of this culture. Waves of immigration to the U.S. have replenished and reinforced the entrepreneurialism inherited from England. Immigrants to America are, by definition pro-active, "get-up-and-goers" willing to take risks for economic opportunity. These virtues lead to success in the free market system.

The culture of high religiosity in America (which we will discuss in a later chapter) is associated with the market virtues of industry, deferred gratification, and voluntary giving. Religion gives people a sense of free will and control over their own destiny—a "can do" spirit that leads them to work hard to rise in the world. Religious people are less likely to say, "I'm stuck being poor," and more likely to believe they can work their way up. This religious mentality is terrific for economic growth and is one reason that Americans work longer hours than the people of any other industrial nation. Maybe it's not the "Protestant Ethic" that drives the spirit of capitalism, but the "religious ethic" more generally.[6] Also note that America's economic success has declined in proportion to a decline in our religiosity. A virtuous culture is essential to economic growth, but we are losing it.

These two essentials not only determine economic growth, but are also symbiotic. That is, a decline in one leads to a decline in the other. As our country loses its cultural values of hard work, thrift, religiosity, and sense of individual responsibility, it then must rely more on government to restrain its excesses, distribute its wealth, and support its people. If we can't regulate ourselves, then the government will take on more regulatory functions. If we can't be charitable voluntarily, the government will redistribute money by force and taxation. All of this means a decline in economic liberty. When moral virtues decline, free market institutions decline as well.

A third but non-essential contributor to American economic growth is an abundance of natural resources. Many people mistakenly believe that the availability of resources is the primary explanation for America's wealth. It is not. Although resources are helpful for growth, there are many rich countries in the world with virtually no natural resources and many poor countries are filled with them. Singapore and Hong Kong are just rocks in the ocean; they have no metals, oil, or minerals, but are still extremely wealthy because they have the two freest economies in the world and a population that practices the virtues Weber identified.

Nonetheless, if the institutional and cultural framework is in place, resources are a bonus to an economy, and that has been true in the United States. America has a diverse climate which means that it can produce a wide variety of products for market exchange. If you ask someone from England, Sweden, Italy, Korea, or most other nations, "what is your

---

6 Barro and McCleary (2003).

climate like?" they can give you a concise answer (e.g., temperate, Mediterranean, tropical, desert), but in America the answer is "all of the above." We have Mediterranean climate in California, tropical climate in Florida and Hawaii, arid deserts in the Southwest, lush prairies in the Midwest, rain forest in the Pacific Northwest, and so on. This means that we can grow almonds, grapes, avocados, timber, wheat, sugar, rice, pineapples, oranges, and a huge variety of other agricultural products within our own borders. Beyond the agriculture we reap above the ground, we also extract oil, copper, iron, silver, gold, natural gas, and minerals from underneath.

Another resource is America's favorable geography. The numerous harbors—the San Francisco Bay, Galveston Bay, Puget Sound, the Mississippi delta, the New York Harbor—are perfect for maritime shipping and expanding wealth-creating trade opportunities. America sits between both the Pacific and Atlantic worlds and enjoys commerce with both. Something just as valuable, especially before the advent of automobiles and trains, are the rivers. The arteries of the Mississippi stretch out to cover almost 2/3 of the U.S., allowing easy trade between the people of most of the country. Favorable resources, including geography, have certainly supplemented America's growth.

## IN THE WORLD

Now that we've explored the nature and causes of America's wealth, let's finish by turning to what this all means for America's place in the world.

Free exchange with the world has made America rich, but has also enmeshed us in more networks of world trade than anyone else in history. We rely on people in Turkey for our clothing, people in China for our toys, people in Japan for our computer games, people in Germany for our cars, and people in Saudi Arabia for our gasoline.

This trade is a double-edged sword when it comes to questions of international conflict. A few years back, Thomas Friedman of the *New York Times* put forward the "Golden Arches Theory of Peace." He noted that countries with McDonald's fast food restaurants within their borders have never gone to war with each other. Friedman didn't propose that we go around the world installing McDonald's restaurants where there are potential enemies, but instead suggested that the trade a McDonald's represents has a pacifying effect. If a nation is sufficiently integrated into the world economy to have a McDonald's, then it is against that nation's interest to go to war with trading partners. For instance, military conflict between China and the U.S. currently makes no sense given our economic interdependence. Why would we try to destroy a nation making us rich? Trade softens hostility and diminishes the national greatness rivalries that have been responsible for so much bloodshed in history.[7]

---

[7] Some have recently questioned this theory, noting that there was substantial trade between opponents in World War I. See Nye (2011).

## Chapter 13

But trade has a darker side too. If we don't go to war with nations we *do trade* with, we are more likely to go to war with those nations that we *do not* trade with. Not only do trade-excluded nations feel aggrieved and belligerent (America's refusal to trade with Japan led straight to Pearl Harbor), but there's also the problem that the enemies of our trading partners become *our* enemies as well. America's entry into World War I, for example, came about because extensive U.S. trade with England upset their German enemies. By trading with and enriching Germany's foe, America became a *de facto* foe as well. Paradoxically, trade creates both peace and war, depending on the context.

Finally, American wealth occasions both admiration and resentment from other countries. Naturally, the nations of the world want to emulate American success. They see the prosperity, openness, and technology of the U.S. and want the same, so they copy the American model.

Yet even as they copy America's success, they still resent it. Some of this resentment probably stems from simple envy, but much of it also comes from American arrogance. The U.S. government has often thrown around its military power recklessly and without the consideration of other nations—the "decent respect for the opinions of mankind" mentioned in the Declaration of Independence. (See the discussion of declining soft power in chapter 24.)

So American power is double-edged: it gives the world a positive model of freedom, democracy, and markets to strive towards, but, like any other form of power, it can lead to arrogance and abuse. Power corrupts, and that can be true of power on the national as well as personal level. We must hope that the U.S. can avoid the jingoistic, nationalistic pride that has led to the decline of previous powerful nations.

In a sense, though, that unfortunate process of decline may have already begun. As we saw above, virtues are necessary for the capitalist system to work and America is abandoning them. Without the habits of deferred gratification, charity, and honesty, America is losing the pre-eminence that it enjoyed throughout the 20$^{th}$ century.

## CONCLUSION

This chapter leaves you with this question: can America get its Weberian moral virtues back and revive the strength of its market system and the prosperity that comes with it? And if so, can the nation possess this greatness without the arrogance that comes with such power? This is a major national challenge, but one that falls upon the disciple-leaders of the 21$^{st}$ century, to meet.

## CHAPTER 13 SOURCES/FURTHER READING

Barro, Robert J. and Rachel M. McCleary. "Religion and Economic Growth," NBER Working Paper No. 9682, issued in May 2003. <http://www.nber.org/papers/w9682>.

Bell, Daniel. *The Cultural Contradictions of Capitalism*. New York: Basic Books, 1976.

Burtless, Gary and Ron Haskins. "Inequality, Economic Mobility, and Social Policy." In Peter H. Schuck and James Q. Wilson, eds., *Understanding America: The Anatomy of an Exceptional Nation*. New York: Public Affairs, 2008.

Diggins, John P. *Max Weber: Politics and the Spirit of Tragedy*. New York: Basic Books, 1996.

DiLorenzo, Thomas. *How Capitalism Saved America: The Untold History of Our Country, From the Pilgrims to the Present*. New York: Crown Forum, 2004.

Federal Reserve Bank of Dallas. "By Our Own Bootstraps: Economic Opportunity & the Dynamics of Income Distribution," Annual Report 1995. <http://www.dallasfed.org/assets/documents/fed/annual/1999/ar95.pdf>

Ferguson, Niall. *The Great Degeneration: How Institutions Decay and Economies Die*. New York: Penguin, 2013.

Franklin, Benjamin. *The Autobiography and Other Writings*. Selected and edited with an introduction by L. Jesse Lemisch. New York: Penguin, 1961.

Friedman, Benjamin M. "The Economic System." In Peter H. Schuck and James Q. Wilson, eds., *Understanding America: The Anatomy of an Exceptional Nation*. New York: Public Affairs, 2008.

Friedman, Thomas L. *The Lexus and the Olive Tree: Understanding Globalization*. New York: Anchor Books, 1999.

Friedman, Thomas L. and Michael Mandelbaum. *That Used to Be Us: How America Fell Behind in the World it Invented and How We Can Come Back*. New York: Farrar, Straus, and Giroux, 2011.

Fukuyama, Francis. *The Great Disruption: Human Nature and the Reconstitution of Social Order*. New York: Free Press, 1999.

_____. *Political Order and Political Decay: From the Industrial Revolution to the Globalization of Democracy*. New York: Farrar, Straus, and Giroux, 2014.

_____. *Trust: The Social Virtues and the Creation of Prosperity*. New York: The Free Press, 1995.

Gordon, John Steele. *An Empire of Wealth: The Epic History of American Economic Power*. New York: Harper Perennial, 2005.

Mandelbaum, Michael. *The Ideas that Conquered the World: Peace, Democracy, and Free Markets in the Twenty-first Century*. New York: Public Affairs, 2002.

Putnam, Robert. *Bowling Alone: The Collapse and Revival of American Community*. New York: Simon & Schuster, 2001.

Rogoff, Kenneth S. and Carmen M. Reinhart. *This Time is Different: Eight Centuries of Financial Folly*. Princeton: Princeton University Press, 2009.

Weber, Max. *The Protestant Ethic & The Spirit of Capitalism: The Relationship Between Religion and the Economic and Social Life in Modern Culture*. New York: Scribner's, 1956.

## Chapter 13

Zeihan, Peter. *The Accidental Superpower: The Next Generation of American Preeminence and the Coming Global Disorder*. New York: Twelve, 2014.

Zernike, Kate. "The Pilgrims Were ... Socialists?" *New York Times*, November 20, 2010.

# Chapter 14

# ECONOMIC CHALLENGES II: VARIETIES OF POLITICAL ECONOMY

## ARTHUR SCHLESINGER: THE VITAL CENTRIST

What are the alternatives to the capitalist economy? What are some of the problems that persist in the free market? What, if anything, can governments do to correct these weaknesses?

This chapter will address these questions with some assistance from Arthur M. Schlesinger, Jr., the great American historian. Schlesinger's father was a history professor at Harvard so it was only natural that young Arthur would follow in his footsteps. From the time he was a child, Arthur was reading and pondering the works of great historians such as Edward Gibbon, Thomas Carlyle, and Charles and Mary Beard. In college, Schlesinger started writing histories of his own and, by age 26, he had won the Pulitzer Prize for his book *The Age of Jackson*. Shortly thereafter, like his father, he was given a professorship at Harvard.

But Schlesinger wasn't only interested in the past; he was also interested in changing the future. He wanted to influence the world through liberal activism. In the 1940s and 50s, he published articles and books championing the Democratic Party and wrote speeches for politicians, such as two-time Presidential candidate, Adlai Stevenson. Eventually, Schlesinger reached a pinnacle of influence as an intellectual advisor to President John F. Kennedy himself.

Like his friend Reinhold Niebuhr, Schlesinger was faced with the dilemma of explaining the tragedy, tyranny, and violence of his time. He wrote a book, *The Vital Center*, diagnosing why the 20$^{th}$ century had been the most violent in history. Schlesinger argued that political problems come primarily from a single source: *extremism*. The terrors of the early 20$^{th}$ century came from extreme right-wing tyrants, like Hitler, or extreme left-wing tyrants, like Stalin. To combat this extremism, said Schlesinger, humans should seek moderation in a position at the liberal middle between the two extremes—"The Vital Center."

Essentially, Schlesinger was arguing for a "Goldilocks" approach to politics. Remember that Goldilocks found Papa Bear's porridge too hot and Mama Bear's porridge too cold, but found Baby Bear's porridge "just right"—neither too hot nor cold. To Goldilocks, both temperature extremes were bad; the best porridge was right in the middle.

To Schlesinger, politics worked the same way. Tyrannical systems of government were like those extreme bowls of porridge. On the extreme left you had communism (e.g., the USSR); on the extreme right you had fascism (e.g., the Nazis); but right in the middle between those extremes you had the vital center: liberalism. Like the baby bear's porridge, liberalism was "just right."

Now, there are some big problems with Schlesinger's theory. First, it was based on bad history. Schlesinger failed to account for the fact that *both* the Soviets and Nazis were socialists (as all totalitarians must be)—they wanted complete control of economic life as a means to control all of society. The U.S.S.R. is short for "Union of Soviet Socialist Republics" and "Nazi" is short for "National Socialist." Halfway between one tyrannical socialism and another is still socialism. There is no place for economic liberty on Schlesinger's spectrum.

Second, the idea that liberalism sits right in the middle, far away from two extremes is self-serving. Nearly everyone, regardless of their political persuasion, believes that they are moderates while their enemies are dangerous "extremists." Conservatives claim this as well as liberals. Who is to say that Schlesinger's liberalism occupied the middle ground and not the conservatism of, say, Eisenhower?

Finally, Schlesinger's theory is based on a mistaken ethical model. Long ago, Aristotle proposed in his work *The Nicomachean Ethics* that all virtues are the middle ground between two extreme vices. Courage, for instance, is the middle ground between cowardice and foolhardiness. This Aristotelian view has a particular appeal to Latter-day Saints who always quote a scripture that admonishes us to seek "moderation in all things."

Unfortunately, this ethical theory is flawed. The "moderation in all things" scripture does not exist, nor would there be such a commandment since there are realms of life where moderation would be highly undesirable.[1] We may want to be moderate in the amount we eat, but the Lord would never ask us to be moderate in our honesty, charity, or covenant-keeping. Clearly the "moderation" argument doesn't always work in ethics or religion, but the question here is: "does it work when applied to economics?"

---

[1] We do find Alma and Paul exhorting us to be "temperate in all things" (Alma 38:10), but this suggests restraint and self-control, not moderation. The word "moderation" is primarily used in the scriptures to render the Greek word for "gentleness" (e.g., Phil 4:5).

# TWO SYSTEMS

To answer this question, we first need to consider what social scientists call the "Politico-Economic Problem"—how to find the economic system that helps a society *best* meet its goals. Note, that we do not search for which economic system is perfect—none is—only for which is the best of many imperfect options.

There have been many modes of economic organization over the course of history (feudal, clan-based, slave-plantation, etc.), but for nations today, there are basically two options: the free market economy and the command economy. Let's take a closer look at each.

## Free Market

The free market economy (sometimes called the "free enterprise" or "capitalist" economy) is based on the principle of liberty. It is defined by private control of property and the non-coercive use of resources. Most importantly, the system operates on the principle of agency. The people of a free market economy choose for themselves how they will buy, sell, invest, and exchange goods and services with one another. Under the market economy, you are free to earn money and donate it to a charity, or buy costly apparel and accumulate possessions. The system means that decision-making happens from the bottom up rather than from the top down, which empowers common people rather than political elites. Most pertinent to our discussion here is that the free market system is *remarkably efficient*.

Before proceeding further, we must dispel a couple of myths. The first is the myth that a free market economy means less government. Many people on both the political left and the right would have you believe that capitalism simply means "getting the government out of the way." That is just not true. A free market economy needs a strong, well-working government in order to function. We learned in the first part of this book that anarchy is not liberty—we would not engage in productive activity if we knew that thieves would just take away the fruits of our labor (that would constitute a "chaos economy," not a free market economy). Without the Rule of Law, there can be no property rights or free exchange and, consequently, little productive economic activity at all.

The myth that "capitalism equals less government" led to some unfortunate economic consequences in the late 20$^{th}$ century. Many economists in the early 1990s believed that since the Soviet Union had collapsed and the government was "out of the way" in Eastern Europe, the free market would flourish. That didn't happen. Communist tyranny simply gave way to oligarchic anarchy. With the bad government gone, kleptocrats moved in to fill the void. This anarchy was as bad for growth as the tyranny it replaced.

The problem of anarchy also explains the poverty of many African nations. Many of them don't have a tyrannical government, but essentially no government at all. This lack of government means that the economy cannot grow. The Rule of Law and a strong government are preconditions of a market economy, not its enemy.

The second myth is that corporate scandals and government-business corruption are features of capitalism. For instance, many historians believe that the Crédit Mobilier railroad bribes during the 1870s, the Teapot Dome scandals of the 1920s, and, most recently, the Enron scandals of the early 2000s happened because of the defects of capitalism. But capitalism, properly understood, means economic freedom under the Rule of Law; these scandals represent the opposite. The Rule of Law protects natural rights, while government corruption and corporate malfeasance (theft, misrepresentation, and fraud) take them away.[2] Under such situations government officials do not leave the market "free," but control and manipulate it for personal gain. Such anti-freedom actions cannot honestly be called "free market" in any sense. Under a free market system, a government would *stop* such illegal abuses through appropriate regulation rather than joining in on them.[3]

**Command Economy**

Let's now consider the alternative to the free market. The command economy (often called "planned" or "socialist") is based on force rather than freedom. The government controls and dictates the use of all property in society and tells people how they must buy, sell, invest, and produce. People are not free to form true communities because the government forces a false "collectivism" upon them. Since there are no property rights, command economies always lack basic freedoms and civil liberties (as in the Soviet Union, Nazi Germany, North Korea, and Cambodia).[4] In a sense, there are only two ways to do things: free or forced. The command economy is based on force.

But coercion is not the only problem. The command economy is also terribly inefficient compared to capitalism. There is a strong, scientifically established correlation between liberty under the Rule of Law and economic prosperity. We talked about Adam Smith's "invisible hand," but it's really not that invisible. Like all theories, we can test Adam Smith's insight to see if it works in practice and see that it passes with flying colors. The wealth of a society rises commensurate with its degree of economic freedom, just as Adam Smith's theory would predict.

# CHINA

We can see the freedom-wealth connection very clearly through several illustrations. Perhaps the most notable example of the past few decades is China. In 1949, the Communists came to power, implemented socialism, and drove the economy into the ground.

---

2 Filmmaker Michael Moore's entire 2009 movie *Capitalism: A Love Story* is based on this misunderstanding.
3 Analogously, we wouldn't condemn the game of baseball itself because some baseball players break the rules. That people cheat under capitalism says nothing about the validity of the capitalist system.
4 Including, of course, religious freedom. Command economies have always tightly controlled thinking and forbidden religions that would compete with the state religion of socialism.

Within ten years, the Chinese were starving by the tens of millions. The Chinese Communist Party continued this command-and-control course for three decades while its people languished in poverty and hardship.[5]

Eventually the people and even the Communist leadership became fed up with the poverty and failure of command economy policies, so in 1978 they began to implement some reforms. Deng Xiaoping, the leader of the Communist Party, allowed a few families to have tiny private-property gardens alongside the government farms. Almost immediately, those little gardens became the most productive agricultural lands in all of China. Seeing this success, Deng decided to extend the opportunity of private ownership elsewhere. He established a number of Special Economic Zones (SEZ's) in coastal cities where he allowed the people to establish private, profit-earning businesses that could trade freely with others both in and out of the country.

The results of Deng's reforms were nothing less than spectacular. Almost overnight, China's economy began to boom beyond anything the world had ever seen. Building on this success, Deng implemented further reforms, expanded the number of SEZ's, and extended property rights. Soon the economy was growing at over 10% per year. Impoverished farm workers moved in droves to the cities (the largest migration in world history) and China began to wake from its economic slumbers.

This program of economic liberalization and reform was, quite simply, the most effective anti-poverty program in the history of the world. Hundreds of millions of Chinese moved from subsistence levels of income to middle class prosperity. Free market reform in China has done more good for the poor than any other humanitarian effort, government program, not-for-profit, or international aid organization over the same period.

China's economy is now the second largest in the world. Failure to implement further reforms over the last decade has led to some recent slowdown, but if the Chinese leadership would increase its commitment to free markets, they would likely overtake the U.S. as the greatest economic power in the world.

## INDIA

The story of India's reform is similar to China's, if not quite as striking. After winning independence from their English overlords in 1947, the Indians decided to throw out everything British, including capitalism. They decided instead to pursue a Soviet Union-style planned economy under their Prime Minister, Jawaharlal Nehru. Predictably, their economy sputtered and their growing population remained mired in poverty and misery. After Nehru's death, his daughter Indira Gandhi doubled down on those failed socialist pol-

---

5   The Communist Party even brainwashed many of the impoverished children in China to think that they had it far better than the "starving children" in capitalist countries. See Chang (1991).

# Chapter 14

icies and it looked as if India was destined for perennial slow growth and stagnation. Many analysts started talking about a "Hindu rate of growth" (trying to blame Indian poverty on its culture).

But then Indira's son Rajiv Gandhi took over as Prime Minister in the 1980s and decided to embark on some cautious economic liberalizations. He removed some of the excessive red tape (often called the "license raj") and allowed greater freedom of trade, investment, and entrepreneurship. The economy began to grow far faster than it had in the previous decades. Then in 1991 a new finance minister, economist Manmohan Singh, launched another round of reforms and the economy grew even more impressively. Mr. Singh later became Prime Minister of India and further expanded the market reforms. The country began to grow almost as fast as China. In spite of their progress towards greater economic liberty, India, like China, has a long way to go to establish a solid free market system. Since they live in a democracy, the people of India control their own economic fate.

## CONTROLLED EXPERIMENTS

The case for the market economy is even stronger when we look at the "controlled experiments" that history has provided. For example, North and South Korea are virtually identical in all variables—ethnicity, resources, traditions, geography, religion, etc. The only difference is their politico-economic systems. South Korea, with its free market economy, is advanced, industrial, free, democratic, and one of wealthier countries in world. North Korea, on the other hand, with its command economy, may be the poorest and most repressed place on earth. The free market system has made that much difference.

There are other notable "experiments" where two similar countries differ widely in wealth because of economic systems: Thailand vs. Burma, West vs. East Germany (pre-1989), Taiwan vs. Mainland China. In each case, the country with the more market-oriented economy has far outperformed its "twin." This is ironic since command economies are almost always implemented in the name of "social justice" and yet, as you can see, there is nothing *less just* than depriving people of freedom and leaving them in poverty, which is what command economies inevitably do.

We have talked before about why free market economies are so efficient, but the ideas are well summed up by historians Ariel and Will Durant, who, after spending decades writing a massive 11-volume history of the world, related the lessons they had learned. One of these lessons was that market economies work because,

> In free enterprise the spur of competition and the zeal and zest of ownership arouse the productiveness and inventiveness of men; nearly every economic ability sooner or later finds its niche and reward in the shuffle of talents and the natural selection of skills; and a basic democracy rules the process insofar as most of the articles to be produced,

and the services to be rendered, are determined by public demand rather than by governmental decree.[6]

The Durants had both begun their careers as socialist supporters of a planned economy, but their study of history convinced them of their error. Humans, they discovered, do what they are rewarded for doing and free markets reward work, innovation, and efficiency.

## MARKET WEAKNESSES

Even though all of the above should be sufficient to convince us, beyond doubt, that the free market economy is superior to a planned economy, the fact remains that economic problems remain under capitalism. The market still has weaknesses. Let's look at the seven primary market weaknesses and what, if anything, governments should do to correct them.

The first market weakness is the problem of *imperfect information*. Remember, the miracle of exchange means that both sides of a transaction win, but this assumes that both parties know what they are getting in an exchange. That is not always a safe assumption. If you dine at Taco Bell, you are usually better off because you get lunch while Taco Bell is better off because they get your money. Both sides win. But what if Taco Bell undercooked the meat and you stayed up all night sick with a stomach bug? Clearly, you were not better off for the exchange and never would have purchased the taco had you known about the sickness it would cause.

In an ideal world, all free market transactions would be win-win, but in reality transactions are often win-lose or even lose-lose because one or both parties don't know exactly what they are getting. As little kids we often got "gypped" when trading comic books or baseball cards, but the truth is that we still, as adults, often get gypped and have what economists call "buyer's remorse." My neighbor once signed up for a two-year TV contract with a satellite company only to find out after installation that it lacked basic network channels. Had he known about this, he never would have signed up. He was a victim of imperfect information and wound up worse off rather than better off after the free transaction.

The second market weakness is *monopoly*. As we saw in previous chapters, one reason for market efficiency is the competition between firms in an industry. As these firms attempt to win customers and capture market share, they drive prices down and quality up. But what if there is no competition? What if one firm buys out all competitors or all of the firms collude?

Now, it's important to note that monopolies are rare in a free market because new entrants or foreign competitors can break them down. Imagine that all the gas stations in Idaho conspired to raise their fuel prices by five dollars. It would only take one defector or enterprising person to start their own gas station and force the other gas stations back into

---

6  Durant and Durant (1968, pp. 58-59).

## Chapter 14

offering competitive prices. If one American car company created a monopoly and raised prices, we would simply buy Japanese or German cars instead. But what if these natural means don't work? We are again stuck with a market weakness.

The third weakness is the problem of *externalities.* Sometimes, a particular transaction affects more than the parties involved (in both good and bad ways). For instance, if I hire a plumber to install a drinking fountain in my house, it's nobody's business but my own and the plumber's—the miracle of exchange makes us both better off. I have my drinking fountain and the plumber has his money. But what if instead of a plumber I hired a band to play an insanely loud all-night house party for me? Then it's the whole neighborhood's problem. I enjoy the music, the band enjoys their money, but the rest of the neighborhood is kept awake by the noise. The transaction between me and the rock band, in other words, creates a public cost problem. People who had nothing to do with our deal nonetheless must "pay" for it.

When people are hurt by a transaction they were not involved in, we call this a "negative externality." A notable example is pollution. Those of us not buying steel must still suffer from the polluted air, impure water, and climate change caused as by-products of steel production.

There are also "positive externalities" in which those not involved in a transaction nonetheless *benefit* from it. For instance, if I hire a landscaper to design and cultivate a beautiful rose garden in my front yard, all of my neighbors get to enjoy the sights and smells without paying for the privilege. You might think that if negative externalities are bad, then positive externalities must be good, but this is not true because it creates the "free rider problem." We have all experienced this. Think of when you have had to do group work in school—some members of the group did very little work because they still received the same grade as everyone else in the group regardless of their contributions. Imagine you live in a four-person apartment and you decide to sign up for a cable TV package that costs $20 a month. This should cost $5 a piece, but one of your roommates says she doesn't want cable and won't pay. The remaining three of you split the bill and pay almost $7 a piece, but your fourth roommate *still gets to watch* without paying. This positive externality is essentially a theft of $2 from the other roommates. Positive externalities create a situation in which some have no incentive to pay for something from which they benefit anyway.

We see this in the public realm all the time. If a man hires a construction company to pave a country road to his house, his neighbors benefit from the road as well, even though they didn't pay for it. You can see how government can step in to fix this problem by providing public goods.[7]

---

[7] This may be the whole rationale for governments to exist. Essential services such as defense and law enforcement cannot be provided privately because of the free rider problem. We require a body with a monopoly on coercive powers (government) to force us through taxation to pay for those essential public goods.

The fourth market weakness is *poverty*. Despite all of the opportunities and wealth a market economy provides, some get left behind. At any given moment, 10% to 15% of Americans live below a basic standard of living. They often lack decent health care, nutritious food, and adequate housing or education. Given how productive capitalism is, it is shameful that many struggle in the midst of plenty.

Fifth, are the instabilities created under the free market. Capitalism, as the economist Joseph Schumpeter pointed out, operates on the principle of "creative destruction"—it constantly pushes towards greater efficiency, creativity, and innovation. That means it always drives out inefficient businesses, old modes of operation, and obsolete technologies. The result is business failure and the loss of jobs.[8] Construction crews bulldoze steel factories in order to erect dot.com high-rise buildings—destroying the old steel worker jobs, and creating new higher-skilled technology jobs. Mom and pop stores lose out to Walmart. Capitalism thrives on the law of the jungle—the fittest firms and jobs survive and grow while the less fit firms and jobs are weeded out.

Of course, this efficiency means that the economy as a whole wins, but particular people lose (in the short term) as their businesses and or jobs give way to more efficient ones. All of this change and creative destruction creates instability, apprehension, and frictional unemployment.

The sixth major market weakness is the problem of inequality. Capitalism rewards effort, smarts, luck, virtue, and skill, but some people have more of these than other people. This creates wildly varying levels of income and wealth. As we saw in the last chapter, free economies generally see a large and growing gap between the richest and poorest, further fueled by the migration of the poor to free market countries.

Seventh, and finally, the market economy is plagued by the weakness of the business cycle. Capitalist economies generally grow, but also experience periodic downturns. During these "recessions" and "depressions" the economy shrinks. The business cycle exacerbates and magnifies many of the other market weaknesses, and virtually everyone, from the CEO to the welfare recipient, suffers. As we shall see, this may be the most serious market weakness of all and may require the most significant government correction.

## SOLUTIONS

So what can we do about all of these problems? Above all, we must remember that all economic systems have them; in fact, most of these problems are far worse under a planned economy. Markets are imperfect because people are imperfect, not because of a "system." Capitalism, with all of its faults, is still the least bad among the available options.

---

8  Many claim that "conservatives" favor capitalism, but capitalism is one of the two most revolutionary forces humans have ever devised—it is hardly "conservative" in any dictionary sense.

But even so, isn't there something we can do to correct these market weaknesses within the framework of capitalism? Can't we seek some kind of "economic middle ground" (analogous to Schlesinger's "Vital Center") in which we retain the freedom and efficiency of the market economy while alleviating some of its weaknesses via appropriate government action?

This question is the source of the most enduring debates among economists. It also creates room for debate among good members of the Church. D&C 134 and the statements of modern prophets make it clear that we believe in private property and the market system, but beyond that, the Lord doesn't give us specifics—he expects us to use our minds and good judgment. This means that good people will often come to different conclusions. Let's look at some of the government solutions to these market weaknesses that economists have proposed.

## INTERNAL CONTROLS

First, a government can exercise internal controls over an economy through inspections, rules, regulations, and licensing requirements. In theory, this can solve the first three market weaknesses. Government can break up monopolies, limit and assign the costs of negative externalities, and provide information to perfect our transactions.

For example, the government can require physicians to have licenses such that we have more perfect information regarding medical transactions. The Food and Drug Administration can inspect products for contamination and make sure your Taco Bell food is sufficiently cooked. Government regulators can require banks to have minimum reserves to prevent bank failure and loss of depositors' money. Through gas taxes the government can limit pollution and force those who cause the pollution to pay for it at the pump. This both creates a disincentive to drive and connects the polluters to the costs of cleanup.

This doesn't mean that such regulations are without problems. Skeptics claim that government regulators can turn into bullies and create bureaucratic red tape that stifles economic creativity, prevents the cost savings of economies of scale, and gives an advantage to those larger businesses that can "capture" the regulators. Furthermore, they say that monopolies are more likely to be *caused* than prevented by governments, and businesses have private incentives to give better information since customers would refuse to buy defective products. Would you ever go back to Taco Bell after getting food poisoning there? Neither would anyone else and Taco Bell would soon be out of business—regulated not by government, but by the discipline of the market.

## PROVIDE BASIC WELFARE

Next, many believe that governments can help solve market weaknesses four to six by providing basic welfare to the less fortunate. The government can skim off some of the resources from the highly efficient, wealth-generating private economy and distribute food, shelter, education, and healthcare to those in need. This can reduce poverty, decrease inequality, and minimize the pain of disruptions. Many also argue that government welfare spending can be seen as an "investment" that helps the poor become productive economic contributors. Basic welfare can also stabilize capitalism since the poor are less likely to revolt if they feel they are well taken care of. Proponents of government welfare say that when the poor are desperate, hungry, and have nothing to lose, they are more likely to rise up against the system.

Critics of the welfare state counter that we can have non-government social safety nets that are non-coercive and more efficient than government ones. Compare, for instance, the LDS church welfare program—which gives a hand up instead of a hand out—to the government programs which, some say, create a cycle of idleness, dependency, and waste. Is it possible that many programs intended to lift people out of poverty actually incentivize them to remain there?

Many also disagree about the form this distribution should take. For example, would it be better to provide education through vouchers or through a government-run school system?

Economists also note that excessive redistribution can hurt the economy by punishing the productive work that causes economic growth. Redistributing the economic pie through heavy taxation may cause the pie itself to shrink, thus making everyone worse off (kind of like killing the goose that lays golden eggs).[9] At what point does confiscation of resources from the wealthy undercut the core incentives of the market system and cause the most productive members of society to reduce their efforts and slow society's economic engines?

There is also the problem of intentions and outcomes. A billion dollars of government anti-poverty spending does not necessarily translate into a billion dollars of real help. The money may go to bureaucrats, fraud, misallocation, and abuse rather than to the truly needy. We should be more concerned about the actual outcomes of these redistributive schemes than intentions. Do we care more about the poor or making ourselves feel "compassionate"?

---

9 This was the famous argument of economist Arthur Laffer. He claimed that you could actually increase government revenues by lowering marginal tax rates if the current rate is higher than that at the revenue-maximizing point.

*Chapter 14*

## EXTERNAL CONTROLS

The final way that some have proposed to remedy market weakness is through *external controls*, i.e., limiting trade with those in other countries. There are people in the United States who might want to buy a car from a manufacturer in Japan or wheat from a farmer in Africa if they feel the products are a better deal, but the government can forbid or penalize such transactions (through embargoes or tariffs) and thereby encourage us to buy from domestic producers.

This is a bad idea. Virtually every economist in the world—left, right, or center—agrees with Adam Smith that international trade is a great engine of growth and when governments limit that trade, the people of both nations suffer. When a government forbids an exchange it prevents both parties from reaping the win-win benefits of that exchange. This proposed "cure" is worse than the weakness itself.

## CONCLUSION

You will notice that in the above discussion of market weaknesses and remedies, we have covered plausible government interventions to correct the first six market weaknesses, but what about the seventh—business cycle and recession? We have saved this one for last because it is the most vexing of all. Economic downturn is such a jarring and problematic issue for capitalism that economists have spent the past century arguing about the proper way to correct it.[10] We will spend the next two chapters considering the two major theories they have proposed.

## CHAPTER 14 SOURCES/FURTHER READING

Acemoglu, Daron and James A. Robinson. *Why Nations Fail: The Origins of Power, Prosperity, and Poverty*. New York: Crown Business, 2012.

Applebaum, Anne. *Gulag: A History*. New York: Doubleday, 2003.

Aristotle. *The Nicomachean Ethics*. Translated by Robert C. Bartlett and Susan D. Collins. Chicago: University of Chicago Press, 2012.

Durant, Will and Ariel Durant. *The Lessons of History*. New York: Simon & Schuster, 1968.

Murray, Charles. *Losing Ground: American Social Policy, 1950-1980*. New York: Basic Books, 1984.

\_\_\_\_\_. "The New American Divide," *Wall Street Journal*, January 21, 2012. <http://online.wsj.com/news/articles/SB10001424052970204301404577170733817181646>.

\_\_\_\_\_. *Coming Apart: The State of White America, 1960-2010*. New York: Crown Forum, 2013.

---

10 Note that the "Austrian School" of economic thought doubts the wisdom of any government interventions at all to combat economic downturn, claiming that all such interventions merely set up the economy for greater failure later.

Pipes, Richard. *Communism: A History*. New York: Modern Library, 2000.

Schlesinger, Arthur M., Jr. *A Life in the 20th Century: Innocent Beginnings*. Boston: Houghton Mifflin, 2000.

———. *Journals: 1952-2000*. New York: Penguin, 2007.

———. *The Vital Center: The Politics of Freedom*. New Brunswick, NJ: Transaction, 1998.

Stigler, George J. *Memoirs of an Unregulated Economist*. New York: Basic Books, 1988.

Sunstein, Cass and Richard Thaler. *Nudge: Improving Decisions About Health, Wealth, and Happiness*. New York: Penguin, 2009.

# Chapter 15

# DEPRESSION AND SOLUTIONS I: KEYNESIANISM

## JOHN MAYNARD KEYNES: GENERAL THEORIST

Now that we've examined market weaknesses and proposed remedies, let's take a closer look at the market weakness that looms larger than all others—the business cycle. Growth under capitalism is not consistent—there are many steps forward but also a few steps back. Those backward steps, "recessions" (or, if they are severe enough, "depressions"), mean the economy shrinks, GDP declines, and human misery increases. Because recession is such a serious problem, economists have dedicated much of their time and energy seeking a solution to it. We will spend the next two chapters looking at the two most widely accepted theories they have come up with.

The first and most well-known theory is called *Keynesianism*. To fully understand Keynesianism in America, we need to know a little bit about John Maynard Keynes himself, the economist who developed this powerful model, and also the Great Depression, the moment in U.S. history when it seemed to display the most explanatory power.

Keynes was a brilliant, educated, wealthy Englishman. His father worked as a banker and his mother was a politician. After graduating from Cambridge University, Keynes went to work in the English Civil Service then the British Treasury, and finally returned to Cambridge as a professor. At Cambridge, Keynes not only asked economic questions, but also turned his keen eye to the question of World War I. He wrote a prescient book that anticipated the consequences of the harsh terms imposed on Germany in 1919. His predictive abilities also brought financial rewards: he made millions investing in the stock market by foreseeing its ups and downs and buying and selling accordingly.

In the years between the wars, Keynes developed the most influential economic theory of the 20th century. He published it in his magnum opus, *The General Theory of Employment, Interest, & Money* and gained the reputation as the greatest economist since Adam Smith. The *General Theory* is a difficult work to read, but its basics are understandable if we look at the real world example it best applies to: The Great Depression.

## THE GREAT DEPRESSION

The 1920s was one of the great boom decades in American history. Americans enjoyed unprecedented riches which were manifest in the materialistic excesses of the age. Warren G. Harding and Calvin Coolidge, though despised today, were beloved in their time as Presidents who oversaw a new era of American mass affluence.

But the party came to a dramatic end in October 1929 when the stock market crashed and sent the American economy into a tailspin. Banks began collapsing by the hundreds, businesses began failing by the thousands, and Americans lost their jobs by the millions. The economy had become so complex that it seemed a mystery as to why this had happened and what, if anything, could be done about it.

America has had economic downturns before and since 1929, but the Great Depression was unique in both its duration and intensity. Unemployment rose to 25%—that meant that ¼ of Americans looking for work could not find it. Today we consider it scandalous if unemployment rises above 6%, but this was over four times worse. Not only were people out of work, they also lost huge amounts of personal wealth: if they had put their money in the stock market, it was mostly wiped out in the crash. If they had put it in the bank, it was mostly wiped out by bank failure. America's GDP declined by 27%, erasing a whole decade of growth.

Unemployment was a by-product of business sluggishness. Few had money to purchase business products. This in turn meant that businesses cut back on their work force who then, in turn, had less money with which to patronize other businesses and so on. A vicious cycle sent more and more businesses into decline.

Farmers were hit particularly hard as they had no cash to pay off their debts. Agriculture is a high-leverage undertaking, meaning farmers must borrow heavily to buy land and equipment and then rely on a good harvest and high prices to pay off their loans. But when farm prices plunged and drought hit the Midwest, farmers had their land seized by the banks that had loaned them money.

Urban Americans suffered as well. They were thrown out of work and into the streets. Men left their families for years at a time, wandering, riding railcars, and hitchhiking looking for anyone who could give them a job. Hungry Americans waited in long lines at city soup kitchens. Worst of all, there was no end in sight. The misery was still in full force a decade later. The country's economic nightmare seemed interminable.

## Herbert Hoover

Where was the government in all of this? What was it doing about the Great Depression? The answer is: more than it had ever done before. The Depression began under the watch of President Herbert Hoover, a remarkable man with a fascinating life story. Hoover had followed the American dream pattern of rags-to-riches. He was born into poverty in Iowa, orphaned at a young age, and then shuffled off to relatives on a farm in Oregon where he learned hard work and thrift. He also excelled academically and received a scholarship to Stanford University where he eventually received a degree in mining engineering.

Then began Hoover's remarkable rise to become one of the richest men in the world. After working as a menial mine laborer, he moved into management and eventually ownership, overseeing mining operations all over the world. His life was full of wealth, fame, adventure, and success (he was even among those besieged during the Chinese Boxer Rebellion of 1899).

After making his millions, Hoover decided to offer his time and talents to his country. President Woodrow Wilson took him up on the offer, asking this great businessman to "engineer" a solution to hunger in Europe after World War I. By all accounts, Hoover's efforts were remarkably successful and millions in war-torn Europe owed him a large debt of gratitude, if not their lives. This cemented his reputation as a brilliant problem-solver. Many, including a young Assistant Secretary of the Navy, wished that he would someday become President.[1] Their wish came true in 1928 when, in a landslide victory, the American people elected Hoover to the nation's highest office. Americans believed that he would be able to engineer solutions to any problems that the country might face.

So when the Great Depression hit, the people of the country were grateful that Hoover, the *wunderkind*, was in the White House. He, of all people, knew how to fix things and steer America back to prosperity and that's just what he set about to do.

As a self-proclaimed "progressive," Herbert Hoover believed in an active, problem-solving government that would intervene extensively to fix the market economy. He involved the government in the private sector further and more dramatically than any of his predecessors ever had by holding wages high, passing public works bills, increasing tariff rates, raising taxes, establishing government controls and programs, and offering public loans to businesses (such as the Reconstruction Finance Corporation). But the more Hoover did, the worse the Depression became and, as a result, he received much of the blame for the poor economy. Perhaps the biggest myth of American history is that Hoover was a "do-nothing" President who just sat back and watched while the Depression worsened. Nothing could be further from the truth.

---

1  This was Franklin D. Roosevelt, the man who later became his nemesis.

## Chapter 15

## Franklin D. Roosevelt

In 1932, Franklin D. Roosevelt (FDR) challenged Hoover for the presidency. Roosevelt's greatest asset was that, temperamentally, he was everything that Hoover was not: whereas Hoover was dour and quiet, FDR radiated optimism; whereas Hoover lacked the ability to sell his policies to the public, FDR was one of the greatest communicators in presidential history; while Hoover was born and raised poor out West, FDR had all the privileges of a wealthy and aristocratic East Coast upbringing. How ironic that Hoover comes down to us as the defender of privilege and FDR the champion of the poor.

Just being "not Hoover" was enough to secure Roosevelt's election. He had promised in his campaign a "New Deal" for the American people, but nobody really knew what that meant, including Roosevelt himself. In the campaign, he actually promised, among other things, to balance the budget and put an end to Hoover's "tinkering" with the private economy. Once he took office, though, it turned out that the New Deal wasn't so "new" after all—it entailed an expansion of the same interventions Hoover had already been doing for four years.

Let's look more closely at the most significant New Deal programs. As we do so, it is important to realize that there are no easy answers to the question of whether or not it "worked." Partisans want to give a simple answer of "yea" or "nay," "good" or "bad," "success" or "failure" to the New Deal, but FDR's program had so many facets that it's impossible to assign it a simple score. Some aspects of the New Deal may have been beneficial for the country overall while other parts may have caused net harm. Some parts helped certain people, but hurt other people.

FDR's first step was to attempt to alleviate the poverty and hardship of indebted farmers who were losing their land (as in John Steinbeck's novel *The Grapes of Wrath*). He passed, with the help of the Democratic Congress, *The Agricultural Adjustment Act* (AAA). The AAA paid farmers to destroy their crops and livestock. It ordered them to take fields full of wheat or corn and set torches to them, or take thousands of gallons of milk and dump it into the street. Why would he order this policy if people in America were going hungry?

The supply-demand graph provides the answer. The problem for farmers was low prices for agricultural goods, so if they destroyed wheat, pork, and milk then the supply would decline and the price would increase—this was, in FDR's opinion, the aid the farmers needed. Whether or not it was a "good" policy depends upon perspective: It was great for the farmers who received government checks and could sell their products for a higher price, but it was bad for poor consumers who had to pay higher food prices and those who had to pay the taxes to fund the subsidy (those high taxes may have also hurt the economy by creating disincentives to produce). As usual, the benefits of government action were highly visible—farmers could trace their good fortune directly to government action—while the costs were mostly *in*visible—urban dwellers couldn't tell exactly why their food prices were going up. This is one reason government action is more popular than inaction and one reason FDR's popularity increased after passage of the AAA.

Another New Deal measure kept wages artificially high. When government imposes a wage increase, it is good for those who have and retain jobs—they get more money per hour—but it is bad for those who don't have jobs because firms can't afford to employ them at the higher rate. This may be one of the reasons the unemployment rate remained stubbornly high throughout the Depression. Again, the benefits were visible and the costs were invisible: those who had jobs were grateful to Uncle Sam for the higher wage, but the unemployed who couldn't get work didn't know who to blame for the lack of jobs. FDR's popularity grew even further.

Next, like Hoover, FDR commissioned an extensive program of public works to create jobs. The government could have simply written checks and given money to the unemployed, but FDR didn't like the idea of people living on the "dole"—he thought it destroyed their dignity and self-respect (something the Prophet of the time, Heber J. Grant, agreed with). FDR wanted to see people earn their assistance, so if the private sector wouldn't hire them, then the government would do so through such programs as the Works Progress Administration (WPA) and the Civilian Conservation Corps (CCC). These programs hired out-of-work Americans to build bridges, dams, prisons, parks, and libraries. The upside was that millions of Americans gratefully received jobs straight from the federal government (causing Roosevelt's popularity to soar even higher); the downside was that the money to pay these workers had to come from higher taxation and debt (which may have dampened private sector hiring).

The next step FDR took to combat the Great Depression was to seize greater control over industry by setting prices, establishing quotas, and having bureaucrats in Washington direct the economy. The National Recovery Administration (NRA), for instance, was set up to steer the economy back to health. Economists today generally agree that government direction is less efficient than market allocation and that the NRA probably delayed the recovery it was designed to hasten. FDR didn't realize that the Supreme Court probably did him a favor when it struck down the NRA as unconstitutional after a few years.

Since the Great Depression largely originated in the financial sector, FDR passed a number of acts to regulate banks and prevent their failure. Among other things, this legislation required banks to hold minimum reserves so they could pay out deposits, mandated bank holidays to calm people down and prevent runs, and established a deposit insurance program (the FDIC) so that people wouldn't panic, knowing that the government would give them their money even if the bank couldn't.

The most enduring of FDR's New Deal efforts was the establishment of a number of relief programs in which the government would give direct assistance to American citizens. Social Security, set up during the Great Depression, is still with us as a form of insurance to help the disabled and elderly. Many economists would approve of such aid, but also understand that raising the taxes necessary to finance welfare programs in the middle of a depression is a bad idea.

Despite all of the above, the New Deal did not end the Great Depression. Long after all of the programs had been implemented, the Depression was still going strong. It is a myth that FDR came riding in on a white horse, launched the New Deal, turned the economy around, and saved the country from economic collapse. Certain New Deal programs may have alleviated some of the harsh effects of the Depression, but they did not end it.

The fact that this myth persists shows the degree to which the New Deal programs and FDR's persona gave the American people hope and optimism in this most difficult economic time. This made FDR's Democratic Party highly popular and it dominated national politics for the next fifty years. From 1860-1932 there had been fifteen Republican Presidential terms and only four Democratic terms, but the popularity of the New Deal reversed that trend. Between 1932 and 1980, there were eight Democratic terms to only four Republican ones and the Democrats also controlled the Congress and Supreme Court during most of that time.

The most lasting consequence of the New Deal was the establishment of the welfare state in America. Before the 1930s, the Federal Government limited itself primarily to military matters, foreign diplomacy, and the regulation of commerce. After the 1930s, the vast majority of Federal Government expenditures and efforts went to distributing money and resources to the citizens. The New Deal gave a new role to the central government which is not only still with us, but has become *the* central role the federal government plays in America today. This was a major achievement.

## KEYNESIANISM

Now that we understand the Great Depression, we are more equipped to understand Keynesianism. In a nutshell, Keynesianism says that economic downturns result from *insufficient demand*—there is just not enough buying going on in the economy. Capitalism is fine, said Keynes, but unstable and given to falling out of balance when human "animal spirits" take over and lead us into over-exuberance. Theoretically, supply and demand will meet at an equilibrium price that clears the market, but Keynes said that the equilibrium gets thrown off when suppliers produce too much. There is over-supply without enough demand to meet all of that production. This means there are many "idle resources" in the economy—the productive assets not being used—and this inefficiency causes economic stagnation.

Let's use an example to illustrate: imagine that you live in the 1920s and it is the era of Lou Gehrig, Babe Ruth, and baseball-mania. To make money you begin manufacturing baseball gloves. Business is going well, people are buying your gloves, and you are getting rich because baseball is all the rage. As customers buy more and more gloves, you produce more and more gloves to meet their demand and get richer and richer until soon you get carried away by your "animal spirits" (excessive zeal) and begin producing so many gloves that they fill up a warehouse. Suddenly, the party stops: you have thousands of gloves that you can't sell because of insufficient demand.

Now, all of your money is tied up in these gloves, but they are just sitting on the shelf gathering dust. They are "idle resources." Instead of using your resources to expand your plant, buy machines, or hire a new workforce, your resources are just sitting there doing nothing—all because you created an excess supply of baseball gloves.

Without resources, you can't pay your bills—rent, money owed to the bank for equipment, electricity costs, etc.—and you go out of business. Your entire factory is now idle. Worse still, all of your employees lose their jobs.

But it doesn't stop there. Your employees used to go to the ice cream shop every day after work, but now they can't afford to because they don't have jobs. This means, in turn, that the ice cream shop doesn't have people coming in to get cones and they have to shut down. This means that the ice cream scoopers can no longer afford to see a movie after work so the movie house shuts down and its employees lose their jobs. The lack of demand problem has a downward-spiraling effect.

Think of all the "idle resources" in the economy now: not just all of the baseball gloves on the shelves, but all of the glove-making machines sitting unused, the workers doing nothing without jobs, the movie projector sitting idle, the ice cream maker doing nothing. All of these assets *could be producing* and making the economy richer, but are instead just sitting there. Why? All because there is too much supply and not enough demand. When there is insufficient aggregate demand, said Keynes, everything else in the economy goes wrong. It is the root of all economic evil.

So what can be done to reverse this downward spiral? Keynes said that government *fiscal policy* (taxing and spending) does the trick. A Keynesian analogy is to think of the economy as a man having a heart attack. We would not just sit by and do nothing while the poor man died, we would pick up the defibrillator and shock him back to life. The government, says Keynes, is like the doctor with the paddles and the economy is like the dying man. The paddles are the tools of fiscal policy—taxing and spending—and can be used, like a defibrillator, to stimulate the economy back to life.

The first fiscal policy tool, the tax cut, reverses the problem of insufficient demand because, when taxes are lower, people have more money in their pockets to purchase the excess supply. For instance, a man could use his tax refund to buy a baseball glove which would mean the employees of the glove manufacturer could then buy ice cream which would mean the ice cream scoopers could buy movie tickets.

The second fiscal policy tool, government spending, can reverse the problem of insufficient demand by having the government step in and pick up the slack. In Keynesian theory, insufficient private-sector demand is filled by public, government-sector demand and it really doesn't matter what the government spends the money on: it can build museums, construct roads, or even hire people to dig holes and fill them back up again. Men paid by the government to build a road can now buy baseball gloves, and glove makers can now buy ice cream, and ice-cream scoopers can now buy movie tickets. Government spending reverses the downward spiral.

But you will notice a problem here: since the government is increasing spending and lowering taxes, don't the basic laws of arithmetic say that the government will then run a budget deficit? Keynes's answer was an emphatic: "*Yes*!" and he believed there was nothing wrong with that. While we all believe that debt and deficits are bad under normal conditions, Keynes said that deficits are desirable during a recession because it makes fiscal stimulus possible. We can worry about paying off those debts once we are out of the recession, but during a recession those budget deficits are just what the doctor ordered.

To those who countered that all of this government activity might have a negative effect on the economy in the long run, Keynes famously responded, "in the long run we are all dead." In other words, we need to focus on the here and now—get demand back into alignment with supply and the rest will take care of itself.

Keynes had offered a persuasive theory of economic downturn and recovery. It has remained attractive to politicians, economists, and the public for many reasons. First, it seems pro-active. It makes us feel that, when beset by economic downturn, we can seize control of our destiny. We don't have to stand by and watch while people lose their jobs and suffer economic misery. Our instinct when bad things happen is to say, "Don't just stand there. *Do something*!" Keynesianism satisfies that instinct.

The second attraction of Keynesianism is that it provides a powerful and convincing explanation of what caused and finally cured the Great Depression. We got into the Depression, says Keynes, because the 1920s were an age of excess and overzealousness. Americans began producing more goods than demand could meet. The economy, thrown out of balance by these animal spirits, came crashing down in 1929. So America sat in the Great Depression for ten years until the government started spending like crazy during World War II. This finally stimulated demand and led to recovery. The government, without knowing it, had implemented Keynes's prescription and thereby shocked the economy out of Depression. Keynes took the puzzle of the Great Depression and turned it into a rational economic problem that could be solved through government action.

The third reason Keynesianism is so popular is that it seems to fit comfortably in the moderate "Vital Center" of economic systems. Its advocates place Keynesianism at the middle ground between the extremes of socialism (complete government control of the economy) and *laissez faire* (no government control of the economy). Like Goldilocks's porridge, it is neither too hot nor too cold. It is a theory of free markets, but markets tempered by

# Depression and Solutions I: Keynesianism

government action. Some even claim that it saves capitalism since its moderate interventions will satisfy the working class and stave off the desire for more radical action.[2]

Fourth, and finally, Keynesianism is popular because it appeals to the most important values of *both* conservatives and liberals today. We sometimes say that conservatives and liberals these days don't agree on anything, but they both agree on Keynesianism. Conservatives, such as George W. Bush, and liberals, such as Barack Obama, like Keynes's philosophy because it gives them a green light to engage in the tax cuts and government spending they would have wanted to do anyway. For this reason, Keynesian economics have dominated American politics since 2001 and you can see why our government has been setting world records for debt and deficits for decades.

We've talked about the strengths of Keynesianism, now what are the weaknesses? First, the whole "debt is good" philosophy sounds intuitively suspicious. We all know that it's bad for individuals to run up big debts, wouldn't that hold for governments too? The "free lunch" philosophy of Keynes just sounds fishy to many people and seems to reward profligacy and punish prudence.

Second, the problem of debt rarely works out as Keynes said it would. Keynes advocated running up debt during a recession and paying off that debt during recovery, but that almost never happens. We live in a democracy where low taxes and high government spending are popular. Politicians get elected by promising us low taxes *and* free benefits (healthcare, prescription drugs, wars, education funding, etc.) at the same time. "We the People" want the government to give us things, but don't want to pay for them even when times are good. So part of the problem with Keynesianism is that we only want to implement half of the theory: we like the debt part (tax cuts and big spending), but don't like the austerity part (tax increases and cutting spending) that must come later.

The third problem of Keynesianism is that the evidence for it is not conclusive. That is, economists haven't yet established a strong correlation between deficits and recovery. If Keynes was right, it should be a simple matter to show through regression analysis that shorter recessions correlate with higher government spending. So far, this evidence has not been forthcoming.

## CONCLUSION

Because of these problems, many economists have sought out alternative explanations for the causes and cures of economic downturns. One brilliant economist believed he had found a better explanation than the one Keynes offered and we will turn to his theory in the next chapter.

---

2  Chapter 14 made clear that it is the free market that lies in the appropriate "middle ground" between the chaos or command alternatives. Whether Keynesianism remains within that middle ground or moves the economy towards the "command" end of the spectrum is a matter of debate.

## CHAPTER 15 SOURCES/FURTHER READING

Black, Conrad. *Franklin Delano Roosevelt: Champion of Freedom.* New York: Public Affairs, 2003.

Buchholz, Todd G. *New Ideas from Dead Economists.* New York: New American Library, 1989.

Jeansonne, Glen. *The Life of Herbert Hoover: Fighting Quaker, 1928-1933.* New York: Palgrave Macmillan, 2012.

Jenkins, Roy. *Franklin Delano Roosevelt.* New York: Henry Holt, 2003.

Kennedy, David M. *Freedom From Fear: The American People in Depression and War.* New York: Oxford University Press, 1999.

Leuchtenburg, William E. *Franklin D. Roosevelt and the New Deal: 1932-1940.* New York: Harper Perennial, 2009.

Miller, Roger LeRoy and Daniel K. Benjamin. *The Economics of Macro Issues.* 6$^{th}$ Edition. Upper Saddle River, NJ: Pearson Prentice Hall, 2013.

Nash, George. *The Life of Herbert Hoover: The Engineer, 1874-1914.* New York: W.W. Norton & Co., 1983. Covers Hoover's pre-political life.

Powell, Jim. *FDR's Folly: How Roosevelt & His New Deal Prolonged the Great Depression.* New York: Random House, 2002.

Reed, Lawrence. "Great Myths of the Great Depression," Cascade Policy Institute, October 2000. <http://cascadepolicy.org/pdf/fiscal/myths.pdf>.

Reich, Robert B. "Economist John Maynard Keynes," *Time*, Mar 29, 1999. <http://content.time.com/time/magazine/article/0,9171,990614,00.html>.

Roosevelt, Franklin D. "The Economic Bill of Rights" (1944). <http://www.fdrheritage.org/bill_of_rights.htm>.

Schlesinger, Arthur M., Jr. *The Age of Roosevelt, Vol. 2: The Coming of the New Deal, 1933-1935.* Boston: Houghton Mifflin, 1958.

Skidelsky, Robert. *John Maynard Keynes: 1883-1946: Economist, Philosopher, Statesman.* New York: Penguin, 2005.

Steinbeck, John. *The Grapes of Wrath.* New York: Viking, 1939.

# Chapter 16

# DEPRESSION AND SOLUTIONS II: MONETARISM

### MILTON FRIEDMAN: CHALLENGING KEYNES

Although Keynesianism became influential in the years following the Great Depression, a competitor theory called "monetarism" came along to challenge it later in the century. The founder and key figure of monetarism was Milton Friedman—perhaps the most influential economist since Keynes.

Friedman was the son of poor Jewish immigrants in New York City. Despite his parents' poverty, Friedman earned a scholarship to study math at Rutgers University and then went to work for the federal government during the Great Depression. This was a turning point in his life. While working in a government price-control office, he came to believe there was waste, inefficiency, fallibility, and hubris among Washington planners. He converted from the socialism of his youth to the free market views he would hold for the rest of his life.

After completing a doctorate at Columbia and taking a position in the economics department of the University of Chicago, Friedman developed a new interpretation of the causes and cures of depressions. He presented this theory in a landmark book—*A Monetary History of the United States*—which he coauthored with Anna Schwartz of the National Bureau of Economic Research.

Schwartz is in many ways even more remarkable than Friedman. She was not only a brilliant economist, but a full time mother as well. She graduated from Columbia with a master's in economics at age 19, married, finished a Ph.D., and then had four children. Each day, after packing lunches and sending her kids off to school, she would sit down to her economics work until they returned.

In their magnum opus, Schwartz and Friedman argued that *monetary* policy, not fiscal

# Chapter 16

policy, explains economic downturns and recoveries. This theory of the Great Depression was so influential that it won Friedman the 1979 Nobel Prize in economics. Coming to know the essentials of monetarism is our task for the remainder of this chapter.

## WHAT IS MONEY?

In order to understand monetarism, we must first understand money. When you think about it, it's really quite remarkable that we carry around little green slips of paper with pictures of dead presidents on them and turn those pieces of paper into hamburgers, shoes, computers, cars, homes, and even skyscrapers. We take money for granted, but we shouldn't—it doesn't exist in the natural world so somebody had to invent it. It stands with fire, the wheel, and electricity as one of the greatest innovations in human history. Different objects have worked as money in different times and places—even shells and tobacco—but most societies in history have used precious metals, such as gold and silver, and today we use printed paper.

Money is such an important invention because it performs three functions that are crucial to economic activity. First, it serves as a *medium of exchange*. If there was no money, people would be forced to barter when making transactions. This would require a "coincidence of wants." For example, if you were a mechanic who wanted a pair of shoes, you would have to spend considerable time and effort finding a cobbler who just happened to need his car fixed. This would make transaction costs high. Instead of spending our time and resources in productive economic activity (fixing cars and making shoes) we would waste time and resources trying to find someone who just happened to have what we want and also just happened to want what we have.

Money means we don't have to do this. Anyone, regardless of what they produce, can give money to the mechanic when they need their car fixed and the mechanic, in turn, can use that money to purchase shoes. In that sense, money works like a lubricant of economic activity—allowing the parts of the economy to work together harmoniously and without friction. Remember, the secret to wealth is free exchange; money, by making exchange easier, makes us considerably richer.[1]

The second function of money is to serve as a *unit of account*. That is, money does for the financial world what inches, feet, yards, and miles do in the spatial world: give a common means of measurement. We sometimes say "you can't compare apples and oranges," but thanks to money you can. If an apple costs twenty-five cents and an orange costs fifty cents, then money has allowed you to see that two apples are worth one orange. This standardized

---

[1] You can see this in the Book of Mormon too as Nephite wealth correlates closely with the availability of currency (gold and silver).

unit of measurement improves our information and helps us make better economic decisions.

The third and final function of money is to serve as a *store of value*. Most economic goods spoil over time, but money can hold its value indefinitely. Perishable goods like milk obviously lose their worth very quickly, but so do non-perishables like shirts (which go out of style) or computers (which become obsolete). If you had tried to "save" by piling up valuable computers in your garage twenty years ago, you would have lost all your savings since they would now be worthless.

Money, on the other hand, retains its value (with an exception we will discuss below) and can be stored. This is why so many societies have used gold as money. It doesn't corrode and stays virtually unchanged for centuries. Archaeologists dig up ancient Greek swords whose iron blades now look like amorphous goo, but their golden hilts still have the perfectly wrought shape they had millennia ago. No wonder that Nephi, who wanted his record to endure for thousands of years, engraved his plates on gold.

The store-of-value function of money is important because capitalism requires saving. It is by saving and investing (through banks, stocks, bonds, etc.), that we are able to pool capital and finance the large productive enterprises that create growth. We can put a little money in the bank each month, store it there, and then years later withdraw a large lump sum to start a business or finance someone else's business. Thanks to money, we don't have to consume our wealth right away, but can accumulate it to use as capital later.

## THE FEDERAL RESERVE

Clearly we need money for our economy to work properly, so where does it come from? Who creates, circulates, and regulates the supply of money in our economy? The answer is: The U.S. Government. The Constitution says in Article I, Section 8: "The Congress shall have power to . . . coin money and regulate the value thereof." This power was greatly expanded in 1913 when President Wilson created the Federal Reserve (sometimes called "The Fed"), a new government agency directly charged with *monetary policy,* i.e., regulation of the money supply. The Fed can, through open market operations and manipulating interest rates, increase or decrease the amount of money in circulation.

Increasing the money supply has two effects. First, a higher money supply means *lower interest rates*. Money, like everything else, is subject to the laws of supply and demand and even has a price. We call the price of money "the interest rate"—the amount you must pay to borrow money from a lender (e.g., a bank). When the supply of money goes up, the price of money (the interest rate) goes down.

This lower interest rate is beneficial to an economy because it spurs economic activity. When interest rates are low and money is cheap, firms can more easily expand, individuals can more easily buy homes, and entrepreneurs can more easily start businesses. This is why

*Chapter 16*

The Fed engages in "quantitative easing" (increased money supply) when the economy is slow.

Second, a high money supply decreases the risk of bank failure. Remember, banks receive our money as deposits but only keep a portion of it on hand. They lend out the rest at interest and that is how they make a profit. This is not a problem unless too many depositors try to withdraw their money at once—we call this a "bank run." Since banks are a core institution in the economy, massive bank failure means failure of the whole system. If the money supply is high, then banks have access to more cash and can survive a bank run. That's another benefit of an expanded money supply.

If a high supply of money spurs economic activity and prevents bank failure, why doesn't The Fed just expand the money supply all the time? The answer is that there are two huge drawbacks to a loose monetary policy.

## ECONOMIC BUBBLES

The first is that a high money supply can create economic "bubbles." When money is cheap, people often borrow heavily to purchase assets that increase in value only because of the buying frenzy itself, not because of the intrinsic value of the asset. In other words, people buy the asset because it is going up in value, and it is only going up in value because people are buying it. It's insubstantial and empty, hence the term "bubble." When these bubbles pop (as they inevitably must—it's a natural market correction), prices come tumbling down, people lose millions, borrowers can't pay off loans, and the economy contracts.

This is how Friedman explained the Great Depression. The Depression, he said, had little to do with lack of demand (as Keynes said) and everything to do with a failure of monetary policy. The Federal Reserve kept the money supply far too high all through the 1920s and this availability of cheap money led people to borrow too heavily. Americans would borrow money to buy stocks, inflating the price of those stocks far beyond their actual value, and then use that inflated stock as collateral to borrow more money (with which to buy more stocks, which they used as more collateral to get more loans to buy more stocks, and so on). By keeping the money supply so high, the Federal Reserve encouraged the reckless borrowing and speculation that inflated this stock market bubble.

Then, in October 1929, the bubble popped. The stock market crashed, investors lost most of their money, borrowers had no cash with which to repay their bank loans, and banks had no cash with which to pay their depositors. This led to massive bank failure and with bank failure came business failure and with business failure came general economic failure—the Great Depression. In a vicious cycle, banks went under, depositors lost their money, and businesses closed their doors for want of cash, investment, and customers.

Then, according to Freidman, The Fed did something even more foolish than before. Right at the moment it should have been *increasing* the money supply to give those banks cash to cover their deposits, it allowed the money supply to *fall* instead. The Fed not only created the Depression by fueling the stock market bubble, but then made it much worse when it could have fixed it.

The Depression was caused by this colossal failure of government, said Friedman, not a failure of the market system itself. As support for his theory, Friedman rightly noted that there had never been a Great Depression before the creation of the Federal Reserve.

So what finally ended the Great Depression according to the monetarist theory? Keynes had claimed that it was the massive government spending of World War II, but Friedman claimed that it was the rapid expansion of the money supply that happened around the same time. Tight money throughout the 1930s kept the country in Depression, but a surge in the money supply at the end of the decade finally jolted the economy back to health.

So which was it and who is right? Was it government spending that ended the Depression or the expanded money supply? Was it fiscal policy or monetary policy? Economists are still debating this question. Some say Keynes, some say Friedman, some say both, and some say neither. Regardless of which view is correct, we must understand both views because they play a crucial role in shaping government economic policy today.

## INFLATION

The creation of bubbles is not the only cost of a high money supply; it also causes *inflation*. One of the great contributions of Friedman and Schwartz was to show that the general level of prices closely follows the quantity of money. They looked at the history of the United States and saw a pattern: every period of falling prices was preceded by a decrease in the money supply, and every period of rising prices was preceded by an increase in the money supply. This general rise in prices is what we call "inflation." To summarize this finding, Friedman coined the famous line, "Inflation is always and everywhere a monetary phenomenon."

Inflation, of course, means that since things generally cost more, your money buys less and has a lower value. By decreasing the value of money, inflation weakens all three of its functions. It weakens the medium of exchange function because people are less willing to accept inflated money in transactions. For example, nobody accepts Zimbabwean dollars because the Zimbabwean government printed so many of them that the money is worthless. Zimbabwe is back to an exchange-killing barter economy. That's a major reason Zimbabwe has become one of the poorest nations on earth.

Inflation also weakens the unit of account function. We can't use money as a measuring stick in transactions when we are unsure of its value. Imagine a carpenter trying to build a house if the length of a foot, inch, or yard kept changing every time he took a measurement—it would be impossible. Prices usually serve as efficient messengers telling us what to produce and consume, but their message is distorted when the value of money is unstable and constantly changing. In other words, inflation exacerbates the already-serious market weakness of imperfect information.

Finally, and most notably, inflation weakens the store of value function of money. We talked before about how most goods spoil and lose their worth, but you can save money because it holds its value indefinitely. Inflation causes money to "spoil" like a moldy loaf of bread or an obsolete television. If money is constantly losing its value, then we don't want to save because our money will be worth less each day it sits in the bank or in our wallet.

In that sense, inflation is a "tax" on savings. If you have saved $100 and the inflation rate is 5%, then the inflation has effectively taken $5 in taxes from you because your hundred dollars buys 5% less than it did the year before.

Worst of all, inflation punishes what we so desperately want to encourage—the Protestant Ethic. Remember, Weber taught us that the virtue of being willing to defer gratification—to put off pleasure now for greater gain later—leads to the saving and capital accumulation that makes capitalism succeed. And yet inflation punishes deferred gratification by reducing the value of saved money. This tax on savings discourages thrift and encourages people to spend their money as quickly as they can. It penalizes those who have been *most responsible* and rewards those who have been *most irresponsible*. Inflation, then, by sapping the Protestant Ethic, in turn saps the spirit of capitalism.

We can see this in our own history. Social scientists have long noted that America reached a turning point in the 1970s—it went from being a nation of savers and lenders to being a nation of spenders and borrowers. There is plenty of blame to go around on this—such as a rise of consumerism—but we must also blame the inflation that took off in the 1970s and punished Americans for saving. Ever since then, American debt, both public and private, has soared.

## STAGFLATION

The inflation of the 1970s also gave credence to Friedman's theory. In previous decades, many of Keynes's disciples believed that there was a tradeoff between inflation and economic stagnation—you had to pick your poison. But Friedman insisted that there could be both inflation and economic stagnation at the same time because the money supply could grow in a time of economic downturn. He predicted that there would come a time of "stagflation"—stagnation and inflation at once.

In the 1970s, his prediction was borne out. Inflation was rampant and the economy was stuck in slow or negative growth. To combat the inflation, political leaders took some silly measures. President Nixon enacted his wage and price controls, which didn't stop inflation, but did create shortages. Nixon's successor, Gerald Ford, tried to get rid of inflation by having Americans wear red buttons that said, "W.I.N."—Whip Inflation Now. Friedman just shook his head at all of this. He knew that wearing pins doesn't stop inflation, government price-fixing doesn't stop inflation, only decreasing the quantity of money does.

Finally, in 1979, President Carter appointed as Fed Chairman a man who understood the problem. His name was Paul Volcker. Shortly after taking office, Volcker began reducing the money supply. As Friedman predicted, the inflation rate began to drop. In the short term this was painful for the American economy and cost Carter re-election, but in the long run it killed the beast of inflation and paved the way for stable money and prosperity in the 1980s and 1990s.

Friedman's theory was put to the test again in 1987. Volcker had just stepped down as Fed Chairman when a stock market crash even worse than that of 1929 occurred. Americans were certain that the "roaring eighties" were crashing into a depression just as the roaring twenties had. And yet depression never came. Few even remember the "Crash of 87" because the economy quickly stabilized and resumed steady growth. Why?

The answer, according to monetarism, is that the new Fed Chairman, Alan Greenspan, reacted exactly as the Fed Chairman should in such a crisis. Whereas the Fed had allowed the supply of money to fall after the crash of 1929, Greenspan flooded the market with liquidity after the crash of 1987. This quick increase in the money supply prevented bank failure, lowered interest rates, and allowed the economy to weather the storm. Then, once the economy was stable and cruising again, he steadily diminished the quantity of money to prevent inflation and speculative bubbles. So ingenious was Greenspan during this crisis that one famous journalist dubbed him "the Maestro"—orchestrating the economy like a master conductor.[2]

After this 1987 episode, Americans began to realize how truly powerful the Fed Chairman was—perhaps the most important financial actor in the world—and were intensely interested in everything he said and did. Greenspan reports in his memoir that it got to the point where the press wouldn't even let him walk to work without shoving dozens of cameras and microphones in his face. Nonetheless, since Greenspan refused to comment on Fed activities, the press was reduced to guessing his actions by reading his facial expression (which never changed) or the size of his briefcase—which varied based on whether or not it contained a sandwich. Strangely, dramatic ups and downs in the world economy hinged on one man's dietary choices.

## CONCLUSION

To summarize the last two chapters, let's use a medical analogy. Both Keynes and Friedman tried, like doctors, to diagnose and cure the "ills" of the economy. According to Doctor Keynes, the economy gets sick (recession) because of market failure—too much supply and

---

[2] Woodward (2001).

not enough demand. According to Doctor Friedman, the economy gets sick because of government failure—a loose monetary policy that creates an asset bubble. According to Keynes, we cure a sick economy through the "medicine" of *fiscal* policy—lowering taxes and increasing government spending to make up for the lack of private-sector demand. According to Doctor Friedman, we cure a sick economy through the "medicine" of *monetary* policy—increasing the money supply to lower interest rates and prevent bank failure.

You may have noticed by now that these two theories are not necessarily in conflict. Friedman did not accept Keynesian theory and Keynes did not know of Friedman's theory, but many economists find merit in both. Our government, since 2001, has been aggressively pursuing both Keynesian *and* Monetarist policies. The fiscal authorities (Congress and the Presidents) have been borrowing and spending like never before, while the monetary authorities (at the Federal Reserve) have been expanding the money supply like never before.

This means that whether or not you agree with these theories, you had better hope and pray that they are right—our government has bet the future of the United States economy on them.

## CHAPTER 16 SOURCES/FURTHER READING

Ebenstein, Lanny. *Milton Friedman: A Biography*. New York: Palgrave Macmillan, 2009.

Friedman, Milton. *Money Mischief: Episodes in Monetary History*. New York: Harcourt Brace Jovanovich, 1992.

Friedman, Milton and Anna Schwartz. *A Monetary History of the United States, 1867-1960*. Princeton: Princeton University Press, 1971.

Friedman, Milton and Rose Friedman. *Free to Choose*. New York: Harvest, 1990.

Greenspan, Alan. *The Age of Turbulence: Adventures in a New World*. New York: Penguin, 2007.

Greider, William. *Secrets of the Temple: How the Federal Reserve Runs the Country*. New York: Simon & Schuster, 1987.

Krugman, Paul. "Who Was Milton Friedman?" *The New York Review of Books*, Feb 15, 2007. <http://www.nybooks.com/articles/archives/2007/feb/15/who-was-milton-friedman/>.

Schwartz, Anna J. "Money Supply," The Concise Encyclopedia of Economics. <http://www.econlib.org/library/Enc1/MoneySupply.html>.

Woodward, Bob. *Maestro: Greenspan's Fed and the American Boom*. New York: Simon & Schuster, 2001.

# Part Three:
## The Cultural Foundations of America

# Chapter 17

# POLITICAL CULTURE I: RELIGION IN AMERICA

### ROGER WILLIAMS: GODLY DISSENT

The dominant force that has shaped American culture is, without question, Christianity. America's Protestant foundations have largely defined its institutions, values, and outlook. No other developed nation has such a high level of religiosity. Why?

To help answer this question we turn to the life of Roger Williams, the man often considered the father of American religious liberty. Williams was born and raised in England and, early in his life, felt called by God to the ministry. He studied theology at Cambridge University, but also discovered that he had the gift of tongues—he easily mastered many European and ancient languages. This gift would later come in handy, as we shall see.

After taking a position as a minister in the Church of England, Williams was disturbed by the lingering "papistry" in the Church. He didn't think that the Church of England's Protestant reforms had gone far enough. With its hierarchy, cathedrals, lavish adornment, and baroque rituals, the Church of England still closely resembled the Catholic Church of Rome. Since Williams, and others like him, wanted to further "purify" the Church of these Catholic vestiges they became known as *Puritans*.

As most Americans know, Puritans were the early settlers of New England.[1] They came to America for two reasons. The first was persecution. The Church of England (Anglican) was the official government religion, so criticizing the Anglican Church, as the Puritans did, was a *de facto* criticism of the government as well. This meant the government would

---

1 The very first New England settlers, the Pilgrims, were Separatists—an even more radical sect who thought the Church was corrupt beyond hope of purification.

oppress these religious dissidents through fines, imprisonment, and floggings. The Puritans escaped this persecution by crossing the Atlantic to America.

Second, many Puritans came to complete the work of the Reformation. They believed that by leaving England and setting up a colony of godliness—a "city upon a hill" that would be a "light to the world"—they could purify the Church of England by example.

Roger Williams was among these Puritan settlers, but he was almost as disturbed by what he saw among New England Puritans as he was by what he had seen in the English Church. The Puritans, who had been objects of religious persecution, had, in America, become religious persecutors themselves. They would banish those of different beliefs, enforce religious observance, and punish "heretics" for their dissidence. The Puritans wanted religious freedom for themselves, but would not extend it to others.

As a minister in the Massachusetts Bay Colony, Williams began to speak out against this hypocrisy. He taught from his pulpit that there are two realms of authority: the realm of governments—civil laws, magistrates, police, armies, courts, and prisons—and the realm of religion—church meetings, sermons, ritual, belief, worship, clerical guidance, and spirituality. Civil authority and religious authority, he said, should be kept strictly separate because government works upon the principle of force. To be legitimate, said Williams, religious convictions had to be freely chosen. If a belief was compelled, then that belief had no validity. He called his position "soul liberty" and argued that Jesus himself had taught this principle in Mark 12:17, saying, "Render to Caesar the things that are Caesar's, and to God the things that are God's."

To the Puritan fathers, this idea of dividing civil and religious authority was a terrible heresy. After all, they reasoned, if we give people freedom in religious matters, they might choose to believe the "wrong" doctrines. Furthermore, church and state had been joined throughout all of history; who was Williams to come along and challenge that? The Puritan fathers demanded that Williams stop teaching soul liberty or face banishment. Williams persisted, so he and his followers were forced to leave Massachusetts. They wandered southward looking for a place to establish a colony of religious freedom. They might have been killed by the local Indians, but Williams, because of his gift with languages, was able to communicate his benign intentions. The Native Americans allowed him to remain and he founded the colony of Providence (Rhode Island).

Although there had been nations with degrees of religious toleration, Rhode Island was the first to offer full religious freedom. All religions were welcome. This included any sect of Protestantism and also Catholicism, Judaism, and even atheism. Williams did not believe it was his business to force anyone to change belief, even those he stridently disagreed with. In this, Williams was remarkably ahead of his time. He anticipated the kind of religiously free society America would one day become.

Williams's own religious beliefs evolved over the course of his life. He was born into the Church of England, then dissented and became a Puritan. After leaving Massachusetts Bay for Providence, he joined the Baptist Sect, only to realize, at the end of his life, that the Baptist religion—centered on baptism by immersion—still lacked the Priesthood authority to perform that ordinance. This epiphany led to his final religious position summarized in this apocryphal quote:

> There is no regularly constituted church of Christ on earth, nor any person qualified to administer any church ordinances; nor can there be until new apostles are sent by the Great Head of the Church for whose coming I am seeking.

Like Jefferson, Williams looked forward to a restoration of the religious truth and authority that had been lost from the earth.

## RELIGIOUS FREEDOM AT THE FOUNDING

At the time of the Founding, Americans had to decide if they wanted to follow Williams's model of religious freedom or the model they had inherited from England in which government supported churches and used compulsion in religious matters. Each individual state had to choose which path it would follow.

As always, Virginia—the most populous state and home to the most prominent Founding Fathers—would take the lead. Two titans of the Founding era came forward to debate this important question.

The first was the great orator Patrick Henry, the patriot and foe of British tyranny who spoke the immortal line, "give me liberty or give me death." Henry proposed that Virginia (and the other colonies) have government sponsorship of religion. His reasoning followed this simple syllogism:

1. *There is no freedom without morality.* Either people will control themselves through internal morality or they must be controlled externally by the government and thereby have less freedom.

2. *Morality depends upon religion.* Strong religious institutions and belief uphold morality. Churches teach that God himself established moral precepts and holds us accountable for our obedience to them.

3. *Conclusion: Government should promote religion.* This will help ensure that people are religious. Morality and freedom are too important to be left to individual choice.

Before moving on, we must note that virtually all of the Founders agreed with Henry's first two propositions. They understood that morality was necessary for freedom and that morality and religion went hand in hand. For example, at the end of his two terms as President, George Washington gave a farewell address to the nation. The father of the country, the most beloved American, the most important and influential man in American history,

## Chapter 17

was finally stepping down and leaving public life forever. He was going home to Mt. Vernon to die and wanted to leave his final, most important advice to the American people. The central theme of his address was the importance of morality and religion.[2] He said,

> Of all the dispositions and habits which lead to political prosperity [freedom], religion and morality are indispensable supports ... And let us with caution indulge the supposition that morality can be maintained without religion. ... Reason and experience both forbid us to expect that national morality can prevail in exclusion of religious principle. It is substantially true that virtue or morality is a necessary spring of popular government. Who that is a sincere friend to it can look with indifference upon attempts to shake the foundation of the fabric?

In other words, Washington accepted Henry's first two suppositions. No religion means no morality, and no morality means no freedom.

John Adams often made similar statements. "Our Constitution was made only for a moral and religious people," he said, "It is wholly inadequate to the government of any other." Even the more skeptical Benjamin Franklin said after the signing of the Constitution, "Without God's concurring aid we shall succeed in this political building no better than the builders of Babel."

So what was wrong with Henry's reasoning? Thomas Jefferson came forward to oppose Henry's proposal and, in the process, gave us the answer. According to Jefferson, Henry was not wrong in his premises (1. & 2.), but in his conclusion (3.).

First, he said, the conclusion did not follow from the premises. Just because something is good and important, it does not mean that government should force us into it. There are many worthy things that are, nonetheless, not the province of government compulsion. For instance, service is good (work for the benefit of others), but compelling people to do service would be slavery (*forced* work for the benefit of others).

Second, said Jefferson, Henry's bill violated the fundamental Lockean principles that America was built upon. By using force in religious matters, governments violate the natural right to liberty. In the state of nature nobody is there to compel you in any way. You can worship a handful of sand, you can pray to the sun, you can deify the sea, you can bow down before a volleyball with a handprint on it, or you can reject religion altogether. In the state of nature you can worship however you want, so freedom of worship is part of our natural right to liberty. Henry's proposal would take part of that freedom away.

Jefferson had a great line that summarized his stance on religious freedom: "The legitimate powers of government extend only to those acts that are injurious to others ... it does me no injury for my neighbor to say there are no gods or twenty gods, it neither picks my pocket nor breaks my leg." In other words, since someone else's beliefs do not affect my

---

2  He emphasized two other themes in his Farewell Address. We shall turn to them in subsequent chapters.

freedom in any way, those beliefs should not be an object of political force. The government is there to protect our natural rights, not take them away, as joining church and state would do.

Third, Jefferson believed that, in the long run, truth can take care of itself. We don't pass laws forcing people to believe the earth is round or that 2+2=4. And why not? Is it not extremely important that people believe correct science or arithmetic? Yes, said Jefferson, but we can best arrive at the truth through a free exchange of ideas, not through compulsion. The human heart and mind, he said, are naturally drawn to the truth and that's the only legitimate way we can arrive at it. Those that try to force opinions on others are those least confident in the truth of their own beliefs. LDS missionaries don't go door to door with guns, compelling people to be baptized. Latter-day Saints understand that the gospel is best served by letting people freely choose or reject our message. That is why we fiercely uphold freedom of religion. Truth can and should take care of itself.

Fourth, Jefferson made the ultimate and irrefutable point that efforts to force religion are simply futile. It's not just that you *should not* force someone to believe a certain way, but that you *cannot*. People will believe what they are going to believe and all of the force in the world can't change that. I can put a gun to your head and make you say that 2+2=5, but I haven't changed your belief, only what you profess to believe. Governments can force our lips, but not our hearts.[3]

Fifth, Jefferson and his friend James Madison made the radical claim that maintaining religious freedom by separating church and state would be better for both church *and* state. Today, those who crusade for separation of church and state usually focus on keeping the government free from the influence of religion. They want to protect the state from the church. But for Madison it was far more important to protect the church from the state. Jefferson and Madison understood that government power, though necessary, has the tendency to corrupt whatever it becomes involved in. "That government is best which governs least," Jefferson often said.[4]

According to Madison, Patrick Henry's plan would backfire. Nothing would drive Americans *away* from religion quicker than to tie it to the government. When church and state are mingled, it brings that which is most sacred—religion—down to the level of that which is most corrupt and base—political power. Henry had said that religion was too

---

[3] If missionaries forced "converts" into a baptismal font at gunpoint then those "baptisms" would be as worthless for salvation as a morning shower. The same holds for the inquisitions and stake burnings of the middle ages.

[4] To illustrate this point, we need only consider the difference in service at a private entity, like a grocery store, to the service at a government agency, like the Department of Motor Vehicles. At the DMV the lines are longer, the service poorer, and the surroundings less pleasant. Why would we want to turn something as precious and important as our church into something like the DMV?

important to be left to the private sphere, but he had it exactly backward—religion was too important to be left to the government.

Jefferson wisely noted that people naturally rebel against that which they are forced to do. As proof, just compare taxes to tithing. Every year in the run-up to April 15th, Americans hire armies of lawyers, accountants, and financial planners to find ways to pay as little tax as possible. People fight their tax obligation with all the energy and resources they can command. But when was the last time someone hired an attorney to get out of paying their tithing? Never. Tithing is based on persuasion (the word), while taxes are based on compulsion (the sword) so we don't react against tithing as we react against taxes. Do we want people to feel about religion as they feel about the IRS (whose favorability among the American people is close to zero)? By bringing force into anything, we create a backlash against it. Joining church and state, Jefferson warned, would turn us away from faith rather than towards it.

Thankfully, Jefferson's argument prevailed in both the short and long terms. In the short term, the Virginia Legislature decided to reject Patrick Henry's bill and accept Jefferson's Statute for Religious Freedom. Jefferson was so proud of this that it is one of the three achievements of his life listed on his tombstone (along with founding the University of Virginia and writing the Declaration of Independence).

In the long term, Jefferson's victory in Virginia set a precedent for the other states. By the 1820s, every state in the union had followed Virginia's lead and abolished their official churches, making religion a matter of private choice. Today we have Thomas Jefferson/Roger Williams-style religious freedom everywhere in America.

## UN-SECULAR AMERICA

On Madison's point about freedom being better for religion, he was far more right than he ever imagined. We now have hard, social scientific data to back up what, for him, was just a hypothesis. In fact, as we shall see below, religious freedom is likely the best explanation for America's high religiosity.

But before getting there, let's look at some of the failed, alternative explanations for why the U.S. remains such a religious nation. The first is the so-called *secularization thesis*. Secularization starts with an "S" and so does Santa Claus: when we are children, our parents tell us that a plump man in a red suit rides around in a flying sleigh on Christmas Eve and delivers presents to all of the kids in the world. It's a fairytale that adults foist upon children because it gets them to behave. Young kids naively believe these stories, but as they get older they outgrow such foolish nonsense.

The secularization thesis says that religion is just Santa Claus for adults. Societies, as they mature and become more sophisticated, outgrow their superstitions, including belief in God. According to the secularization thesis, the more modern, advanced, educated, and scientific a society is, the less religious it will be.

This explanation just doesn't fit the facts. Note that the United States has become *more* religious over the past 200 years at the same time as it has been pushing back the boundaries of science and modernity more than any other country. The U.S. remains, in many ways, the most cutting-edge technological society in the developed world, and yet is also the most religious. The secularization thesis cannot account for this. Furthermore, religious Americans have been, on average, slightly *more* educated than secular Americans, not less. The secularization thesis has no answer to this falsifying data, nor can it explain the current experience of China, which is modernizing at record pace, and yet, at the same time, undergoing a mass religious awakening. China is a far more modern *and* religious place than it was fifty years ago. Contra the secularization thesis, modernity and secularism do not go hand in hand.

The next attempt to explain religion came from Karl Marx. The Marxist thesis says that religion is a tool of economic oppression. Marx saw all of history as a conflict between haves and have-nots. The rich attempt to glut themselves on the labor of the poor by feeding them myths about God, angels, and salvation so that they won't recognize and revolt against their exploited condition. Religion, said Marx, is a colossal fraud for the working class—the "opiate of the masses"—which gives poor people a false escape from a harsh reality. (Also note that Marx's arguments had been anticipated by Korihor 2000 years earlier; see Alma chapter 30.) In the Marxist thesis, religion is something lower-class people adhere to because they have been duped into it by the scheming, unbelieving upper class.

The Marxist theory is also falsified by the facts. The rich are actually *more* religious than the poor. Church attendance is much higher among the middle and upper classes than among the lower class. America is far richer than many European countries, and yet also far more pious. The reality is the opposite of what Marx's theory would predict.

Another failed attempt to explain religion in society came from the great psychiatrist Sigmund Freud. According to Freud, people believe in God because of mental weakness and poor mental health. Mental hospitals are populated with delusional people who think they are Napoleon Bonaparte, Shirley Temple, or knights fighting fire-breathing dragons. To Freud, this same kind of craziness explains why people believe in God, angels, and revelation—religious people are deluded by mass neurosis. For Freud, the mentally weaker you are, the more religious you will be. (Korihor anticipated this argument as well, calling belief in Christ the product of a "frenzied mind.")

This explanation fares no better than the other two. When we turn to the medical data, we find that the religious are actually *more* mentally stable, healthy, and well-adjusted than the unreligious. The reality is the exact opposite of what Freud predicted. Some psychiatrists have actually prescribed religious observance for depressed clients since religion increases their happiness and diminishes their sense of isolation and anxiety. In other words, religion *reduces* rather than *produces* mental instability.[5]

While the above three theories fail to explain American religiosity, there are two theories that are far more plausible. The first is what we might call the "zealous seeds" thesis. It says that America is religious because of its early settlers. The most religious and zealous Europeans (e.g., Roger Williams, the Puritans, the Pilgrims) were unpopular and forced to immigrate to America. They were so religious that they couldn't stand Europe and Europe couldn't stand them. That meant that America was populated, from the beginning, by religious crusaders and these early immigrants established a hyper-religious culture that later Americans have inherited and assimilated into. The seeds of Puritan zealotry have grown into a forest of religious fervor. This religiosity, built into the "DNA" of American culture, has been passed down and strengthened over the centuries.

The second plausible explanation for American religiosity is the "religious economy" theory (i.e., market explanation), which says that America is religious for the same reason that it is rich: the free market. This is where Madison was so prescient. When the government does not interfere in the "buying" and "selling" of religion, it has the same result as in economic life—vibrant competition and abundance. It might rub some of us the wrong way to treat religion as a "product" to be produced and consumed, but the metaphor works well in explaining social behavior and that is what concerns us here.

Why would freedom of religion (a free market) lead to higher religiosity? To understand this, we go back to the supply and demand graph. On the supply-side, churches "sell" religion and, in a country with religious freedom, many churches will enter the marketplace to "compete" for market share. They try to get as many people as they can to "buy" their religion. That competition creates a better product for the same reason that the grocery store gives better service than the DMV. It's not that better people work at the grocery store, it's that the store has competitors which force it to work hard to attract customers. In the same way, churches in countries with religious freedom (like the U.S.) have to compete for spiritual business and must provide an excellent spiritual product.

In Europe, by contrast, the governments have traditionally forced people to support pastors and pay them regardless of what they do. This means that the pastor (like the DMV manager) has little incentive to provide a quality product. Many clergymen in European history have simply bought a book of sermons to read perfunctorily each Sunday, and then spent the rest of the week engaging in hobbies. Few want to attend such religious services, so it is no wonder that Europeans hardly go to church anymore. By paying the pastors and supporting religion (as Patrick Henry wanted to do in Virginia), the European governments have killed the very religiosity they were trying to cultivate.

On the demand side, the free market of religion means that there are many different

---

5 Lennox (2011, 77-78).

religions competing for "customers," so different people can find a different religious "product" that works for them. Some people prefer Lutheranism, some Congregationalism, some Catholicism, some Islam, some Judaism, and some Buddhism. Under a free market, everyone can "buy" the religion that they like best.

## CANDY BAR ANALOGY

Let's use an analogy to help us understand the theory of the religious market. Imagine that we are not talking about the relationship between church and state, but between candy bar and state. Think what would happen if the American government made Almond Joy the official government candy bar, with all of the subsidies and special privileges that entailed. The other candy bars would not be able to compete with Almond Joy and would go out of business. Now those who prefer Almond Joy to all other candy bars would still buy them, but those who prefer Snickers, Twix, Hershey, Mr. Goodbar, Milky Way, and others would buy far fewer candy bars because the ones they like best would not be available. The joining of candy bar and state would reduce the demand for candy bars and the number of candy bars consumed would decline.

The supply side of candy bars would also suffer. Since Almond Joy would have no competitors and would receive government money no matter what quality of chocolate bar they produced, they would have no incentive to make candy that people would want to buy. They would become lazy, start skimping, become indifferent to quality, use inferior ingredients, and who could blame them? They would be paid through government compulsion regardless of whether or not anyone wanted their candy bars. Even those who preferred Almond Joy would consume less under this scenario because the quality of the candy bar would have suffered.

Contrast that hypothetical situation to what we actually have. In our free market of candy bars, all of the companies have to compete and improve their quality in order to attract customers. Every person can find a candy bar that they like best. Under the free market, many more candy bars will be consumed and much better candy bars will be produced.

The same vibrancy that characterizes the candy bar market in America also characterizes the market for religion. Pastor Rick Warren in Orange County has to give the best sermons, best spiritual advice, and best sense of community to his parishioners if he wants to attract and retain them. Because of his effectiveness in all of this, thousands show up to his mega-church every Sunday and millions buy his books and multimedia.

As you can see, James Madison was spectacularly correct and Patrick Henry spectacularly wrong. Henry thought that government force would make us *more* religious, but, as with so many government actions, the actual effects were the opposite of the intended effects. Henry feared that if government did not force religion on the people, religion would decline, but Madison understood that religion would decline if government *did* force it on the people.[6] Madison intuitively knew that you cannot go wrong with liberty no matter what the domain (religion, commerce, speech, etc.). Freedom strengthens while coercion weakens.

So powerful is the market paradigm in explaining American religiosity that today it has gained widespread acceptance among scholars and the media. For instance, Andrew Higgins of the *Wall Street Journal* wrote,

> In America, where church and state stand apart, more than 50% of the population worships at least once a month. In Europe, where the state has often supported -- but also controlled -- the church with money and favors, the rate in many countries is 20% or less.[7]

There is little doubt that religious freedom is partially responsible for high American religiosity.

## THE RELIGIONS WE DEMAND

Although America is clearly "consuming" more religion than other advanced nations, the question remains: which religions do they tend to choose? Which supplies of religion does the public demand? The answer is counter-intuitive.

In the early 20th century, American churches were confronted with the problem of modernity: scientific challenges to faith, changes in cultural norms, and new sexual permissiveness. The mainstream Christian churches decided they would try to increase their "market share" by accommodating modernity and changing their doctrines and practices to fit the times. They reduced donation requirements, became lax about chastity, cut down on church attendance expectations, threw out Sabbath day observance, and jettisoned biblical literalism. They reasoned that by modernizing and making their religion easier to live, new members would join their churches in droves.

The exact opposite occurred. As they lifted restrictions and jumped on the world's bandwagons, their membership rolls plummeted and have been in steady decline ever since. Each new accommodation to the world (most recently ordaining practicing homosexuals and performing gay marriages) drives out more members.[8]

As Americans leave the mainstream Christian churches they turn instead to those religions that have *not changed* to fit the times. Those churches that have kept donation

---

[6] Adam Smith himself made this point in *The Wealth of Nations*.
[7] Wiggins (2007).
[8] An analog in the world of soft drinks was Coke's infamous attempt at "modernizing" its product to fit new tastes back in the 80s. It flopped, but Coke was smart enough to reverse course and go back to its previous formula. Thus Coke, unlike the mainstream churches, retains a high market share and is gaining customers worldwide.

requirements high, retained strict codes of chastity, kept dietary laws, demanded Sabbath observance, maintained doctrinal purity, and made high worship and service demands (such as weekly church meetings and two year missions) have grown the fastest in recent decades. This includes religions like Evangelical Christianity, Catholicism, Mormonism, and Islam.

This is surprising to many: you would think that the easier it is to live a religion, the more people would want to join it. President Hinckley explained why it is otherwise when talk show host Larry King asked him to explain growing LDS membership. People want an anchor in a turbulent world, the prophet said, not a barometer. We go to church to hear what God wants *us* to do, not to tell God what we want *Him* to do. How much truth could a religion have if that "truth" was constantly changing to accommodate the whims of a corrupt world? How much conviction can a church's teachings inspire if those teachings are subject to the caprices of popular fashion? What kind of God would switch His divine demands to fit our human fads? Would such a being even be worthy of our worship? We can get the doctrine of "do whatever you want" from the media, but we expect our churches to teach the opposite. We go to church to escape the moral depravity of our society, not to be told to indulge in it. No wonder the "modernizing" churches are losing their members so quickly.

## MEANING OF "SEPARATION OF CHURCH AND STATE"

We've now established the importance of separating church and state, but many religious people are uncomfortable with that phrase. It sounds like something that might come from radicals in an anti-religious organization. Does it mean that the government must establish atheism as the official state religion? Does it mean that voters can't listen to their religious conscience when casting their ballots? Does it mean that politicians must throw out their religious beliefs when making public decisions? The Reverend Martin Luther King, Jr. used Christianity to argue for an end to racial discrimination. Rep. Dick Gephardt said he was a Democrat because his Christian faith led him to be concerned for the poor while George W. Bush said he was a Republican because his Christian faith taught him that all people everywhere were deserving of liberty.[9] Does "separation of church and state" require that we put a stop to this?

Clearly not and this is not what Jefferson, Madison, Williams, or the Founding Fathers had in mind. The Founders themselves believed in a large role for religion in America. Washington constantly invoked God's aid during every phase of the Founding and often made reference to "Divine Providence" in his speeches. Even Jefferson, one of the least orthodox of the Founders, attended church services in the nation's capital and referenced

---

9  The struggle for abolition, Civil Rights, progressive-era reforms and every other liberal cause has been based in Christianity, so it is strange that religious voters today more commonly call themselves conservatives.

## Chapter 17

God repeatedly in the Declaration of Independence (Jefferson made even more references to God in the original draft before the committee edited them out).

Furthermore, Washington's army included paid chaplains to minister to the soldiers and pray for their efforts in the war—a government-sponsored religious activity which persists in the military today. George Washington and all subsequent Presidents have taken their oaths of office on the Bible and have declared, "so help me God" at the end of their oath. Clearly, the Founders didn't intend for "the separation of church and state" to mean banishing God from public life.

To understand what it means and to clear up the confusion surrounding this much-invoked phrase, we must realize that there is a big difference between *church* and *God*. We do believe in a separation of *church* and state, but not necessarily a separation of *God* and state. Government should be neutral towards particular churches, but not necessarily towards religion in general.

## THE CONSTITUTION ON RELIGION

Since we must walk with care the fine line between separating church and state and banishing religion, where can we turn for guidance? The Constitution is the logical starting point and its First Amendment give us two important clauses that define the relationship that exists between religion and the government in America. It says, "Congress shall make no law respecting an establishment of religion," a clear command to separate church and state at the national level. But right after that, the Constitution adds, "or prohibiting the free exercise thereof."[10]

These two clauses, right next to each other in the First Amendment, are in constant tension. When it comes to religion-government relations, liberals today tend to focus on the "Establishment Clause" and conservatives tend to focus on the "Free Exercise Clause." Almost all of our debates about religion in government grow out of the tug of war between these two important principles.

To illustrate this tension, let's look at some examples. Many disagree over the use of religious language in public life, as in political speech or in official government emblems. Some ignorant people go on to cable news and say, "The Founding Fathers put 'under God' into the pledge of allegiance so who are we to take it out?" But the Founders didn't put it there; the Congress did in the 1950s. This came about because of the Cold War. Americans and their elected officials decided that the U.S. needed to set itself apart from the "godless Communists" in Soviet Russia. Our American faith in God, they said, could be a bulwark against Communism and an asset in our struggle for freedom. By putting the words "under God" in

---

10 Also note that beyond these references, the Constitution does not mention religion except to say that there will be no religious test for office, meaning that anyone, regardless of their faith, is permitted to stand for election.

the pledge of allegiance, Americans could show that they recognized a higher power than the state as the object of worship—making the nation less susceptible to the totalitarianism that had taken over the Soviet Union.

But others oppose this religious civic language on the grounds that it will backfire. If we use God in our political symbols, then won't we come to identify our nation with God and God's will? Won't we then be *more* rather than less susceptible to government/totalitarian control? After all, if our government is God's government, then we can't legitimately oppose its actions. How can you criticize government policy or the party in power if they are acting "Under God"? Our liberty, remember, depends upon checking and limiting the government's power, but some say that once we associate our government with God, that will be less likely. God, after all, doesn't need checks, balances, or limitations. As you can see, both sides have a strong case.[11]

What about government funding religious schools? This became an issue in the 1960s when the federal government expanded its scope and power into new realms. Education had previously been the province of local governments, but the national government started funding schools and taking a more active role in controlling local education. When the U.S. government started handing out money to secular, public schools, the Catholic schools held out their hands as well. Their request for funds was denied on the grounds that to give them money would be to "establish religion," but the Catholic schools responded that, by *not* giving them funds, they were implicitly establishing the non-religion of the public schools. If the government could give money to secular, unreligious schools, but none to religious schools, they said, then it would openly discriminate against religion in favor of secularism and thereby violate the Free Exercise Clause.

What about prayer or Bible reading in public schools? In the 19th and early 20th centuries, few questioned the acceptability of either. In fact, the Northwest Ordinance of 1787, which laid down rules for admitting new territories and states, declared that one of the purposes of public schools was to teach religion and morals. Each day before class, public school teachers all over America would invoke God's aid before class and then teach the pupils from the Bible. In the 1960s, many Americans began to challenge this. The Supreme Court decided in *Engel v. Vitale* (1962) and *Abington School District v. Schempp* (1963) that school-sponsored prayers and Bible reading violated the Establishment Clause. If a public school teacher prays or teaches the Bible on public, taxpayer-funded property, then the government is indirectly subsidizing prayer and biblical religion and thereby establishing that religion. Proponents of school prayer and Bible study said that prohibiting these activities violated one's right to free exercise of religion—the people of a community should be able to pray or read their sacred book whenever and wherever they want.

---

11 The First Presidency has sided in some instances with those wanting to keep religious symbols in public life. See First Presidency (1979).

*Chapter 17*

The Latter-day Saints were most directly involved in questions of church and state in the 19th century when some Church members practiced plural marriage as a tenet of their religion even as the 1862 Morrill Act made polygamy illegal in Utah. The Saints fought this law in the courts until it came to a head in the *Reynolds vs. U.S.* decision of 1879 in which the Supreme Court declared that "Laws are made for the government of actions, and while they cannot interfere with mere religious belief and opinions, they may with practices."

All of the above examples show that when it comes to religion in public life, both sides have powerful arguments. We should be grateful that we have both perspectives in politics to remind us of these principles and perhaps check the excesses of one another.

## CONCLUSION

While we may not be able to give final answers to specific questions about religion-government relations, we Latter-day Saints have important insights into the issue. First, our church teaches religious freedom as a core doctrine. The Eleventh Article of Faith declares, "We claim the privilege of worshiping Almighty God according to the dictates of our own conscience, and allow all men the same privilege, let them worship how, where, or what they may." The prophet Joseph Smith said on many occasions that he was a strong proponent of religious freedom and that "if he were the Emperor of the world and had control over the whole human family he would sustain every man, woman and child in the enjoyment of their religion."[12] All prophets since him have re-affirmed this principle. At its heart, religious freedom is based on the Golden Rule—Do unto others as you would have them do unto you (Matthew 7:12). Respecting others in their unique beliefs protects the likelihood that we will be protected when our beliefs are not in line with the majority. Roger Williams's idea of "soul liberty" is not just a nice idea to Latter-day Saints; it is a religious imperative.

But beyond this basic truth, we can disagree on specifics. Both the Establishment and Free Exercise clauses are key elements of our American institutions. While God has revealed broad principles of religious freedom to us, he has not commanded us in all particulars, which is why he gave us the ability to reason and discuss, so that we might apply these truths as best we can. Even as we accept the general principles given us by Williams, Jefferson, and Madison, there is still room for disagreement in how to apply them. We can only come to the correct perspective if we are humbly willing to listen to alternative points of view—something severely lacking in our political discourse today.

It is up to us as Latter-day Saints not just to uphold true political principles, but to help temper the tone of the discussion of the world and bring the respect and civility to the

---

12 Madsen (1992). This gives lie to the popular notion that Joseph Smith was a theocrat bent on establishing a political kingdom of God on earth.

conversation that has been lacking. As we do this, all of us—Democrats, Republicans, and independents—might learn something and become wiser.

## CHAPTER 17 SOURCES/FURTHER READING

Allitt, Patrick. *Religion in America Since 1945: A History*. New York: Columbia University Press, 2003.

Bloom, Harold. *The American Religion: The Emergence of the Post-Christian Nation*. New York: Simon & Schuster, 1992.

Brooks, Arthur C. *Gross National Happiness: Why Happiness Matters for America--and How We Can Get More of It*. New York: Basic Books, 2008.

Bryson, Bill. *At Home: A Short History of Private Life*. New York: Doubleday, 2010.

Butler, Jon. *Awash in a Sea of Faith: Christianizing the American People*. Cambridge, MA: Harvard University Press, 1990.

Church Newsroom. "Religious Freedom." The Church of Jesus Christ of Latter-day Saints. <http://www.mormonnewsroom.org/official-statement/religious-freedom>.

First Presidency of the Church of Jesus Christ of Latter-day Saints. "The First Presidency Warns Against 'Irreligion'" *Ensign*, May 1979.

Gaustad, Edwin S. *A Religious History of America*. San Francisco: Harper-San Francisco, 1990.

Grossman, Cathy Lynn. "Charting the Unchurched in America," *USA TODAY*, March 7, 2001.

Higgins, Andrew. "In Europe, God Is (Not) Dead: Christian groups are growing, faith is more public. Is supply-side economics the explanation?" *Wall Street Journal*, July 14, 2007. <http://online.wsj.com/news/articles/SB118434936941966055>.

Iannaccone, Laurence R. "Introduction to the Economics of Religion," *Journal of Economic Literature* Vol. XXXVI (September 1998), pp. 1465-1496.

Jefferson, Thomas. "Letter to The Danbury Baptist Association," January 1, 1802. <http://www.loc.gov/loc/lcib/9806/danpre.html>.

Madsen, Truman G. "Smith, Joseph: Teachings of Joseph Smith," *Encyclopedia of Mormonism*. 1992. <http://eom.byu.edu/index.php/Trials_of_Joseph_Smith#Legal_Trials_of_Joseph_Smith>.

Marty, Martin E. *Pilgrims in Their Own Land: 500 Years of Religion in America*. Boston: Little, Brown, & Co., 1984.

Maxwell, Neal A. "Meeting the Challenges of Today," BYU Devotional, October 10, 1978. <http://speeches.byu.edu/?act=viewitem&id=909>.

Meacham, Jon. *American Gospel: God, the Founding Fathers, and the Making of a Nation*. New York: Random House, 2006.

Micklethwait, John and Adrian Wooldridge. *God is Back: How the Global Revival of Faith is Changing the World*. New York: Penguin, 2009.

Miller, Perry. *Errand into the Wilderness*. Cambridge, MA: Belknap Press of Harvard University Press, 1956.

# Chapter 17

———. Roger Williams: *His Contribution to the American Tradition*. Indianapolis: Bobbs-Merrill, 1953.

Noll, Mark A. *A History of Christianity in the United States and Canada*. Grand Rapids, MI: Eerdmans, 1992.

———. *America's God: From Jonathan Edwards to Abraham Lincoln*. New York: Oxford University Press, 2002.

———. *Religion & American Politics: From the Colonial Period to the 1980s*. New York: Oxford University Press, 1990.

Oaks, Dallin H. "Preserving Religious Freedom," Talk at Chapman University, February 4, 2011. <http://www.mormonnewsroom.org/article/elder-oaks-religious-freedom-Chapman-University>.

———. "Religious Values and Public Policy," *Ensign*, October 1992.

Shah, Timothy Samuel. "Born Again in the USA," *Foreign Affairs*, October 2009.

Sims, Andrew. *Is Faith Delusion?: Why Religion is Good for Your Health*. London: Continuum, 2009.

Stark, Rodney and William Sims Bainbridge. *A Theory of Religion*. New Brunswick, NJ: Rutgers University Press, 1996.

Washington, George. Farewell Address, 1796.

Wuthnow, Robert. "Religion." In Peter H. Schuck and James Q. Wilson, eds., *Understanding America: The Anatomy of an Exceptional Nation*. New York: Public Affairs, 2008.

# Chapter 18

# POLITICAL CULTURE II: IDEOLOGY IN AMERICA

### GROVER CLEVELAND: PRINCIPLE ABOVE PARTY

Americans today are stuck in a flawed paradigm of politics. Our political culture is largely framed by a misleading binary that pits the ideology of "conservatism" on the one side against the ideology of "liberalism" on the other. Instead of thinking in terms of right and wrong, Americans are trapped thinking in terms of right and left.

One exemplary American who defied these simplistic categories was President Grover Cleveland—largely forgotten by history and only remembered, if at all, as the U.S. President who served two non-consecutive terms (he was elected in 1884, defeated in 1888, and elected again in 1892). But we should revere Cleveland for the integrity and character he brought to the White House. His guiding principle in office was not "right-wing" or "left-wing" ideology, but the public good.

Cleveland was born in New Jersey, raised in Clinton, New York, and eventually practiced law in Buffalo. While working as an attorney, Cleveland gained a reputation for two attributes: hard work and rugged honesty. He was always willing to put in the necessary effort to give his clients the best possible representation and would always tell the truth regardless of consequences.

The people of Buffalo saw Cleveland's honesty and work ethic and decided these traits were exactly what they needed to fix the problems of the time. The late 19th century was an age of political corruption and one-party rule. Politicians often exchanged public favors for private gain. Graft, bribery, and kickbacks were rampant. To combat this, the people elected Cleveland Mayor of Buffalo and then Governor of New York. Unlike so many others, Cleveland remained honest in spite of the temptations of political power. He worked

# Chapter 18

tirelessly for reform by taking on the corrupt forces in the legislature and big city machines. He rejected the idea that it is OK to tell little white lies for the "greater good," or to claim to believe something one does not in order to please voters. This rare honesty led the Democratic Party to nominate Cleveland for President.

Cleveland's party affiliation worked against him. The Democrats were the party of the South and had lost their political influence with their defeat in the Civil War. Since the Republicans, the party of the North, controlled all three branches of government without opposition, they succumbed to the corruption that comes with unchecked power.

## E.L. GODKIN AND THE MUGWUMPS

Many Americans, disgusted with this corruption, left the Republican Party altogether. Among them was E.L. Godkin, one of the leading journalists of the time and founder of the liberal magazine *The Nation*. Godkin had supported the Republicans his whole life because they had been the party of "liberalism"—which back then meant limiting government to its core functions of securing rights to life, liberty, and property. By working to end slavery and thereby gaining property rights for African-Americans, Lincoln and the Republicans had proven themselves the champions of liberalism.

But as the tide of corruption rose, Godkin and others like him felt that the Republican Party had lost its way. He decided instead to support the Democrat Grover Cleveland, believing him to be the more liberal candidate. Those like Godkin who defected to Cleveland became known as "Mugwumps" and, thanks to their efforts, Cleveland was elected President—the only Democrat to achieve the nation's highest office between the Civil War and World War I.

Although Godkin was temporarily stung by the Republican Party's betrayal of liberalism, even worse was the betrayal of liberalism itself that happened near the end of his life. Liberalism had once stood for individual rights and limited government, but around the turn of the century Godkin saw that it began to stand for expanded government power. In one of his last articles, "The Eclipse of Liberalism" (1900), Godkin claimed that liberalism, a philosophy that "freed men from the vexatious meddling of governments," was "a declining, almost a defunct force." "On the other hand," he said, "there is a faction of so-called Liberals who so little understand their traditions as to make common cause with the Socialists." Liberalism, he ruefully noted, was evolving into the opposite of what it had once been.

Godkin's dilemma is an ongoing dilemma for all of us and our country. Political parties and ideologies disappoint us. They constantly evolve in what they stand for and force us to continually re-evaluate our relationship to them. Understanding ideology, party, and their evolutions in America is our goal for this chapter.

## IDEOLOGY

You often hear the term "ideology" thrown about in political discussion. Even more often you hear people talk about the ideologies of "conservatism" and "liberalism." What do these terms mean?

Ideology is just a way to simplify politics. There are literally thousands of issues out there to consider—e.g., income tax, trade with China, marijuana laws, criminal punishment, regulation of meat processing, abortion, gay marriage, prescription drugs, gun control, immigration, military action in Syria, diplomacy with Iran—and it's much easier to choose a package of positions, an *ideology*, than it is to think about the issues individually. Many conceptualize ideologies by placing them on a binary (two-sided) political spectrum with one ideology on the left side and another ideology on the right.

Scholars trace the origin of the political spectrum back to the French Revolution of 1789 where a national assembly convened to debate the nature of the new French government. Some of the representatives supported the monarchy and sat on the right-hand side of the chamber while others opposed the monarchy and sat on the left. Thus was born the binary conception of politics.

The ideological spectrum found its way to America and we still use it today with "conservatives" on the right and "liberals" on the left. The position in the middle between the two sides we call "moderate." This binary spectrum constitutes the most common framework that people use to think about and discuss political issues and candidates. It lies at the core of American political culture.

## POLITICAL PARTIES

Differences of ideology lead to the formation of political parties, which are simply institutions that people organize, join, and support in order to advance their ideological agenda. Currently, the Republican Party tries to advance conservatism while the Democratic Party tries to advance liberalism. Working through parties, people can 1) unite various constituencies into a more powerful whole, 2) raise money for their causes, and 3) put forward candidates for office who will try to enact them.

Since America has almost always had two dominant political parties we often speak of the country as having a "two-party system." This two-party system probably formed and persisted because of the winner-take-all nature of elections in the U.S. Rather than apportioning seats in legislative bodies by the share of the vote received, the candidate with the most votes in a district takes a single seat. The Electoral College is also winner-take-all, with one presidential candidate receiving all of a state's electoral votes.

Many countries do not have a two-party system. Some democracies have multiparty systems in which legislators come from three or more parties and must form coalitions to pass legislation, while non-democratic countries, such as China and North Korea, have one-party systems.

## HISTORY OF IDEOLOGY IN AMERICA

America's two-party system took shape almost as soon as the country began. During George Washington's first term, Treasury Secretary Alexander Hamilton proposed controversial policies to strengthen the federal government, such as the creation of a national bank, funding national and state debts, and subsidizing industry through higher taxes. Many Americans, like Thomas Jefferson, opposed these policies as a dangerous concentration of government power. Those on Hamilton's side, who called themselves Federalists, proposed legislation, while those on Jefferson's side, who called themselves Republicans, opposed this legislation.

So ideology in the early Republic had, on the one side, the conservatives led by Hamilton who wanted to expand federal government power, and on the other side the liberals led by Jefferson who wanted to limit federal government power. In the early $19^{th}$ century, the torch of Hamiltonian conservatism was carried by Henry Clay and the Whigs while the torch of Jeffersonian liberalism was carried by Andrew Jackson and the Democrats.

This ideological split couldn't last, though. Ideologies and the parties that house them evolve because America evolves. As new issues come to the forefront, parties and ideologies change to capture positions on these new political questions. In the mid $19^{th}$ century, that new issue was slavery.

Hamilton and Jefferson both opposed slavery, but they did not make it a political issue, believing it would die out of its own accord (after all, that's what eventually happened in most Western nations). The rise of cotton as the basis of the southern economy extended slavery's life in America and then, when the U.S. acquired new western lands, the question arose as to whether or not slavery should be allowed to expand into those territories.

Conservatives, who belonged to the Democratic Party and were led by Senator Stephen A. Douglas, believed in *popular sovereignty*—the idea that slavery should expand according to the will of the local citizens. Liberals, who belonged to the newly formed Republican Party and were led by Abraham Lincoln, believed that slavery should be confined to the South where it already existed, but not extended to any new territories. This was the state of ideology and the parties in the mid $19^{th}$ century.

The ideological split represented by Lincoln and Douglas came to an end because the North won the Civil War. This had two consequences: 1) it led to the abolition of slavery, which ended the question of slave expansion as a national issue, and 2) it gave unchecked power to the Republicans, which resulted in the major corruption previously discussed.

The new divide in ideology pitted liberal reformers of the Democratic Party, exemplified by Grover Cleveland and supported by the Mugwumps, against conservative Republicans who wished to support business and remain loyal to the party that had saved the Union. Republicans simply tried to scare voters away from Cleveland and the Democrats by labeling them the party of "Rum, Romanism, and Rebellion."[1]

The rise of American industry in the late 19th century and the success of Cleveland liberals in reducing corruption led Americans to focus on some new concerns. The plight of the working poor had become much more visible in a newly industrialized America and many wished to take political action to remedy the problem. Industrialization had also made America the most powerful nation in the world, and many came to believe that the U.S. could use this military might to solve international problems. Those who wanted to use the Federal Government to solve problems of injustice both at home and abroad called themselves "liberals." To Godkin's chagrin, liberalism had now completely flipped its meaning: the American ideology of limited government had now become the ideology of expanded government.

This new liberalism cemented its definition and gained popularity in the 1930s when The Great Depression exacerbated the condition of the poor. The decade also saw the rise of fascist dictators around the world, such as Mussolini, Hirohito, and, of course, Hitler. Liberals like President Franklin Roosevelt were eager to use American might to defeat these dictators.

So ideology in the early 20th century pitted liberals, who largely belonged to the Democratic Party and revered FDR, against conservatives, who largely belonged to the Republican Party and followed Senator Robert Taft (the most notable critic of FDR's foreign and domestic policies). Roosevelt expanded government power to help the disadvantaged at home and defeat tyrants abroad, while Taft and the conservatives opposed these actions, believing the Federal Government still posed a threat to freedom, and that the U.S. should mind its own business in international affairs.

FDR's new liberal philosophy was remarkably popular, and Democrats dominated politics for the next few decades. But something happened after World War II that caused the ideologies and parties to evolve once again: the rise of international communism. Initially, liberal Democrats continued as the foreign policy interventionists ("hawks") wanting to confront this tyranny, but the Vietnam War debacle caused them to rethink their position. Liberals gradually abandoned the hawkishness of FDR, Truman, and JFK, and became more peace-oriented ("doves"). As the liberals stepped down, conservatives stepped up and became the staunch anti-communists who would "get tough" with the Soviet Union and defeat communism in the world.

This switch in foreign policy meant that late 20th century ideology was different than it had been in the first half of the century. Liberals, still in the Democratic Party and now

---

1 A reference to the recent secession led by southern Democrats and the Democratic Party's Irish constituency, which was known for Roman Catholicism and heavy drinking.

represented by Senator George McGovern, continued to believe in expanded government at home, but became more isolationist in foreign affairs. Conservatives, meanwhile, had found a hero for their new philosophy in Ronald Reagan. Like Taft, Reagan believed in limiting government power in the domestic sphere—less regulation, lower spending, and lower taxes—but unlike Taft (and like FDR), he believed in expanding federal government power in military and foreign affairs.

In the 21$^{st}$ century we largely remain within this framework, but new social issues (such as gay marriage, immigration, and abortion rights) have entered the equation with liberals being more libertarian on these questions and conservatives being more restrictive. Ideologies continue to evolve, though, and with each day that passes, the meanings of "liberal" and "conservative" change to fit new circumstances and pressures.

This whirlwind tour through the history of American parties and ideologies should be sufficient to convince you that the only constant in American political culture is change. It should also be sufficient to convince you that there are some big problems with the binary political spectrum that frames American politics as a contest of left-right ideologies.

## PROBLEMS WITH IDEOLOGY

The first major problem with American ideologies is that their very meanings are uncertain. "Conservative" and "liberal" are nothing more than labels attached to constantly shifting bundles of positions. There is no unifying philosophy or core principle behind them. If you ask 1,000 people "what is a liberal [or conservative]?" you will get 1,000 different answers. If you go to the dictionary, it will tell you that a liberal is one who favors change and a conservative is one who favors preservation, and yet liberals want to *preserve* entitlements, abortion rights, higher tax rates, and the environment, while conservatives want to *change* the Middle East, entitlement spending, deficits, Roe v. Wade, and government economic restrictions. Clearly, conservatives and liberals *both* want to change or conserve depending on the issue.[2] As you can see, ideologies are not philosophies, but just jumbled packages of political positions with nothing connecting them but a label.

This lack of essence explains why ideologies vary so radically in what they mean over time. Even if you were able to come up with a long list that included everything conservatives or liberals believe right now, that list would soon be obsolete as the ideologies evolved into something else.

Ideologies also mean different things in different places. In the U.S., hardcore anti-com-

---

2 Some will claim that if conservatives want change, it's only to go *back* to a previous state of affairs. But this ignores the ways in which liberals constantly pine for the past as well—the higher tax rates and economic equality of the 1950s, the fewer security restrictions before September 11, 2001, the greater economic regulations of the 1970s, and the communalism of the early 1800s. Even Karl Marx, the most notorious "Leftist" in history, wanted to return to the state of communism that existed before the advent of private property.

munists have been more identified with conservatism, and yet in China communists *themselves* are called "conservatives" (while those who wish to free up markets from state control are considered "liberals"). If you go to France or Australia and mention conservative President Ronald Reagan, they will call him a "liberal," which in those countries means a believer in free markets. As you can see, ideologies vary not only by time, but also by place.

The second major problem with the political spectrum is that it misleads us by limiting our perspective and making us prone to groupthink. When we see the world in terms of left-right, we are likely to accept positions because they are those of a socio-ideological group, not because they are correct. We simply let our ideology do our thinking for us.[3] This comes from laziness. It is far easier to say "ditto" to our peer group or a talk show host than it is to actually do the hard work of reasoning through the issues.

Shouldn't we seek what is correct regardless of the label attached? Shouldn't we just vote for the best candidate with the best views and not worry about who is tagged "conservative" or "liberal" or who is Republican or Democrat? Inasmuch as signing on to everything a party stands for is a substitute for making up our own minds, then the bumper sticker that says, "Vote Republican [or Democrat]: it's easier than thinking" is true. Nothing turns people into intellectual zombies as quickly as ideology.

The political spectrum also oversimplifies. The world of politics is far more complex than two sides. There are an infinite number of issues and an infinite number of ways to approach each one, and yet our political culture is saturated with the idea that all of politics boils down to a simple choice between just two options: left or right.

The persistence of something as misleading as the political binary can be explained by the "narrative fallacy"—the human need to impose a coherent story on chaotic facts, even when the story doesn't fit. Economist Nassim Taleb well expressed the problems of this thinking when he said, "The next time a Martian visits earth, try to explain to him why those who favor allowing the elimination of a fetus in the mother's womb also oppose capital punishment. Or try to explain to him why those who accept abortion are supposed to be favorable to high taxation but against a strong military. Why do those who prefer sexual freedom need to be against individual economic liberty?" This, he says, is the "absurdity of clustering."[4]

To see how truly ridiculous the political spectrum is, imagine that you showed up to the grocery store tomorrow and the clerk met you outside with two carts full of products and said, "which will it be today: Cart A, or Cart B?" You would be puzzled and say, "neither." You would almost certainly see products you liked and did not like in both carts. You would also see that many good products were found in neither cart. Far better than accepting a

---

[3] For instance, how many conservatives simply went along with the Iraq War because it was the "conservative" thing to do, and how many liberals opposed the Iraq War because it was the "liberal" thing to do? Should they not have considered this policy based on its own merits rather than the label attached to it?

[4] Taleb (2007, pg. 16).

pre-selected basket of random groceries is going inside the store and choosing what you want based on your own personal tastes, thinking, and preferences. Just as it would be silly to think that there are only two packages of groceries (or outfits, hobbies, friends, music, or movies), so it is silly to limit ourselves to two packages of issues in politics.

By accepting the political spectrum we also put ourselves in a conceptual prison that prevents the outside-the-box thinking that our country desperately needs. Since the conservative-liberal binary leads us to believe that there are only two ways to approach an issue, it prevents us from conceiving of other options that may be more adequate to solve political problems. Often the answer is found neither on the "right" nor the "left" (or a compromise between them), but outside the spectrum altogether. Numerous studies have also shown that groups composed of people of diverse political perspectives far outperform those of a monolithic perspective. This shouldn't surprise us since we arrive at truth not by declaring in favor of a dogma, but by subjecting ideas to critical examination (considering new evidence and alternative paradigms). Ideology prevents us from doing this by telling us we don't need to pursue truth, but already have all the answers. This is the opposite of humility and nothing could be more harmful to the pursuit of truth, which we desperately need in politics today.

We should be creating new ideas in politics, not buying into old ones packaged with thousands of others. Disciple leaders are the ones who will have to come up with these new ideas, so the sooner they can think beyond the stifling "conservative-liberal" paradigm, the better.

The third major problem with the political spectrum is that it creates hostility, prejudice, and polarization. It creates in our minds an "us vs. them" mentality in which one ideology is that of the heroes and the other ideology is that of the villains. We slap labels on people and then judge them accordingly, something the scriptures specifically command us not to do. An ideological label is a poor reason to give someone our respect or disrespect, and yet that's where the political spectrum leads us.[5]

This labeling ultimately produces hatred, incivility, and destruction of general decency. Instead of talking respectfully and trying to learn from others in politics, ideologues call names and tear down. Politics is a tricky, complex world—we need all of the humility we can muster in order to arrive at the best answers. But ideology leads us to believe that since we already *have* all the answers, all that remains is to destroy the "enemies on the other side" who stand in our way. In this mode of operation, we cannot find common ground or develop creative, pragmatic solutions to political problems.

Countless times, the prophets have commanded us to avoid contention, but ideology

---

[5] Ideologism—hatred of those who carry an alternative political label—is a form of bigotry as insidious as racism—hatred of those who carry an alternative racial label. Just as pride, hatred, and laziness drive racism, so pride, hatred, and laziness drive ideologism. Keep this in mind the next time you are tempted to derisively label someone a "liberal" or "conservative."

magnifies this unfortunate natural-man tendency. You can see this on sad display every evening on cable news. Adherents to the "two sides" scream and vilify one another in a never-ending, unfruitful excuse for public discourse. This hatred has the same source and effects as racism or any other kind of prejudice. The natural man, in his pride, needs to create "others" to hate, compare himself with, and feel superior to.

Although it would be nice if there were simply a "good guy" side in politics that had all of the answers, that's just not the way it is. That is why the prophets, although they have occasionally endorsed particular political positions, have never endorsed an ideology. In fact, here is what an official Church release said in 2009,

> Individual members [of the Church] are free to choose their own political philosophy and affiliation. Moreover, the Church itself *is not aligned with any particular political ideology or movement. It defies category.* Its moral values may be expressed in a number of parties and ideologies . . . The need for civility is perhaps most relevant in the realm of partisan politics . . . the Church views with concern the politics of fear and rhetorical extremism that render civil discussion impossible. Latter-day Saint ethical life requires members to treat their neighbors with respect, regardless of the situation. The Church hopes that our democratic system will facilitate kinder and more reasoned exchanges among fellow Americans than we are now seeing [italics added].[6]

Elder Dallin H. Oaks also noted the inadequacy of our binary political categories when he wrote,

> Those who govern their thoughts and actions solely by the principles of liberalism or conservatism or intellectualism cannot be expected to agree with all of the teachings of the gospel of Jesus Christ. As for me, I find some wisdom in liberalism, some wisdom in conservatism, and much truth in intellectualism—but I find no salvation in any of them.[7]

## HOW TO PROCEED

At this point, you may be thinking to yourself: "This is silly. Why do we even have ideologies and political parties if they constantly change, limit our thinking, and create hostility? Shouldn't we just do away with this whole idea of two sides and learn to think for ourselves?"

If this is what you think, you are in good company. The Prophet Joseph Smith warned members of the Church against political parties and asked that they look to people and principles instead. He said of the two major parties of his time,

---

6  Church Newsroom (2009).
7  Oaks (1991, p. 207).

## Chapter 18

> We care not a fig for Whig or Democrat; they are both alike to us, but we shall go for our friends, our tried friends, and the cause of human liberty, which is the cause of God ... We [shall act] in the cause of humanity and equal rights—the cause of liberty and the law.[8]

If it is good enough for Joseph Smith to evaluate issues on whether or not they advance liberty (rather than party or ideology), shouldn't it be good enough for us too?

The Founding Fathers also didn't like political parties. They saw them as vile "factions" that divided the country and corrupted politics. The Constitution says nothing about political parties (or ideology) because the Founders hoped that parties wouldn't form. They instead hoped the American people would choose candidates based on their virtue and wisdom, not the party they belonged to.

As President, Washington positively despised the party system that split his cabinet. Like a parent scolding bickering children, Washington had to constantly admonish Hamilton, his Treasury Secretary, and Jefferson, his Secretary of State, to stop fighting. Washington became so frustrated that he dedicated much of his Farewell Address to warning the people against the divisive party spirit that created contention and turned good people against each other. Jefferson eventually made overtures in this direction as well when he said at his 1801 inaugural, "we are all Republicans, we are all Federalists."

In fact, Jefferson and Hamilton never even recognized that they belonged to political parties. They believed instead that they were the guardians of the republic, protecting it against apostates who wanted to destroy liberty or the federal system.

## VALUE OF TWO PARTIES

If the Founders hated political parties and if parties do all of the rotten things mentioned above, why do we even have them? The answer is that in the 1820s Americans began to accept the two-party system as a legitimate part of the democratic system. The leader in this way of thinking was none other than future president Martin Van Buren. Van Buren explained that a two-party system could actually strengthen our democracy by having one party govern while the other party opposed. Some may call this "divisive," but it has the healthy effect of checking those in power and keeping them accountable. The division of power is the secret to freedom, and inasmuch as each party checks the power of the other, then the two-party system can help preserve liberty.[9]

Van Buren also noted, like Madison, that factions are an inevitable part of a free society, but, unlike Madison, he saw that parties themselves are not factions, but a means to *channel*

---

8 *History of the Church* 4:480, Dec. 1841.
9 Remember that the corruption of the late 19th century came about because the Republicans had no organized opposition.

the factions into larger groups, thus creating compromises that dilute their dangers. Parties don't encourage factions, said Van Buren, they help neutralize them.[10] One modern political scientist echoed Van Buren in these terms:

> The Founding Fathers deplored parties (or "factions," as they called them), and hoped that the country would be preserved from them. In actuality, the parties, once they began developing in the distinctively American manner, became guardians of the principles of the Fathers: guarantors of the diffusion of power and a stalwart defense against the unrestrained plebiscitary democracy which the Fathers judged to be the greatest of all political dangers.[11]

There are other reasons to accept the two-party system beyond those given by Van Buren. First, parties can serve to improve our information as voters. Yes, we need to do our own thinking and pick our own positions, but hundreds of candidates run for office each year—congresspersons, senators, mayors, city councilpersons, school board members, superintendents, sheriffs, state representatives, and so on. Few of us have time to exhaustively research every candidate to find out their views, but the parties serve a "branding" function that helps us in political decision-making.[12] Without knowing much about a particular candidate, we can still have a pretty good idea of what they stand for simply by noting their party. If we know which party we prefer, then we can usually know which candidate we prefer without having to spend our lives researching them.

Second, the two-party system serves a moderating, stabilizing function. When we have two candidates in an election it creates a "middle" that the candidates must move towards in order to be elected. This makes it less likely that an extremist will win. Candidates who run on a Communist or Nazi platform in America are almost certain to be defeated because the majority of Americans would shun such extremist candidates

Finally, a two-party system helps preserve the majority rule principle that is the linchpin of democracy itself. When there are two parties in an election, a candidate must receive at least 50% of the vote to win. This means that most of the people will have voted for the winner and even those who voted for the loser are more likely to accept the victor as legitimate because it was the choice of "the people." If there weren't two parties and candidates, but three parties instead, then a candidate could be elected with only 34% of the votes, meaning their election wouldn't have represented "the will of the people" (a majority).

---

10 See Hofstadter (1969).

11 Burnham (1959, 60).

12 It's a little like using a brand name to buy a pair of shoes. If you know you like the cost, performance, comfort, and durability of Adidas, for instance, then you don't need to research every pair of shoes at the store, you can just select a pair carrying the Adidas brand name and be confident that it will generally be what you want. Parties allow us to do that in politics.

*Chapter 18*

## THIRD PARTIES

While our two-party system is fairly robust, there have been periodic third-party challenges in U.S. history. Usually these third parties have had no effect at all. The third-party candidate runs for election, does not win, and does not affect the outcome (e.g., the 1980 presidential candidacy of John Anderson). At other times, the third party is incorporated into one of the major parties, as happened in the 1890s when the People's Party was swallowed up by the Democratic Party. Sometimes a third party will displace a major party, as when the Republicans displaced the Whigs in the 1850s.

But unfortunately, third parties in U.S. history have sometimes hurt the democratic process by thwarting majority will. For example, there were four major candidates in the 1860 presidential election, meaning that Lincoln was elected with only 40% of the vote. This gave his presidency a sense of illegitimacy and was enough for Southerners to secede from the Union. The Civil War—easily the greatest calamity in the nation's history—was at least partly caused by the breakdown of our two-party system.

Third-party candidates have continued to hurt our country in more recent years. In the year 2000, Ralph Nader's third-party presidential run cost Al Gore the election and put George W. Bush in the White House with less than 50% of the popular vote. Since more Americans had voted against Bush than for him, there was a sense throughout his two terms that he wasn't a legitimate president. Even before he had taken office, Bush was already controversial and despised. In that sense, much of the divisiveness and partisan bitterness over the past decade can be traced to a third party.

Even as the Church has always distanced itself from a particular party or ideology, it *has* supported the two-party system itself. There was even a time, as the Church was trying to gain mainstream political acceptance at the turn of the 20th century, when Church leaders systematically *assigned* members to the two parties so that they could fully participate in the American political system.

## CONCLUSION

As you can see, there is real value to the two-party system even as there are real problems with the binary ideological thinking that comes with it. Is there a way we can have our cake and eat it too? Can we possibly keep the advantages of our two-party system while also avoiding the pitfalls of ideology?

The answer, of course, is "yes." The ultimate takeaway from this chapter is that we can and should reject the simplistic left-right spectrum, but still support the two-party system. As the Church's statement says above, the principles of the gospel defy any narrow political category; they are too rich to be pigeonholed into any of the imperfect "philosophies of men" that pass for political ideologies today. Both contain some truth, but many falsehoods, so keep them at arm's length.

We should instead, as Joseph Smith counseled, evaluate policies based on their merits, not on their labels. Ask yourself, "What political position advances the principles of liberty under the Rule of Law?" then vote for or belong to a party on that basis. If the positions the two sides put forward are inadequate, then find creative, independent ideas that will contribute to liberty and the public good.

If we can keep loyalty to the gospel above loyalty to party or ideology, then we can view politics with a critical lens that will allow us to be willing to change our minds, see past the partisan cheerleading, and have compassion and charity towards those we may disagree with. Those are goals worth pursuing.

## CHAPTER 18 SOURCES/FURTHER READING

Brodsky, Alyn. *Grover Cleveland: A Study in Character*. New York: St. Martin's Press, 2000.

Burnham, James. *Congress and the American Tradition*. Chicago: Regnery, 1959.

Church Newsroom. "The Mormon Ethic of Civility," Church of Jesus Christ of Latter-day Saints, October 16, 2009. <http://www.mormonnewsroom.org/article/the-mormon-ethic-of-civility>.

Diggins, John P. *Up From Communism: Conservative Odysseys in American Intellectual Development*. New York: Columbia University Press, 1975.

First Presidency. "Letter on Political Participation," Church of Jesus Christ of Latter-day Saints, September 22, 2008. <http://www.mormonnewsroom.org/article/first-presidency-issues-letter-on-political-participation>.

Forcey, Charles. *The Crossroads of Liberalism: Croly, Weyl, Lippmann & The Progressive Era, 1900-25*. New York: Oxford University Press, 1961.

Godkin, E.L. "The Eclipse of Liberalism," *The Nation* (August 9, 1900).

Graff, Henry. *Grover Cleveland*. New York: Times Books, 2002.

Haidt, Jonathan. *The Righteous Mind: Why Good People Are Divided by Politics and Religion*. New York: Pantheon, 2012.

Hartz, Louis. *The Liberal Tradition in America*. New York: Harcourt Brace, 1955.

Hofstadter, Richard. *The Idea of a Party System: The Rise of Legitimate Opposition in the United States, 1780-1840*. Berkeley: University of California Press, 1969.

Jeffers, H. Paul. *An Honest President: The Life and Presidencies of Grover Cleveland*. New York: Perennial, 2000.

Lewis, Hyrum. "The Myth of American Conservatism," *Journal of the Historical Society* (12:1), 27-45.

Mattson, Kevin. *When America Was Great: The Fighting Faith of Liberalism in Postwar America*. New York: Routledge, 2004.

## Chapter 18

Morris, Edmund. *Colonel Roosevelt*. New York: Random House, 2010.

Nevins, Allan. *Grover Cleveland: A Study in Courage*. New York: Dodd, Mead, 1932.

Oaks, Dallin H. *The Lord's Way*. Salt Lake City: Deseret Book, 1991.

Schuck, Peter H. *Why Government Fails So Often, and How It Can Do Better*. Princeton: Princeton University Press, 2014.

Smith, Rogers M. "Beyond Tocqueville, Myrdall, and Hartz: The Multiple Traditions in America," *American Political Science Review* 87 (Sept 1993): 549-66.

Taleb, Nassim Nicholas. *The Black Swan: The Impact of the Highly Improbable*. New York: Random House, 2007.

# Chapter 19

# EXCLUSION & INCLUSION I: DIVERSITY, IMMIGRATION, & THE CREED

## JAMES WILSON: SCOTTISH-BORN AMERICAN

James Wilson is one of the "forgotten founders" of American history. He was a key player in the creation of the United States, but often overshadowed by giants like Washington, Franklin, and Jefferson. Wilson was born in Scotland and, in 1765, he immigrated to Pennsylvania where he took up the study of law. He proved himself a brilliant legal mind and eventually taught at the University of Pennsylvania.

Wilson was one of the foremost patriots in the years leading up to independence and a fierce defender of his adopted country against British authority. He was one of the few Founding Fathers to have signed both the Declaration of Independence and the Constitution. In the early republic, he pushed hard for democracy and served as one of the original six justices of the United States Supreme Court.

Although Wilson was not born in America, he was an important American who played a key role in each phase of the Founding. This chapter will explore how all of us, immigrants or not, become Americans. As with Wilson, our status as Americans has little to do with our place of birth, but everything to do with the ideals that America stands for.

## AMERICAN DIVERSITY

One of the wonders of America is its remarkable diversity. It is a land of myriad races, ethnicities, backgrounds, and religions. This is on display every four years at the Olympic Games. When a Chinese diver stands up to the platform, she looks Chinese. When a Kenyan runner steps up to the starting line, he looks Kenyan. When a Swedish gymnast ascends the balance beam, she looks Swedish. But the Americans look like Chinese, Kenyans, Swedes, and all other nationalities. You wouldn't even be able to tell Americans apart from other nationalities without their uniforms.

American diversity originates in immigration. From the beginning, the U.S. has been a nation of immigrants.[1] This immigration has been ongoing, but has occurred primarily in four waves. The first wave occurred during the colonial era when the immigrants came mostly from England. They formed the population base of the Founding era and had names like Washington, Jefferson, and Adams. There were, of course, immigrants from other countries (such as Scotland, Germany, and France), but the vast majority came from England. This explains why English is the predominant U.S. language and why American institutions are largely English in origin.

The next wave occurred in the mid 19$^{th}$ century. This time, the immigrants came from all over Northwestern Europe, but particularly Ireland as the Irish fled the ravages of the Great Potato Famine. This added not only to the ethnic diversity of America, but also to the religious diversity since the Irish were primarily Catholic.

In the late 19$^{th}$ and early 20$^{th}$ century, America entered the third wave of immigration. These "new immigrants" of the third wave still came largely from Europe, but this time from Eastern and Southern Europe—e.g., Russia, Greece, Italy, the Balkans, Poland. The religious mix of America now included large numbers of Jews and Orthodox Christians.

The passage of the Immigrant Act of 1924 restricted immigration, but it resumed in full force after the loosening of immigration laws in the 1960s. This launched a fourth wave of immigration that we are still in the midst of today. Those coming to America now hail largely from Asia and Latin America. These immigrants bring more Catholicism along with Asian religious traditions (such as Buddhism, Confucianism, Hinduism, and Sikhism).

It is also important to remember that the diversity of America was supplemented by a forced "immigration" of Africans during the years of the slave trade. African-Americans are a valuable part of the American mosaic, even if the slave origins were involuntary and detestable.

The value of diversity is becoming increasingly clear. Not only does it bring greater pluralism, which strengthens democracy, but also enriches culture, improves decision-making, and makes it more likely to find solutions to problems. Diverse groups generally outperform monolithic groups in almost any cognitive task since the exchange of ideas improves and expands the number of mental tools the group can draw from.[2]

But diversity can also lead to division and strife. It can cause a fracturing of national

---

[1] The exception, of course, are the Native Americans, but even they immigrated to America, only much earlier. The Navajos, for example, moved down from Canada before Columbus's arrival.

[2] Page (2007).

unity and a decline in social capital (or public trust).³ Americans have used three primary approaches to deal with this challenge: nativism, assimilation, and multiculturalism.

## NATIVISM

Nativism deals with diversity by trying to stop it. Nativists say that America is defined by a particular race and religion. In order to be a good, pure American, one must be a WASP (White Anglo-Saxon Protestant) and those who fall outside of this classification—blacks, Jews, Catholics, Asians, etc.—should be kept on the margins of society or out of the country altogether. Sadly, Nativism has a long history in American life and found its fullest expression in the "Know Nothings"⁴ of the 1850s who formed the "American" political party in order to stop Irish immigration and the "baneful influence" of their ethnicity and Catholic religion.

The nativist tendency comes from *ethnocentrism*, a "belief in the inherent superiority of one's own ethnic group or culture." It means privileging your group simply because it's yours and refusing to see beyond the confines of a particular perspective.

While nativism comes from ethnocentrism, ethnocentrism itself comes from pride—that recurrent vice of the Nephites which led to their ultimate downfall.⁵ At its core, pride means elevating ourselves above others and diminishing them to make ourselves feel superior by contrast (See Helaman 6:17 and D&C 58:41). Pride carries with it other sins, such as self-centeredness, conceit, boastfulness, arrogance, and haughtiness. Since it means measuring intellect, opinions, works, wealth, and talents against those of others, pride makes every man an adversary. As C.S. Lewis put it, "Pride gets no pleasure out of having something, only out of having more of it than the next man . . . It is the comparison that makes you proud: the pleasure of being above the rest. Once the element of competition has gone, pride has gone."⁶

Because of its origins in pride, Nativism is not an option for Latter-day Saints. Let's consider the other two options.

---

3 Putnam (2007).
4 When asked about the activities of their organization, the semi-secret group was told to respond, "I know nothing."
5 Nativism can also come from fear. Members of the Church can struggle with tendencies toward nativism when they look for neighborhoods with high concentrations of LDS members or worry about their child playing with another child on the block who has been trained differently. Motivations that produce nativism are often founded in the fear that allowing an influx of people who differ markedly from the majority may dilute or change treasured features of the status quo. One may try to limit immigration of a group out of hatred and pride, but could also love and respect different people while still worrying about the impact that the fusion of cultures might have.
6 Lewis (1952, pp. 109-10).

## Chapter 19

## ASSIMILATION

Assimilation deals with diversity by unifying various peoples under a common culture often symbolized by a "melting pot"—a single national identity which Americans, for all of their differences in skin color, national origin, or religion, melt into. This pot is the American Creed.

You will remember from Part I that the American Creed comprises the values of the Founding: equality, rights, and democracy. Under the melting pot view, these values—rather than race, ancestry, territory, or religion—define what it means to be an American. Immigrants become fully American by adopting the American Creed as their own.

The Creed is controversial because it has specifically Anglo-American origins. The principles of the Founding were the product of a unique English legacy of liberty that was transplanted to, and strengthened on, American soil (see Chapter 5). The Puritan settlers brought with them the English tradition of dissenting Protestantism. They believed in respecting God's authority, not man's, which led them to distrust government and give greater weight to individual rights and decisions over the prerogatives of governments, elites, or collectives.

## MULTICULTURALISM

Since not everyone in America is of English ancestry, not everyone is Protestant, and not everyone accepts equality, rights, individualism, property, and democracy, many reject assimilation. They propose a multi-cultural model of diversity instead. This is sometimes symbolized as a "salad bowl."

Multiculturalism says that there is no single American identity, but many distinctive American identities. Americans should not melt into one set of values, but embrace a multiplicity of values. Rather than celebrate our being Americans, the multiculturalists say, we should celebrate being "hyphenated Americans" (e.g., Anglo-American, Irish-American, Chinese-American, African-American, Polish-American).

There may be merit to this point of view, but if it means discarding the principles of the Founding, which we believe are inspired, Latter-day Saints may need to reject elements of this approach as well and go with the melting pot. Not only would this be in line with true principles, it would also be in line with the American mainstream. Assimilation is by far the most popular and predominant model of American identity. President Franklin Roosevelt voiced this standard melting pot viewpoint during World War II, when he said,

> The principle on which this country was founded and by which it has always been governed is that Americanism is a matter of the mind and heart; Americanism is not,

and never was, a matter of race and ancestry. A good American is one who is loyal to this country and to our creed of liberty and democracy.[7]

More recently, President Obama invoked the Creed, saying,

> We have a core set of values that are enshrined in our Constitution, in our body of law, in our democratic practices, in our belief in free speech and equality, that, though imperfect, are exceptional.[8]

## CURRENT IMMIGRATION

Most racial minorities and recent immigrants also accept the melting pot view. This is important to note in light of the wave of immigration we find ourselves in the midst of.

Immigration today has many advantages. First, accepting new immigrants is a deeply ingrained American tradition. As a nation of immigrants, America, by definition, welcomes new immigrants as part of its identity. It further adds to the diversity that makes our country interesting and strong.

Immigration to America also gives economic opportunity. Most of the immigrants who arrive in this country are poor and fleeing economic and political oppression. The golden rule seems to require that we allow them the same opportunities we enjoy.

Most economists also believe that immigrants help boost American economic growth. Immigrants generally work hard, fill important labor demands, and push up the country's GDP.

As you can see, there are many reasons to welcome new immigrants to America, but there are also some drawbacks. Since most of the immigrants who come to America are poor, they place a burden on the public sector. Immigrants and their children use more in public services (schools, welfare rolls, public assistance, government healthcare) than they pay out in taxes. Immigration also tends to drive both poverty and inequality upward. Adding millions of new immigrants to the ranks of the poor each year increases the poverty rate and the gap between the highest and lowest income groups. Poverty and inequality are also associated with higher crime rates, drug use, low education, and other social pathologies we are trying to solve. It's important to note that these problems are generally not permanent, as later generations of immigrants are able to break free of the poverty, but it is a problem in the short term (the first two generations). Since many of the current immigrants arrive here illegally, many Americans also feel that this immigration undermines the Rule of Law.[9]

---

7 Roosevelt (1943).

8 Obama (2009).

9 Modern immigration also has some wrinkles that make crafting policy toward it even more challenging than was the case a century ago, e.g., an expanded system of entitlements, the increased visibility of terrorism, a

# Chapter 19

The consensus among Americans is favorable to immigration, so long as it is legal and done in reasonable amounts. While our political system is paralyzed in a right-left division that can only conceive of the immigration debate in terms of "more" or "less," perhaps we should think outside the binary and consider instead what *kind* of immigration is best. We may want to think less about how many immigrants to admit, and more on finding those who: 1) have the skills our economy needs, 2) find themselves under the greatest oppression, 3) can add the most economic value, and 4) would be most likely to help reduce rather than add to our public debt. We are in desperate need of a paradigm shift on the immigration debate.

## CONCLUSION

We've now talked about the inclusion of immigrants as full Americans, but what about the history of exclusion and discrimination in the U.S.? How has America lived up to (or failed to live up to) its Creed by allowing *all* Americans full participation in the rights and privileges guaranteed by the Declaration? This will be the topic of our next chapter.

## CHAPTER 19 SOURCES/FURTHER READING

Appiah, K. Anthony, et. al. *Multiculturalism: Examining the Politics of Recognition*. Princeton: Princeton University Press, 1994.

Citrin, Jack. "Political Culture." In Peter H. Schuck and James Q. Wilson, eds., *Understanding America: The Anatomy of an Exceptional Nation*. New York: Public Affairs, 2008.

Hayden, Tom. "The Port Huron Statement of Students for a Democratic Society." 1962. <http://coursesa.matrix.msu.edu/~hst306/documents/huron.html>, accessed Jan 20, 2014.

Huntington, Samuel P. *American Politics: The Promise of Disharmony*. Cambridge, MA: Harvard University Press, 1981.

\_\_\_\_\_. *Who Are We? The Challenges to America's National Identity*. New York: Simon & Schuster, 2004.

Lewis, C.S. *Mere Christianity*. New York: Macmillan, 1952.

Obama, Barack. "The President's News Conference in Strasbourg." April 4, 2009. <http://www.presidency.ucsb.edu/ws/?pid=85959>.

Page, Scott E. *The Difference: How the Power of Diversity Creates Better Groups, Firms, Schools, and Societies*. Princeton: Princeton University Press, 2007.

Putnam, Robert. "*E Pluribus Unum*: Diversity and Community in the Twenty-first Century," *Scandinavian Political Studies* vol. 30, no. 2 (2007), 137-174.

---

new emphasis on multiculturalism. These forces make immigration a far more challenging issue than it was in pre-World War II times.

Roosevelt, Franklin D. Speech Activating the 442nd Regimental Combat Team. February 1, 1943. <http://www.homeofheroes.com/moh/nisei/index3_442nd.html>.

Schlesinger, Arthur M., Jr. *The Disuniting of America: Reflections on a Multicultural Society.* New York: Norton, 1992.

Schuck, Peter H. "Immigration." In Peter H. Schuck and James Q. Wilson, eds., *Understanding America: The Anatomy of an Exceptional Nation.* New York: Public Affairs, 2008.

Sipress, Joel M. "Relearning Race: Teaching Race as a Cultural Construction," *History Teacher* 30 (February 1997): 175-185.

# *Chapter 20*

# EXCLUSION & INCLUSION II: FULFILLING THE FOUNDING

### ELIZABETH CADY STANTON: "UNLOCKEING" WOMEN'S RIGHTS

In the last chapter we learned about the American Creed and how it serves to define and unify the country by *including* Americans of various national backgrounds, religions, ethnicities, and races as full participants in American life. In this chapter, we will see that, historically, America has not lived up to the ideals of the Creed and has instead *excluded* many groups from the principles of the Founding. The Creed advocates equality, rights, and government by consent, but many groups have been denied all three. Heroes throughout U.S. history have protested this hypocrisy by calling for the nation to make good on its founding promises.

One such hero was Elizabeth Cady Stanton, a brilliant 19th century New Yorker. Stanton wanted to grow up and practice law like her father so she excelled in school and mastered mathematics, classics, languages, and other subjects. But as her male classmates were heading off to college at Yale or Union or Columbia, she was told that, despite having been the brightest student at her school, she could not attend college because of her gender. She gained a fundamental sense of the injustices of exclusion early in her life.

Nonetheless, she understood that education begins, not ends, in the classroom. She couldn't go to law school and receive formal legal training, but she could daily enter her father's law library and, with guidance and intensive study, became one of the most learned legal minds in America.

Like most women, Stanton married and had children, but she wasn't through crusading for greater inclusion. She, like her husband, was an abolitionist who wished to rid the world of slavery. Together they would attend abolitionist conferences where men would take turns standing and speaking out against the systematic oppression of blacks. When Stanton felt she had something to add, she would also stand to speak, only to be told to sit back down and be silent because she was a woman. This made her conscious not only of American exclusion, but also hypocrisy. How ironic that abolitionists could claim to believe in equal rights and yet deny it to someone right in their midst. America, she saw, had the greatest ideals in the world, but was hypocritical for failing to live up to these ideals when it came to women.

## MARTIN LUTHER KING, JR.

In the next century, another great figure also witnessed American hypocrisy, but this time in matters of race. Martin Luther King, Jr. was born in Atlanta in 1929 to a middle class family. His father was a minister and a leader among his fellow blacks. This was not coincidental. To understand why ministers have always played a key role in African-American life we have to go all the way back to the southern slave system.

On the plantation, every minute of a slave's life was controlled by the master—eating, sleeping, working, recreation. Their lives were entirely regimented except for one brief moment: church meetings. The masters were usually Christians who believed that it was their responsibility to "Christianize" their slaves. However, it was unthinkable that the slaves would go to the white church so the master would allow his slaves to have their own little church meeting while he was gone. They would all assemble in the cabin of one of the slaves (this is where the title "Uncle Tom's Cabin" comes from) and there learn the Bible, sing hymns, and be taught basic Christian precepts.

In these few precious moments, the slaves had a modicum of freedom where they could develop an institution independent of their masters. The most literate, intelligent, and charismatic slave would emerge as the leader and serve as minister. Thus, they had a natural slave leader that was not a white-appointed overseer.

Slavery ended after the Civil War, but the freed slaves were left without any institutions—such as banks, social clubs, commercial establishments, political parties—except for one: *their church*. This was the one organization that they carried with them out of bondage so the church had to take on functions beyond spiritual ones. It became an all-purpose institution and the minister of the church became an all-purpose leader. He had to be a minister, but also lead in all other economic, political, and cultural matters, such as finance, activism, welfare, and entrepreneurism.

As the 19th century gave way to the 20th, this role for the black church and minister remained. No wonder a gifted man like Martin Luther King, Sr. would choose the ministry—the most prestigious and influential position in the black community—and no wonder that his talented son would follow him into this profession.

Martin Luther King, Jr., received a college education and then completed a Ph.D. in theology at Boston University. From there he took up a pastorate in Montgomery, Alabama and was thrown into the midst of the Civil Rights struggle, a quintessentially American quest to gain equality for all.

Some have claimed that because King often criticized America, he was "anti-American" and "unpatriotic." Nothing could be further from the truth. It was because he so deeply believed in the American ideals of freedom, equality, and consent of the governed that he criticized his country for failing to include all persons in those promises. King's critique of America was grounded in his commitment to America's founding principles. In the last public address of his life, he kept saying, "somewhere I read . . . " and then listed the rights guaranteed in the Constitution that blacks were often denied. In his most famous speech, he articulated "a dream" that America would "rise up and live out the true meaning of its creed." His highest political commitments were to the truths found in the Declaration; he just wanted America to make good on those truths.

Both Stanton and King identified a fundamental American hypocrisy—a hypocrisy that persists not because America is so bad, but because its ideals are so good. The American principles of equality, liberty, rights, and representation have become the aspiration of the whole world. With such high ideals to live up to, the U.S.A. has naturally fallen short.[1]

In this chapter we turn to three specific groups who have been especially denied full participation in these American ideals: racial minorities, the poor, and women. In other words, oppression has happened according to the categories of race, class, and gender. In many ways, the entirety of American history can be conceived of as a vast struggle to "fulfill the Founding" by ending these exclusions.

## Race

The quest to include African-Americans in the ideals of the Founding took place in two phases. The first phase culminated in the Civil War and Reconstruction and was largely led by President Abraham Lincoln. As you might expect, Lincoln introduced no new political principles in extending rights to blacks; he simply referenced the longstanding American ideals of natural rights and equality.[2] If, as Locke and the Founders said, rights came from our status as humans with agency ("endowed by their Creator") then, Lincoln reasoned, these rights had to apply to all regardless of skin color. Does someone of a darker skin with African ancestry have free will? Is he human? Is he a child of God? Then, according to the

---

1 Myrdal (1962).
2 See Brookhiser (2014).

Declaration of Independence, he possesses all of the natural rights that anyone else would have.

Some slaveholders protested that slavery was justified because blacks were less intelligent than whites (a false, but common belief at the time). Lincoln didn't disagree; he just turned the point back on the slaveholder and asked, "Is there anyone in the world smarter than *you*? Then, by your very own logic, the first person who comes along with higher intelligence has the right to make *you* his slave." If dark skin is justification for slavery, then can't we be enslaved by the first person who comes along with fairer skin? Lincoln's point was that neither intelligence nor skin color (nor any other secondary characteristic) could justify natural rights: only our status as humans created in God's image could. Inasmuch as all races belong to a common humanity, then all races have the same natural rights and the government should guarantee and enforce those rights (against slaveholders or any others who would take them). Such was the philosophy of the Founding that Lincoln helped extend to persons of all races in America. In that spirit, he issued the *Emancipation Proclamation* of 1863, which freed the slaves in the South.

Of course, Lincoln was assassinated before the full abolition of slavery, so his fellow Republicans continued the work after his death. During the post-Civil War phase of U.S. History that we call "Reconstruction" (1865-1877), they passed a series of Amendments to the U.S. Constitution that they hoped would grant full legal equality to African-Americans. *The 13th Amendment,* passed in 1865, abolished slavery in the U.S. once and for all (not just in the South); the *14th Amendment,* passed in 1868, gave full citizenship to all regardless of race; and the *15th Amendment,* passed in 1870, gave blacks (in theory) the same right to vote as white Americans.

But, as often happens, the intentions of government action didn't match the actual outcomes. Powerful racist forces, in the South especially, conspired to prevent blacks from enjoying their full rights as Americans. A series of southern-state Jim Crow Laws kept the blacks segregated and legally inferior, while terrorist organizations, such as the Ku Klux Klan, intimidated and inflicted violence upon them. In spite of Lincoln, the Civil War, and Constitutional Amendments, the promises of equality mentioned in the Declaration were still not fully realized.

A notorious 1896 Supreme Court decision, *Plessy v. Ferguson,* upheld the Jim Crow laws. It was undeniable that America's founding principles demanded equality, said the Court, but the races could be kept separate (segregated) but equal at the same time. This was manifestly untrue: blacks were consigned to attend inferior schools, frequent inferior public facilities, and even use inferior restrooms. *Plessy* upheld the lingering legal oppression of blacks that the Civil War, Lincoln, and the 13th-15th Amendments had hoped to end.

This state of affairs continued for over fifty years. Most white Americans felt that they had done enough for the cause of southern blacks. Almost all had sacrificed loved ones in the Civil War that brought slavery to an end. That, they reasoned, was enough. Furthermore, the first half of the 20th century was one of the most challenging times ever (with World War I, the Great Depression, World War II, and the beginnings of the Cold War) and the American people felt they had more pressing matters to attend to than ending the second-class status of African-Americans.

This is why extending American ideals to all races required a second phase—The Civil Rights movement of the 1950s and 60s led by Martin Luther King, Jr. After World War II ended and the Cold War had settled into a stalemate, Americans were finally willing to listen to those calling for equality. The first step came in 1954 when the Supreme Court overturned the *Plessy* decision with *Brown v. Board of Education,* which stated that "separate but equal" was unconstitutional. Integration of schools, for starters, was necessary to fulfill the American promise of equality.

Building on the momentum of *Brown v. Board,* Martin Luther King, Jr., who had recently emerged as the most popular black leader, launched further actions to secure Civil Rights. How could he and his confreres, limited in resources and political power, challenge the entrenched segregationist forces in America?

They had three tools at their disposal that they used to great effect. First, they had the power of the free market. Nobel-Prize winning economist Gary Becker has shown that the market does not care about skin color or any other arbitrary distinction, but only about value and efficiency. Even racists don't ask about the skin color of those who make the shoes they buy. They only care if those shoes are durable, comfortable, and offered at a reasonable price. Enduring racial inequality depends upon anti-market government actions (such as slave laws and Jim Crow Laws) to uphold racist privileges.

America's market economy meant that blacks had the freedom to engage or not engage in economic transactions with anyone they wished, which gave them the power of the boycott (a tool the Founding Fathers also used). This was most visible in Montgomery, Alabama where Civil Rights leaders called for a boycott of segregated buses. Blacks in the 1960s south were economically disadvantaged and so were more reliant on mass transportation than whites, but this in turn meant that the bus companies were reliant on them for business.

Blacks were also systematically discriminated against on buses—any time a white passenger boarded and needed a seat, a black passenger had to rise and move to the back. So King asked the black community of Montgomery to do something difficult—walk to work instead of taking the bus. They did so knowing that this would mean a long, exhausting walk of many miles (both before and after a long, exhausting day of work) and sacrificing the precious little free time they had outside of their jobs.

Once the bus companies saw what was going on they realized they were losing customers and would go out of business if things didn't change. King and the boycotters had forced their hand and, with some legal help, the boycott worked and served to end bus segregation. Score another one for Civil Rights and the power of economic liberty.

The second tool they had at their disposal was *civil disobedience*—public defiance of unjust laws. Now, some have decried civil disobedience as mere "law-breaking" and don't we, as Latter-day Saints, believe in "obeying, honoring, and sustaining the law"? Yes, but there are a few key distinctions between civil disobedience and breaking the law. First, the essence of breaking the law is profiting without getting caught. Someone who steals a diamond necklace from a store in the middle of the night is trying to enrich himself and wants to get away unpunished. With civil disobedience it is the exact opposite—the whole point is to get caught. The person disobeys the law not to get gain, but to send a message of the injustice of the defied law. This requires that they complete their action publicly, notify the aggressor of their intentions, and receive legal punishment for their actions.

Accordingly, the Civil Rights activists held "sit-ins" at "whites only" restaurants, participated in "freedom rides" on segregated buses, and coordinated public disobedience of Jim Crow laws. It worked just as they intended—they received no material benefit and were fined and thrown in jail for their actions. King, in fact, wrote his *magnum opus* while imprisoned in Birmingham. But as the protestors were arrested and carried off to prison, the TV cameras and reporters captured this for the rest of the country, touching the hearts of Americans and turning them from apathy to sympathy. Through the messages sent by civil disobedience, average Americans saw that fulfilling the Founding required abolishing the institutional racism and segregation that still existed in the nation.

As their final tool, King and the Civil Rights crusaders had the constitutional right of freedom of assembly. This meant that they could get their message out through well-publicized rallies. It was at one such assembly, the 1963 march on Washington, that King gave his famous "I Have a Dream" speech. Americans heard and were persuaded by his moving and timeless words that invoked the authority of the Founders: "I have a dream that one day this nation will rise up and live out the true meaning of its creed: 'We hold these truths to be self-evident: that all men are created equal.'"

All of these efforts bore political fruit. In 1964, with bipartisan consensus, Congress passed and the President signed a *Civil Rights Act* that ended systematic, public discrimination. A year later, a federal *Voting Rights Act* secured the right to vote regardless of race. Certainly inequities and racial discrimination remain in America, but the mid-1960s were a second great step towards overcoming those injustices and granting fuller inclusion in the principles of the Founding to people of all races.

## Class

Let's now turn to the next category of exclusion: class. At the time of the Founding there had been property-owning requirements to vote. Even so, America was still uniquely democratic because widespread land ownership meant that most free males could have a say in politics. But over time, that began to wane. America was growing rapidly through natural increase and immigration. This meant that the amount of land available for settlement was not keeping up with the growing population and the percentage of Americans eligible to vote was declining. In the 1820s, this became a visible problem and President Andrew Jackson represented a movement to uphold and extend America's democratic traditions by giving a political voice to those too poor to own land.

Jackson and others pointed out that America was founded on the principle of "government by the consent of the governed." Since those who did not own land were as governed and subject to laws as anyone else, then, according to the American Creed, they should have a right to give their consent to that government at the ballot box. Locke's philosophy demanded that the right to vote be given to all regardless of wealth.

On this principle, the states moved one by one to abolish their property-owning requirements. A poor, free man now had the same voting power as a rich man. For this reason, historians often refer to the 1830s as the era of "Jacksonian Democracy," an age when a crucial principle of the Founding—government by the consent of the governed—was expanded to include poor Americans.

## Gender

But if we take seriously the principle of government by the consent of the governed, then Jacksonian Democracy did not go far enough: women were still excluded and they made up over half of the American population. This is where Elizabeth Cady Stanton came in. Her greatest achievement was to follow the founding principles of John Locke to their logical conclusion in matters of gender, thus doing for women what Lincoln and King had achieved for African-Americans.

Stanton noted that Locke's philosophy maintained that people have rights by virtue of their status as free human beings created in God's image. Females, she pointed out, were obviously free human beings and would have the same rights as males in the state of nature. Consequently, women should have those same rights in society. Weren't women also governed and subject to the laws just like men? Yes, so according to the Declaration they *must* have the right to give their consent to the government and its laws through suffrage (voting rights).

To this end, Stanton and other like-minded women, gathered in Seneca Falls, New York in 1848 for a convention. This convention marks the beginning of the women's suffrage movement in America and it was there that Stanton presented her Declaration of Women's Rights, which demanded that women be included in the ideals put forward in the Declaration.

Stanton also understood, like Locke, that property rights were foundational to other

## Chapter 20

rights. Until women had the right to own and control meeting places, printing presses, and resources independent of their husbands or the government, then they couldn't fully realize their rights to life or liberty. So that's where Stanton aimed her first efforts. Noting that women were often subject to taxes but denied the right to vote, she invoked the most notable slogan of the Founding: "no taxation without representation." Until they had the right to vote, women were subjected to the same injustices as the generation of 1776 had been under King George III. In all of this, Stanton was essentially saying that if a man believed in the principles of the Founding, then he had to believe in women's rights as well.

Some opposed Stanton saying that women were "virtually represented" through their husbands or that they were "too virtuous" to be sullied by the corrupt realm of politics. But Parliament had made the same argument of "virtual representation" at the time of the Founding and it didn't work any better then. And if high virtue was reason enough to exclude someone from politics, then the most moral and virtuous of men (such as Washington and Lincoln) should also have been denied political participation.

Stanton's airtight reasoning and political efforts generated successes during her lifetime and after. She was directly responsible for the passage of women's property ownership laws in New York (other states followed). That was the foot in the door that eventually led to voting rights in select territories (Wyoming and Utah first), the drafting of a suffrage bill, and, finally, the passage of the *19th Amendment* to the U.S. Constitution, which gave women the same voting rights as men.

## LIMITS TO DEMOCRACY?

So far we have assumed that extending rights, particularly the rights of the governed to give their consent, is always a worthy goal, but are there limits? Lincoln, King, Stanton, Jackson and others worked to fulfill the Founding by addressing the problem of the exclusion of certain groups, but can efforts to extend voting rights go too far?

These are interesting and important debates in current political discourse. Until 1971, Americans under the age of 21 were not able to vote. This changed because young men, aged 18-20, were being sent in droves to die in the jungles of Vietnam. In a sense, they were more "governed" (controlled by the government) than any other segment of society and if they were old enough to die for a government policy, weren't they old enough to have a say in that policy too? Government "by the consent of the governed" demanded the voting age be lowered and this happened in 1971 through the *26th Amendment*.

But why stop at 18? Why not give 17-year-olds or 14-year-olds the right to vote? We can answer this, once again, by appealing to our founding principle of "government by the consent of the governed." Those under the age of 18 are not fully governed—they cannot enter into legal contracts or even be arrested and tried for crimes like adults can—so they do not yet have the right of consent (voting).

Many incarcerated criminals also lack full voting rights. Some believe that, regardless of one's crimes, they should be allowed a say in politics since they are completely governed by the state's penal system, which tells them when to wake up, where to go, what to do, when to eat, what to eat, and so forth. If we believe in government by the consent of the governed, shouldn't criminals have as much right to vote as anyone else?

To answer this we must consult the Declaration of Independence, which tells us that governments exist on the principle of the social contract. Felons, by violating the law, have broken the contract. They have deprived others of their rights to life, liberty, or property so they are punished with a commensurate loss of their own rights, including the right to vote.

## WHY DON'T AMERICANS VOTE?

By far the largest politically unrepresented group in America are those indifferent citizens who choose not to vote. Why is it that America, the most democratic nation on earth whose voting rights were so hard won, nonetheless has a voter turnout rate of about 50%? Why is it that only half of those who have the right to vote actually exercise that right at election time?

The first reason is cynicism. From a utilitarian point of view, one vote doesn't matter. It has almost never been the case that any single voter made a difference in a major election. Even if you sat out every election of your lifetime, the results would be exactly the same, so why vote if you make no difference? This is a problem in all democracies, but is more pronounced in the United States with our winner-take-all election system and Electoral College.

Many Americans also hold the cynical belief that it doesn't matter who is elected. Politicians usually break their campaign promises and ignore the will of the people anyway—new politicians, same bad policies. Because of this, many of us conclude that there really is no point to voting.

The response to this cynicism is that we don't vote because it has a utilitarian benefit for us personally or even because it will change the outcome. We vote because it is our civic duty. Upon the "duty-based" (deontological) approach to ethics, people should do what they would want universalized: do what is right regardless of consequences. Since we want to live in a voting democracy, we should exercise our right to vote as a way to uphold and support that system.

The second reason voter turnout is low in the United States is that voting is voluntary. Many nations have laws requiring their citizens to vote, but not the United States. Our very freedom in America leads to an unfortunate use of that freedom in low voter turnout. The complexity of voter registration in this country also discourages many from going to polls on election day.

Third, America's tradition of limited government reduces incentives to vote. Since our national government has had less direct influence on the lives of the citizens, Americans have cared less than those in other democracies what that government does.

Finally, and most importantly, Americans vote in low numbers because of demography. America is a young country with a comparatively high birthrate and many young immigrants. It is simply a fact that older people vote at a higher rate than younger people so a younger country will have, by the laws of mathematics, lower voter turnout. The above four explanations help us understand why Americans vote in low numbers, even as we try to extend the vote to excluded groups.

## CONCLUSION

What about continuing debates over discrimination? Most of us agree that the government should not discriminate against someone (for office, voting, employment, or military service) based on national origin, race, religion, or gender, but what about *private* discrimination? What if an anti-Mormon owns a house and would prefer not to rent that house out to members of the Church of Jesus Christ of Latter-day Saints? Should they be permitted to discriminate in this way with their own property? What about not renting a home to Jews, blacks, Muslims, or any other group? Such discrimination, most of us believe, would be wrong, but don't natural rights mean the right to do things people deem wrong?

Of course most people oppose discrimination *against* minority races, but what about discrimination *in favor* of those same races? Some say *affirmative action* policies are necessary to redress past wrongs and give greater equality of opportunity. Since centuries of discrimination have created systematic barriers and disadvantages (such as low income) for minorities, shouldn't we take positive (affirmative) steps towards righting those wrongs rather than merely ceasing discriminatory behaviors? Others oppose affirmative action saying that every discrimination in favor of one group (say, Mormons) would be a *de facto* discrimination against another group (say, Catholics). They also say that affirmative action policies are ineffective and actually harm minority groups by reinforcing negative stereotypes. This important debate continues.

Racial minorities, even though they now have full citizenship rights, still wield disproportionately less economic and cultural power. Women are generally under-represented in high paying professions while men are generally over-represented in prison and homelessness. Should we do something about these inequities if we truly believe in fulfilling the Founding? If so, what? Contrary to what ideologues will say, there are no easy answers to these questions. But find answers we must if we are to continue the project begun by the Founders and include the excluded into the high ideals of America.

## CHAPTER 20 SOURCES/FURTHER READING

Branch, Taylor. *America in The King Years*, 3 vols. New York: Simon & Schuster, 1989-2006.

Brookhiser, Richard. *Founders' Son: A Life of Abraham Lincoln*. New York: Basic Books, 2014.

Catton, Bruce. *The American Heritage Short History of the Civil War*. New York: Dell, 1960.

Chesnutt, Charles W. "The Sheriff's Children" (1889). <http://www.chesnuttarchive.org/works/Stories/sheriff.html>.

Donald, David Herbert. *Lincoln*. New York: Touchstone, 1996.

Douglass, Frederick. *Narrative of the Life of Frederick Douglass, An American Slave* (1845). <http://www.gutenberg.org/files/23/23-h/23-h.htm>.

Daniel, Feller. *The Jacksonian Promise: America, 1815-1840*. Baltimore: Johns Hopkins University Press, 1995.

Frady, Marshall. *Martin Luther King, Jr.: A Life*. New York: Penguin, 2002.

Ginzberg, Lori D. *Elizabeth Cady Stanton: An American Life*. New York: Hill and Wang, 2010.

Howe, Daniel Walker. *What Hath God Wrought: The Transformation of America, 1815-1848*. New York: Oxford University Press, 2007.

King, Martin Luther, Jr. "Letter from a Birmingham Jail" (1963). <http://www.africa.upenn.edu/Articles_Gen/Letter_Birmingham.html>.

McPherson, James M. *Battle Cry of Freedom: The Civil War Era*. New York: Oxford University Press, 1988.

Myrdal, Gunnar. *An American Dilemma: The Negro Problem and Modern Democracy*. New York: Pantheon, 1962.

Oates, Stephen B. *With Malice Toward None: A Life of Abraham Lincoln*. New York: Harper & Row, 1977.

Patterson, Orlando. "Black Americans." In Peter H. Schuck and James Q. Wilson, eds., *Understanding America: The Anatomy of an Exceptional Nation*. New York: Public Affairs, 2008.

Raboteau, Albert J. *Slave Religion: The "Invisible Institution" in the Antebellum South*. New York: Oxford University Press, 1978.

Schlesinger, Arthur M., Jr. *The Age of Jackson*. Boston: Little, Brown, & Co., 1945.

Stanton, Elizabeth Cady and Susan B. Anthony. *Selected Papers of Elizabeth Cady Stanton and Susan B. Anthony*. edited by Ann D. Gordon. New Brunswick, N.J.: Rutgers University Press, 2003.

Wilentz, Sean. *The Rise of American Democracy: Jefferson to Lincoln*. New York: Norton, 2006.

# Chapter 21

# TECHNOLOGY, SOCIALIZATION, COMMUNICATION I: POSSIBILITIES

### HENRY DAVID THOREAU: TRANSCENDENTALISM

Technology is foundational to American life and culture. To introduce the promise and perils of technology, we turn to the great American essayist Henry David Thoreau. Born and raised in early 19$^{th}$ century Boston, Thoreau graduated from Harvard, and then took a teaching position in a local school. His life was adequate, but he felt stifled and limited by urban society. Everything seemed so artificial and compartmentalized. Everywhere he looked he saw buildings, roads, businesses, factories, and, worst of all, machines. The emerging modern world was based on machine production, machine transportation, and machine recreation. It seemed that even people themselves were becoming insignificant cogs in a vast machine that deprived them of will and autonomy.

This frustration with modern life led Thoreau to quit his job and retreat into the wilderness. Thoreau's account of this experience became the 1854 American classic, *Walden*. In the introduction he said,

> I went to the woods because I wished to live deliberately, to front only the essential facts of life, and see if I could not learn what it had to teach, and not, when I came to die, discover that I had not lived. I did not wish to live what was not life, living is so dear; nor did I wish to practice resignation, unless it was quite necessary. I wanted to live deep and suck out all the marrow of life, to live so sturdily and Spartan-like as to put to rout all that was not life, to cut a broad swath and shave close, to drive life into a corner, and reduce it to its lowest terms.

*Chapter 21*

Thoreau was not alone in his feeling about the need to rejuvenate the human spirit in defiance of the technological world. Other Americans of the time who shared his feelings were called "Transcendentalists." Among the Transcendentalists were poets Emily Dickinson and Walt Whitman and philosopher-essayist Ralph Waldo Emerson.

## ROMANTICISM

Transcendentalism was the American version of a larger trans-continental movement called *Romanticism*. At its core, Romanticism was a backlash against the *Enlightenment*. Enlightenment thought, which dominated the late 18$^{th}$ century, conceived of the universe in machine-like terms and said that one can understand nature the same way one understands a clock: by prying it open and analyzing the constituent parts. Isaac Newton, the greatest figure of the Enlightenment, used reason and analysis to "dis-cover" (uncover) laws of motion and gravity that had always been there, but hidden. To Enlightenment thinkers, science is the means by which we gain important knowledge, reason holds the key to understanding, and analyzing this "machine" universe of ours is how we arrive at truth.

But is that view totally adequate to human needs? The Romantics didn't think so and, chances are, neither do you. Imagine for a moment that you come home from a date and tell your roommates about what a wonderful time you had and how you think you are in love. Suddenly, one of your roommates pipes up and says, "Technically, what you perceive of as 'love' is actually a chemical exchange in your brain that creates a pattern of neural discharge according to external stimuli which, in turn, produces a sensation of euphoria that you interpret as amorous feeling." Would you accept this "scientific analysis" of love from your roommate? If not, then you agree with the Romantics.

Enlightenment rationality can explain much, but it has limits. Science is silent on that which is most important—those transcendent elements of life such as value, emotion, free will, spirit, and beauty. The Enlightenment, said the Romantics, must be kept in its place because its mechanical view can have a deadening, soul-destroying effect. Instead of looking to science for transcendent truth, we should look to literature, art, or poetry. The Enlightenment thinker would have us believe that if we want to understand humanity, we should examine brain scans, dissect bodies, or observe brain patterns that can be quantified and analyzed. The Romantic would counter that there is far more about the meaning of humanity in Shakespeare, Yeats, or Byron than in the laboratory.

Romantics like Thoreau thought that we could fight the Enlightenment through a retreat to nature. Why do Americans go camping? We live in comfortable homes with thermostats set to ideal temperatures down to the very degree, we sleep on mattresses carefully engineered to caress us to sleep with a perfect balance of firmness and softness, and we can summon hot, delicious food from our kitchens any time we want. Why do we leave all of this, venture into the woods, eat canned food burnt over an open fire, get bit by mosquitos,

# Technology, Socialization, Communication I: Possibilities

and sleep in a nylon sack on hard, cold ground? The Romantics explained that we do it to replenish the soul and fight the monsters of an all-encompassing, conformist, technological society.

One of the greatest expressions of the Romantic point of view is found in Mary Shelley's novel *Frankenstein*. We think of Frankenstein as a common Halloween monster, but Shelley had much deeper purposes in mind when she wrote her book. Frankenstein, remember, was not the monster. Dr. Frankenstein was the protagonist of the story, but also the villain because he was an Enlightenment scientist to whom nothing was transcendent—even humans were mere materials to work with. To Dr. Frankenstein, science could do no wrong.

But it did go terribly wrong, and that's the main theme of Shelley's book. In his scientific disregard for humanity, Frankenstein created a tragic monster that killed his loved ones and haunted him to his death. More than a horror story, *Frankenstein* is a parable of the Romantic point of view.

Dr. Frankenstein went into nature to confront his monsters and we might say the same of Thoreau. Frankenstein lost his battle and Shelley feared that the human race as a whole would do the same by letting science slip out of our control. The monster, science, can have terrible consequences if not kept within its bounds.

We find this same theme in ancient literature and myth—such as Icarus flying too close to the heavens, heathens erecting the Tower of Babel, or Prometheus bringing fire to the world. They all provide us with a common warning: science and technology, while appealing and useful, can have many unfortunate, *unintended consequences*. [1]

In this chapter and the next, we will pursue this theme further. First by taking a holistic view of science and technology and seeing how it impacts human society in general, and then by looking at how technology has had unintended consequences on American life in particular.

## TECHNOLOGICAL VIEW OF HUMAN HISTORY

Let's begin with the big picture—the long technological view of world history. The first *homo sapiens* made their living much as animals do—by hunting and gathering. They killed prey and gathered roots, nuts, and berries and, by so doing, either had enough to eat or died according to the Darwinian logic that governs the natural world. Hunter-gatherers wandered about looking for food in little bands based purely on kinship. They had no formal government or social order beyond the rule of a chief they followed because of his charisma,

---

[1] Romanticist themes are also found in our pop culture, as in the movie *Dead Poet's Society* about young men who find themselves stifled by rigid parents and a conformist boarding school. Their teacher, played by Robin Williams, encourages them to challenge this rote existence through poetry, literature, drama, and spontaneity. They eventually revive the Dead Poet's Society and retreat at nights to a cave where they find precious moments of autonomy and self-expression.

prowess, or position in the family. They were constantly on the move and finding food was the sole occupation of everyone in the group.

## AGRICULTURAL SOCIETY

Then, in what was the most consequential technological moment in history, somebody (probably in the Middle East) figured out that humans didn't need to just wander around and hope to *find* food, they could *produce* food by raising it themselves. Instead of hoping that their tribe might find a few stalks of wheat, these clever people decided to put the seeds in the ground, divert water from the river, and then let the wheat stalks grow as cultivated crops to consume at their whim. Instead of tracking wild animals, they enclosed and bred animals themselves to slaughter whenever they wanted. *Voilà*: humans had invented agriculture. They now had a surplus of food rather than just a subsistence level.

This wasn't just important because it meant that they had more to eat, it also meant, for the first time in history, an extensive division of labor. Most people, about 80%, were involved in food production, but the other 20% became carpenters, masons, soldiers, merchants, etc. The wealth-producing process of specialization and trade described by Adam Smith started to take off at this point.

This division of labor also meant the beginning of religion and philosophy. Agricultural societies could now afford to pay a class of people to ask the big questions: Who are we? Where did we come from? What are we doing here? What is the cosmos? What should we be doing with our lives? What is right and wrong? Humans, with their surplus of food (and therefore time), now invented writing, which meant they could transmit knowledge across space and time. Thus was born literacy, education, historical consciousness, and culture.

Another great change was that agricultural peoples were sedentary instead of nomadic. They no longer had to wander in search of their food, but could stay put. This was convenient, but it also left them vulnerable to plunder and attack by others. For protection, they had to create governments and cities. They vested monarchs with power and, with their surplus resources, supported armies and built walls around their homes to protect them from external and internal chaos.

Because the source of their wealth was in agriculture and agriculture depends upon cultivable land, power in this society resided with landholders. Those who controlled land controlled food production—the foundation of their entire society. The kings, aristocrats, and lords maintained power by controlling land either directly or indirectly.

## INDUSTRIAL SOCIETY

The next big turn in human technological history occurred around the year 1700. Throughout the pre-modern era, if someone wanted work done, they either had to do it themselves or harness an animal to do it. If they wanted a millstone turned, for instance, they could turn it themselves or lash the turning lever to the back of a beast.

Starting in the middle ages, humans realized that they didn't have to rely solely on biological muscle power (animal or human); they could exploit *inanimate* sources of power. Instead of pushing the millstone themselves, they could put a wheel into a stream and attach it to a shaft that would rotate the millstone and grind the wheat. By the 1700s, Europeans had figured out that they could take little black rocks (coal), light them on fire, heat up water, and use the steam pressure to rotate a piston that could turn the wheel and mill the grain.

But why stop there? Why not use inanimate power to weave fibers together into cloth or, eventually, create steel beams, manufacture pairs of shoes, and create an infinite variety of consumer goods? Thus was born the machine, the factory, and industrial society. We often call this machine-age the *modern era*.

Notice that under this new system, humans were no longer solely or even primarily producing food. These factories pumped out non-food, physical consumer goods, such as light bulbs, pencils, jeans, sunglasses, cars, hats, and sprinkler heads—tangible, physical products that humans could use.

At this point, power shifted from landlords to capitalists. The most important production in the modern age no longer depended upon land, but upon capital: the tools, factories, and machines used to produce more goods. The owners of capital, men like Andrew Carnegie, had remarkable wealth and power.

## POSTINDUSTRIAL SOCIETY

Of course Americans no longer live in pre-modern societies, but we no longer live primarily in modern societies either. Americans have now entered the "postmodern" or "post-industrial" age. This new age was brought about by the most recent human technological revolution: we call it the *information revolution*.

In the postmodern present, society is not only moving away from agricultural production, but industrial production as well. Fewer and fewer people in America work in factories and ever less of our economy is dedicated to producing industrial goods. We fight against this because we don't understand it. We are angered that we buy our industrial goods from China instead of making them ourselves, but fail to realize that this is simply a function of our post-industrial transition. The decline of manufacturing is not, in that sense, something to lament. If our rubber hose says, "Made in China," it means that China is doing our industrial work for us so we can focus on post-industrial production.

This new post-industrial society is fascinating. As we move away from producing food and industrial products, we increasingly create something that *isn't even physical*—information. Post-industrial workers spend most of their lives producing little patterns of ones and zeroes that don't exist in the material world; they exist in the platonic realm of cyberspace. We might look at these patterns on computer screens or printed pages, or download them to disks, but ultimately, their existence is intangible.

This is puzzling: most of today's college graduates will spend their lives making something that nobody will ever touch. Since the most valuable product in this new age is *information*, people pay CEO's, programmers, financiers, lawyers, and engineers millions of dollars to produce patterns of binary code. So the primary site of production in our age is no longer the farm or even the factory, but the office.

Those who have the most power in this new age are not those who own land or capital, but those who possess *knowledge* and technical expertise. What's great about this is that anyone can acquire knowledge and it is unlimited in supply. That is one reason the prophets have been hammering home the theme, "get all the education you can," for the past few decades. They are not prophets for nothing; they see the direction history is moving. Bill Gates didn't get rich and influential by owning land or factories, but by his expertise in producing patterns of binary code that we call operating systems. Warren Buffet didn't become the world's richest man by owning farmland or factories, but by having knowledge of finance.

But it's even more puzzling when we consider what we can do with information once it is produced. If you lived in a pre-modern society and produced wheat or lived in a modern society and produced steel, you had to move these goods physically from the site of production to the site of consumption. Post-industrial products (information) move near the speed of light. We can move our most valuable products anywhere in the world instantaneously at the press of a button (indeed, billions of dollars' worth of information may be travelling through the wireless airwaves in the very room where you are sitting at this moment). This is mind-boggling in its implications.

It gets even stranger: industrial products can be *reproduced and replicated* instantaneously and infinitely *at no cost*. It would be nice if we could go to our car, hit "Control + C" and "Control + V," and have a second (or ten thousandth) copy of the car, but that's exactly what we can do with the information products that are even more valuable than cars. For instance, a Hollywood blockbuster film, which can be downloaded digitally, costs tens of millions of dollars to make, and yet we can make all of the copies of it that we want for free (not legally, of course, but we'll turn to that perplexing issue later).

We know that in the 18$^{th}$ century, humans invented machines to do their physical labor, but in the 20$^{th}$ century, humans invented machines to do their mental labor. These machines don't just work for us, they *think* for us.

The story of the origin of such machines is an essential but under-appreciated part of American history. During World War II, America was trying to develop more accurate missiles to bring the war to a speedier end. This required extensive mathematical calculation so the government started hiring mathematicians and math clerks—usually women since the men were off fighting. They called these young women "computers" since they spent their day doing computations with pencil, paper, slide-rules, and chalkboards.

It wasn't enough. We needed more computing power than these humans could give so some scientists came up with an idea: if we can get machines to do physical work in the war (e.g., jeeps, tanks, rifles, aircraft carriers), why can't we have machines do mental work as well? The government gave the go-ahead to scientists at the University of Pennsylvania to build a "thinking machine"—a computer that would be non-human.

The computer they built was clumsy, slow, and enormous—constructed with thousands of vacuum tubes that filled up a big room—but it had two important characteristics that still define computer technology today: first, it would be based on binary code, and second, it would be programmable (originally programmed using switches and punch cards). By the time this machine (ENIAC) was finished, the war had ended, but the information age was just beginning as experts began to make improvements on their new invention. Eventually, the transistor replaced the hot, bulky, expensive vacuum tubes and all of the computing power that used to take up many rooms could be wired onto a teeny silicon chip the size of your fingernail. They called it a "microchip" because, compared to what it replaced, it was, indeed, micro.

From that point on, the computers would get smaller and smaller and more and more powerful (while always keeping the core characteristics of binary language and programmability). IBM, HP, Microsoft, Apple, Google, and other computer companies have continued pushing forward information technology. Computing power has climbed so high that we now carry around thinking machines in our pockets that are far more powerful than ENIAC. And whereas ENIAC cost so much that only the government could afford it, now even most "starving college students" own multiple computers (laptops, iPods, tablets, smartphones). These little thinking machines allow us to produce, share, and access infinite amounts of information at the speed of light. This computer revolution explains the post-industrial society we now inhabit.

Most relevant for our purposes here, this revolution was launched and is centered in America. While the agricultural revolution took place in the Middle East, and the industrial revolution occurred in England, the information revolution is moving forward in places like San Jose, Seattle, and even Boise. America is leading the way in this next great turn in human history.

The post-industrial revolution also has relevance for the gospel. Atheists of the 21$^{st}$ century are still advancing arguments based on the old industrial-age paradigm that conceived of everything as matter in motion. Humanity has now moved far beyond this. We now recognize information, a non-material entity, as being as fundamental to reality as matter. The information revolution is now proving what the scriptures have long told us: everything is

# Chapter 21

full of "intelligence" (a word that the first computer scientists used before coming up with the word "information"). Information is embedded in everything from atoms to microorganisms. Physicists even conceive of quarks, the sub-sub atomic particles that compose the whole universe, as tiny "quantum computers."

Information is even implanted in every one of our cells. Each strand of DNA, we are now finding out, is a mega software program of almost unfathomable complexity and power containing instructions on how to make arms, legs, brains, noses, etc. Even many atheists submit that this suggests some kind of "higher intelligence" that has "programmed" life.[2] Here we humans invented computers in the 20$^{th}$ century only to find out shortly thereafter that God had done it first. We have been walking around for thousands of years with software code embedded in the cells of our bodies, but we didn't even have a conception of software until recently.

"Intelligence" in the scriptures may refer to the immaterial order/information in nature and the ordering powers that God and his children possess. Intelligence can comprehend and create information. Intelligence is everywhere—it's a scientific fact. Programs require programmers. Designs require designers. Creations require creators. The fingerprint of God is everywhere. Don't look for God in the deep, dark corners of the universe (or in the gaps of scientific knowledge) when He is so omnipresent in everything—the light that shineth in all things.

## THE ADVANTAGES

Now that we've taken a quick tour through technological history, we return to our original question: what are the benefits of scientific and technological advance? We could list hundreds, but let's summarize in just a few key points.

The first advantage of technology is that it gives us new products that your parents and grandparents couldn't have imagined at your age. For example, you carry around a phone in your pocket, but it is also a little movie studio, web browser, calculator, multimedia player, video game system, and more. Think of all the other devices that make our lives comfortable: light bulbs, washing machines, cars, televisions, microwave ovens, central heating and air conditioning, indoor plumbing, etc. Each eases our burdens and allows us more leisure, but those are just the recent inventions. If we reach back hundreds of years we find fire, the wheel, the printing press, the engine, the lever, and others.

The miracle of new products is particularly visible in the realm of medicine, where new

---

2   Author Robert Wright, for instance, suggests that the existence of the complex "computer code" that is DNA points to some kind of "universal programmer" (Wright (2000)). Francis Crick, the co-discoverer of DNA, assumed that this code must have been created by extraterrestrial beings and transported to earth (Crick (1982)). Philosopher Thomas Nagel argues that the evidence for mind independent of matter is now overwhelming (Nagel (2012)).

treatments, preventive care, and surgical procedures have extended lives remarkably. You have seen this even in your own lifetimes. HIV used to be an immediate death sentence, but today people with the virus continue to live for decades. Cancer also used to mean almost certain, immediate death, but today over half of cancer patients live out their normal life spans. Vaccines for polio, smallpox, and other deadly diseases have saved countless lives. Women used to take a calculated risk of death in deciding to have children, but in the first world that is a thing of the past. From all of this, Americans in the year 2000 can expect to live *twice as long* as Americans did in 1900. This is just a small sampling of the new possibilities available through technological advancement.

But it's not only the quality of what technology gives; it's also the quantity. Technology is a major part of the magic of free exchange. As people specialize, they innovate and magnify many times the goods they create. Notice how little of our income is spent on food today compared to previous eras. Agricultural technology has multiplied the amount of food available many times over. It is not just that humans invented shoes, cars, and computers, but we have *more* shoes, cars, and computers with each passing generation.

Finally, and most importantly from a gospel perspective, science and technology give us greater light and knowledge. They satisfy that inherent human desire to know. The best part of our nature thirsts after knowledge and leads us to seek education. Students will forget most of what they learn, but developing a passion for acquiring knowledge and wisdom has eternal benefits. The scriptures even tell us,

> Whatever principle of intelligence we attain unto in this life, it will rise with us in the resurrection. And if a person gains more knowledge and intelligence in this life through his diligence and obedience than another, he will have so much the advantage in the world to come (D&C 130:18-19).

All of the material possessions science gives us will be rotting away on this temporal planet centuries from now, but our knowledge will persist and be of value as we continue our eternal progress.

The Glory of God is intelligence, so increasing in intelligence, through science or otherwise, makes us more like God. Most scientists don't know this, but in gathering data, developing theories, and conducting tests in laboratories, they are doing God's work. That is why they find it so rewarding. Science gives greater knowledge, greater knowledge is godly, ergo, science is godly and moves us towards eternal growth and godhood.[3] Philosopher Henri

---

3 Murray (2014). This is a gospel principle, but you can also find it in American pop culture. In an episode of Star Trek the Next Generation, Commander Riker is in conversation with a member of a seemingly all-powerful race called The Q who can snap their fingers and teleport or make any object they wish appear. These powerful tricksters get bored and toy with the crew of the *Enterprise* for entertainment. But on this occasion, Q doesn't want to play with Riker, but wants to *learn* from him. Riker can't believe it. What could the all-powerful Q possibly learn from him? He's a mere barbarian by comparison. Q responds that this is precisely the point: humans have the concept of advancement and are constantly learning and progressing.

*Chapter 21*

Bergson caught a glimpse of this truth on the last page of his masterwork, *The Two Sources of Morality and Religion*, by saying, the more we learn the more we find that "the universe . . . is a machine for the making of gods."[4] God's plan is all about exaltation; science, when done right, is exalting.

## SCIENCE AND RELIGION

This may strike you as surprising since you have probably heard of the "war" between science and religion in which every bit of ground gained by one side is a loss for the other. Actually, this "war" is a fiction dreamt up by those who understand neither science nor religion. One of the great eternal principles of our faith tradition is that all truth is part of one great whole—regardless of the source. As a young man, Henry Eyring, Sr., who would become a Princeton professor and one of the greatest American chemists,[5] was about to head off to college at the University of Arizona when his father took him aside and said, "You are going to learn many things at the University, but I want you to know that anything you learn that is true is part of the gospel." Truth, in whatever field and from whatever source, is *gospel* truth.

In fact, sociologist Rodney Stark argues that science grew directly out of Christian religion. The fathers of science—e.g., Bacon, Newton, and Galileo—believed that they could glorify the rational Creator of the universe by discovering the workings of His creations. Johannes Kepler, after formulating the laws of planetary motion, fell to his knees and thanked God for revealing his glories to a humble servant.[6] Christianity is not against science (as some atheists and fundamentalists believe), but, according to Stark, is the very outlook that created and sustains science.

The reality is that from Copernicus to Einstein nearly all of the revolutionary scientific thinkers were religious believers and sometimes profoundly so.[7] Often they were religious eccentrics like Newton or pantheists like Einstein, but believers they were. Study and faith are two different methods for acquiring knowledge, but they have a common precondi-

---

Science, says Q, has taken humans from the caves to the stars in just a few thousand years. Humankind has surpassed pre-modern and industrial man and someday will even surpass the Q. Gene Rodenberry, the creator of Star Trek, was an atheist, but he was unwittingly communicating a profound truth about eternal progress

4 Bergson (1935, pg. 317).

5 His "reaction rate theory" was one of the great scientific breakthroughs of the 20th century as it brought the insights of quantum physics to bear on chemistry.

6 Some misguided scientists today make a discovery and conclude, "Since science can explain it, God didn't do it." Kepler's reaction was the opposite: "since science can explain it, then my discovery reveals a rational God behind it."

7 This was even true of Darwin at the time he put forward his theory of evolution by natural selection. See Darwin (1859).

tion—humility—and a common purpose—greater truth. Science and religion are complementary, not conflicting.

The idea of a science-religion "war" also comes from those who have ulterior motives. Some people don't like the restrictions God places on their behavior, so they invoke the authority of science to justify immorality. Faith begins as "a desire to believe" (Alma 32:27) and they desire to believe that God does not exist; i.e., their atheism is a matter of faith. It's no coincidence that the leading "New Atheists" of today (and, as noted above, there is nothing "new" about their arguments), not only crusade against belief in God, but also advocate sexual promiscuity. The original "New Atheist," Korihor, did the same at the time of Alma. If you find someone who says they have "lost their testimony" because of something they learned in science, Church history, or what have you, watch closely and you may find that they didn't really *think* their way out of the church, but *sinned* their way out. The intellectual reasons for rejecting the gospel are often *ex-post* justifications for actions contrary to gospel teachings.

## CONCLUSION

It should be clear that religion has nothing to fear from science, but that doesn't mean that science poses no dangers to other realms of human activity. Technological "advances" have often had profound, unintended consequences on American life. It's to these that we will turn in our next chapter.

## CHAPTER 21 SOURCES/FURTHER READING

Armand M. Nicholi, Jr. *The Question of God: C.S. Lewis and Sigmund Freud Debate God, Love, Sex, and the Meaning of Life*. New York: Free Press, 2002.

Baldwin, Carliss Y. and Kim B. Clark. *Design Rules: The Power of Modularity*. Cambridge, MA: M.I.T. Press, 2000.

Bateman, Merrill J. "Nothing Shall Be Withheld," BYU-Idaho Devotional, 22 May 2007.

Bell, Daniel. *The Coming of Postindustrial Society*. New York: Basic Books, 1976.

Bergson, Henri. *Creative Evolution*. Arthur Mitchell, trans. New York: Modern Library, 1944.

\_\_\_\_\_. *The Two Sources of Morality and Religion*. Garden City, NY: Doubleday, 1935.

Collins, Francis S. *The Language of God, The: A Scientist Presents Evidence for Belief*. New York: Free Press, 2006.

Crick, Francis. *Life Itself: Its Origin and Nature*. New York: Simon & Schuster, 1982.

Eyring, Henry J. *Mormon Scientist: The Life and Faith of Henry Eyring*. Salt Lake City: Deseret, 2007.

Eyring, Henry. *The Faith of a Scientist*. Salt Lake City: Bookcraft, 1967.

Faust, James E. "The Shield of Faith," LDS General Conference, April 2000.

Gilder, George. *Microcosm: The Quantum Revolution in Economics and Technology*. New York: Simon & Schuster, 1989.

Gleick, James. *The Information: A Theory, A History, A Flood*. New York: Vintage, 2012.

Kelley, Kevin. *Out of Control: The Rise of Neo-Biological Civilization*. New York: Addisson-Wesley, 1994.

Larsen, Timothy. "War Is Over, If You Want It: Beyond the Conflict Between Faith and Science," *Perspectives on Science and the Christian Faith*, vol. 60, no. 3 (Sep 2008), 147-155.

Lennox, John C. *Gunning for God*. Oxford: Lion Hudson, 2011.

Lindsey, Brink. *The Age of Abundance: How Prosperity Transformed America's Politics and Culture*. New York: HarperCollins, 2007.

Murray, Charles. *The Curmudgeon's Guide to Getting Ahead: Dos and Don'ts of Right Behavior, Tough Thinking, Clear Writing, and Living a Good Life*. New York: Crown Business, 2014.

Nagel, Thomas. *Mind and Cosmos: Why the Materialist, Neo-Darwinian Conception of Nature is Almost Certainly False*. New York: Oxford University Press, 2012.

Numbers, Ronald L. *Galileo Goes to Jail and Other Myths About Science and Religion*. Cambridge: Harvard University Press, 2010.

Plantinga, Alvin. *Where the Conflict Really Lies: Science, Religion, and Naturalism*. New York: Oxford UP, 2011.

Postrel, Virginia. *The Future and Its Enemies*. New York: Free Press, 2011.

Ridley, Matt. *The Rational Optimist: How Prosperity Evolves*. New York: HarperCollins, 2010.

Sacks, Jonathan. *The Great Partnership: God, Science and the Search for Meaning*. London: Hodder & Stroughton, 2011.

Shelley, Mary. *Frankenstein, or the Modern Prometheus* [1818]. New York: Barnes & Noble, 1993.

Stark, Rodney. *For the Glory of God: How Monotheism Led to Reformations, Science, Witch-hunts, and the End of Slavery*. Princeton: Princeton University Press, 2003.

Thoreau, Henry David. *Walden; or, Life in the Woods* [1854]. Mineola, NY: Dover, 1995.

Toffler, Alvin and Heidi. *The Third Wave*. New York: Bantam, 1980.

Willard, Dallas, ed. *A Place for Truth: Leading Thinkers Explore Life's Hardest Questions*. Downer's Grove, IL: Intervarsity Press, 2010.

Wright, Robert. *NonZero: The Logic of Human Destiny*. New York: Vintage, 2000.

# Chapter 22

# TECHNOLOGY, SOCIALIZATION, COMMUNICATION II: LIMITS

## HENRY ADAMS: PROPHET OF MODERNITY

If anyone could have been considered an heir of American royalty, it was Henry Adams. His father had been a congressman and diplomat in the service of Abraham Lincoln and both his grandfather and great-grandfather had been presidents of the United States. But unlike his ancestors, Adams chose to observe and analyze political life rather than participate in it.

As a professor of history at Harvard Adams looked backward with admiration upon the great statesmen of the early republic, but looked forward with fear. As the 20th century dawned, he saw the rise of new technologies (e.g., electricity, phones, automation, automobiles, airplanes), which, he believed, would unleash unforeseen destruction on the world. While most social theorists of the time predicted ever-greater peace and happiness, Adams believed that the 20th century would be one of unprecedented violence.

His reasoning was simple: technology increases *power*, but not *morality*. All power requires moral control, and yet here was far more power in human hands with no commensurate increase in human goodness.[1] People were ethically inadequate to the task of taming the forces they had unleashed. Instead of seeing science in terms of steady progress, Adams compared it to the Second Law of Thermodynamics in which order naturally degenerates into chaos.

In this chapter, we will consider the ways in which Adams had a point. We will look at

---

1 We could see proof of this decline, he thought, simply by contrasting the politicians of his time (the late 19th century), such as Hays, Garfield, and Arthur, to those of the founding generation, such as Washington, Adams, and Jefferson.

some of the major technologies that have shaped American life, for better and worse, and some of the major critiques of technology that those in the American tradition have offered.

## MACRO TECHNOLOGY IN AMERICA

Adams had particular reason to fear for the United States, because it was (and remains) the most technologically innovative land in the world. According to Author William Bernstein, there are four primary conditions for technological innovation:

- Laws securing property rights
- Safe havens for scientific rationalism
- Efficient capital markets
- Mechanisms for improved transportation and communication[2]

All of these conditions can be subsumed under a single, overarching principle that has run throughout this book: the Rule of Law. A society under the Rule of Law has secure property rights, protects the free inquiry of scientific rationalism, allows efficient capital allocation through the free market, and, of course, a free society is more likely to have more developed transportation and communication. Economists Daron Acemoglu and James Robinson have even shown that both the agricultural and industrial revolutions came about because of strong Rule of Law institutions that provided incentives for innovation.[3]

This explains why America, a land blessed with the Rule of Law under the Constitution, has been the leading technological nation for over a century. It also explains why industrialization took hold so quickly in the USA and why America has been at the forefront of the information revolution.

When the first settlers to America arrived, they introduced efficient, large-scale agriculture that replaced the primarily hunter-gathering practices of the Native Americans. Then, right at the time of the Founding, one of the most remarkable thefts in the history of the world occurred: an Englishman named Samuel Slater stole the secrets of industrialization from his home country. The English were the first to make the jump to machine power, but were very protective of their industrial knowledge. They feared that if competitor nations found out their secrets, those nations would become just as rich and strong so they made it a crime for anyone to take this industrial knowledge from their island.

Slater disregarded this restriction. While working in an English factory, he memorized as much as he could of the design and structure of the machines. Eventually, he snuck away to America, sought out a wealthy Rhode Islander named Brown, and, together, they recre-

---

2 Bernstein (2004).
3 Acemoglu and Robinson (2012).

ated the English factory system in America. Within 100 years English fears were realized: the USA had become the greatest industrial power in the world.

## SPECIFIC TECHNOLOGIES IN USA

During the industrial and post-industrial phases in American history, there have been countless inventions that have changed the country in dramatic ways. Below, we will look at some of the most important ones and see that even though they improved life for many, Henry Adams's fears were justified. Each technological innovation has had unintended consequences that altered the political, cultural, and economic life of the country—often for the worse.

## COTTON GIN

In the early 19th century, a brilliant tinkerer named Eli Whitney invented the cotton gin. It had always been difficult to process cotton because of the pesky seeds tightly embedded in the cotton fibers, but Whitney's machine made it possible to remove these seeds merely by turning a hand crank. This unleashed a worldwide cotton boom. People everywhere wanted to wear this soft, comfortable fabric instead of heavy, itchy wool. This is exactly what Whitney had hoped for.

What he had not hoped for was the strengthening of American slavery that came with this increased cotton production. The gin, by increasing the efficiency of forced labor, re-energized the slave system in the American South (which had been dying out) and contributed to the American Civil War. Of course Whitney never thought to himself, "I'm inventing this machine to kill 620,000 Americans and perpetuate slavery for countless others," but that was the result anyway. He had, in a sense, created a Frankenstein monster: the cheap, comfortable fabric allowed by the cotton gin had a terrible and unforeseen human cost.

## BARBED WIRE

Barbed wire seems a simple enough invention, yet it greatly altered American geography. For generations, cowboys, Indians, pioneers, and settlers had wandered freely over the American West. It was difficult to lay claim to huge chunks of land because there was little timber available for fencing. Barbed wire allowed ranchers to contain their herds on carefully defined property. Acre by acre, the open plains of the American West were carved up into small units. Thousands of homesteaders were given the opportunity to own land, but the great plains now exist only as a patchwork of enclosed farms, not the wide-open space of the 19th century. Barbed wire is one of the main culprits.

## Chapter 22

## TELEGRAPH AND RAILROAD

In 1815, when Samuel Morse tapped out the first ever telegraph message, information could suddenly travel at the speed of light. Before Morse, people could only communicate as fast as they could physically travel, but with the telegraph humans were unshackled from the constraints of material speed and could connect across vast distances.[4] The seeds of the post-industrial age were already planted.

Shortly after the introduction of the telegraph, railroads emerged as a means of rapid transportation. Church members traveling to Utah previously had to spend months crossing the plains by foot, often with incredible suffering. Now, they could simply purchase a ticket, climb into a rail car, take a nap, and wake up in Zion. The completion of the Transcontinental Railroad in 1869 also helped tie the country together, joining the west coast to the east and ensuring the USA would be one national unit instead of many (as in Europe, which developed before such innovations).

But along with this transportation and communication revolution came a new rootlessness to America. Ease of travel made Americans more nomadic: they would leave their ancestral homes and live far from families and hometown friends. Americans have always been a restless, mobile people, but the railroad magnified this tendency. The bonds of community, which served as a source of strength, meaning, and even a social safety net, were weakened by these technologies that made life so convenient.

## REAPER

The railroad contributed to the urbanization of America, but so did Cyrus McCormick's mechanical reaper. McCormick understood that the bottleneck to farming was the harvest. The abundance of arable land in America meant that a farmer could plant and plow almost as many crops as he wanted, but harvesting those crops was a different matter. It was near impossible to find and pay enough workers to gather the crops into the barn before they froze or spoiled in the field.

McCormick solved this problem with his ingenious machine, the McCormick Reaper, which did the harvesting work of dozens of field hands in far less time. Farmers could now plant almost as much as they wanted. Food production and affordability shot up, contributing to American health and wealth. As farmers exported their goods, the American Midwest became the "breadbasket of the world."

The Reaper also meant that farms became larger and more capital intensive. No longer could you compete as a farmer with a small plot of land and simple tools. Mechanized farming also required fewer workers. Before McCormick, around 80% of Americans worked in

---

4  Exceptions were long-distance visual signaling systems, like the smoke signals of Native-Americans or the semaphore-flag communication of Mongolian armies.

agriculture, now that number is close to 2% and the crop yield is higher than ever before. Children of farmers, who were essential agricultural workers in previous generations, had nothing to do. Logically, they moved and found work in the cities. McCormick didn't set out to destroy small family farms and create big cities in America, but that was one of the unforeseen results of his invention.

## ASSEMBLY LINE

Many credit Henry Ford with fully developing the assembly-line process of manufacturing, in which each worker completes a single small part of a large project. The process is remarkably efficient and has raised the standard of living of Americans, provided higher wages, and given us many more factory-produced goods than we otherwise would have had.

The assembly line also changed the nature of work itself. Karl Marx noted that industrial capitalism destroys the worker's relationship to that which he produces and turns the worker into yet another commodity, like the machine itself. There is much validity to this critique. Before the factory, makers of durable goods were artisans—such as coopers, gunsmiths, potters, and silversmiths—who would begin with raw materials and, with the skill acquired over years of apprenticeship, work those materials into a fine, finished product. There was a sense of satisfaction in having created a good from start to finish. The assembly line, making workers into so many cogs in the machine, destroyed this more craft-oriented mode of production even as it raised living standards. In industrial societies, the warmer master-apprentice relationship was replaced by the colder employer-employee relationship.

## AUTOMOBILE

The transportation advantages brought by the advent of the automobile are obvious: people can move about with more speed, convenience, and flexibility than ever before. Few of us would want to go back to traveling by foot or horse, but think of how cars have altered American home life. Before the automobile, people usually lived and worked in the same place (e.g., living in an apartment above the storefront). How could they do otherwise? But the automobile allowed Americans to separate the two: they could live in one place and work in another. Thus were born the suburbs. Cities have a high cost of living, but also better paying jobs. Cars allowed people to receive the high salary of city work, but enjoy the cheap living of suburban life. Think of the miles of tract-home developments that sprawl out from America's cities. These would have been unlikely without the automobile.

Interestingly, the historical data also shows that booms in automobile purchases correlate with increased sexual promiscuity—yet another unintended consequence of this technology. We'll look more closely at the negative consequences of the sexual revolution below.

## MASS MEDIA

Through most of history only the wealthy could afford cultural pursuits. They had the money and leisure to buy art, attend the opera, listen to fine music (it had to be performed live), read literature, or watch dramatic productions. But technology has changed all that. The poor today can afford to listen to Mozart, hang a Da Vinci print on their walls, or check out opera DVD's from their local library. High culture is now available to the masses.

But critics charge that mass culture simply means debased culture. Rich and poor alike watch the same television shows and movies, listen to the same music, read the same newspapers, and enjoy the same art, but instead of watching a Goethe drama and listening to Bach, we watch reality TV and listen to country or rap. Has mass media really been a step forward for America? Many would say no.

## AIR CONDITIONING

We all know that air-conditioning makes us more comfortable on a hot day, but consider what it did to American demography. The American Southwest used to be almost uninhabitable in the summers. Temperatures in places like Phoenix or Las Vegas can rise to 120° F and before the invention of air conditioning there was nothing anyone could do about it. Those in cold climates could make fires, build shelter, and don more clothes, but those in hot climates had no escape from the summer heat.

When humans invented a way to cool the air in enclosed spaces, the Southwest suddenly became a more attractive place to live. You could get all of the benefits of warm weather year-round and then bear the summers by staying indoors in air-conditioned rooms. Millions began migrating south and west to the Sunbelt. The population center of the United States has been moving in a southwesterly direction ever since.

## NUCLEAR POWER

Nuclear energy has obvious benefits and drawbacks. It is a cheap, efficient, and relatively clean way to generate electricity. Despite high-profile nuclear meltdowns, it is also safe compared to alternatives like coal (far more people die in mining accidents than in nuclear accidents).

We also know that nuclear technology can be used to make bombs so powerful that they can destroy the entire human race. Interestingly, this threat of human-wide destruction may be responsible for decreasing conflict between the great powers in recent decades. Ever since the rise of the nation state, the great powers have gone to war with one another every generation or so, but this has not happened since World War II. Nuclear weapons have made the stakes of war too high. Could it be that these most destructive weapons of war have, paradoxically, given us greater peace? Science Fiction writer Ray Bradbury thought so. He said in a 1966 interview,

> I prophesy a golden age as the result of the hydrogen bomb, in which this one science-fictional device will enable us to get along beautifully without war. We've been so busy being terrified by the Bomb, we haven't realized what a godsend it is. I predict there will be no more gigantic wars . . . We'll go on having these guerrilla excursions, here and there in the world, but we've stopped a lot of wars in the last twenty years because of this science-fictional device.[5]

## CONTRACEPTION

The rise of convenient contraceptives brought on hugely ironic consequences. In the 1960s, the birth control pill was approved and released to wide acclaim. Not only would it allow family planning, many believed that it would also give women full control over reproduction and reduce the number of unwanted pregnancies.

Actually, the opposite happened. The out-of-wedlock birthrate shot upward with the sexual revolution that coincided with the new availability of birth control. "Consequence-free" sex was supposed to liberate women, but in fact, it made them more captive; teen pregnancies often meant dashed hopes for college, career, and family. Many became welfare recipients and were chained to a life of the dole and dependency.

Beyond that, the social consequences of sexual promiscuity have been disastrous. Today over 40% of children are born to single parents, which has exacerbated virtually every social pathology. Many remarkable women raise successful children by themselves, but those who grow up without a father are statistically more likely to use drugs, engage in criminal activity, have lower educational attainment, live in poverty, and, worst of all, have children out of wedlock themselves. This creates a cycle of dependency that accounts for many of the major problems in our country and, most tragically, those hardest hit are the poor. This explains much of the inequality that has been on the rise since the early 1970s.[6]

---

5  Bradbury (2004, p. 33).
6  Latter-day prophets saw this problem coming in the 1950s and warned that the "judgments of God" awaited us if ignored the law of chastity. The nation didn't listen and has been paying the price for the last half century. We see the prophesied "judgments of God" every time we turn on the news and see persistent poverty, rising gang activity, growing inequality, a failing education system, and drug wars. The world says that the prophets are behind the times, but the opposite is the case: social scientists are just recently discovering what the prophets have been telling us for centuries. The gospel provides simple, although not easy, answers for even the most difficult social problems.

*Chapter 22*

## INFORMATION AGE CHALLENGES

The personal computer is perhaps the most important American invention of all as it has launched us into the information age and radically altered the way we work and play. But unintended by any computer inventor are the major challenges to agency, rights, and the Rule of Law that information technology has created.

The first challenge is insularity. Today we can get away with only interacting with like-minded people. In politics, conservatives and liberals don't get their news from traditional journalism or network TV, but from web pages that serve as echo chambers to reinforce what they already believe. Instead of engaging contrary views and opinions to expand perspectives and think independently, Americans increasingly just double down on the views they start out with. When we do engage those of alternative persuasions, the anonymity of information age communication makes this communication more antagonistic and course. This poses a potential threat to the Rule of Law since democracy requires flexibility, compromise, pluralism, and high-level thinking in order to work.

The second challenge is biotechnology's blurring of the distinction between human and non-human. For instance, we now have the capacity to clone human beings. Would these clones qualify for full human rights? What about clones created purely for organ harvesting and without higher brain function? What about embryos that could be used for life-saving stem-cell research? Do human embryos have the natural rights that fully developed people do?

Advances in computer technology may also lead us to ask, "at what point do computers themselves have rights and should the protection of law extend to intelligent non-humans?" Latter-day Saints who understand that rights don't come from computational ability or complex wiring, but from our status as children of God, will not face this dilemma, but others in the information age will.

A third challenge to the Rule of Law in the information age is pervasive monitoring. Cameras, drones, and satellites watch us constantly. Almost every American carries video technology in their pocket. At a moment's notice, anyone can pull out a camera phone, capture our actions on film, and post it on YouTube for the whole world to see. Many believe that our natural right to liberty entails a right to privacy, and yet there is now less privacy than ever before. We are under ever-increasing surveillance by the government, private organizations, and each other. Every internet site we visit is tracked, every purchase we make becomes part of a cataloged history, every movie we rent or library book we check out all becomes part of vast databases that are followed, monitored, and used to entice us with further products. Perhaps Orwell was a little premature in the gloomy picture presented in *1984*, but was he really wrong?[7]

---

7  For more on protests against techno-surveillance, see Leonard (2014).

A fourth threat to the Rule of Law in the post-industrial age is the facilitation of theft. Information is the product of highest value in our current stage of human development, and yet information is infinitely replicable and can be transmitted at the speed of light. This means that we can quickly copy digital information for ourselves, but without leaving less for anyone else.

If information is the fruit of someone's labors, then they have a natural right to it. Those valuable sets of 1's and 0's that we experience as designs, essays, songs, movies, and business plans can be copied and distributed without cost. This is theft, but seems harmless. Since property rights are crucial for the Rule of Law, economic growth, and technological innovation, this is a scary prospect. Our liberty and prosperity could depend upon our finding ways to define property rights in the digital age.[8]

Finally, while it's true the post-industrial age means less physical pollution (e.g., chemicals in rivers, trash in fields, smoke in the sky), the information age brings its own forms of pollution, such as computer viruses, email spam, pornography popups, and video game violence. Pollution hasn't disappeared in the post-industrial age, it has just taken on new, subtler, and perhaps more damaging forms, particularly since new pollution can lead to new addictions. How to clean up our digital environment is yet another challenge America will face in the coming years.

## CRITIQUES

We've now run through a sampling of technologies in America, seen the negative, unintended consequences they can have and the challenges they pose to the future. All of this technological downside has generated a backlash from a number of critical perspectives that we must now consider.

The first is the *Luddite* Critique which claims that new technologies destroy jobs. Luddism first emerged in industrializing England, where hand weavers (supposedly led by a man named Ludd) saw that they were being displaced by machines that could do their work better and faster, thus making their trade obsolete. The weavers had spent their entire lives perfecting their craft and yet a new technology suddenly appeared and made their skills worthless. The Luddites took matters into their own hands: they went into the factories and literally began smashing the hated machines, trying (in vain it turns out) to save their jobs.

Modern-day Luddites continue to claim that technology destroys jobs and makes skills obsolete. They are correct in a sense. Each new technology has costs to someone some-

---

8  We may find that non-monetary incentives will drive innovation in the information age. Notice, for instance, how many people cooperate in creating open-source products without any financial recompense (contributors to Wikipedia, for instance). The satisfaction of creating an information artifact and knowing it will be used by millions of people may be incentive enough. This fact may reduce the need for clearly defined property rights in the digital realm.

where. The light bulb put candle-makers out of work, the automobile made blacksmithing obsolete, and the Internet is currently throwing newspaper printers out of jobs.

But what Luddites fail to see is that this destruction is what economist Joseph Schumpeter called *creative* destruction. Yes, each new technology destroys old jobs, but it opens up many more in their place: candle-makers out, light bulb engineers in; blacksmiths out, automotive workers in; newspaper reporters out, web designers in. Generally, the new jobs are of higher quality than the old, even if there are short-term costs to specific people whose skills are no longer useful. There is usually a net overall benefit to society as people retrain and hold better jobs than those of previous generations.

Second is the Social Critique which opposes some technology on the grounds that it destroys interpersonal relationships. The strength of our social relations largely determines how happy and meaningful our lives are, and yet social media, these critics claim, make our relationships shallow, mediated, and transitory. Whereas agricultural Americans interacted face-to-face in community events, front porch conversations, sewing circles, and barn raisings, postmodern Americans connect in a virtual world of digital reality (e.g., texts, emails, videogames, websites, and chat rooms).

A group of literary figures called "The Southern Agrarians" criticized technology on these grounds in their 1930 book *I'll Take My Stand*. They argued that technology was bringing the fragmented, lonely individualism of the industrial North to the ordered, happy, communal South. They "took their stand" against this threat, hoping to preserve agricultural community against industrial anomie.

The Amish have their own version of the social critique. They have decided that sacrificing community for convenience isn't worth it; they reject most aspects of modern life in order to preserve the richness and simplicity of their pre-modern communities. Their credo became, "come out from among them, and be ye separate" (2 Corinthians 6:17).

But is it not possible that technology can also strengthen social bonds? Families and friends separated by thousands of miles can now connect instantaneously via social media. Such connections may be less rich and authentic than the personal, face-to-face relationships of previous eras, but they are better than no relationships at all. Many people feel that Facebook, Skype, Twitter, Instagram, and Snapchat allow them to make and maintain *more* social connections than they would otherwise have. What we have lost in relationship quality, they say, we may have made up for in quantity.

Third, the Green Critique says that technology kills the planet. Each new invention just gives humans more power to pollute and ravage the earth. Humans created the printing press, which required cutting down forests for paper; humans created factories and automobiles, which belch pollutants into the atmosphere; and humans created fossil-fuel mining, which scars a once-beautiful landscape. Those in the environmental movement often look with suspicion on technology for this reason.

But even as technology finds new ways to destroy the planet, it also finds new ways to heal it. Notice, for instance, that our major cities have *less* air pollution than they did a generation ago, thanks to higher fuel efficiency, cleaner energy, and de-industrialization. There is more forested land in the U.S. today than there was in the past (a trend we can expect to continue as we communicate increasingly through electronics rather than on paper). Post-industrial society is cleaner than industrial society, so each innovation that takes us in that direction is a step towards a cleaner, greener planet. When you compare the pollution of automobiles to the waste products of the horses they replaced, perhaps even industrialization improved the environment.

Finally, the Romantic Critique (perhaps the most important of all) says that technology wastes our time, diminishes the authenticity of our experiences, and reduces our ability to think. In short, technology destroys our very souls. New technologies simply mean we spend more of our lives on mind-numbing, time wasting entertainment or social media instead of engaging in productive and rewarding activities.

This is the most legitimate critique of all. We talked earlier about the Transcendentalists, but many recent Americans have also made Romanticist arguments. Sci-fi stories portray a future in which robots or machines "take over," turn us into mindless drones, and threaten our humanity.[9] Hippies of the 1960s waxed romantic in excoriating the bland, conformist world of a middle-class America pampered by suburban technological conveniences. They rejected their parents' professions, politics, technology, and science and took to the road in their Volkswagen vans, looking for authentic experience. We can appreciate their yearning, even if we reject their "solution" in sex, drugs, and rock n' roll.

Modern researchers have also found that information technology, like the Internet, can reduce cognitive ability. Nicholas Carr has pointed out that those who spend more time online have improved visual-spatial skill and the ability to make quicker judgments based on patterns, but these advantages are more than outweighed by the disadvantages that heavy internet usage creates: superficial reading, weak analysis, lower comprehension and retention of information, diminished ability to reflect deeply, and an inbuilt bias towards vivid information.[10]

The Romantic Critique has also come from modern prophets and apostles. Dallin H. Oaks warned that, in the information age, "Technology toys like video games and the Internet are already winning away the time of our children and youth . . . Some young people are amusing themselves to death—spiritual death."[11] D. Todd Christofferson added that, "much

---

9 Examples include *Brave New World, Terminator, Bladerunner, Wall-E, 1984, War Games, The Matrix,* and *Attack of the Clones.*
10 Carr (2010).
11 Oaks (2007).

of what passes for entertainment today is coarse, degrading, violent, mind-numbing, and time wasting."[12]

David A. Bednar not only warned against the perils of technology, he also offered a key for discerning between its appropriate and inappropriate uses:

> I offer two questions for consideration in your personal pondering and prayerful studying: 1. Does the use of various technologies and media invite or impede the constant companionship of the Holy Ghost in your life? 2. Does the time you spend using various technologies and media enlarge or restrict your capacity to live, to love, and to serve in meaningful ways?[13]

## CONCLUSION

All of the above should be sufficient to help us see that the question for Latter-day Saints isn't whether or not to accept technology, but *how to use it*. We live in a world saturated with technologies and can enjoy the benefits they offer. At the same time, by recognizing the risks and critiques mentioned above, we can avoid some of the errors that societies and individuals make if they place undue faith in technology. Scientific advance is valuable, but should be kept in its proper place and used appropriately. The task for disciple-leaders is to learn how to keep the benefits of science and technology, minimize the drawbacks, and guide others to do the same.

## CHAPTER 22 SOURCES/FURTHER READING

Adams, Henry. *The Education of Henry Adams* [1919]. New York: Modern Library, 1944.

Akerlof, George A. & Janet L. Yellin. "An Analysis of Out-Of-Wedlock Births in the United States," Brookings Policy Brief Series, #4 of 186, August 1986. <http://www.brookings.edu/research/papers/1996/08/childrenfamilies-akerlof>, accessed Jan 27, 2014.

Bayles, Martha. "Popular Culture." In Peter H. Schuck and James Q. Wilson, eds., *Understanding America: The Anatomy of an Exceptional Nation*. New York: Public Affairs, 2008.

Bednar, David A. "Things as They Really Are." *Ensign* (June 2010).

Bernstein, William J. *The Birth of Plenty: How the Prosperity of the Modern World Was Created*. New York: McGraw-Hill, 2004.

Bradbury, Ray. *Conversations with Ray Bradbury*. Edited by Steven L. Aggelis. Jackson, MS: University Press of Mississippi, 2004.

Carr, Nicholas. *The Shallows: What the Internet Is Doing to Our Brains*. New York: W.W. Norton, 2010.

---

12 Christofferson (2010).
13 Bednar (2010).

Foucault, Michel. *Discipline and Punish: The Birth of the Prison* [1977]. Translated by Alan Sheridan. New York: Vintage, 1995.

Fukuyama, Francis. *Our Posthuman Future: Consequences of the Biotechnology Revolution*. New York: Farrar Straus Giroux, 2002.

Howe, Melissa J.K. and Linda J. Waite. "The Family." In Peter H. Schuck and James Q. Wilson, eds., *Understanding America: The Anatomy of an Exceptional Nation*. New York: Public Affairs, 2008.

Lasch, Christopher. *The True and Only Heaven: Progress and its Critics*. New York: W.W. Norton, 1991.

Leonard, Andrew. "The tech protests get personal — and ugly" Salon.com January 22, 2014. <http://www.salon.com/2014/01/22/the_tech_protests_get_personal_and_ugly/>.

Nisbet, Robert A. *The Quest for Community: A Study in the Ethics of Order and Freedom*. New York: Oxford University Press, 1953.

Oaks, Dallin H. "Good, Better, Best," LDS General Conference, October 2007. <https://www.lds.org/general-conference/2007/10/good-better-best?lang=eng>

Orwell, George. *Animal Farm and 1984*. Boston: Houghton Mifflin Harcourt, 2003.

Postman, Neil. *Amusing Ourselves to Death: Public Discourse in the Age of Show Business*. New York: Penguin, 1986.

_____. *Technopoly: The Surrender of Culture to Technology*. New York: Vintage, 1992.

Schumpeter, Joseph. *Capitalism, Socialism, and Democracy*. New York: Harper & Bros., 1942.

Twelve Southerners. *I'll Take My Stand* (1930). Baton Rouge: LSU Press, 2006.

Wolfe, Tom. *Hooking Up*. NY: Farrar Straus Giroux, 2000.

# Chapter 23

# AMERICA & THE WORLD I: HISTORY

## GEORGE KENNAN: CONTAINMENT

We turn in these final two chapters to America's place in the world, especially the past and present of U.S. foreign policy. Among the most important figures in this story is George Kennan, the great diplomat and architect of Cold War strategy. Kennan grew up shy and bookish in Milwaukee and did well enough in school to earn a scholarship to Princeton. After acquiring the necessary skills in writing and foreign language in college, he served on the U.S. Foreign Service's first diplomatic team to Soviet Russia.

While in the Soviet Union, Kennan became enthralled with Russian culture and society. He enjoyed their plays, ballet, and architecture and devoured the works of writers like Dostoevsky, Tolstoy, and Chekov. He even learned the language well enough to translate for Stalin himself.

Although Kennan loved Russian culture, he detested its politics. He saw that communism was an oppressive system that was impoverishing and enslaving the people and threatening peace. Kennan was in Moscow right after World War II when Stalin started behaving like Hitler. The Nazi conquest of Poland, Czechoslovakia, and Ukraine had set off World War II, but now Stalin was conquering those same places. Had America defeated Hitler only to see him replaced by a new tyrant to the east?

Americans wondered what to do. They had just finished the bloodiest war in history and were understandably loathe to go to war again, but did that mean they had to stand by and watch while the Soviets brought more and more countries under their dominion? Some said America should do nothing; others said America should invade Russia to overthrow Stalin just as it had overthrown Hitler.

Kennan had a different idea—a kind of middle ground between these two extremes. He proposed an approach to communism that came to be known as *containment*. In a communication to the State Department called "The Long Telegram" he said that the U.S. should neither to go to war with Russia nor sit passively by. The Soviet Union, he said, was unstable because communism (and not capitalism, as Marx had claimed) was riddled by contradictions and would eventually collapse of its own weight. Since the flawed Soviet economic system could not last, the U.S. didn't need to go and roll back communism because, with time, it would die of its own accord.

Nor could the U.S. sit back and let more nations fall under Soviet control. The oppression and threat to global liberty was too great. The U.S. should accept communism where it had already taken hold (as in Russia), but should apply strategic counterforce when the Soviets attempted to expand into new regions. Thus, said Kennan, America could "contain" the spread of global communism.

This theory found widespread acceptance in the U.S. government. President Truman himself bought into the ideas of Kennan's Long Telegram and adopted containment as the basis of his foreign policy approach that we call the "Truman Doctrine."

Containment worked as a Cold War policy and Kennan lived to see his theory vindicated with the collapse of the Soviet empire in 1989, but the Cold War is long over and Americans are left to meet new global challenges. We discussed previously the government's internal (domestic) role—protecting natural rights—but now we must consider our government's external role. How should it behave towards the other nations of the world? Over these final two chapters, we will address this question by looking at some theories of international relations as well as the history of American foreign affairs.

There are two dimensions to determining America's global role: *how much* intervention and *what kind* of intervention? To what extent should the United States be involved politically in the rest of the world and what form should this involvement take? These questions are usually answered in terms of interventionism-isolationism and realism-idealism.

## INTERVENTIONISM

The *interventionist* position says that since America is quite simply the most powerful political/military entity of all time, staying out of the world's political affairs is a pipe dream. Whether we like it or not, our power makes us the *de facto* world leader and we should seize this mantle of leadership and guide the world accordingly. America has a responsibility, says the interventionist, to accept that burden of leadership and intervene to make the world a better place. If we fail to shape the world, then the world will shape us.

Besides that, interventionists believe America can do a number of great things with her power. First, the U.S. can establish "national greatness" through military assertion. A "foreign policy of national strength and moral assertiveness abroad," say leading conservatives, can create a muscular, nationalist ethos that will "physically and spiritually unify the nation" and give purpose and meaning to its citizens.[1]

Second, they say, America can solve many of the world's problems with her power. There is injustice, tyranny, poverty, and oppression all over the globe and the interventionist believes that America should step in to stop these horrors. If there is genocide in Rwanda and tribes are killing each other by the thousands, can we really just stand back and say, "It's none of our business"? If Iraqis are suffering under the ruthless domination of Saddam Hussein, can we really just say it's their problem and not ours? Does not the parable of the Good Samaritan demand that we make it our business to help others in need? To the interventionist, the answer is "yes." America can and should step in to stop evil around the world with its mighty military.

Third, the interventionist believes that we can further American interests through military intervention. We can keep trade routes open, establish new markets, and gain access to necessary raw materials (such as oil). Interventionism is not only morally right, but economically beneficial, they say.

## IDEALISM

To justify their position, interventionists frequently invoke the doctrine of foreign policy *idealism*—a philosophy that sees international relations in terms of good and evil. Superman is a perfect symbol of the idealist mentality: Superman defeats villains in Metropolis to establish "truth, justice, and the American way," and idealists believe America should do the same in the world. The red and blue colors on Superman's costume are not coincidental—he is a projection of the idealist/interventionist conception of America so popular at the time he was invented.

The same could be said of Spiderman, another hero who wears the colors of the American flag. The central theme of the original Spiderman films was, "with great power comes great responsibility," and, for the idealist-interventionist, the same could be said of America. The desire for freedom burns in the heart of every human being, says the idealist, and American power means we have the responsibility to remove oppression around the world. People are fundamentally good and under the right conditions any nation can live "happily ever after" with freedom and prosperity.

## REALISM

Foreign policy *realism*, on the other hand, is far more cynical and sees foreign relations not in terms of good v. evil, but in terms of self-interest. We can't hope for the triumph of

---

[1] Brooks and Kristol (1997).

good in the world, but only for stability and peace through balancing the power of nations against one another.

Whether America pursues realist or idealist policies has depended upon the U.S. President—the figure who stands at the head of the military and the State Department and thereby determines the direction of American foreign policy during their terms.

## ISOLATIONISM

Isolationism disagrees with the interventionist on each of these points. The isolationist says that the American government should stay out of the world's affairs and mind its own business—a good rule of thumb for individuals as well as nations. While we might trade with people of other nations and persuade them to adopt better political and economic institutions, it is ultimately not right to intervene with our military. Each nation should choose its own political destiny and it is wrong for other nations to "meddle" and impose an agenda from the outside.

While the interventionist says we can achieve "national greatness" through military action, the isolationist says (with Master Yoda), "War does not make one great." America's greatness comes from its freedom and ideals, not the wars it fights.

What about solving the world's problems? To the isolationist, these problems are not ours. We have enough problems to worry about at home and our government should focus its efforts there. While the interventionist invokes the parable of The Good Samaritan, the isolationist invokes the Golden Rule. Would we want foreign nations to invade *our* country with *their* military to solve *our* problems of racial strife or economic inequality? If we wouldn't want other nations to bring their military in to "solve" our problems, is it right for us to go around "solving" theirs? The principle of "Do unto others as you would have others do unto you," demands that we respect the sovereignty of other nations and stay out, especially since even well-intentioned foreign interventions can backfire.

What about using the U.S. military to advance our interests in the world? The isolationist would say that nothing is more in America's interest than peace. The costs of military intervention in blood and treasure do not justify a slightly lower price at the gas pump. The American military exists to defend America, not pursue ostensible interests in nations around the globe.[2]

Is America a Superman-Good Samaritan or is America an isolationist follower of the Golden Rule? That is among the central questions for American foreign relations today. Most of us are somewhere in the middle between these two extremes, but lean towards

---

[2] Note that the isolationist-interventionist debate is usually only about America's *military* involvement with the world. Most isolationists and interventionists alike have no problem with America engaging the world culturally, economically, and diplomatically (through trade, negotiation, exchange, travel, missionary work, and so forth).

either more or less American military intervention and lean towards either realism or idealism in foreign policy philosophy.

## ISOLATIONIST BEGINNINGS

The history of America in the world might be conceived of as a long, gradual movement from isolation to intervention. The U.S. began wanting as little political connection with other nations as possible, but today we have a major military presence in every region of the globe.

The degree of American military involvement today was unthinkable to the Founding Fathers since they created the country in a quest for isolation. Remember, it was the wars between France and England that led to the taxation that stirred up the colonists to rebellion and independence. In that sense, the nation was born in the attempt to escape the bloodshed and costs of European entanglements.

This isolationism was hard to maintain. In the early republic, the vortex of the France-England rivalry threatened to suck America in. Presidents Washington, Adams, and Jefferson struggled constantly to keep the nation neutral, but the French and British would draft American sailors, seize American ships, and block American trade.

France tried to entice the young nation into an alliance by claiming that it was "a sister republic," but Washington saw the French Revolution for the anarchic bloodbath that it was and refused to create a formal alliance (as illustrated in the Citizen Genet Affair). The English then assumed that America's rejection of France meant that it would ally with England. When this turned out not to be the case, the angry English began seizing American ships and sailors to the point that Washington, trying to avoid war, dispatched Supreme Court Chief Justice John Jay to negotiate Jay's Treaty. This put a stop to the depredations, but conceded so much to the English that France was angered and threatened war. That was the situation Washington bequeathed to Adams who struggled his whole presidency to keep the new nation out of war with France. He almost didn't succeed and actually called Washington out of retirement to head the American military for a final time.

Washington was so concerned about foreign entanglement that he made it the third of the three great themes of his Farewell Address (the other two were the importance of religion and the danger of political parties). Trade liberally with all nations and seek goodwill, said Washington, but do not favor one nation over another lest we become drawn in to their wars. America finally fought a war with England, The War of 1812, to achieve what Washington had advocated: isolation from the squabbles between European powers.

After the War of 1812, a new president, James Monroe, pursued an ambitious policy that he hoped would ensure American isolation for decades to come—The Monroe Doctrine. With the help of Secretary of State John Quincy Adams, Monroe proclaimed that any European intervention in the Western Hemisphere would be considered an attack on the

United States itself and grounds for war. This was a bold proclamation, but Monroe felt it necessary because constant European meddling in the "New World" would inevitably draw the USA back into European conflicts. The Monroe-Adams gamble worked: the Europeans generally did not call the American bluff and left the Western Hemisphere alone.

Later, when John Quincy Adams became President, he was even more explicitly isolationist. In many formal speeches he stated that America had no business intervening in the affairs of foreign nations, even to "spread freedom." America, he said, is the example of liberty for nations around the globe, but "defender only of her own." What about foreign tyrants? "America," Adams famously declared, "goes not abroad in search of monsters to destroy." This early isolationism bought the nation almost a century of peace from European wars.

America spent these first decades of the $19^{th}$ century defining itself in terms of geography and ideals. Jefferson bought Louisiana from France, Adams secured Florida from Spain, and Polk annexed Texas, seized the southwest from Mexico, and purchased the northwest from England. Through morally questionable means, America quadrupled in size and acquired its enduring shape during the mid-$19^{th}$ century.

America not only defined itself in terms of its land during these years, but also in principles. The Civil War was fought to abolish slavery and thereby cement and extend the principles of the Declaration of Independence. All of the nation's military actions from 1815 to 1898 were internal (the Civil War) or contiguous (the Mexican-American War) rather than the kinds of overseas foreign interventions that Washington had warned against.

## TRANSITION TO INTERVENTION

Why did American isolation come to an end? At the end of the $19^{th}$ century, America found itself among the most powerful nations in the world. The economy had been booming, immigrants had swelled the population, the national borders had expanded, and, by 1898, Americans could translate all of this size into military might.

American leaders decided to use this power to follow the pattern of European nations and establish an empire. This beginning of U.S. interventionism occurred under President William McKinley who took the nation into the Spanish-American war in order to seize the vestiges of Spain's once-mighty empire in the Philippines, Cuba, and Puerto Rico. Around the same time, the U.S. annexed Hawaii and other pacific islands. Like England, France, and Russia, the United States entered the imperial game by carving up parts of the world and imposing political dominion on foreign peoples. McKinley justified this empire in idealist terms saying that America had a responsibility to "uplift," "Christianize," and bring American values to foreign peoples.

After President McKinley was killed by an anarchist in 1901, his Vice President, Theodore Roosevelt, took the helm of state and continued steering American foreign policy in the same interventionist directions. But Roosevelt was more of a realist. For instance, he negotiated an end to the Russo-Japanese war in hopes of preventing either side from becoming too powerful and threatening stability in the Pacific. Rather than siding with either nation as the "good guy," Roosevelt became involved to achieve a balance of power that would ultimately protect the United States in the Pacific. Roosevelt also expanded American naval strength with the "Great White Fleet" and used it to cow Japan and Russia into docility.

After Roosevelt and his successor William Howard Taft came the highly consequential presidency of Woodrow Wilson. During Wilson's time in office, the European nations went to war with each other yet again; this time it was the worst war in history. They simply called it The Great War, but we know it as World War I. Wilson had little interest in foreign affairs and even won re-election on the platform, "He kept us out of war." But the interventionist temptation was too great. After the Germans infringed on U.S. trading rights and sunk vessels carrying American citizens, Wilson entered the war on the side of the allies. He did not rationalize this intervention on the grounds of self-defense or balance of power, but on the grounds of spreading American values, to "make the world safe for democracy." This was the most notable (but not the last) example of Superman-style idealism in American history.

World War I didn't end as Wilson had hoped, so during the 1920s America tried briefly to move back to isolation. Never again, Americans said, would they send their sons off to die in a fruitless European war. To this end, the Harding and Coolidge Administrations signed a number of treaties, such as the Washington Conference Treaty for Disarmament and the Kellogg-Briand Pact, that they hoped would prevent war forever after.

It didn't work. In spite of Wilson's League of Nations and all of the nice pieces of paper making war "illegal," Hitler re-armed Germany, embarked on European conquest, and allied with the Japanese empire. America was, once again, drawn into a European conflict.

Franklin Roosevelt is often considered one of our greatest presidents not only because he led the country during World War II, but also because his approach satisfied both idealists and realists alike. In the War, America defeated villains and spread "truth, justice, and the American way" to lands in both Europe and Asia, but also stabilized the regions and protected American interests.

World War II also marked the end of any serious attempts at isolation. Since 1941, America has, for better or worse, taken a leading and highly interventionist role in world affairs. Interventionism began under McKinley in the 1890s, but was cemented as policy in the 1940s under FDR.

Chapter 23

# COLD WAR

At the end of World War II, Roosevelt died and left Harry Truman as President. Truman had to confront the Soviet Expansion mentioned at the beginning of the chapter. America's former ally had become a dangerous adversary, made even more so when Russia acquired nuclear weapons in the late 1940s. Thus began the fifty-year "Cold War," a period of mistrust and tension between the U.S. and the Soviet Union.

As a realist, Truman began to intervene furiously in the world to balance power against the Soviets and implement Kennan's containment doctrine. He sent troops to Korea to prevent communism from spreading in Asia, sent money and aid to Europe in the form of the Marshall Plan to prevent Europe from falling to communism, and sent military resources to countries such as Greece to help them combat communist insurrection. America, Truman felt, had no choice but to intervene far and wide in the world to prevent Soviet Communism from destabilizing the world and threatening the United States.

Truman left office in 1952, but his policies continued under his Republican successor, Dwight D. Eisenhower. To the frustration of many Republicans of the time, Eisenhower did not intervene idealistically to liberate countries under communist domination, but instead continued Truman's realist containment policies during his eight years in office.

Presidents John F. Kennedy and Lyndon Johnson did the same in the 1960s, but that's when containment hit a snag. In order to contain communism in Southeast Asia, Kennedy and Johnson sent troops to Vietnam. It was a disaster. The Vietnam War killed tens of thousands of Americans in a futile effort to prevent communist advance in Indochina and impose American-style government on a people that didn't want it. Isolationist sentiments, so discredited by Pearl Harbor, began to creep back into circulation. Many, especially those who couldn't remember World War II, felt that America's military power was often a force for evil rather than good in the world and they wanted to bring the troops home. This became a guiding theme of George McGovern's 1972 presidential campaign and still guides much foreign policy thinking today.

When America finally withdrew from Vietnam in the 1970s, isolationists were gratified, but many others felt that America was losing its greatness while communism was gaining the upper hand in the world. President Richard Nixon worked for détente (relaxing of tensions) with the Soviet Union and even went to China and fraternized with Mao Zedong, one of the worst tyrants in history. Many were disturbed by this realism that seemed to mark a retreat from America's moral leadership in the world.

These sentiments led to the election of Ronald Reagan who promised that America would no longer just contain communism but would defeat it. When asked what his strategy for the Cold War would be, Reagan responded: "We win, they lose." To that end, he engaged in an enormous arms buildup to defeat the Russians the same way his hero, FDR, had defeated the Germans and Japanese. He brought back Wilsonian idealism and framed the Cold War in these terms, even calling the Soviet Union an "evil empire."

This assertive idealism continued throughout Reagan's first term (1981-1985), but then something interesting happened in his second term: Reagan reversed course. The idealist crusader began to negotiate arms reduction treaties with Soviet Premier Mikael Gorbachev and openly recanted his "evil empire" statement.

Whatever it was—Reagan's military buildup, moralism, or negotiation—it seems to have worked. Just as Reagan left office in 1989, the Cold War came to an end. The Soviet Union crumbled, the Berlin wall came down, and America entered a new era in which it was the only superpower.

## CONCLUSION

This brings us up to the present. Kennan had provided us with answers of how to engage the world during the Cold War, but it ended decades ago and America is still groping for a coherent strategy of how to proceed in this new unipolar (one power) world. What is the nation's place in the world today and what should its foreign policies look like? These questions will be the subject of our final chapter.

## CHAPTER 23 SOURCES/FURTHER READING

Adams, John Quincy. "Speech to the U.S. House of Representatives," July 4, 1821. <http://millercenter.org/president/speeches/detail/3484>.

Ambrose, Stephen A. *Rise to Globalism: American Foreign Policy, since 1938*. New York: Penguin, 1997.

Brooks, David and William Kristol. "A Return to National Greatness: A Manifesto for a Lost Creed," *The Weekly Standard*, March 3, 1997.

Burnham, James. *Containment or Liberation? An Inquiry into the Aims of United States Foreign Policy*. New York: John Day, 1953.

Clark, J. Reuben. "Concerning America, and Liberty, and its Price," *Improvement Era*, July 1940.

Dallek, Robert. *The American Style of Foreign Policy: Cultural Politics and Foreign Affairs*. New York: Knopf, 1983.

Diamond, Martin. *The Spirit of Democracy: The Struggle to Build Free Societies Throughout the World*. New York: Times, 2008.

Ferguson, Niall. *Colossus: The Price of America's Empire*. New York: Penguin, 2004.

———. *The War of the World: Twentieth-Century Conflict and the Descent of the West*. New York: Penguin, 2006.

Gaddis, John L. *George Kennan: An American Life*. New York: Penguin, 2011.

———. *The Cold War: A New History*. New York: Penguin, 2005.

Heilbrunn, Jacob. *They Knew They Were Right: The Rise of the Neocons*. New York: Doubleday, 2008.

Herring, George C. *From Colony to Superpower: U.S. Foreign Relations since 1776*. New York: Oxford, 2008.

Hobsbawm, Eric. *The Age of Extremes: A History of the World, 1914-1991*. New York: Pantheon, 1994.

Isaacson, Walter and Evan Thomas. *The Wise Men: Six Friends and the World They Made-Acheson, Bohlen, Harriman, Kennan, Lovett, McCloy*. New York: Simon & Schuster, 1986.

Kagan, Robert. *Dangerous Nation: America's Place in the World from Its Earliest Days to the Dawn of the Twentieth Century*. New York: Knopf, 2006.

Kennan, George F. *Memoirs, 1925-1950*. Boston: Atlantic Monthly Press, 1967.

\_\_\_\_\_. "Long Telegram," U.S. State Department, 22 February 1946. <http://www2.gwu.edu/~nsarchiv/coldwar/documents/episode-1/kennan.htm>.

\_\_\_\_\_. *The Kennan Diaries*. Edited by Frank Costigliola. New York: W.W. Norton & Co., 2014.

Krauthammer, Charles. "The Unipolar Moment," *Foreign Affairs*, Vol. 70, No. 1, (1990/1991), pp. 23-33.

LaFeber, Walter. *The American Age: United States Foreign Policy at Home and Abroad*. New York: Norton, 1994.

Lukacs, John. *George Kennan: A Study of Character*. New Haven: Yale UP, 2007.

McDougall, Walter. *Promised Land, Crusader State: The American Encounter with the World Since 1776*. Boston: Houghton Mifflin, 1997.

Monroe, James. "Seventh Annual Message to Congress," December 2, 1823. <http://www.ourdocuments.gov/doc.php?doc=23&page=transcript>.

Morris, Edmund. *Dutch: A Memoir of Ronald Reagan*. New York: Modern Library, 2000.

Patterson, James T. *Grand Expectations: The United States, 1945-1974*. New York: Oxford University Press, 1996.

\_\_\_\_\_. *Restless Giant: The United States from Watergate to Bush vs. Gore*. New York: Oxford University Press, 2005.

Thompson, Nicholas. *The Hawk and the Dove: Paul Nitze, George Kennan, and the History of the Cold War*. New York: Henry Holt, 2009.

Truman, Harry. "Presidential Address to Congress," 12 March 1947. <http://www.ourdocuments.gov/doc.php?doc=81&page=transcript>.

Wilson, Woodrow. "Speech before Congress," April 2, 1917. <http://www.ourdocuments.gov/doc.php?doc=61&page=transcript>.

Wood, Gordon. *Empire of Liberty: A History of the Early Republic, 1789-1815*. New York: Oxford University Press, 2009.

# Chapter 24

# AMERICA & THE WORLD II: APPROACHES

## FRANCIS FUKUYAMA: THE END OF HISTORY

Francis Fukuyama became one of the world's foremost thinkers by diligence and connections with the right people. He attended Cornell University, where he studied under legendary political philosopher (and bestselling author) Allan Bloom and then went to Harvard for graduate study with Samuel Huntington, one of the country's top political scientists. After completing his doctorate in the late 1980s, Fukuyama took a position at the RAND Corporation in California, doing defense policy research and analyzing world affairs.

The most notable trend of the time was the growth of freedom and democracy in the world. Gorbachev was reforming the Soviet Union, Eastern Europe was breaking free of the grip of totalitarianism, Tiananmen Square protestors signaled democratic stirrings in China, and Asian "tigers" like South Korea and Taiwan were moving toward representative government.

In a 1989 article entitled, "The End of History?" Fukuyama developed an influential theory to explain this remarkable development. He argued that the world was converging on a single political model—liberal democracy. Fascism had been defeated decades before, communism was headed to the ash heap of history, and monarchy, theocracy, and dictatorship—although they persisted in some countries—had long since been discredited. In a simple Darwinian sense, democratic capitalism was winning out over all "less fit" competitors.

Fukuyama explained this in terms of historical logic and human nature. He said that people have two primary desires, which in turn drive history. First is the desire for physical goods, such as food, shelter, medical care, and toys. Second is *thymos,* or the need for *recognition.* It's not enough for people to have a shirt to wear and keep them warm, it must be

# Chapter 24

a fashionable shirt carrying a name-brand logo. It's not enough to have a house to live in, the house must be large and set on a hill where everyone can see it. It's not enough to have a well-working car, the car must look flashy and convey an image. In all of this, we want status and recognition—thymos.

To Fukuyama, those two basic human desires explain why the world would inevitably converge on liberal democracy. Capitalism had been scientifically proven to deliver more material goods to people, satisfying their physical desires, while democracy gives people equal status before the law and therefore satisfies their desire for recognition. Since other forms of government do not adequately fulfill these two basic needs, they are unstable with inner contradictions that will eventually lead them to crumble. But liberal (capitalist) democracy, by satisfying both physical and thymotic needs, stands as the ultimate destination of all societies—it is the "end of history."[1]

## CLASH OF CIVILIZATIONS

Not everyone agreed with Fukuyama's assessment. Three years later, Fukuyama's old teacher at Harvard dissented and offered an alternative paradigm for thinking about foreign affairs. According to Samuel P. Huntington, the world was not converging, but diverging in new ways. Yes, the Cold War divisions of ideology had ended, but this would simply give way to *new* divisions along cultural lines. Huntington believed that transnational cultural units called "civilizations" would create world conflict in the coming years. Just as empires had replaced tribes, nations had replaced empires, and ideological blocs had replaced nations, now civilizations were poised to replace ideological blocs as the organizing units that would define world affairs.

Contra Fukuyama, Huntington argued that modernization and globalization would not lead to a happy convergence of peoples around the globe, but would lead instead to resentment and dislocations. The main component of culture, he noted, is religion and as people sought identity and meaning in a materialist, globalizing world, they would turn to ancient religious traditions with all of the associated doctrines and dogmas. As peoples of the world came into contact, it would lead to conflict between these broad religious-cultural units, meaning ancient hatreds would revive, cultural groups would attempt to reclaim lost territory, and religious believers would fight for their faith tradition against all competitors. This was the "clash of civilizations" from the title of his thesis.

---

1 Many have misunderstood what Fukuyama meant by "the end of history." Clearly, he didn't mean that there would be no more human actions, historical events, or even wars; he simply meant that mankind's political evolution had come to an end.

## GREAT POWER POLITICS

In contrast to Fukuyama and Huntington, John Mearsheimer's "Tragedy of Great Power Politics" paradigm (2001) saw the revival of nation states as the dominant world players in the 21st century. This return of national competition, said Mearsheimer, would mean a return to the suspicion, paranoia, and war characteristic of the international anarchy that existed from the rise of the nation state in the 17th century to the beginning of the Cold War in the 1940s. Like Huntington, Mearsheimer believed conflict would characterize the future, but unlike Huntington, he saw the source of this conflict, not in culture, but in national identity.

## WHO IS RIGHT?

Each of these three theories is a powerful *international relations paradigm*. These paradigms, or conceptual maps, structure and aid our thinking about world affairs. Just as physical maps guide us when we take a trip or hike, conceptual maps guide us in decisions about diplomacy, war, cultural exchange, and trade.

All three paradigms have had their day in the sun. In the 1990s, the world seemed to be following a trajectory consistent with Fukuyama's theory. The Berlin Wall came down, the Soviet Union collapsed, and throughout the world a global free-market revolution continued apace. As Fukuyama predicted, liberal democracy was on the march. It was only a matter of time, it seemed, before all nations in the world joined the United States and other liberal democracies at "the end of history."

The Islamic terrorist attacks against the United States on September 11, 2001 made Huntington appear to be a prophet in that decade. Islamic Civilization, it seemed, was going to war against Western Civilization, just as he had predicted. Perhaps the end of history was not so near. Perhaps cultural divisions and conflicts had, in fact, replaced the Cold War ideological divisions.

In the 2010s, with the resurgence of nationalism (seen in Brexit, the rise of populism in America, and the strain on the European Union), it appears that Mearsheimer's theory is most relevant. Fukuyama and Huntington thought that the nation-state would have diminishing influence in the 21st century, but so far the opposite has been the case.

## CHALLENGES

So why does it matter and who cares about these international relations paradigms? We should all care because it matters a great deal. How we conceive of the world determines how we interact with the world.[2] If we get the conceptual map wrong, as the United States

---

2 The guiding paradigm during the Cold War was, of course, George Kennan's containment theory explained

did in Vietnam, then the policy that follows will be wrong too. Just as a bad road map will get us lost on a trip, so a bad conceptual map will get us lost in foreign relations. We need accurate paradigms to be able to meet the international challenges our country faces today.

One obvious challenge is the threat of terrorism. Religious fanatics, extremist ideologues and others try to kill innocent Americans in order to generate fear and anarchy in our society. The attacks of September 11, 2001 were the most notable example and the American response generated the most controversial foreign policy decisions of recent decades (e.g., the Iraq War).

There is also the problem of nuclear proliferation. Many fear that if tyrannical regimes, such as Iran and North Korea, get their hands on nuclear weapons, they could use them to destroy free countries (e.g., South Korea or Israel) or commit terrorism. Imagine the body count if the 9/11 hijackers would have had access to nukes.

Regional instability is another challenge. This is particularly acute in the Arab world, where popular uprisings have revealed signs of democratic hope, but so far have largely led to a merry-go-round of dictators. This has made the region unpredictable, anarchic, dangerous, and potentially destabilizing to world order.

Finally, there is the challenge of rising competitors. America is currently the most powerful nation in the world, but many are concerned that a non-democratic nation might overtake us. The rise of China, while encouraging for the economic opportunity and trade it provides, may mean that a non-democratic, one-party state will become as powerful as the United States and exercise a less-than-benign influence on the world.

## THREE FORMS OF POWER

To meet each of these above challenges, America has three forms of power at its disposal: political (military), economic (financial), and "soft" (cultural). As of now, America is far and away the most dominant nation in the world in all three power categories.

In the economics section of this book, we learned that the U.S. is easily the wealthiest nation in history, controlling 30% of the world's resources. In international relations, we can use this economic clout by giving or withholding aid, or opening up and cutting off trade relations. Through economic sanctions or gifts, the U.S. can try to get other nations to do what it wants.

Most importantly, though, economic power translates into military power. America uses its wealth to purchase tanks, bombs, aircraft, ships, machine guns, and soldiers. Since the military spending of the United States is nearly as great as the rest of the world combined, the country has military might never before matched in human history. The U.S.

---

in Chapter 23.

has more ability to compel other countries into compliance with foreign policy wishes by destructive force than any nation has ever had before.

Perhaps more influential than either economic or military power is what international relations scholars call "soft power"—the ability to persuade foreigners to do something. Every day, people around the world are exposed to American ideas about democracy and liberty, science and technology, and even ways of doing business. This can shape their hearts and minds even more powerfully than tanks, bombs, and dollars. American culture can "sell" people on the USA and get them to "want what we want them to want" by example. If the old adage, "the pen is mightier than the sword," is correct, then soft power is the most important power of all.

## UNIPOLARITY

Scholars refer to the current world situation—in which the United States has unrivaled dominance in all three realms—as *unipolarity*. In the past, there has been bipolarity (as with the USSR and the USA during the Cold War) and multipolarity (as during the 19th century when many European nations competed for dominance), but since the world has become globalized there has never been a unipolar world with a single nation standing unchallenged in all three realms of power.

## ARE WE DECLINING?

The question for Americans today is: "Can it last?" All of the great powers throughout history have eventually collapsed. Rome dominated the Mediterranean world at the time of Christ, but by the 5th century the Roman Empire had split in half and was falling to barbarian invaders. China was the dominant power in Asia from 1000 to 1500 AD, but then fell into a slumber from which it is only now beginning to waken. England dominated the world in the 19th century, but by the early decades of the 20th century had to call upon the USA for help to survive against its continental rivals. Will the USA follow the same path?

The popular assumption today is that it will. Most people say that America has already started to slide in all three forms of power and it is only a matter of time until other nations (e.g., China, a united Europe, or perhaps even India) catch up and overtake us.

There are reasons behind this assumption. America appears to be declining in economic power. The financial crisis of 2008, according to many economists, was not just another blip on America's strong economic record, but a major turning point that marks the beginning of a new age of slow growth and stagnation.[3] Even though we are now many years out from the "Great Recession," unemployment remains stubbornly high and "underemployment" is

---

3  Gordon (2016).

higher still. Our nation is setting a world record for public debt and many scholars believe that such high levels of debt will eventually lead to economic calamity.[4]

As we discussed earlier, economic power correlates closely with economic freedom. By any standard America's economic liberty has been in decline since the beginning of this century. There is plenty of blame to go around since this decline has occurred under both conservative Republican and liberal Democratic administrations. Is it any surprise that our growth has slowed so remarkably when it is merely following the drop in economic freedom that growth so closely tracks?

This decline in economic power, says Yale historian Paul Kennedy, will inevitably be accompanied by a decline in military power.

> It has been a common dilemma facing previous 'number-one' countries that even as their relative economic strength is ebbing, the growing foreign challenges to their position have compelled them to allocate more and more of their resources into the military sector, which in turn squeezes out productive investment and, over time, leads to the downward spiral of slower growth, heavier taxes, deepening domestic splits over spending priorities, and a weakening capacity to bear the burden of defense.[5]

Kennedy's "Imperial Overstretch" thesis came out in the Reagan years when many believed the Japanese economy would overtake America's. But even though Kennedy was wrong (and widely derided) in the short term, this does not mean he was wrong in the longer term.

Finally, America is also weakening in soft power. Our culture is no longer as attractive to nations around the world as it once was. In 1989, Chinese pro-democracy protestors at Tiananmen Square fashioned a model of the Statue of Liberty as the symbol of the rights they were fighting for. Today, by contrast, we see few referring to America as a beacon of liberty in the world. Anti-Americanism has risen and polls show that favorable views of America have declined almost everywhere in the 21$^{st}$ century. The once-heroic nation that saved the world from fascism in the 1940s is now widely seen as a threat to world peace.

To many, this soft power has declined because of our "arrogant" foreign policy. By going it alone in foreign affairs without regard for international opinion, they say, America has gained a reputation as a bully. Since nobody likes a bully, few want to imitate or follow the American path.

To others, America's decline in soft power is simply a result of envy. People dislike the USA, they say, because of our power, freedom, and greatness. They hate America for the same reason that high school students hate the head cheerleader or the star basketball player.

---

4  See, for example, Rogoff and Reinhart (2009). Because of some data errors, this book is controversial, but its overall point remains. Also see Friedman and Mandelbaum (2011).
5  Kennedy (1987, p. 533).

Whether envy or bullying has occasioned the world's ire, nearly everyone agrees that American soft power has also declined because of the debasement of our culture. Violence, promiscuity, and materialism pervade our popular media and this is the image we project to the rest of the world. As people in other nations associate this filth with the USA, they naturally recoil from imitating or being favorable to American interests. According to political scientist James Q. Wilson,

> The greatest barrier to American influence on the world today is probably not our system of government or even our unequalled military power, but our popular culture. We export, to great individual but no collective applause, blue jeans, Big Macs, rock and hip-hop music, Web-based pornography, and motion pictures that often celebrate violence and a shallow adolescent culture.[6]

Given what the perception of American culture has become, it is understandable that fewer people in the world want to follow America's lead.

Many of us, though, believe that all of this decline talk is premature. Yes, there are startling signs of America slipping in power and influence, but this has happened before and the nation has always bounced back. The United States is founded on robust principles that have survived far worse crises than our current ones. We have every reason to expect that the greatness of America will continue. A setback now does not signify a long-term trend. For that reason, it is safe to assume that American "bounce-back" is at least as likely as American decline.

## CONCLUSION

But here's the final, and in many ways most important, point of the book: this bounce-back won't happen on its own. It will require action by the American people themselves. The future is open and indeterminate so decline or rebound is something the nation will have to choose and the choices of the nation are disproportionately influenced by its leaders. *That is where you come in.*

As a disciple-leader of the future, *you* must decide how to respond to these challenges and the threat of American decline. *You* must decide what kind of power to use, how to use it, and where to use it. *You* must decide which paradigm is most accurate to the world situation and most useful in determining policy. The future of the world is in your hands.

In this book you have learned history, now it is time for you to go and shape it. The principles of constitutionalism, free markets, and cultural uplift are worth striving for, but a rudderless nation will not be up to the task. Only if disciples influence the world for the better in political, economic, and cultural matters can the trends of American decline be halted and reversed.

---

6  Wilson (2006).

*Chapter 24*

## CHAPTER 24 SOURCES/FURTHER READING

Beinart, Peter. *The Good Fight: Why Liberals—And Only Liberals—Can Win the War on Terror and Make America Great Again.* New York: HarperPerennial, 2008.

Beveridge, Albert. "The March of the Flag," September 1898. <http://www.historytools.org/sources/beveridge.html>.

Cohen, Eliot. "The Military." In Peter H. Schuck and James Q. Wilson, eds., *Understanding America: The Anatomy of an Exceptional Nation.* New York: Public Affairs, 2008.

Cohen, Tyler. *The Great Stagnation.* New York: Dutton, 2011.

Fukuyama, Francis. *America at the Crossroads: Democracy, Power and the Neoconservative Legacy.* New Haven: Yale University Press, 2006.

_____. *The End of History and the Last Man.* New York: Avon, 1992.

Gibbon, Edward. *Decline and Fall of the Roman Empire*, 6 vols. 1776-1789.

Gordon, Robert J. *The Rise and Fall of American Growth.* Princeton: Princeton University Press, 2016.

Hubbard, Glenn and Tim Kane. *Balance: The Economics of Great Powers from Ancient Rome to Modern America.* New York: Simon & Schuster, 2013.

Huntington, Samuel P. *The Clash of Civilizations and The Remaking of World Order.* New York: Simon & Schuster, 1996.

_____. *The Third Wave: Democratization in the Late Twentieth Century.* Norman: University of Oklahoma Press, 1991.

Joffe, Joseph. *The Myth of America's Decline: Politics, Economics, and a Half Century of False Prophecies.* New York: W.W. Norton & Co., 2014.

Kaplan, Robert. *The Coming Anarchy: Shattering the Dreams of the Post Cold War.* New York: Vintage, 2000.

Kennedy, Paul. *The Rise and Fall of the Great Powers.* New York: Vintage, 1987.

Kupchan, Charles A. *The End of the American Era: U.S. Foreign Policy and the Geopolitics of the Twenty-First Century.* New York: Vintage, 2002.

Mead, Walter Russell. *Power, Terror, Peace, and War: America's Grand Strategy in a World at Risk.* New York: Knopf, 2004.

Mearsheimer, John J. *The Tragedy of Great Power Politics.* New York: W.W. Norton, 2001.

Nye, Joseph. *Soft Power: The Means to Success in World Politics.* New York: Public Affairs, 2004.

_____. *The Future of Power.* New York: Public Affairs, 2011.

Oren, Michael B. *Power, Faith, and Fantasy: America in the Middle East 1776 to the Present.* New York: W.W. Norton, 2007.

Zakaria, Fareed. *The Post-American World.* New York: W.W. Norton, 2008.

v

# BIBLIOGRAPHY

Abcarian, Robin. "American Exceptionalism: We think we're special. Is that so wrong?," *Los Angeles Times*, September 12, 2013. <http://articles.latimes.com/2013/sep/12/local/la-me-ln-american-exceptionalism-20130912>, accessed Feb 2, 2014.

Acemoglu, Daron and James A. Robinson. *Why Nations Fail: The Origins of Power, Prosperity, and Poverty*. New York: Crown Business, 2012.

Adams, Henry. *The Education of Henry Adams* [1919]. New York: Modern Library, 1944.

Adams, John Quincy. "Speech to the U.S. House of Representatives," July 4, 1821. <http://millercenter.org/president/speeches/detail/3484>.

Adams, John to H. Niles, February 13, 1818. <http://www.constitution.org/primarysources/adams-niles.html>.

———. *The Portable John Adams*. Edited by John Patrick Diggins. New York: Penguin, 2004.

Akerlof, George A. & Janet L. Yellin. "An Analysis of Out-Of-Wedlock Births in the United States," Brookings Policy Brief Series, #4 of 186, August 1986. <http://www.brookings.edu/research/papers/1996/08/childrenfamilies-akerlof>, accessed Jan 27, 2014.

Allitt, Patrick. *Religion in America Since 1945: A History*. New York: Columbia University Press, 2003.

Ambrose, Stephen A. *Rise to Globalism: American Foreign Policy, since 1938*. New York: Penguin, 1997.

Andrus, Hyrum L. and Helen Mae Andrus, eds. *They Knew the Prophet*. Salt Lake City: Bookcraft, 1974.

Appiah, K. Anthony, et. al. *Multiculturalism: Examining the Politics of Recognition*. Princeton: Princeton University Press, 1994.

Applebaum, Anne. *Gulag: A History*. New York: Doubleday, 2003.

Appleby, Joyce. *The Relentless Revolution: A History of Capitalism*. New York: W.W. Norton, 2010.

Ariely, Dan. *Predictably Irrational: The Hidden Forces That Shape Our Decisions*. New York: HarperCollins, 2008.

Aristotle. *The Nicomachean Ethics*. Translated by Robert C. Bartlett and Susan D. Collins. Chicago: University of Chicago Press, 2012.

Armand M. Nicholi, Jr. *The Question of God: C.S. Lewis and Sigmund Freud Debate God, Love, Sex, and the Meaning of Life*. New York: Free Press, 2002.

# Bibliography

Articles of Confederation and perpetual Union between the states of New Hampshire, Massachusetts-bay Rhode Island and Providence Plantations, Connecticut, New York, New Jersey, Pennsylvania, Delaware, Maryland, Virginia, North Carolina, South Carolina and Georgia (1781).

Bailyn, Bernard. *The Ideological Origins of the American Revolution*. Cambridge, MA: Harvard University Press, 1967.

_____. *The Peopling of British North America: An Introduction*. New York: Vintage, 1986.

Baldwin, Carliss Y. and Kim B. Clark. *Design Rules: The Power of Modularity*. Cambridge, MA: M.I.T. Press, 2000.

Barro, Robert J. and Rachel M. McCleary. "Religion and Economic Growth," NBER Working Paper No. 9682, issued in May 2003. <http://www.nber.org/papers/w9682>.

Bastiat, Frédéric. *The Law*. Irvington-on-Hudson, New York: Foundation for Economic Education, 1998.

Bateman, Merrill J. "Nothing Shall Be Withheld," BYU-Idaho Devotional, 22 May 2007.

Beard, Charles. *An Economic Interpretation of the Constitution of the United States* [1913]. Mineola, NY: Dover, 2004.

Beard, Charles and Mary. *History of the United States*. New York: Macmillan, 1921.

Becker, Gary. *The Economics of Life: From Baseball to Affirmative Action to Immigration, How Real-World Issues Affect Our Everyday Life*. New York: McGraw-Hill, 1997.

Becker, Jasper. *Hungry Ghosts: Mao's Secret Famine*. New York: Henry Holt, 1996.

Bednar, David A. "Things as They Really Are." *Ensign* (June 2010).

Beeman, Richard. *Our Lives, Our Fortunes and Our Sacred Honor: The Forging of American Independence, 1774-1776*. New York: Basic Books, 2013.

_____. *Plain, Honest Men: The Making of the American Constitution*. New York: Random House, 2009.

Behravesh, Nariman. *Spin-Free Economics: A No-Nonsense, Nonpartisan Guide to Today's Global Economic Debates*. New York: McGraw-Hill, 2009.

Beinart, Peter. *The Good Fight: Why Liberals—And Only Liberals—Can Win the War on Terror and Make America Great Again*. New York: HarperPerennial, 2008.

Bell, Daniel. *The Coming of Postindustrial Society*. New York: Basic Books, 1976.

_____. *The Cultural Contradictions of Capitalism*. New York: Basic Books, 1976.

Benson, Ezra Taft. "Born of God," General Conference of the Church of Jesus Christ of Latter-day Saints, October 1985.

_____. "Our Divine Constitution," *Ensign*, November 1987.

_____. "The Constitution—A Glorious Standard," *Ensign*, May 1976.

_____. "The Proper Role of Government," *Conference Report*, October 1968, pp. 17-22.

_____. *This Nation Shall Endure*. Salt Lake City: Deseret Book, 1977.

Benson, Jackson J. *John Steinbeck, Writer: A Biography*. New York: Penguin, 1990.

Bergh, Albert Ellery, ed. *The Writings of Thomas Jefferson*. 19 Volumes. Washington, D.C.: Thomas Jefferson Memorial Foundation, 1904.

Bergson, Henri. *Creative Evolution*. Arthur Mitchell, trans. New York: Modern Library, 1944.

_____. *The Two Sources of Morality and Religion*. Garden City, NY: Doubleday, 1935.

Berlin, Isaiah. *Two Concepts of Liberty*. New York: Oxford University Press, 1958.

Bernstein, William J. *The Birth of Plenty: How the Prosperity of the Modern World Was Created*. New York: McGraw-Hill, 2004.

Beveridge, Albert. "The March of the Flag," September 1898. <http://www.historytools.org/sources/beveridge.html>.

Black, Conrad. *Franklin Delano Roosevelt: Champion of Freedom*. New York: Public Affairs, 2003.

Bloom, Harold. *The American Religion: The Emergence of the Post-Christian Nation*. New York: Simon & Schuster, 1992.

Bobrick, Benson. *Angel in the Whirlwind: The Triumph of the American Revolution*. New York: Penguin, 1997.

Boorstin, Daniel. *The Americans: The Colonial Experience*. New York: Vintage, 1964.

_____. *The Americans: The Democratic Experience*. New York: Random House, 1973.

_____. *The Lost World of Thomas Jefferson*. Chicago: University of Chicago Press, 1993. Covers Jefferson's intellectual outlook.

Bowen, Catherine Drinker. *Miracle at Philadelphia: The Story of the Constitutional Convention, May to September 1787*. Boston: Little, Brown, & Co., 1966.

Bradbury, Ray. *Conversations with Ray Bradbury*. Edited by Steven L. Aggelis. Jackson, MS: University Press of Mississippi, 2004.

Branch, Taylor. *America in The King Years*, 3 vols. New York: Simon & Schuster, 1989-2006. This trilogy is perhaps the best treatment of King and the Civil Rights movement.

Brodsky, Alyn. *Grover Cleveland: A Study in Character*. New York: St. Martin's Press, 2000.

Brookhiser, Richard. *Alexander Hamilton, American*. New York: Free Press, 1999.

_____. *Founders' Son: A Life of Abraham Lincoln*. New York: Basic Books, 2014.

_____. *Founding Father: Rediscovering George Washington*. New York: Free Press, 1996.

_____. *Gentleman Revolutionary: Gouverneur Morris: The Rake who Wrote the Constitution*. New York: Free Press, 2003.

_____. *James Madison*. New York: Basic Books, 2011.

_____. *The Adamses: America's First Dynasty*. New York: Free Press, 2002.

Brooks, Arthur C. *Gross National Happiness: Why Happiness Matters for America--and How We Can Get More of It*. New York: Basic Books, 2008.

Brooks, David and William Kristol. "A Return to National Greatness: A Manifesto for a Lost Creed," *The Weekly Standard*, March 3, 1997.

Bryson, Bill. *At Home: A Short History of Private Life*. New York: Doubleday, 2010.

## Bibliography

Buchholz, Todd G. *From Here to Economy: A Shortcut to Economic Literacy.* New York: Dutton, 1995.

\_\_\_\_\_. *New Ideas from Dead Economists.* New York: New American Library, 1989.

Budziszewski, J. *What We Can't Not Know: A Guide.* Dallas: Spence Publishing, 2003.

Burnham, James. *Congress and the American Tradition.* Chicago: Regnery, 1959.

\_\_\_\_\_. *Containment or Liberation? An Inquiry into the Aims of United States Foreign Policy.* New York: John Day, 1953.

\_\_\_\_\_. *The Machiavellians.* New York: John Day, 1943.

\_\_\_\_\_. *The Managerial Revolution: What is Happening in the World.* New York: John Day Company, Inc., 1941.

Bushman, Richard L. *Joseph Smith: Rough Stone Rolling.* New York: Random House, 2007.

Butler, Jon. *Awash in a Sea of Faith: Christianizing the American People.* Cambridge, MA: Harvard University Press, 1990.

\_\_\_\_\_. *Becoming America: The Revolution before 1776.* Cambridge, MA: Harvard University Press, 2000.

Butterfield, L. H. ed. *Letters of Benjamin Rush* Vol. II. Princeton: The American Philosophical Society, 1951.

Calhoun, John C. *A Disquisition on Government* (1848). New York: Peter Smith, 1943.

Carr, Nicholas. *The Shallows: What the Internet Is Doing to Our Brains.* New York: W.W. Norton, 2010.

Catton, Bruce. *The American Heritage Short History of the Civil War.* New York: Dell, 1960.

Catton, Bruce and William B. Catton. *The Bold and Magnificent Dream: America's Founding Years, 1492-1815.* Garden City, NY: Doubleday, 1978.

Chang, Jung. *Mao: The Unknown Story.* New York: Knopf, 2005.

\_\_\_\_\_. *Wild Swans.* New York: Doubleday, 1991.

Chernow, Ron. *Alexander Hamilton.* New York: Penguin, 2004.

\_\_\_\_\_. *Washington: A Life.* New York: Penguin, 2010.

Chesnutt, Charles W. "The Sheriff's Children" (1889). <http://www.chesnuttarchive.org/works/Stories/sheriff.html>.

Christensen, Joe J. "Greed, Selfishness, and Overindulgence," *Ensign,* May, 1999.

Christofferson, D. Todd. "Moral Discipline," General Conference, October 2009.

\_\_\_\_\_. "Reflections on a Consecrated Life." *Ensign* (Nov. 2010).

Chua, Amy & Jed Rubenfeld. *The Triple Package: How Three Unlikely Traits Explain the Rise and Fall of Cultural Groups in America.* New York: Penguin, 2014.

Church Newsroom. "Religious Freedom." The Church of Jesus Christ of Latter-day Saints. <http://www.mormonnewsroom.org/official-statement/religious-freedom>.

# Bibliography

———. "The Mormon Ethic of Civility," Church of Jesus Christ of Latter-day Saints, October 16, 2009. <http://www.mormonnewsroom.org/article/the-mormon-ethic-of-civility>.

Churchill, Winston. *History of the English Speaking Peoples*. Edited by Henry Steel Commager. New York: Barnes & Noble, 1994.

Clark, J. Reuben. "Concerning America, and Liberty, and its Price," *Improvement Era*, July 1940.

Cohen, Tyler. *The Great Stagnation*. New York: Dutton, 2011.

Collins, Francis S. *The Language of God, The: A Scientist Presents Evidence for Belief*. New York: Free Press, 2006.

Collinson, Patrick. *The Reformation: A History*. New York: Modern Library, 2004.

Constitution of the United States of America (1787).

Cook, Quentin L. "Restoring Morality and Religious Freedom," *Ensign*, September 2012.

Countryman, Edward. *The American Revolution*. New York: Hill & Wang, 2000.

Covey, Stephen R. *The Seven Habits of Highly Effective People*. New York: Simon and Schuster, 1989.

Crick, Francis. *Life Itself: Its Origin and Nature*. New York: Simon & Schuster, 1982.

Crunden, Robert. *A Brief History of American Culture*. New York: Paragon House, 1998.

Custis, George Washington Parke. *Recollections and Private Memoirs of Washington*, edited by Benson J. Lossing. New York: Derby & Jackson, 1860.

Dallek, Robert. *The American Style of Foreign Policy: Cultural Politics and Foreign Affairs*. New York: Knopf, 1983.

Darwin, Charles. *On the Origin of Species* (1859). New York: Signet Classics, 2003.

De Tocqueville, Alexis. *Democracy in America* (1830). New York: Penguin, 2003.

Declaration of Independence (1776).

Diamond, Martin. *The Spirit of Democracy: The Struggle to Build Free Societies Throughout the World*. New York: Times, 2008.

Diggins, John P. *John Adams*. New York: Henry Holt, 2003.

———. *Max Weber: Politics and the Spirit of Tragedy*. New York: Basic Books, 1996.

———. *Up From Communism: Conservative Odysseys in American Intellectual Development*. New York: Columbia University Press, 1975.

———. *Why Niebuhr Now?* Chicago: University of Chicago Press, 2011.

DiLorenzo, Thomas. *How Capitalism Saved America: The Untold History of Our Country, From the Pilgrims to the Present*. New York: Crown Forum, 2004.

Donald, David Herbert. *Lincoln*. New York: Touchstone, 1996.

Douglass, Frederick. *Narrative of the Life of Frederick Douglass, An American Slave* (1845). <http://www.gutenberg.org/files/23/23-h/23-h.htm>.

Dubner, Steven J. and Stephen Leavitt. *Freakonomics: A Rogue Economist Explores the Hidden Side of Everything*. New York: William Morrow, 2005.

———. *Superfreakonomics*. New York: William Morrow, 2009.

## Bibliography

Durant, Will and Ariel Durant. *The Lessons of History*. New York: Simon & Schuster, 1968.

Dweck, Carol S. *Mindset: The New Psychology of Success*. New York: Random House, 2006.

Ebenstein, Lanny. *Milton Friedman: A Biography*. New York: Palgrave Macmillan, 2009.

Ellis, Joseph J. *American Creation: Triumphs and Tragedies at the Founding of the Republic*. New York: Knopf, 2007.

_____. *Founding Brothers: The Revolutionary Generation*. New York: Vintage, 2002

_____. *His Excellency: George Washington*. New York: Knopf, 2004.

Eyring, Henry J. *Mormon Scientist: The Life and Faith of Henry Eyring*. Salt Lake City: Deseret, 2007.

Eyring, Henry. *The Faith of a Scientist*. Salt Lake City: Bookcraft, 1967.

Faust, James E. "The Shield of Faith," LDS General Conference, April 2000.

Fawcett, Stanley E., ed. *God's Prophets Speak*. Springville, UT: Horizon, 2004.

Federal Reserve Bank of Dallas. "By Our Own Bootstraps: Economic Opportunity & the Dynamics of Income Distribution," Annual Report 1995. <http://www.dallasfed.org/assets/documents/fed/annual/1999/ar95.pdf>

Daniel, Feller. *The Jacksonian Promise: America, 1815-1840*. Baltimore: Johns Hopkins University Press, 1995.

Ferguson, Niall. *Colossus: The Price of America's Empire*. New York: Penguin, 2004.

_____. *Civilization: The West and the Rest*. New York: Penguin, 2011.

_____. *The Ascent of Money: A Financial History of the World*. New York: Penguin, 2008.

_____. *The Great Degeneration: How Institutions Decay and Economies Die*. New York: Penguin, 2013.

_____. *The War of the World: Twentieth-Century Conflict and the Descent of the West*. New York: Penguin, 2006.

Ferling, John. *Almost A Miracle: The American Victory in the War of Independence*. New York: Oxford University Press, 2009.

_____. *Setting the World Ablaze: Washington, Adams, Jefferson, & The American Revolution*. New York: Oxford University Press, 2000.

Fernandez-Armesto, Felipe. *The Americas: A Hemispheric History*. New York: Modern Library, 2003.

First Presidency of the Church of Jesus Christ of Latter-day Saints. "The First Presidency Warns Against 'Irreligion'" *Ensign*, May 1979.

_____. "Letter on Political Participation," Church of Jesus Christ of Latter-day Saints, September 22, 2008. <http://www.mormonnewsroom.org/article/first-presidency-issues-letter-on-political-participation>.

Flexner, James T. *George Washington: The Indispensable Man*. Boston: Little, Brown, 1974.

Forcey, Charles. *The Crossroads of Liberalism: Croly, Weyl, Lippmann & The Progressive Era, 1900-25*. New York: Oxford University Press, 1961.

Foucault, Michel. *Discipline and Punish: The Birth of the Prison* [1977]. Translated by Alan Sheridan. New York: Vintage, 1995.

Fox, Frank and Clayne Pope. *American Heritage: An Interdisciplinary Approach*. 5th edition. Dubuque, IA: Kendall/Hunt, 1990.

_____. *City Upon a Hill*. Provo, UT: BYU Academic Publishing, 2007.

Fox, Richard. *Reinhold Niebuhr: A Biography*. New York: Pantheon, 1985.

Frady, Marshall. *Martin Luther King, Jr.: A Life*. New York: Penguin, 2002.

Franklin, Benjamin. Examination Before The House of Commons (1766).

_____. *The Autobiography and Other Writings*. Selected and edited with an introduction by L. Jesse Lemisch. New York: Penguin, 1961.

Fried, Charles. *Modern Liberty and the Limits of Government*. New York: W.W. Norton, 2007.

Friedman, Charles. *Law in America: A Short History*. New York: Modern Library, 2002.

Friedman, Milton. *Capitalism and Freedom*. Chicago: University of Chicago Press, 1962.

_____. *Money Mischief: Episodes in Monetary History*. New York: Harcourt Brace Jovanovich, 1992.

Friedman, Milton and Anna Schwartz. *A Monetary History of the United States, 1867-1960*. Princeton: Princeton University Press, 1971.

Friedman, Milton and Rose Friedman. *Free to Choose*. New York: Harvest, 1990.

Friedman, Thomas L. and Michael Mandelbaum. *That Used to Be Us: How America Fell Behind in the World it Invented and How We Can Come Back*. New York: Farrar, Straus, and Giroux, 2011.

Friedman, Thomas L. *The Lexus and the Olive Tree: Understanding Globalization*. New York: Anchor Books, 1999.

_____. *The World is Flat: A Brief History of the Twenty-First Century*. New York: Farrar, Straus, and Giroux, 2005.

Fukuyama, Francis. *America at the Crossroads: Democracy, Power and the Neoconservative Legacy*. New Haven: Yale University Press, 2006.

_____. *Our Posthuman Future: Consequences of the Biotechnology Revolution*. New York: Farrar Straus Giroux, 2002.

_____. *The End of History and the Last Man*. New York: Avon, 1992.

_____. *The Great Disruption: Human Nature and the Reconstitution of Social Order*. New York: Free Press, 1999.

_____. *Trust: The Social Virtues and the Creation of Prosperity*. New York: The Free Press, 1995.

_____. *The Origins of Political Order: From Prehuman Times to the French Revolution*. New York: Farrar, Straus, and Giroux, 2011.

_____. *Political Order and Political Decay: From the Industrial Revolution to the Globalization of Democracy*. New York: Farrar, Straus, and Giroux, 2014.

Gaddis, John L. *George Kennan: An American Life*. New York: Penguin, 2011.

_____. *The Cold War: A New History*. New York: Penguin, 2005.

Gaustad, Edwin S. *A Religious History of America*. San Francisco: Harper-San Francisco, 1990.

Gibbon, Edward. *Decline and Fall of the Roman Empire*, 6 vols. 1776-1789.

# Bibliography

Gilder, George. *Microcosm: The Quantum Revolution in Economics and Technology.* New York: Simon & Schuster, 1989.

Ginzberg, Lori D. *Elizabeth Cady Stanton: An American Life.* New York: Hill and Wang, 2010.

Givens, Terryl and Fiona. *The God Who Weeps: How Mormonism Makes Sense of Life.* Salt Lake City: Ensign Peak, 2012.

Gleeson-White, Jane. *Double Entry: How the Merchants of Venice Created Modern Finance.* New York: W.W. Norton & Co., 2012.

Gleick, James. *The Information: A Theory, A History, A Flood.* New York: Vintage, 2012.

Godkin, E.L. "The Eclipse of Liberalism," *The Nation* (August 9, 1900).

Gordon, John Steele. *An Empire of Wealth: The Epic History of American Economic Power.* New York: Harper Perennial, 2005.

Gordon, Robert J. *The Rise and Fall of American Growth.* Princeton: Princeton University Press, 2016.

Graff, Henry. *Grover Cleveland.* New York: Times Books, 2002.

Greenspan, Alan. *The Age of Turbulence: Adventures in a New World.* New York: Penguin, 2007.

Greider, William. *Secrets of the Temple: How the Federal Reserve Runs the Country.* New York: Simon & Schuster, 1987.

Gress, David *From Plato to NATO: The Idea of the West and its Opponents.* New York: Free Press, 1998.

Grossman, Cathy Lynn. "Charting the Unchurched in America," *USA TODAY*, March 7, 2001.

Haidt, Jonathan. *The Righteous Mind: Why Good People Are Divided by Politics and Religion.* New York: Pantheon, 2012.

Hamilton, Alexander. *Alexander Hamilton: Writings.* Edited by Joanne B. Freeman. New York: Library of America, 2001.

Hamilton, Alexander, James Madison, and John Jay. *The Federalist Papers.* Edited by Clinton Rossiter. New York: Penguin, 1961.

Hannan, Daniel. *Inventing Freedom: How the English-Speaking Peoples Made the World Modern.* New York: HarperCollins, 2013.

Hartz, Louis. *The Liberal Tradition in America.* New York: Harcourt Brace, 1955.

Hayden, Tom. "The Port Huron Statement of Students for a Democratic Society." 1962. <http://coursesa.matrix.msu.edu/~hst306/documents/huron.html>, accessed Jan 20, 2014.

Hayek, Friedrich Von. *The Road to Serfdom.* Chicago: University of Chicago Press, 1944.

_____. *The Constitution of Liberty.* Chicago: University of Chicago Press, 1978.

Hazlitt, Henry. *Economics in One Lesson.* New Rochelle, NY: Arlington House, 1979.

Heilbroner, Robert L. *The Worldly Philosophers: The Lives, Times, and Ideas of the Great Economic Thinkers.* New York: Simon & Schuster, 1980.

Heilbroner, Robert L. and Lester Thurow. *Economics Explained: Everything You Need to Know About How the Economy Works and Where It's Going.* New York: Simon & Schuster, 1998.

Heilbrunn, Jacob. *They Knew They Were Right: The Rise of the Neocons.* New York: Doubleday, 2008.

Herring, George C. *From Colony to Superpower: U.S. Foreign Relations since 1776.* New York: Oxford, 2008.

Higginbotham, Donald. *The War of American Independence.* Boston: Northeastern University Press, 1983.

Higgins, Andrew. "In Europe, God Is (Not) Dead: Christian groups are growing, faith is more public. Is supply-side economics the explanation?" *Wall Street Journal*, July 14, 2007. <http://online.wsj.com/news/articles/SB118434936941966055>.

Hirsch, E.D. *Cultural Literacy: What Every American Needs to Know.* Boston: Houghton-Mifflin, 1987.

Hitchens, Christopher. *Thomas Jefferson: Author of America.* New York: HarperCollins, 2005.

_____. *Thomas Paine's Rights of Man.* New York: Atlantic Monthly Press, 2006.

Hobbes, Thomas. *Leviathan* (1651). New York: Penguin, 1982.

Hobsbawm, Eric. *The Age of Extremes: A History of the World, 1914-1991.* New York: Pantheon, 1994.

Hofstadter, Richard. *The Idea of a Party System: The Rise of Legitimate Opposition in the United States, 1780-1840.* Berkeley: University of California Press, 1969.

Howe, Daniel Walker. *What Hath God Wrought: The Transformation of America, 1815-1848.* New York: Oxford University Press, 2007.

Hubbard, Glenn and Tim Kane. *Balance: The Economics of Great Powers from Ancient Rome to Modern America.* New York: Simon & Schuster, 2013.

Huemer, Michael. *The Problem of Political Authority: An Examination of the Right to Coerce and the Duty to Obey.* New York: Palgrave Macmillan, 2013.

Hume, David. *Political Essays.* Edited by Charles William Hendel. New York: Liberal Arts Press, 1953. (1741, 1752).

Huntington, Samuel P. *American Politics: The Promise of Disharmony.* Cambridge, MA: Harvard University Press, 1981.

_____. *Who Are We? The Challenges to America's National Identity.* New York: Simon & Schuster, 2004.

_____. *The Clash of Civilizations and The Remaking of World Order.* New York: Simon & Schuster, 1996.

_____. *The Third Wave: Democratization in the Late Twentieth Century.* Norman: University of Oklahoma Press, 1991.

Iannaccone, Laurence R. "Introduction to the Economics of Religion," *Journal of Economic Literature* Vol. XXXVI (September 1998), pp. 1465-1496.

Ip, Greg. *The Little Book of Economics.* Hoboken, NJ: Wiley, 2010.

Isaacson, Walter and Evan Thomas. *The Wise Men: Six Friends and the World They Made-Acheson, Bohlen, Harriman, Kennan, Lovett, McCloy.* New York: Simon & Schuster, 1986.

## Bibliography

Isaacson, Walter. *Benjamin Franklin*. New York: Simon & Schuster, 2003.

Jeansonne, Glen. *The Life of Herbert Hoover: Fighting Quaker, 1928-1933*. New York: Palgrave Macmillan, 2012.

Jeffers, H. Paul. *An Honest President: The Life and Presidencies of Grover Cleveland*. New York: Perennial, 2000.

Jefferson, Thomas. "Letter to The Danbury Baptist Association," January 1, 1802. <http://www.loc.gov/loc/lcib/9806/danpre.html>.

_____. *The Writings of Thomas Jefferson*. New York: Derby & Jackson, 1859.

Jenkins, Roy. *Franklin Delano Roosevelt*. New York: Henry Holt, 2003.

Joffe, Joseph. *The Myth of America's Decline: Politics, Economics, and a Half Century of False Prophecies*. New York: W.W. Norton & Co., 2014.

Johnson, Paul. *A History of the American People*. New York: Harper Perennial, 1999.

_____. *George Washington: The Founding Father*. New York: HarperCollins, 2005.

_____. *The Offshore Islanders: A History of the English People*. London: Orion, 1972.

_____. *The Renaissance: A Short History*. New York: Modern Library, 2000.

Kagan, Robert. *Dangerous Nation: America's Place in the World from Its Earliest Days to the Dawn of the Twentieth Century*. New York: Knopf, 2006.

Kahneman, Daniel. *Thinking Fast and Slow*. New York: Farrar, Straus and Giroux, 2013.

Kaplan, Robert. *The Coming Anarchy: Shattering the Dreams of the Post Cold War*. New York: Vintage, 2000.

Kelley, Kevin. *Out of Control: The Rise of Neo-Biological Civilization*. New York: Addisson-Wesley, 1994.

Kennan, George F. *Memoirs, 1925-1950*. Boston: Atlantic Monthly Press, 1967.

_____. "Long Telegram," U.S. State Department, 22 February 1946. <http://www2.gwu.edu/~nsarchiv/coldwar/documents/episode-1/kennan.htm>.

_____. *The Kennan Diaries*. Edited by Frank Costigliola. New York: W.W. Norton & Co., 2014.

Kennedy, David M. *Freedom From Fear: The American People in Depression and War*. New York: Oxford University Press, 1999.

Kennedy, Paul. *The Rise and Fall of the Great Powers*. New York: Vintage, 1987.

King, Martin Luther, Jr. "Letter from a Birmingham Jail" (1963). <http://www.africa.upenn.edu/Articles_Gen/Letter_Birmingham.html>.

King, Ross. *Brunelleschi's Dome: How a Renaissance Genius Reinvented Architecture*. New York: Penguin, 2000.

_____. *Machiavelli: Philosopher of Power*. New York: HarperCollins, 2007.

Kotkin, Joel. *The City: A Global History*. New York: Modern Library, 2005

Krauthammer, Charles. "The Unipolar Moment," *Foreign Affairs*, Vol. 70, No. 1, (1990/1991), pp. 23-33.

# Bibliography

Krugman, Paul. "Who Was Milton Friedman?" *The New York Review of Books*, Feb 15, 2007. <http://www.nybooks.com/articles/archives/2007/feb/15/who-was-milton-friedman/>.

_____. *Pop Internationalism*. Cambridge, MA: M.I.T Press, 1996.

Kupchan, Charles A. *The End of the American Era: U.S. Foreign Policy and the Geopolitics of the Twenty-First Century*. New York: Vintage, 2002.

LaFeber, Walter. *The American Age: United States Foreign Policy at Home and Abroad*. New York: Norton, 1994.

Landes, David. *The Wealth and Poverty of Nations*. New York: Norton, 1999.

Larsen, Timothy. "War Is Over, If You Want It: Beyond the Conflict Between Faith and Science," *Perspectives on Science and the Christian Faith*, vol. 60, no. 3 (Sep 2008), 147-155.

Lasch, Christopher. *The True and Only Heaven: Progress and its Critics*. New York: W.W. Norton, 1991.

Lee, Susan. *Susan Lee's ABZs of Economics: Basics to Buzzwords--Everything you Need to Know in Plain English*. New York: Simon and Schuster, 1987.

Lennox, John C. *Gunning for God*. Oxford: Lion Hudson, 2011.

Leonard, Andrew. "The tech protests get personal — and ugly" Salon.com January 22, 2014. <http://www.salon.com/2014/01/22/the_tech_protests_get_personal_and_ugly/>.

Leuchtenburg, William E. *Franklin D. Roosevelt and the New Deal: 1932-1940*. New York: Harper Perennial, 2009.

Lewis, C.S. *Mere Christianity*. New York: Macmillan, 1952.

Lewis, Hyrum. "The Myth of American Conservatism," *Journal of the Historical Society* (12:1), 27-45.

Lindsey, Brink. *The Age of Abundance: How Prosperity Transformed America's Politics and Culture*. New York: HarperCollins, 2007.

Lipset, Seymour Martin. *American Exceptionalism: A Double-Edged Sword*. New York: W.W. Norton, 1997.

Livesay, Harold C. *Andrew Carnegie and the Rise of Big Business*, 2d ed. NY: Longman, 2000.

Locke, John. *Second Treatise of Government* (1689).

Lukacs, John. *George Kennan: A Study of Character*. New Haven: Yale UP, 2007.

Machiavelli, Niccolò. *Discourses on Livy* (1531). Translated by Harvey C. Mansfield and Nathan Tarcov. Chicago: University of Chicago Press, 1998.

_____. *The Prince* (1532). New York: Penguin, 2003.

Madison, James. *Notes of Debates: In The Federal Convention of 1787*. Oxford, OH: Ohio University Press, 1985.

Madsen, Truman G. "Smith, Joseph: Teachings of Joseph Smith," *Encyclopedia of Mormonism*. 1992. <http://eom.byu.edu/index.php/Trials_of_Joseph_Smith#Legal_Trials_of_Joseph_Smith>.

_____. *Presidents Of The Church: Insights Into Their Lives And Teachings*. Salt Lake City: Deseret Book, 2004.

_____. *Five Classics*. Salt Lake City: Eagle Gate, 2001.

# BIBLIOGRAPHY

Magnusson, Sally. *The Flying Scotsman: A Biography of Eric Liddell*. New York: Quartet Books, 1981.

Malone, Dumas. *Jefferson the Virginian*. Boston: Little, Brown & Co., 1948.

Mandelbaum, Michael. *The Ideas that Conquered the World: Peace, Democracy, and Free Markets in the Twenty-first Century*. New York: Public Affairs, 2002.

Mankiw, Greg. *Principles of Economics*. Fifth Edition. Mason, OH: Cengage Learning, 2008.

Marsden, George. *Jonathan Edwards: A Life*. New Haven: Yale University Press, 2003.

Marty, Martin E. *Pilgrims in Their Own Land: 500 Years of Religion in America*. Boston: Little, Brown, & Co., 1984.

Marty, Martin. *Luther*. New York: Penguin, 2004.

Mattson, Kevin. *When America Was Great: The Fighting Faith of Liberalism in Postwar America*. New York: Routledge, 2004.

Maxwell, Neal A. "Meeting the Challenges of Today," BYU Devotional, October 10, 1978. <http://speeches.byu.edu/?act=viewitem&id=909>.

McCarthy, Cormac. *The Road*. New York: Vintage, 2007.

McCarty, Marilu Hurt. *The Nobel Laureates: How the World's Greatest Economic Minds Shaped Modern Thought*. New York: McGraw-Hill, 2001.

McCraw, Thomas K. *The Founders and Finance: How Hamilton, Gallatin, and Other Immigrants Forged a New Economy*. Cambridge, MA: Belknap Press, 2012.

McCullough, David. *1776*. New York: Simon and Schuster, 2005.

_____. *John Adams*. New York: Simon & Schuster, 2001.

McDonald, Forrest. *We The People: The Economic Origins of the Constitution*. Chicago: University of Chicago Press, 1958.

McDougall, Walter. *Promised Land, Crusader State: The American Encounter with the World Since 1776*. Boston: Houghton Mifflin, 1997.

McPherson, James M. *Battle Cry of Freedom: The Civil War Era*. New York: Oxford University Press, 1988.

Meacham, Jon. *American Gospel: God, the Founding Fathers, and the Making of a Nation*. New York: Random House, 2006.

Mead, Walter Russell. *God and Gold: Britain, America, and the Making of the Modern World*. New York: Knopf, 2007.

_____. *Power, Terror, Peace, and War: America's Grand Strategy in a World at Risk*. New York: Knopf, 2004.

Mearsheimer, John J. *The Tragedy of Great Power Politics*. New York: W.W. Norton, 2001.

Micklethwait, John and Adrian Wooldridge. *God is Back: How the Global Revival of Faith is Changing the World*. New York: Penguin, 2009.

_____. *The Company: A Short History of a Revolutionary Idea*. New York: Modern Library, 2003.

Middlekauff, Robert. *The Glorious Cause: The American Revolution, 1763-1789*. New York: Oxford University Press, 1982.

Mill, John Stuart. *On Liberty* [1859]. Mineola, New York: Dover, 2002.

Miller, Perry. *Errand into the Wilderness.* Cambridge, MA: Belknap Press of Harvard University Press, 1956.

_____. Roger Williams: *His Contribution to the American Tradition.* Indianapolis: Bobbs-Merrill, 1953.

Miller, Roger LeRoy and Daniel K. Benjamin. *The Economics of Macro Issues.* 6th Edition. Upper Saddle River, NJ: Pearson Prentice Hall, 2013.

Mischel, Walter. *The Marshmallow Test: Mastering Self-Control.* Boston: Little, Brown, and Company, 2014.

Monroe, James. "Seventh Annual Message to Congress," December 2, 1823. <http://www.ourdocuments.gov/doc.php?doc=23&page=transcript>.

Montesquieu, Charles de. *The Spirit of the Laws* (1748). Edited by Anne M. Cohler, Basia Carolyn Miller, and Harold Samuel Stone. New York: Cambridge University Press, 1989.

Morone, James A. and Rogan Kersh. *By the People: Debating American Government.* New York: Oxford University Press, 2013.

Morris, Edmund. *Colonel Roosevelt.* New York: Random House, 2010.

_____. *Dutch: A Memoir of Ronald Reagan.* New York: Modern Library, 2000.

Morris, Ian. *Why the West Rules (for now).* New York: Farrar, Straus, and Giroux, 2010.

Murray, Charles. "The New American Divide," *Wall Street Journal,* January 21, 2012. <http://online.wsj.com/news/articles/SB10001424052970204301404577170733817181646>.

_____. *Coming Apart: The State of White America, 1960-2010.* New York: Crown Forum, 2013.

_____. *Losing Ground: American Social Policy, 1950-1980.* New York: Basic Books, 1984.

_____. *The Curmudgeon's Guide to Getting Ahead: Dos and Don'ts of Right Behavior, Tough Thinking, Clear Writing, and Living a Good Life.* New York: Crown Business, 2014.

Myrdal, Gunnar. *An American Dilemma: The Negro Problem and Modern Democracy.* New York: Pantheon, 1962.

Nagel, Thomas. *Mind and Cosmos: Why the Materialist, Neo-Darwinian Conception of Nature is Almost Certainly False.* New York: Oxford University Press, 2012.

Nasar, Sylvia. *Grand Pursuit: The Story of Economic Genius.* New York: Simon & Schuster, 2011.

Nash, George. *The Life of Herbert Hoover: The Engineer, 1874-1914.* New York: W.W. Norton & Co., 1983. Covers Hoover's pre-political life.

Neuhaus, Richard, ed. *Reinhold Niebuhr Today.* Grand Rapids, MI: William B. Eerdman's, 1989.

Nevins, Allan. *Grover Cleveland: A Study in Courage.* New York: Dodd, Mead, 1932.

Niebuhr, Reinhold. *The Children of Light and the Children of Darkness: A Vindication of Democracy and a Critique of Its Traditional Defense.* Chicago: University of Chicago Press, 1944.

_____. "Why the Christian Church is Not Pacifist," in *The Essential Niebuhr,* edited by Robert McAfee Brown. New Haven: Yale University Press, 1987, pp. 102-119.

_____. *Moral Man & Immoral Society: A Study in Ethics.* New York: Charles Scribner's Sons, 1932.

# Bibliography

———. *The Irony of American History*. New York: Charles Scribner's Sons, 1952.

———. *The Nature and Destiny of Man*. New York: Charles Scribner's Sons, 1953.

Nisbet, Robert A. *The Quest for Community: A Study in the Ethics of Order and Freedom*. New York: Oxford University Press, 1953.

Noll, Mark A. *A History of Christianity in the United States and Canada*. Grand Rapids, MI: Eerdmans, 1992.

———. *America's God: From Jonathan Edwards to Abraham Lincoln*. New York: Oxford University Press, 2002.

———. *Religion & American Politics: From the Colonial Period to the 1980s*. New York: Oxford University Press, 1990.

North, Douglass C. *Understanding the Process of Economic Change*. Princeton: Princeton University Press, 2005.

Nozick, Robert. *Anarchy, State, and Utopia*. New York: Basic Books, 1974.

Numbers, Ronald L. Galileo *Goes to Jail and Other Myths About Science and Religion*. Cambridge: Harvard University Press, 2010.

Nye, Joseph. *Soft Power: The Means to Success in World Politics*. New York: Public Affairs, 2004.

———. *The Future of Power*. New York: Public Affairs, 2011.

Oaks, Dallin H. "Good, Better, Best," LDS General Conference, October 2007. <https://www.lds.org/general-conference/2007/10/good-better-best?lang=eng>

———. "Preserving Religious Freedom," Talk at Chapman University, February 4, 2011. <http://www.mormonnewsroom.org/article/elder-oaks-religious-freedom-Chapman-University>.

———. "The Divinely Inspired Constitution," *Ensign*, February 1992.

———. *The Lord's Way*. Salt Lake City: Deseret Book, 1991.

———. "Religious Values and Public Policy," *Ensign*, October 1992.

Oates, Stephen B. *With Malice Toward None: A Life of Abraham Lincoln*. New York: Harper & Row, 1977.

Obama, Barack. "The President's News Conference in Strasburg." April 4, 2009. <http://www.presidency.ucsb.edu/ws/?pid=85959>.

Oren, Michael B. *Power, Faith, and Fantasy: America in the Middle East 1776 to the Present*. New York: W.W. Norton, 2007.

Orwell, George. *Animal Farm and 1984*. Boston: Houghton Mifflin Harcourt, 2003.

Oviatt, Joan. "I Have Learned to Sing": President Heber J. Grant's Struggle to Sing the Hymns of Zion," *Ensign* (September 1984).

Padover, Saul. *Jefferson: A Great American's Life and Ideas*. New York: Penguin, 1952.

Page, Scott E. *The Difference: How the Power of Diversity Creates Better Groups, Firms, Schools, and Societies*. Princeton: Princeton University Press, 2007.

Paine, Thomas. *Common Sense* (1776).

———. *The American Crisis* (1776).

## Bibliography

Patterson, James T. *Grand Expectations: The United States, 1945-1974*. New York: Oxford University Press, 1996.

_____. *Restless Giant: The United States from Watergate to Bush vs. Gore*. New York: Oxford University Press, 2005.

Pipes, Richard. *Communism: A History*. New York: Modern Library, 2000.

Plantinga, Alvin. *Where the Conflict Really Lies: Science, Religion, and Naturalism*. New York: Oxford UP, 2011.

Popper, Karl. *The Open Society and Its Enemies*. Princeton: Princeton University Press, 2013.

Porter, Bruce D. *War and the Rise of the State: The Military Foundations of Modern Politics*. New York: Free Press, 1994.

Postman, Neil. *Amusing Ourselves to Death: Public Discourse in the Age of Show Business*. New York: Penguin, 1986.

_____. *Technopoly: The Surrender of Culture to Technology*. New York: Vintage, 1992.

Postrel, Virginia. *The Future and Its Enemies*. New York: Free Press, 2011.

Potter, David. *People of Plenty: Economic Abundance and the American Character*. Chicago: University of Chicago Press, 1958.

Powell, Jim. *FDR's Folly: How Roosevelt & His New Deal Prolonged the Great Depression*. New York: Random House, 2002.

Putnam, Robert. *Bowling Alone: The Collapse and Revival of American Community*. New York: Simon & Schuster, 2001.

Raboteau, Albert J. *Slave Religion: The "Invisible Institution" in the Antebellum South*. New York: Oxford University Press, 1978.

Randall, Willard Sterne. *George Washington: A Life*. New York: Henry Holt & Co., 1998.

_____. *Thomas Jefferson: A Life*. New York: Henry Holt & Co., 1993.

Rawls, John. *A Theory of Justice*. Cambridge, MA: Belknap Press, 1999.

Reed, Lawrence. "Great Myths of the Great Depression," Cascade Policy Institute, October 2000. <http://cascadepolicy.org/pdf/fiscal/myths.pdf>.

Reed, Leonard. *I, Pencil: My Family Tree as told to Leonard E. Read*. Irvington-on-Hudson, NY: The Foundation for Economic Education, Inc., 1958.

Reich, Robert B. "Economist John Maynard Keynes," *Time*, Mar 29, 1999. <http://content.time.com/time/magazine/article/0,9171,990614,00.html>.

Ridley, Matt. *The Rational Optimist: How Prosperity Evolves*. New York: HarperCollins, 2010.

Roberts, J.M. *A History of Europe*. New York: Penguin, 1997.

Rogoff, Kenneth S. and Carmen M. Reinhart. *This Time is Different: Eight Centuries of Financial Folly*. Princeton: Princeton University Press, 2009.

Romney, Marion G. "First Presidency Message: Rule of Law," *Ensign* (February 1973): 2.

_____. "Political Thought and Life of J. Reuben Clark Jr.," BYU Devotional, November 21, 1972. <http://speeches.byu.edu/?act=viewitem&id=371>.

## Bibliography

\_\_\_\_\_. "Socialism and the United Order Compared," *Conference Report*, April 1966, pp. 95-101.

Roosevelt, Franklin D. Speech Activating the 442nd Regimental Combat Team. February 1, 1943. <http://www.homeofheroes.com/moh/nisei/index3_442nd.html>.

\_\_\_\_\_. "The Economic Bill of Rights" (1944). <http://www.fdrheritage.org/bill_of_rights.htm>.

Ruggiero, Guido De. *The History of European Liberalism*. Boston: Beacon, 1927.

Sacks, Jonathan. *The Great Partnership: God, Science and the Search for Meaning*. London: Hodder & Stroughton, 2011.

Schlesinger, Arthur M., Jr. *The Age of Roosevelt, Vol. 2: The Coming of the New Deal, 1933-1935*. Boston: Houghton Mifflin, 1958.

\_\_\_\_\_. *The Disuniting of America: Reflections on a Multicultural Society*. New York: Norton, 1992.

\_\_\_\_\_. *The Age of Jackson*. Boston: Little, Brown, & Co., 1945.

\_\_\_\_\_. *A Life in the 20th Century: Innocent Beginnings*. Boston: Houghton Mifflin, 2000.

\_\_\_\_\_. *Journals: 1952-2000*. New York: Penguin, 2007.

\_\_\_\_\_. *The Vital Center: The Politics of Freedom*. New Brunswick, NJ: Transaction, 1998.

Schuck, Peter H. *Why Government Fails So Often, and How It Can Do Better*. Princeton: Princeton University Press, 2014.

Schuck, Peter H. and James Q. Wilson, eds. *Understanding America: The Anatomy of an Exceptional Nation*. New York: PublicAffairs, 2008.

Schumpeter, Joseph. *Capitalism, Socialism, and Democracy*. New York: Harper & Bros., 1942.

Schwartz, Anna J. "Money Supply," The Concise Encyclopedia of Economics. <http://www.econlib.org/library/Enc1/MoneySupply.html>.

Shah, Timothy Samuel. "Born Again in the USA," *Foreign Affairs*, October 2009.

Shelley, Mary. *Frankenstein, or the Modern Prometheus* [1818]. New York: Barnes & Noble, 1993.

Sims, Andrew. *Is Faith Delusion?: Why Religion is Good for Your Health*. London: Continuum, 2009.

Sipress, Joel M. "Relearning Race: Teaching Race as a Cultural Construction," *History Teacher* 30 (Feb 1997): 175-185.

Skidelsky, Robert. *John Maynard Keynes: 1883-1946: Economist, Philosopher, Statesman*. New York: Penguin, 2005.

Smith, Adam. *The Theory of Moral Sentiments* (1759). New York: Penguin, 2009.

\_\_\_\_\_. *The Wealth of Nations* (1776). New York: Modern Library, 1994.

Smith, Joseph. Correspondence with John C. Calhoun (1843). *History of the Church* 6:155-60.

\_\_\_\_\_. *Lectures on Faith*. Salt Lake City: Deseret Book, 1985.

Smith, Rogers M. "Beyond Tocqueveille, Myrdall, and Hartz: The Multiple Traditions in America," *American Political Science Review* 87 (Sept 1993): 549-66.

Sowell, Thomas. *Basic Economics: A Common Sense Guide to the Economy*. 4th Edition. New York: Basic Books, 2011.

\_\_\_\_\_. *Economic Facts and Fallacies*. Second Edition. New York: Basic Books, 2011.

Stanton, Elizabeth Cady and Susan B. Anthony. *Selected Papers of Elizabeth Cady Stanton and Susan B. Anthony*. edited by Ann D. Gordon. New Brunswick, N.J.: Rutgers University Press, 2003.

Stark, Rodney and William Sims Bainbridge. *A Theory of Religion*. New Brunswick, NJ: Rutgers University Press, 1996.

Stark, Rodney. *For the Glory of God: How Monotheism Led to Reformations, Science, Witch-hunts, and the End of Slavery*. Princeton: Princeton University Press, 2003.

Steinbeck, John. *The Grapes of Wrath*. New York: Viking, 1939.

Stewart, David O. *The Summer of 1787: The Men who Invented the Constitution*. New York: Simon & Schuster, 2007.

Stigler, George J. *Memoirs of an Unregulated Economist*. New York: Basic Books, 1988.

Sunstein, Cass and Richard Thaler. *Nudge: Improving Decisions About Health, Wealth, and Happiness*. New York: Penguin, 2009.

Surowiecki, James. *The Wisdom of Crowds*. New York: Doubleday, 2004.

Taleb, Nassim Nicholas. *The Black Swan: The Impact of the Highly Improbable*. New York: Random House, 2007.

Taylor, Alan. *American Colonies*. New York: Viking, 2001.

Tetlock, Philip. *Expert Political Judgment: How Good Is It? How Can We Know?* Princeton: Princeton University Press, 2006.

Thompson, Nicholas. *The Hawk and the Dove: Paul Nitze, George Kennan, and the History of the Cold War*. New York: Henry Holt, 2009.

Thoreau, Henry David. *Walden; or, Life in the Woods* [1854]. Mineola, NY: Dover, 1995.

Tice, Richard. "Greed: When Enough Is Not Enough," *Ensign*, June, 1989.

Tierney, John. "Do You Have Free Will? Yes, It's the Only Choice," *New York Times*, March 22, 2011, pg. D1.

Toffler, Alvin and Heidi. *The Third Wave*. New York: Bantam, 1980.

Tomasi, John. *Free Market Fairness*. Princeton: Princeton University Press, 2012.

Truman, Harry. "Presidential Address to Congress," 12 March 1947. <http://www.ourdocuments.gov/doc.php?doc=81&page=transcript>.

Twelve Southerners. *I'll Take My Stand* [1930]. Baton Rouge: LSU Press, 2006.

Walker, Ronald W. *Qualities That Count: Heber J. Grant As Businessman, Missionary, and Apostle*. Provo: BYU Press, 2003.

Washington, George. Farewell Address (1796).

Weber, Max. *The Protestant Ethic & The Spirit of Capitalism: The Relationship Between Religion and the Economic and Social Life in Modern Culture*. New York: Scribner's, 1956.

Wilentz, Sean. *The Rise of American Democracy: Jefferson to Lincoln*. New York: Norton, 2006.

Willard, Dallas, ed. *A Place for Truth: Leading Thinkers Explore Life's Hardest Questions*. Downer's Grove, IL: Intervarsity Press, 2010.

Wills, Garry. *James Madison*. New York: Henry Holt, 2002.

# Bibliography

Wilson, James Q. "American Exceptionalism," *The American Spectator*, October 2, 2006. <http://spectator.org/articles/46395/american-exceptionalism>, accessed February 2, 2014.

Wilson, James Q. and John J. DiIulio, Jr. *American Government*. 8th edition. Boston: Houghton Mifflin Company, 2001.

Wilson, Woodrow. "Speech before Congress," April 2, 1917. <http://www.ourdocuments.gov/doc.php?doc=61&page=transcript>.

Wolf, Martin. *Why Globalization Works*. New Haven: Yale University Press, 2004.

Wolfe, Tom. *Hooking Up*. NY: Farrar Straus Giroux, 2000.

Wood, Gordon. *Empire of Liberty: A History of the Early Republic, 1789-1815*. New York: Oxford University Press, 2009.

\_\_\_\_\_. *The American Revolution: A History*. New York: Random House, 2002.

\_\_\_\_\_. *The Creation of the American Republic*. New York: Norton, 1969.

\_\_\_\_\_. *The Radicalism of the American Revolution*. New York: Random House, 1993.

Woodward, Bob. *Maestro: Greenspan's Fed and the American Boom*. New York: Simon & Schuster, 2001.

Wright, Robert. *NonZero: The Logic of Human Destiny*. New York: Vintage, 2000.

Zakaria, Fareed. *The Future of Freedom: Illiberal Democracy at Home and Abroad*. New York: W.W. Norton, 2003.

\_\_\_\_\_. *The Post-American World*. New York: W.W. Norton, 2008.

Zeihan, Peter. *The Accidental Superpower: The Next Generation of American Preeminence and the Coming Global Disorder*. New York: Twelve, 2014.

Zernike, Kate. "The Pilgrims Were ... Socialists?" *New York Times*, November 20, 2010.

Zimbardo, Philip. *The Lucifer Effect: Understanding How Good People Turn Evil*. New York: Random House, 2007.